ASSOCIATIONAL LIFE IN AFRICAN CITIES

Popular Responses to the Urban Crisis

Edited by

Arne Tostensen – Inge Tvedten – Mariken Vaa

Nordiska Afrikainstitutet 2001

Indexing terms

Associations

Civil society

Cities

Community participation

Governance

Housing

Services

Non-governmental organisations

Religious institutions

Africa

Cover illustration: Adriaan Honcoop
Printed in Sweden by Elanders Gotab, Stockholm 2001

ISBN 91-7106-465-6

Contents

Preface

The first conference under the auspices of the research programme *Cities, Governance and Civil Society in Africa* was convened in Bergen, Norway at the end of August 1998. The conference was entitled "Associational life in African Cities: Urban Governance in an Era of Change" and organised by the Nordic Africa Institute in conjunction with the Chr. Michelsen Institute.

The thematic background to the conference was the multitude of voluntary associations that has emerged in African cities in recent years. In many cases, they are a response to mounting poverty, failing infrastructure and services, and, more generally, weak or abdicating urban governments. Some associations are new, in other cases, existing organisations are taking on new tasks. Important research questions are: under what circumstances and in what contexts have people organised themselves, and how are local and central governments responding to popular collective action for urban development? One preliminary observation based on the papers presented in Bergen is that urban associations in Africa are a flourishing field of research. But there is still a dearth of studies on how central and local governments deal with urban civil society.

Many people contributed towards making the conference a success, first and foremost, the authors of papers, the discussants and the other participants. On the practical side, thanks are due to the conference secretaries Ingrid Andersson and Benedicte Solheim. We also want to thank the Board of the Chr. Michelsen Institute for providing supplementary funding from the "The Anniversary Fund of the Norwegian Bank for the Chr. Michelsen Institute".

The conference in Bergen started off with a public lecture by Mark Swilling: "The Challenge of Urban Governance in Africa" A revised version of this lecture is now being published under the title "Re-casting institutional transformation in local government—the learning paradigm" in Pieterse, E., Parnell, S. and Swilling, M., (eds) *South African Reconstruction: Making Developmental Local Government Work,* University of Cape Town Press, 2001. Altogether, 23 papers had been prepared for the conference, drawing on material from no less than 19 different African countries. Of the 17 chapters in this book, 16 are revised versions of papers presented in Bergen, while Chapter 1 and the introductions to the sub-sections were written after the conference was held.

The preparation and publication of this book involves the efforts of many people. First, we would like to thank the contributors for their industry and, gradually, their patience in responding to yet another set of suggestions for the revision of their chapters by the editors. Annabelle Despard translated Cheikh Gueye's chapter from French. Richard Moorsom did a language check on the whole manuscript. Daniel Talje drew up the List of acronyms and the Glossary. Ingrid Andersson, assistant to the programme *Cities, Governance and Civil Society in Africa* has performed a variety of tasks. Among other things, she has kept track of authors and manuscripts, checked bibliographical references and helped constructing the index. Finally, an anonymous referee for our publication department has contributed many insightful comments and suggestions.

Uppsala and Bergen, March 2001

Arne Tostensen   *Inge Tvedten*   *Mariken Vaa*

CHAPTER 1
The Urban Crisis, Governance and Associational Life

Arne Tostensen, Inge Tvedten and Mariken Vaa

The first section of this chapter reviews briefly some central features of African urbanisation and some salient characteristics of the current urban crisis. Africa is one of the least urbanised regions in the world, but cities and towns grow faster here than anywhere else, and large-scale urbanisation is a fairly recent phenomenon. The crisis consists of shortage of housing and jobs, widespread poverty, severe environmental problems, failing services and inadequate local government structures.

Then follows a discussion of civil society and governance, offering some conceptual clarifications and a consideration of how civil society pertains to urban governance. Civil society is defined as the public realm of organised social activity located between the state and the family, regardless of normative orientation. The normative character and function of civil society is a matter of empirical investigation. Governance, on the other hand, refers to *practices* rather than formal institutions and can be understood as the general manner in which people are governed—but not exclusively by the institutions of government.

The chapter concludes with a discussion of the changing role of urban associations in Africa. A brief review of earlier research traditions is followed by an assessment of urban associations and how they have recently taken on new functions which present new opportunities and challenges for government and the governed. They have a large potential for finding collective solutions to common problems. But there is also a need for a critical analysis of the role of associations in urban development, particularly with regard to how they incorporate the poor and how they are gendered.

CENTRAL FEATURES OF AFRICAN URBANISATION

The urbanisation process in Africa has over the years been subject to a variety of reactions and interpretations: strange mixtures of neglect or negative attention and of misconceptions of what it is about. National governments have perceived the high rates of urban population growth as deeply problematic and have generally shied away from formulating any comprehensive policies for urban development. Rather, they have tacitly accepted the colonial legacy of urban containment, or embraced donor agencies' sometimes ill founded warnings against 'urban bias'. International and bilateral donors have until recently concerned themselves only to a limited degree with urban processes (Milbert, 1999).

There are, of course, considerable variations in patterns of urban development across the African continent, and in how it has been described and interpreted. It may be useful to remember that the term 'urbanisation' in itself commonly carries two distinct meanings. Urbanisation is both a change in the pattern of settlement and a social process (O'Connor, 1983:17). Geographers and demographers have primarily studied African towns and cities in relation to some dimension of settlement, where cities are seen as locations and as elements in a system of settlements. Anthropologists, sociologists and historians are more preoccupied with social structure and the dynamics of change in social relations and institutions (Peil and Sada, 1984; Coquery-Vidrovitch, 1988).

Development economics has only recently recognised the importance of cities for economic development (Harris, 1992; World Bank, 2000). However, since the mid-1980s, there has been an increasing interest among researchers from a variety of disciplines in urbanisation as an aspect of development, and a concomitant concern with urban management or government, and more recently, what is labelled problems of urban governance. (Stren and White, 1989; Stren, 1994; Rakodi, 1997; Swilling, 1997). Partly, this turn in research interest reflects an increasing awareness among donors and lending institutions that there is indeed some link between urbanisation and development, and that the extreme poverty and other burdens of misery carried by large segments of the urban population in the developing countries are not likely to go away by simply ignoring the fact that cities exist and continue to grow. But it should also be borne in mind that for more than half a century, social scientists have been studying African cities independently of fashions in development thinking, focusing on how the urban experience reshapes social relations, how urbanites create new institutions and redefine and accommodate old ones.

For most African cities, as for each individual country, there is a dearth of basic demographic data. For many countries, figures for national, regional and city populations are estimates or projections based on census data that may be 20 to 30 years old. What is known about the nature and scale of urban change in Africa is, therefore, to a large extent based on studies of particular cities, sectors or neighbourhoods, whose representativeness is difficult to ascertain. There is, however, a fairly widespread consensus on the following features: Africa is one of the least urbanised regions in the world; cities and towns are growing faster here than anywhere else; and large-scale urbanisation is a fairly recent phenomenon.

The overall level of urbanisation in Africa, defined as the per cent of the population living in settlements of a certain size, was estimated to be 34 per cent in 1995. But there are important differences both between regions and within sub-regions in their level of urbanisation. North Africa and Southern Africa were both 48 per cent urbanised in 1995, West and Middle Africa were close to the average for the continent, and the East African region had only 22 per cent living in cities. (Rakodi, 1997:33). These figures are based on UN estimates (UN, 1998).

Rates of urban population growth may have slowed down somewhat, but are still very high, particularly in the least urbanised parts of the continent. Predictions for 2000–2005 indicate that Africa as a whole will have an annual growth rate of its urban population of 4.5 per cent. It will be highest in East Africa, which is now the least urbanised sub-region, and lowest in Southern and North Africa, where urbanisation levels are around 50 per cent already (Becker, Hamer and Morrison, 1994:34). In the years immediately following independence, some cities grew at a considerably faster rate than at present, particularly in countries where the colonial government had restricted movement through pass laws and similar measures. Lusaka, Zambia, is recorded to have grown by 15 per cent annually in the 1960s (Jere, 1984).

The high rates of urban population growth are usually, and sometimes mistakenly, attributed to the annual inflow of rural migrants to the city. With extremely high growth rates, as in the case of Lusaka mentioned above, in-migration has obviously played an important role. But years of in-migration of primarily young people will later result in high rates of natural growth. The largest cities grew very rapidly in the early post-independence period due to rural-urban migration. At the turn of the century, growth rates are lower and natural increase is the major element. In the developing world as a whole annual city growth rates have been attributed to 35 per cent in-migration, 50 per cent natural growth and 15 per cent changes in city boundaries (Harris, 1992).

The third distinctive feature of African urbanisation as a pattern of settlement is that really large cities are a rather recent phenomenon. In 1950, only five African cities had more than 200,000 inhabitants: Ibadan, Addis Ababa, Lagos, Leopoldville (now Kinshasa) and Khartoum. Forty years later, in 1990, 25 cities in Africa had more than one million inhabitants, with Cairo and Lagos included among the 30 largest cities in the world (UNCHS, 1996:13, 17). Some cities have grown more than tenfold over the last few decades.

But if large cities are a recent phenomenon in Africa the continent is not without urban traditions. Far from all African cities originate in the colonial era. Cairo and Alexandria may be the only African cities dating back to antiquity, but there has been continuous urban settlement in various parts of sub-Saharan Africa for more than a thousand years. Best known are the Islamic cities of the savannah belt in West Africa. Some of these were capitals of empires, others were religious centres or nodal points of trans-Saharan trade routes. But they were not the only pre-colonial urban centres. The trading posts on the coast of East Africa, some of which are important urban centres today, predate the colonial occupation by several centuries (Vennetier, 1976; O'Connor, 1983).

The urban crises

According to the *Global Report on Human Settlements 1996*, the background document to the UN Habitat II conference in Istanbul: "...from the early 1960s, when most African countries obtained formal independence, to the mid-1990s, African cities have changed in at least four major ways: their size, their spatial organisation or morphology, the quality and distribution of public services and infrastructure, and their employment base" (UNCHS, 1996:86).

The rapid population growth of most cities in Africa has already been mentioned. The demand for jobs, housing and services is immense. Physical infrastructure is crumbling, and schools and health services are woefully inadequate. Most African cities also have severe environmental problems, partly linked to transport and production, but primarily to inadequate shelter conditions and service provision. A large, if varying, proportion of the urban population is housed in unauthorised and unserviced settlements. In some cities, up to 90 per cent of the new housing stock has been provided informally.

The urban employment base is changing, from employment in the public sector and in private but formal enterprises to self-employment or wage work in the unregistered economy. Increasing numbers seek their livelihood in the informal economy, where statistics are not collected. Incomes may vary, but on average they are probably lower than in the formal economy. Formal employment is not a guarantee against poverty, however. Regular wages have decreased in real terms over the last couple of decades, so that a wage income is no longer sufficient to support a family, sometimes not even an individual. The various structural adjustment programmes imposed on most African countries over the last 15–20 years have entailed a whole range of measures intended to liberalise the national economy, and have hit urban households harder than rural ones. Reduced food subsidies, devaluation, raised producer prices for agricultural products, combined with wage freezes and cutbacks in the public sector, have marginalised large segments of the urban population. Many urban households eke out their livelihoods by combining wages, casual work, trade, support from relatives and running up debts (Aina, 1997).

Poverty is widespread, and is not confined to the unemployed or occasionally employed day-workers. The urban poor in sub-Saharan Africa are a differentiated, often fragmented, complex and varied group (Aina, 1997; Vaa, Diallo and Findley, 1989). There is also reason to believe that the scale of urban poverty is underestimated and that the number of urban people in poverty is growing at a faster rate than the number of poor rural people (Wratten, 1995). With declining real wages and widespread unemployment among men, women's earnings have become the main source of livelihood for many households. The proportion of women who are sole providers for their families is increasing, but research on this phenomenon and its implications for gender relations is so far very limited (Moser and Peake, 1995). Gender aspects of urban poverty are rarely analysed beyond counting women-headed households, a very heterogeneous category. The poverty of urban populations is reflected in various ways: inadequate diet, worsening housing conditions, sometimes also lower school attendance, and a growing incidence of child labour. There have for some time been signs that infant mortality increase in the poorest sections of some cities (Hardoy, Cairncross and Satterthwaite, 1990).

There is a general consensus, not only among researchers, that African cities are in crisis, and that the crisis consists of failing services and inadequate local government structures, shortage of housing and jobs, severe environmental problems, widespread poverty and increasing inequalities (Stren and White, 1989; Rakodi, 1997). It is interesting to note, however, that while

African governments, civil servants and observers such as journalists normally attribute the urban crisis to explosive urban growth and adverse economic circumstances, a more widely held view in the various research communities is that this crisis is a result of failures in government. Since independence, states have failed to provide institutional and legal frameworks for the overall development of cities. Instead, individuals and firms are exposed to obstructionist legal norms, corrupt civil servants and pervasive informality. One consequence is inefficiency and low productivity in urban enterprises. But, as there is a close association between urbanisation and economic growth, mal-functioning cities also have negative macro-economic consequences.

Generally, local authorities have until recently been unresponsive to the mounting urban crises. Local and national governments have not been able to devise new regulatory frameworks which would serve urban residents better in their pursuit of livelihoods, shelter and services. Various policy measures launched by central governments have in many cases exacerbated the situation. During the last decade, however, some countries have taken steps to decentralise and make local government more democratic and accountable. At the same time, the monopoly of state institutions is being challenged by urban residents themselves. Voluntary associations and *ad hoc* groups have proliferated, serving a variety of purposes.

ASSOCIATIONAL LIFE IN AFRICAN CITIES

The current usage of concepts such as civil society and associational life is diverse and lacking in clarity. A multitude of terms is being used interchangeably and inconsistently, often without precise definition. Furthermore, usage varies from one country to another. This lack of clarity does not result only from careless definition of concepts. Indeed, authors disagree substantively over the meanings of the terms applied; conceptualisation is contested and the outcomes—laced with ideological content or epistemological significance—may have far-reaching implications for analysis. This state of affairs causes confusion and may lead—at best—to ambiguous analysis.

Apart from the concept of civil society, the notion of governance is a source of confusion as well. Whereas the donor community tends to affix the adjective 'good' to add a normative dimension, the academic community is inclined to take a neutral stand. Our ambition here is not to provide a definitive typology of forms and types of associational expression. Rather, our more modest aim is to seek somewhat greater clarity and consistency of usage.

Civil society: Between the state and the household

This is not the place to delve into a lengthy discussion of the philosophical and historical origins of the concept of civil society. Others have done that far better than we could hope to manage within the present space (e.g. Keane, 1988; Pelczynski, 1984). It will suffice here to delineate the main strands of current thinking (cf. Van Rooy, 1998; Sjögren, 1998). These strands are not necessarily discrete; rather, in many cases they overlap and can be seen as reflecting differences of emphasis.

Some writers attach great importance to the values and norms considered to be inherent in civil society, the emphasis being placed on 'civil' (Shils, 1991). In this sense civil society is seen as a carrier of positive values such as trust, tolerance and co-operation; civil society becomes synonymous with the good society (Van Rooy, 1998:12). This strong normative bent is akin to the notion of communitarianism, which stresses solidarity and cohesion within communities based on fundamental moral principles—without the help or intrusion of the state (Etzioni, 1993). Robert Putnam's seminal analysis of 'social capital' in Italy considers it a social glue, which has much in common with Amitai Etzioni's communitarianism (Putnam, 1993). It follows from these notions that whatever goes on in civil society must be in the public interest.

Another strand vaguely defines civil society as a collective noun—a description of the sum of organisations and activities that contribute to the civility of public life in one form or another. A normative element is generally present, albeit not always expressed explicitly. The assumption is that the sheer presence of a diversity of organisations leads to the promotion of a common good. The plethora of non-governmental organisations (NGOs) found world-wide and the donor community appear to espouse this euphoric view.

A third conceptualisation views civil society as a sphere, a space or an arena for action by divergent interests, struggling against each other or against the state, or simply engaging in self-contained activities of various kinds. Within this strand one tendency emphasises the relationship to the state, where various groups try to pressurise the state into taking a certain course of action or adopt a specific policy, or to hold the state accountable for its action or inaction. Another current stresses the defensive stance of civil society in asserting its autonomy and fending off state interference in its activities.

A fourth understanding describes civil society as a historical moment: a societal conjuncture in which a set of prerequisites are in place. Those prerequisites include the primacy of the individual, being autonomous, and exercising rights within a shared public space based on agreed rules and norms that are generally observed. In this conception civil society is viewed as a specific product of historical and cultural conditions.

A fifth posture sees civil society as essentially an anti-hegemonic project against modern liberalism and capitalism. It is considered the antithesis of Francis Fukuyama's thesis about 'the end of history' (Fukuyama, 1992). One strain puts the accent on the 'alternative' visions of society, through quasi-clandestine forms that seek to disassociate from a society considered to have derailed. Examples of such associational expressions are the deep-ecological section of the environmental movement, some gender-based organisations, religious fundamentalisms and fellowships, and a collection of dispositions drawing on the ideology of various brands of anarchism. Some of these assume anti-Western attitudes as a reaction against the spread of consumerism through the homogenising processes of globalisation.

A widespread view—not least in the donor community—places civil society in direct opposition to a centralised or autocratic state as a countervailing power. This notion stems from two interrelated experiences over the past four decades: (a) the abysmal performance of the state, particularly in Africa, in producing what is generally referred to as development, however defined, the main causes identified as bureaucratisation, corruption and mismanagement; and (b) the equally devastating failure of state institutions of governance to function democratically. In the ensuing profound crisis citizens have turned to civil society sources of legitimacy and action. Likewise, donors have become disillusioned in their dealings with corrupt and inefficient states and have looked elsewhere for channels of assistance. 'Rolling back the state' and giving room for associational pluralism have been seen as the answer to the crisis. This anti-statist stance has took root in tandem with a corresponding faith in the market as the key to economic recovery.

Relative to the above strands of thinking about civil society we need to define our own stand. Along with Robinson and White, we take exception to the above-mentioned idyllic depiction of civil society (1997:3):

> Actual civil societies are complex associational universes involving a vast array of specific organisational forms and a wide diversity of institutional motivations. They contain repression as well as democracy, conflict as well as co-operation, vice as well as virtue; they can be motivated by sectional greed as much as social interest. Thus any attempt to compress the ideas of civil society into a homogeneous and virtuous stereotype is doomed to fail. It is also intellectually harmful not only because it misrepresents the reality of civil societies, but also because it distorts development discourse more broadly by encouraging similarly simplified but overwhelmingly negative conceptions of other societal agencies, whether state or market.

Subscribing to this criticism of civil society as a virtuous stereotype, we see the multitude of organisational forms and expressions as ambiguous and contradictory in value terms. The uncritical, inherently virtuous stereotype is rather a reflection of wishful thinking on the part of the donor community, a favourable self-projection by sections of civil society itself, or an ideology-tainted representation by segments of the academic community. We submit that civil society is neither inherently virtuous nor inherently vicious; it can be either, neither or both. We are inclined, at the level of general definition, to underscore the ambiguity of civil society but ultimately its normative nature or function is subject to empirical investigation, not a matter to be determined *a priori* (Tostensen, 1993).

Thus, we define civil society as the public realm of organised social activity located between the state and the private household (or family)—regardless of normative orientation. However, organisations whose principal objective is profit-making—i.e. enterprises—do not form part of civil society, nor do organisations seeking state power, i.e. political parties. Civil society is an arena of diverse activity, some but by no means all of which counterpoised to the state. Much associational life may be entirely neutral *vis-à-vis* the state. Civil society organisations may also enter into co-operation with state agencies, either directly through joint ventures or through a tacit understanding about a

13

division of labour. When associations engage in co-operation there is a possi-bility or risk of co-optation by the state. Whatever the nature of the relation-ship between civil society and the state it may have a legitimising or delegiti-mising effect on the exercise of state power.

A typology of associational life?

Above, the terms civil society and associational life have been used inter-changeably to denote the general phenomenon under discussion. From a gen-eral notion of civil society, it may be necessary to specify its manifestation in various forms of associational life. The classification attempts are many. Most of them are deficient in one way or the other, mainly because they are geared towards non-academic uses or biased towards the particular research prob-lems at hand and thus stop short of a generic schema. Some of the definitional problems stem from the diverging conceptualisations of civil society at the general level. The bulk of the literature on civil society in Africa has centred on the role associations play in democratisation processes (see e.g. Rothchild and Chazan, 1988; Bratton, 1989 and 1989b; Hyden and Bratton, 1992; Harbeson et al., 1994; Kasfir, 1998). Far less attention has been paid to the role of associational life in urban governance (Stren and Kjellberg Bell, 1995; Swilling, 1997).

Associations playing a role in urban governance often take the form of NGOs, or they have ties to NGOs. It may therefore be useful to look at recent work on defining and classifying voluntary associations. In his analysis of so-called development NGOs, Tvedt (1998) discusses four types of definitions of voluntary organisations. His discussion is based on Salamon and Anheier's work (1992) on the non-profit sector. They identify four types of definitions: (a) the legal; (b) the economic/financial; (c) the functional; and (d) the struc-tural-operational.

As most countries require organisational expressions of civil society to register in order to operate legally, it would seem reasonable to consider all registered organisations *bona fide* elements of civil society. Although the neat-ness of this legal definition may seem attractive—particularly for donors in search of partners—there are several problems with it. First, the legislation in terms of which registration is required has been enacted by the state. As such it should be seen to represent the state's interest in controlling civil society organisations by defining the parameters for their operation in terms of man-agement and financial conditions. Second, many organisations of civil society are denied registration on account of not conforming to the legal stipulations. Others may have been de-registered owing to the displeasure of the state. Third, a host of people involved in the informal or quasi-formal activities of civil society never bother to seek registration or choose not to do so. From a comparative perspective too, the legal approach has weaknesses as the legal framework may vary considerably from one country to another.

The economic/financial definition takes its cue from the revenue base of civil society organisations. It is suggested that those deriving more than a cer-tain percentage of their income from domestic public sources or foreign donors, say 50 per cent, cannot be said to be part of civil society. Such a funding structure negates the very essence of civil society as being rooted in popular activity. The implication is that such a funding bias will make an organisation too dependent on the state to be a genuine expression of civil society; its independence will be seriously curtailed. Whereas this revenue base criterion no doubt says a lot about the independence organisations enjoy *vis-à-vis* the state or donors, its strict application would probably exclude the majority of formal associations in Third World countries. Pervasive poverty is not a good basis for sustaining financially independent civil society organisations over periods of time. They may have to secure core or earmarked funding from public sources, donors or benevolent patrons. In either case independence would be in jeopardy. However, the collection of independent means from a wide variety of sources is probably only feasible on an *ad hoc* basis for smaller community based projects, such as a school, a health clinic or the like.

The functional definition stresses the stated purposes, objectives and functions of NGOs. They tend to champion a cause on behalf of a real existing membership or a presumed constituency, most often vaguely defined as 'the people', 'the community', 'the poor' or 'the grassroots'. They may be small and entirely based on voluntary work or large with a paid staff supplemented by volunteers. They may operate at local, national or international levels. A major problem with this definition is that it takes at face value the stated objectives of these organisations rather than an analysis of their actual functions.

The fourth definition—the structural-operational one—emphasises basic structure and operation. Tvedt lists five constituent criteria that need to be satisfied to qualify for genuine NGO status: they must be formally constituted, though not necessarily legally registered, be non-governmental in basic structure, and organisationally distinct from the state. Organisations must be self-governing, i.e. with a structure of elected officers who are accountable to a constituency. They must be non-profit making and largely based on voluntary work.

These are important dimensions of associations, which should not be neglected in the analyses. But as definitional criteria of civil society they are too restrictive, since they fail to capture more loosely knit networks, which may be crucial elements of the survival strategies of the poor, in rural areas as well as in towns (Wellman, 1999). Admittedly, such networks exhibit a low degree of formalisation but they do constitute *organised* activities. Some social scientists see these networks as important sources of 'social capital' (Portes, 1998). The frequency of interaction between the members of networks may vary considerably, which, in turn, yields flexibility. At times networks may remain dormant, as a latent organisational resource to be activated and mobilised in times of need. Or they may be operative continuously, as a permanent feature of the social life of its members. The latter would hold true, for instance, in the case of commercial exchange networks and webs of mutual help at the local level.

These networks are often based on ascribed (kinship, ethnicity) as distinct from acquired (religion, business) properties, sometimes in combination with other characteristics. Ascription is a particularly important aspect of civil societies in Africa. The reach of networks may be confined to local communities (e.g. urban centres) or span continents to include diaspora populations (Sowell, 1996). Thus they may extend great distances—indeed globally—and sometimes control considerable financial resources.

The typology discussed by Tvedt also puts too much emphasis on the internal self-government of civil society organisations. Although many such organisations in developing countries are based on membership, many of them are not—particularly in Africa. Rather, people gravitate towards these associations on the basis of functional or ascriptive identities. In many cases it may be more accurate to speak of adherents or followers than members, their loyalty being measured in terms of participation rather than formal enrolment and payment of membership fees. Leaders are often self-proclaimed rather than elected. Thus, the internal procedures for handling the affairs of the organisation tend to become blurred. As a corollary, the principles of accountability and transparency are rarely observed.

The fact that ascription is a prevalent criterion of social organisation in Africa would suggest that management styles are likely to deviate from those of organisational cultures based on Weberian precepts. Neo-patrimonial sentiments and clientelism are so pervasive in Africa—even sometimes emerging as informal structures within formalised organisations—that one would expect them to characterise civil society too. Drawing on his experiences from Kenya, Wachira Maina (1998) maintains emphatically that the literature tends to overlook how general conflicts and cleavages in African societies are reproduced and reflected in civil society. For instance, cases abound of NGOs ridden by ethnic cleavage. Indeed, some civil society organisations are formed on the basis of such sentiments as their distinguishing feature. Such parochial bases and orientations may not be well liked by the donor community but they are a living reality in Africa, even within organisations whose appearance may be different.

In some respects, however, Maina goes further in his definitional discussion than we are inclined to do. First, he asserts that the assumed boundaries between the state and civil society are rather porous, often blurring into each other. He also points out that the state may use certain civil society organisations as vehicles for its hegemonic project within its territorial jurisdiction. On occasion, states also admit to applying dual-track diplomacy in pursuing foreign policy, i.e. using NGOs as complementary instruments of foreign policy whenever state agencies are deemed to have a disadvantage—typically in sensitive matters such as human rights and democratisation (Tostensen and Grünfeld, 1999). While we agree with Maina that there is a considerable grey area between state and civil society it is hardly a definitional issue; rather, it is matter of empirical investigation.

Like ourselves, Maina has reservations about Tvedt's and other authors' emphasis on formalisation. He argues (Maina, 1998:137) for:

> ... a shift in perspective from a preoccupation with organisations and institutions to an activity view of civil society. Those who focus on organisational forms and institutions do great injustice to civil society in Africa. Much that is

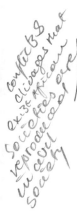

both interesting and transformative in the continent occurs outside or at the periphery of formal organisational life. Spontaneous protests, laxity and lack of discipline and active non-co-operation with the State are important civic activities ... Spontaneous, non-confrontational methods ... are safer ways of registering one's disagreement with the government than more robust public activities such as protest marches, placard-waving and burning effigies (emphasis added).

By extending the definition of civil society to 'an activity view' Maina runs the risk of rendering it inoperational. For expressions of civil society activity to be subjected to analysis they must be identifiable, i.e. be discernible over time with a modicum of organisational 'staying-power'. Loose networks may be short-lived and sometimes difficult to identify, and spontaneity is the antithesis of organisation. Maina's definition becomes meaningless because it encompasses virtually everything that goes on outside of the state. Besides, what may appear to be spontaneous activities are, in reality, often instigated by organised forces.

Civil society encompasses a battery of widely different associational activities: professional societies; trade unions; confederations of employers; chambers of commerce; chess clubs, debating clubs, choirs, youth clubs and similar social activities; charities; non-governmental organisations engaged in development work; adoption agencies; neighbourhood organisations; organisations promoting sectional interests; advocacy organisations working for a variety of causes from environmental conservation to human rights protection; clandestine societies; self-help groups; loose networks promoting livelihoods or causes; churches and religious groupings; ethnic associations; welfare associations; rotating savings and credit societies; burial societies; community based organisations; co-operative unions; and many more. This multiplicity of associational forms is found at local, national and international levels.

Similarly, acronyms abound and add to the confusion—there is a virtual explosion of terms with more or less serious, satirical or derogatory connotations: NGO (non-governmental organisation); PVO (private voluntary organisation); PVDO (private voluntary development organisation); CBO (community based organisation); CSO (civil society organisation); QUANGO (quasi-non-governmental organisation); GONGO (government non-governmental organisation); GANGO (gap-filling non-governmental organisation); CO (charitable organisation); PO (people's organisation); GO (grassroots organisation); IO (independent organisation); PO (private organisation); VO (voluntary organisation); AGO (anti-government organisation); NGI (non-governmental individual); MONGO (my own non-governmental organisation), and many more.

On top of this plethora of acronyms some authors have added adjectives to denote functions or objectives, such as 'reformist' (i.e. seeking to change a system or improve the situation of citizens); 'nominal' (to suggest that the beneficiaries are privileged groups who use civil society organisations opportunistically to further their own narrow interests); 'empowering' (i.e. seeking to empower a particular constituency); 'popular'; 'welfare'; 'relief'; 'educational', 'advocacy', 'watchdog', 'public-service', 'charity', 'family', etc. Bogus

NGOs may earn labels like 'politician's' (exploited by a politician for political gain); 'briefcase' (meaning an entrepreneurial individual whose 'office' is his briefcase); 'bureaucrat's' (used for financial gain by a bureaucrat), and so on. The problem of classification is further compounded by the fact that most NGOs pursue multiple objectives and it is often difficult to ascertain which objective is the overriding one.

Is it possible to establish a typology of this hodgepodge of activities? Hardly. The dimensions and variables are so numerous that a comprehensive, generic typology would be too rich in permutations to serve as a useful, let alone an economical tool to use. Its complexity would defeat its purpose. Failing to establish an exhaustive typology, we would like, however, to reiterate our general definition of civil society and summarise the additional criteria discussed above. We define civil society as the public realm of organised social activity located between the state and the private household (or family)—with the following additional specifications:

- Civil society is a neutral collective noun for an array of organised activity in an area for action at local, national and transnational levels.
- The concept of civil society has no normative import by definition; it is neither inherently virtuous nor vicious. It may contain any sort of normative orientation in an ambiguous and contradictory fashion. The normative character and function of civil society cannot be determined *a priori*; rather, it is a matter of empirical investigation.
- Organisations whose principal objective is profit-making—i.e. enterprises—do not form part of civil society, nor do organisations seeking state power, i.e. political parties.
- The relationship of civil society to the state is varied. Civil society may be a countervailing power to the state, indeed, an anti-state force. Alternatively, it may take a collaborative stance *vis-à-vis* the state and thus risk co-optation. Or, it may be seen as a separate sphere of activity—as non-state rather than anti-state.
- Civil society contains informal as well as formal elements; however, with a modicum of organisation. Loose networks qualify as civil society organisations, but spontaneous activities do not.
- The basis of membership in civil society organisations may be ascriptive or acquired properties.

Urban governance

The term 'governance' has, like that of civil society, been used and misused. It has a variety of meanings. Ambiguity still surrounds the concept. Arguably, in the 1990s the donor community left a strong imprint and established an almost hegemonic meaning of the term with a strong normative bent. The World Bank in particular, followed by most other donors—multilateral and bilateral alike—was preoccupied with governance issues in the wake of the poor performance by many countries in pursuing structural adjustment programmes in the 1980s (Bräutigam, 1991). Although donors have normally added the adjective 'good' to denote a positive normative content, 'governance' in its naked form may also be used to mean 'good governance'.

The twin concepts of transparency and accountability are generally considered an integral part of 'good governance'. Transparency refers to openness in public administration and access to information from the public sector agencies. It entails that decision-making and processing of cases and documents should not be disguised or withdrawn from public scrutiny. In its most basic sense accountability means that public officials and others in positions of trust should, as a matter of principle, be held to account for their actions and be sanctioned if not performing according to established norms and standards of proper civil service behaviour.

The governance debate within the donor community has centred on rather technical or managerial aspects of governance, initially shying away from the full political implications in terms of democratic institutions and practice. The international financial institutions were concerned primarily with the implementation of stabilisation and structural adjustment policies in the economic sphere. However, they gradually came to realise that agreeing with the governments in question on substantive economic policies did not necessarily mean straightforward implementation. At first, faltering implementation was attributed to lack of technical competence and capacity, not to the wider political environment in which implementation was to take place. It was only well into the 1990s that democratisation was put firmly on the agenda, based on the acknowledgement that it was not enough to 'get the prices and policies right' and adhere to management practices in accordance with the precepts of 'good governance'; it was also necessary to 'get the politics right'.

We prefer to use governance as a neutral term to denote a broad category of management practices, distinguishable from the more specific term of government. The latter refers to the overtly political institutions of a given polity: the legislature, the executive (including the civil service), and the judiciary, plus other institutions comprising the state apparatus. Governance, on the other hand, refers to *practices* rather than formal institutions and as noted above, can be understood as the general manner in which people are governed—but not exclusively by the institutions of government. The nature of governmental institutions has a bearing, of course, on the quality of governance, but government and governance should not be conflated as identical phenomena. Furthermore, the way in which governance is exercised largely reflects the prevailing political culture, i.e. notions about how people relate to one another in political and public life. Thus, governance is as much about legitimacy as it is about pure administration and management.

It should be noted that practices of 'governance' take place also outside the institutions of government, e.g. within informal activities and civil society. Organisations of civil society may exercise governance internally and on behalf of various constituencies. In this sense, governance is a particularly useful concept in the analysis of the dynamics of urban areas; it is capable of incorporating analyses at both formal and informal levels, including such pervasive phenomena as patronage, clientelism, corruption and empowerment. Since the involvement of civil society in urban governance has largely come about on account of the deficiencies of urban authorities, an urban governance approach is suitable for covering the gap-filling functions of associational life, and collaboration between NGOs and local authorities, as well as the struggles between them.

McCarney et al. (1995:95ff) define governance, as distinct from government, as "the relationship between civil society and the state, between rulers and the ruled, the government and the governed." They see accountability, transparency, responsiveness, real participation, empowerment of groups in civil society and public consultation as central elements in the governance concept. They distance themselves from the erstwhile state-centred use of the term, and emphasise, instead, that the notion of governance permits the incorporation of forces and factors in analyses that were previously considered to be marginally involved in policy formulation, implementation, outcome and impact. McCarney et al. (1995:99–100) contend that:

> [f]or urban analysis, the adoption of the notion of governance leads to a shift away from statist perspectives which predominantly focus on constructs such as administration, management, and even local government in its bureaucratic sense. Governance incorporates elements which, in conventional terms, are often considered to be outside the public policy process. These include the private sector, civil associations, community organisations and social movements. Use of this concept also transcends the institutional and technocratic dimensions of the public policy arena, and accommodates an exploration of political dynamics.

An approach to urban analysis based on governance allows all the stakeholders in the unfolding processes to be taken on board, not only state actors. It permits scrutiny of the nature and role of various agents of civil society, in terms of their organisational form, mode of operation, awareness of and participation in processes of policy formulation, planning and implementation. In short, the governance concept encompasses all the relevant actors and ingredients in urban development.

THE CHANGING ROLE OF URBAN ASSOCIATIONS

Having discussed the magnitude and characteristics of the urban crisis in Africa and clarified conceptual issues related to civil society and associations, there is a need for a critical assessment of the role of associations in urban development. Currently perceived as perhaps *the* solution to the urban problem by governments and aid organisations alike, through the so-called "enabling approach" (UNCHS/Habitat 1996:424), it is important to take a closer look at their strengths and limitations.

With the broad definition of associations adopted here, urban associations are heterogeneous institutions involved in a range of activities including community management, provision of social services and infrastructure, finance and credit, and religious and social affairs. They may be large or small, formal or informal, horizontal or vertical, and base their financial existence on voluntary contributions, membership fees or external funding. Though difficult to quantify, associations of one type or another exist in practically all urban societies and the large majority of urban dwellers will be involved in at least one of them—usually several.

The effectiveness of local associations in serving their members and communities depends on a number of features reflecting their structure, membership and function. Key issues seem to be the degree of community initiation, their internal heterogeneity, the extent to which members participate actively in decision-making, and the contribution made by members in cash or kind. For many associations with a broader mandate, the extent of external funding will also be important for what they can accomplish.

Finally the political and economic context in which the associations function is important for their ability to contribute to the well-being of their members and the development of their communities. An "enabling framework" gives government a central role in setting the stage for urban development, while leaving room for a multiplicity of large and small initiatives, investments and expenditures by local associations. A disabling framework leaves little room for local initiatives and hampers popular participation. Other external agencies (such as aid organisations) can bring knowledge, expertise, capital and advice, but without local participation these initiatives are not likely to respond to the needs and priorities of the communities and associations themselves.

Urban associations are nothing new, and urban anthropology has been concerned with them since the very beginning of the sub-discipline. Louis Wirth in his seminal (albeit much criticised) article "Urbanism as a Way of Life" published in 1938 argued that what he saw as the disintegration of social organisation in urban areas compelled the urbanite to get involved in urbanised groups and associations. "It is largely through the activities of voluntary groups, be their objectives economic, political, educational, religious, recreational or cultural, that the urbanite expresses and develops his personality, acquires status and is able to carry on the round of activities that constitute his life career" (Wirth, 1938:12).

The somewhat negative view of urban life presented by Wirth emphasised divisiveness and fluidity in the urban normative order. It was followed by a proliferation of studies showing that urban areas also contain strong social groups and networks and well adapted households and family units. The city also gave room to individual innovation and entrepreneurship and considerable power and influence (Lewis, 1965; Southall, 1973; Fox, 1977). Much of this work referred to the important role of informal associations and networks in the urban context, largely compensating for the traditional institutions and patterns of social relations known from rural areas.

Many of these studies went out of their way to demonstrate the positive aspects of urban life, losing sight of the difficult situation in which an increasing number of urbanites found themselves. Among the more detailed and sober analyses of the role of associations and networks in the emerging African cities are the Rhodes-Livingstone studies from the Copperbelt in Zambia (Epstein, 1967; Mitchell, 1969), and the University of Natal studies from Port Elizabeth in South Africa (Mayer, 1963; Pauw, 1963). The former emphasised the importance of urban associations as links to the rural areas of origin, while the latter focused on the importance of associations for survival strategies in town as links with rural areas gradually weakened.

The early literature refers primarily to associations with socio-cultural objectives, acting as catalysts for people from the same ethnic group or area of origin in their struggle to settle in a new and hostile urban environment. They included burial societies, church associations and sports clubs. Urban associations were also generally seen as based on ideas and ideologies from the rural areas, with elders (often tribal leaders) in central positions and membership being voluntary and informal.

Towards political independence and before the present urban crisis became apparent, many associations took on more political roles, developing into labour movements (as in Zambia and Kenya) or resistance movements (as in Angola and Mozambique). Leaders with traditional roots were often replaced by younger political entrepreneurs with objectives beyond the immediate social group. Urban associations played an important role in the struggle for independence in many countries in Africa, as they have more recently in the transition towards more democratic regimes.

Post-independence urban Africa saw a retreat to associations of a more private and social nature, including professional associations, with new single-party governments embarking upon ambitious urban development programmes and seeing some of the larger associations as political threats. With an enhanced number of second and third generation urbanites, associations also increasingly turned their attention to issues related to their urban life situation, with less emphasis on maintaining links to their rural areas of origin. In line with this, credit societies and professional associations became more common. Many studies also show a trend towards broader and more heterogeneous membership bases.

The onset of the urban crisis in the mid-1980s, with shortages of housing and jobs, growing poverty and inadequate urban services as important manifestations, seems to have had a dramatic impact on the number and nature of associations in urban areas. Their role increasingly became centred on providing urban services that the state could not deliver (such as housing, water and sanitation) and catering for the more immediate needs of the expanding urban informal settlements through associations ranging from community security societies to religious and other spiritual associations.

From this stage onward, the existence and role of urban associations also caught the attention of governments and aid organisations. The notion of good governance and the perceived role of civil society in development led to support to established locally-based associations, and to the establishment of more formal CBOs and NGOs at an intermediate level between the local community and state. In fact, the involvement of associations came to be seen as a precondition for successful project design and sustainability through "partnerships". The interest culminated in the mid-1990s with the World Bank adopting the notion of 'social capital', defining it as "the ability of actors to secure benefits by virtue of membership in social networks [], normally given structure through the creation of local associations" (World Bank, 1999:3–4).

With the external interest in civil society and associations came more funding, and with more funding came requirements for formal structures and accountability. The process of formalisation of associations has implied new opportunities both economic and political, but also a danger of their becoming detached from their popular base. The involvement of external bodies (governments, international donors and NGOs) has also revealed an inadequate understanding of the role and potentials of local associations.

In many urban contexts associations have become influential actors in the development process at the national, regional and local levels. Enhanced political legitimacy and access to funding have turned them into operative entities attracting well-qualified people. In many countries associations have established formal networks (around housing, credit, informal businesses, etc.) rendering them even more effective. The linkages between many local associations/NGOs have also strengthened their competence and capacity. There are numerous examples throughout Africa of associations that have made important contributions to their members' well-being and home areas.

Having said this, the process of formalisation has also in many cases led to more vertically organised associations characterised by hierarchical relationships and unequal power distribution among their members. Enhanced efficiency and accountability have taken place at the expense of member participation, and many associations have become more elitist and more homogeneous with respect to occupation, economic status and level of education. They have also become more dependent on external actors, who influence objectives as well as organisational forms in the process.

Despite the external attention devoted to civil society, the large majority of voluntary associations in Africa are still informal, work on a small scale and have limited resources. While retaining their popular base and being more horizontal in their organisation, their scope for making an impact are more constrained due to inadequate funding from both external sources and membership fees. There are also a number of examples of associations having disintegrated under pressure to grow and become more formalised.

There are two key issues regarding the changing role of urban associations. One is the extent to which associational life includes the poorest sections of the urban population. With the formalisation and commercialisation of many associations, the thresholds for becoming a member, making an active contribution and benefiting from associational activities are likely to have become higher. Understanding processes of inclusion and exclusion in this respect is important.

A second critical issue concerns how associational life is gendered. The partial exclusion of women in the early phases of urban associational life was related to their traditionally marginal roles in many rural societies. Women in urban areas have subsequently acquired a stronger position, due to their involvement in the informal economy and their status as principal breadwinners in many poor urban households, but their changing status and role are not necessarily reflected in associational life. Specific women's groups proliferate, but there are indications that larger and more influential associations continue to be male-dominated domains.

Despite the growing importance of urban associations, informal networks within kin-groups, neighbourhoods, or gender and age groups and links with rural areas probably still play a more significant role for the urban population in their struggle for survival than do associations. Such networks are important for access not only to material resources, but also to social security and fulfilment of socio-cultural obligations. Having said this, associations and other organisations may have an unfulfilled potential for securing positive outcomes and a better future for the urban residents by finding collective solutions to common problems. Local associations are potentially not only agencies of structural transformation for the urban poor, but also a place where lessons on autonomy, empowerment, popular participation and democracy are learnt (Aina 1990:6).

Associational life in African cities today is characterised by a wide range of organisations with a variety of functions and objectives. As we see it, the role of civil society and urban associations in development is at a crossroads. The challenge is not only to re-establish links with the populations on which associations originally based their existence, but also to establish more effective and equal partnerships with external actors. This requires a better understanding of urban associations among governments, donors and the private sector , as well as more accountable leadership of the associations themselves. In creating such an enhanced understanding, there is an obvious need for more independent research.

References

Aina, Tade Akin, 1990, "Understanding the Role of Community Organisations in Environmental and Urban Contexts", *Environment and Urbanisation*, Vol. 2, No. 1.

—, 1997, "Governance and Urban Poverty in Africa: Challenges to Policy and Action", paper presented at *The International Forum on Urban Poverty*, Florence, Italy, November 9–13, 1997.

Becker, Charles M., Andrew M. Hamer and Andres R. Morrison, 1994, *Beyond Urban Bias in Africa*. Portsmouth: Heinemann and London: James Currey.

Bratton, Michael, 1989a, "Beyond the State: Civil Society and Associational Life in Africa", *World Politics*, Vol. XLI, No 3.

—, 1989b, "The Politics of Government–NGO Relations in Africa", *World Development*, Vol. 17, No. 4.

Bräutigam, Deborah, 1991, *Governance and Economy: A Review*. Policy Research Working Paper (WPS 815), Washington DC: World Bank.

Coquery-Vidrovitch, Catherine, 1988, *Processus d'urbanisation en Afrique, Vol. 1 et 2*. Paris: L'Harmattan.

Epstein, A.L., 1967, "Urbanisation and Social Change in Africa", *Current Anthropology*, Vol. 8.

Etzioni, Amitai, 1993, *The Spirit of Community: The Reinvention of American Society*. New York: Simon & Schuster.

Fox, Richard, 1977, *Urban Anthropology. Cities in their Cultural Context*. Engelwood Cliffs: Prentice Hall.

Fukuyama, Francis, 1992, *The End of History and the Last Man*. Harmondsworth: Penguin Books.

Harbeson, John, Donald Rothchild and Naomi Chazan (eds), 1994, *Civil Society and the State in Africa*. Boulder, CO: Lynne Rienner.

Hardoy, Jorge, E. Sandy Cairncross and David Satterthwaite (eds), 1990, *The Poor Die Young*. London: Earthscan.

Harris, Nigel (ed.), 1992, *Cities in the 1990s: The Challenge for Developing Countries*. London: UCL Press.

Hyden, Goran and Michael Bratton (eds), 1992, *Governance and Politics in Africa*. Boulder, CO: Lynne Rienner.

Jere, Harrington, 1984, "Lusaka: Local Participation in Planning and Decision-making", in Payne, Geoffrey K. (ed.), *Low-Income Housing in the Developing World*. Chichester: John Wiley & Sons.

Kasfir, Nelson (ed.), 1998, *Civil Society and Democracy in Africa: Critical Perspectives*. London: Frank Cass.

Keane, John (ed.), 1988, *Civil Society and the State. New European Perspectives*. London: Verso.

Lewis, Oscar, 1965, "Further Observations on the Folk-Urban Continuum and Urbanisation with Special Reference to Mexico City", in Hauser, P.M. and L.F. Schnore (eds), *The Study of Urbanisation*. New York: Random House.

Maina, Wachira, 1998, "Kenya: The State, Donors and the Politics of Democratisation", in Van Rooy, Alison (ed.), *Civil Society and the Aid Industry: The Politics and Promise*. London: Earthscan.

Mayer, Philip, 1963, *Townsmen and Tribesmen*. Cape Town: Oxford University Press.

McCarney, Patricia, Mohamed Halfani and Alfredo Rodriguez, 1995, "Towards an Understanding of Governance The Emergence of an Idea and its Implications for Urban research in Developing Countries", in Stren, Richard and Judith Kjellberg Bell (eds), *Perspectives on the City, Urban Research in the Developing World*, Vol. 4. Toronto: University of Toronto Press.

Milbert, Isabelle (with Vanessa Peat), 1999, *What Future for Urban Co-operation. Assessment of post Habitat II strategies*. Geneva: Graduate Institute of Development Studies and Swiss Agency for Development and Co-operation.

Mitchell, J.C. (ed.), 1969, *Social Networks in Urban Situations. Analysis of Personal Relationships in Central African Towns*. Manchester: Manchester University Press.

Moser, Caroline O.N., and Linda Peake, 1995, "Gender" in Stren, Richard and Judith Kjellberg Bell (eds), *Perspectives on the City, Urban Research in the Developing World*, Vol. 4. Toronto: University of Toronto Press.

O'Connor, Anthony, 1983, *The African City*. London: Hutchinson.

Pauw, B.A., 1963, *The Second Generation*. Cape Town: Oxford University Press.

Peil, Margaret with Pius O. Sada, 1984, *African Urban Society*. Chichester: John Wiley & Sons.

Pelczynski, Z.A., 1984, *The State and Civil Society. Studies in Hegel's Political Philosophy*. Cambridge: Cambridge University Press.

Portes, Alejandro, 1998, "Social Capital: Its Origins and Application in Modern Sociology", in *Annual Review of Sociology*, Vol. 24.

Putnam, Robert D., 1993, *Making Democracy Work. Civic Traditions in Modern Italy*. Princeton, NJ: Princeton University Press.

Rakodi, Carole, (ed.), 1997, *The Urban Challenge in Africa: Growth and management of its large cities*. Tokyo, New York and Paris: United Nations University Press.

Robinson, Mark and Gordon White, 1997, *The Role of Civic Organisations in the Provision of Social Services: Towards Synergy*. Research for Action 37, World Institute for Development Economics Research (WIDER), Helsinki.

Rothchild, Donald and Naomi Chazan, (eds), 1988, *The Precarious Balance: State and Society in Africa*. Boulder, CO: Westview Press.

Salamon, L.M. and H.K. Anheier, 1992: "In Search of the Non-profit Sector I: The Question of Definition", *Voluntas*, 3, 3.

Shils, Edward, 1991, "The Virtue of Civil Society", *Government and Opposition*, Vol. 26, No. 1.

Sjögren, Anders, 1998, "Civil Society and Governance in Africa—an Outline of the Debates", Working Paper No. 1 from the *Research Programme on Cities, Governance and Civil Society in Africa*. Uppsala: Nordic Africa Institute.

Southall, Aidan (ed.), 1973, *Urban Anthropology. Cross-Cultural Studies of Urbanisation*. New York: Oxford University Press.

Sowell, Thomas, 1996, *Migrations and Cultures: A World View*. New York: Basic Books.

Stren, Richard, 1994, "Towards a Research Agenda for the 1990s. An Introduction", in Stren, R. (ed.), *Urban Research in the Developing World: Africa*. Vol. 2. Centre for Urban and Community Studies, University of Toronto.

Stren, Richard and J. Kjellberg Bell (eds), 1995, *Perspectives on the City, Urban Research in the Developing World*, Vol. 4. Toronto: University of Toronto Press.

Stren, Richard E. and Rodney R. White (eds), 1989, *African Cities in Crisis*. Boulder, San Francisco and London: Westview Press.

Swilling, Mark (ed.), 1997, *Governing Africa's Cities*. Johannesburg: Witwatersrand University Press.

Tostensen, Arne and Frederik Grünfeld, 1999, *Options and Trade-offs: Means and Measures in the Implementation of Norwegian Human Rights Policy*. Oslo: Ministry of Foreign Affairs. Studies on Foreign Policy Issues. Report 4:99.

Tostensen, Arne, 1993, "The Ambiguity of Civil Society in the Democratisation Process", in Ofstad, Arve and Arne Wiig (eds), *Development Theory: Recent Trends*. Proceedings of the Norwegian Association of Development Research Annual Conference 1992. Bergen: Chr. Michelsen Institute, Report R 1993:6.

Tvedt, Terje, 1998, *Angels of Mercy or Development Diplomats? NGOs and Foreign Aid*. Oxford: James Curry.

UN, 1998, *World Urbanisation Prospects. The 1996 Revision*. New York: United Nations.

UNCHS/HABITAT, 1996, *An Urbanizing World*. Global Report on Human Settlements 1996. Oxford: Oxford University Press.

Vaa, M., S. Findley and A. Diallo, 1989, "The Gift Economy: A Study of Women Migrants' Survival Strategies in a Low-Income Bamako Neighbourhood", *Labour, Capital and Society*, 22:234–60.

Van Rooy, Alison (ed.), 1998, *Civil Society and the Aid Industry: The Politics and Promise*. London: Earthscan.

Vennetier, Pierre, 1976, *Les villes d'Afrique tropicale*. Paris: Masson.

Wellman, Barry, 1999, "The Network Community: An Introduction", in Barry Wellman (ed.), *Networks in the Global Village: Life in Contemporary Communities*. Boulder CO: Westview.

Wirth, Louis (1938), "Urbanism as a Way of Life", *American Journal of Sociology* (44).

World Bank, 1999, *Does Social Capital Help the Poor? A Synthesis of Findings from Local Level Institutions Studies in Bolivia, Burkina Faso and Indonesia*. Washington: World Bank.

—, 2000, *Entering the 21st Century*. World Development Report *1999/2000*, Oxford: Oxford University Press, Ch. 6.

Wratten, Ellen, 1995, "Conceptualising Urban Poverty", *Environment and Urbanisation*, Vol. 7, No. 1, April 1995, pp. 11–36.

SECTION I

COPING THROUGH INFORMAL NETWORKS

Informal networks form an important part of associational life in African cities. Due to their low degree of formalisation networks are often hard to trace by outsiders, such as bureaucrats or researchers. Indeed, networks are less frequently studied than their more formalised counterparts. Yet, they are a living reality and a crucial element in the coping strategies of the urban poor. This section seeks to highlight the role of mutual assistance networks among the urban poor in Africa, exemplified by experiences from Guinea-Bissau, Senegal, South Africa and Swaziland.

All the contributions of this section deal with networks in one way or another. The common denominator is the exploitation of existing networks for resource mobilisation. In this manner mutual-help networks are means to acquiring material resources to alleviate urban poverty. Beyond poverty alleviation at the most basic level social networks may also constitute a 'productive resource' to be utilised in extensive trading arrangements across Africa and beyond, within which large amounts of goods and money circulate.

Taking her cue from empirical observations in Bissau, the capital city of Guinea-Bissau, Ilda Lourenço-Lindell argues in favour of a network approach to urban studies. She asserts that informal networks of mutual assistance, notwithstanding their loose nature, are critical in the coping strategies of poor urbanites. Being embedded in webs of social relationships, people gain access to niches of the urban informal economy, find places to live, and are sustained through crises. Lourenço-Lindell conceptualises participation in such networks as 'informal rights', stressing the reciprocity involved over time. However, she is careful to underscore the differential ability of urban dwellers to exercise their informal rights, and to pinpoint that both co-operation and conflict are inherent in these networks.

While recognising the vulnerability of the urban poor—i.e. insecurity, exposure to risk and inability to recover—Lourenço-Lindell sees informal networks as a social resource to be exploited in order to reduce vulnerability. Networks are particularly important in efforts to recover from material shocks; hence, poor people invest in such webs of social relationships as an insurance policy of sorts.

At the empirical level Lourenço-Lindell shows the importance of networks in rice production and fish mongering in Bissau. Not only are network intermediaries important in getting access to resources like land, labour and information, but also in distributive processes once the products are available. The mode of operation of these networks defies the logic of an impersonal market; basically, they rest on sets of cultural rights and obligations.

AbdouMaliq Simone's comparative study of Soumbedioune in Greater Dakar, Senegal and the inner city of Johannesburg, South Africa, emphasises the extreme fluidity of informal networks, which defies formalisation and produces a situation of near 'invisibility'. The fluidity and 'invisibility' of these networks turn them into singularly flexible tools for responding to windows of opportunity, as and when they appear. It is precisely the *ad hoc* nature of networks that help them to maintain flexibility and to widen the range of options available in changing circumstances. In this manner vulnerability is reduced.

The source of cohesion of the networks is partly found in entrenched traditions, ethnicity and religion, and partly in adaptations to modernity that add new elements and modify their modes of operation. In Soumbedioune, for example, religious networks play a prominent role, but they are reinforced and/or modified by modern patterns of migration. The *turuq*—Islamic Sufi-based brotherhoods—constitute linchpins in the management of Senegalese identity, but they are also networks extending far beyond the borders of Senegal. While initially engaged in local trading in groundnuts and consumables, they have gradually embarked upon with commercial activities world-wide.

By contrast, the networks operating in the inner city of Johannesburg are not based on religious ties. With the repeal of the influx control laws of the apartheid regime migrants have moved into the big cities in great numbers, not only from areas within the borders of South Africa but also from the Southern African sub-region and the African continent at large. The networks are generally based on these migratory patterns. However, friction has arisen between the indigenous South Africans and 'alien' immigrants. With xenophobic overtones, the former seek to fend off competition by constricting the operations of the latter.

The contribution by Miranda Miles discusses the role of informal networks in the coping strategies of poor women in Swaziland. In vulnerable positions on the lower rungs of the employment ladder individuals, households and communities mobilise whatever resources they command to eke out a living. Apart from the tangible assets at their disposal, women create and draw on networks to enhance their resilience and chances of survival. These informal reciprocity networks derive largely from long-standing rural traditions of communal work parties, which are recreated in the city to form a basis for acquisition of resources within an urban setting. The source of cohesion in the city is generally kinship, friendship or home area origin ('homegirl network').

Within the framework of a rudimentary social welfare system, coupled with increasingly tenuous urban-rural ties, the female urbanites rely on the informal networks for their survival. Miles refers to a common mechanism for mobilising resources: rotating savings and credit systems whose members contribute a certain amount on a regular basis. After a specified time each member may take out the collectively saved amount. The right to withdraw money from the common pool thus rotates among the members. The funds may be used for any purpose, at the discretion of each member: burials, school fees, medication, utilities, etc. Networks may also be utilised to acquire land, employment (mostly domestic work), shelter, market stalls, etc. Although most networks prove useful in securing some sort of tangible asset, they should not be underestimated as sources of moral support and comfort. As such they serve a therapeutic function in terms of psychological well-being.

CHAPTER 2

Social Networks and Urban Vulnerability to Hunger

Ilda Lourenço-Lindell

INTRODUCTION

Dwellers in many African cities face difficult challenges. They have seen their cities grow at unprecedented rates, felt the heightened competition for resources and witnessed the failure of their governments to provide basic services and jobs. They have also experienced how structural adjustment policies have severely cut their real incomes, made them redundant and deprived them of affordable education, health services and even food. As a result larger social groups are being affected by increased material poverty, and new groups are becoming vulnerable. But urbanites have not yet been defeated by these increasing strains and are responding to the changes in a variety of ways. They are forming organisations to fill in the gaps in service provision and press for greater social justice, and also becoming engaged in webs of mutual exchange of goods and services. Not surprisingly, the informalisation of economic activities has reached new heights and associational life seems to be booming in many African cities.

While the general concern of this volume is with organised associational activity in urban Africa, this particular paper deals with less formalised forms of co-operation in the form of networks of assistance and their role in coping with the increasing stresses of urban life. A focus on social networks has not been as fashionable as the focus on more formalised groups including community based associations, at least partly as a result of the emphasis currently being given to the potential role of such groups in urban management and democratisation. The aim of this paper is not to question the importance of such associations, but to remind ourselves that there are informal structures operating in African cities which sustain the lives and livelihoods of many disadvantaged people and offer them a measure of security. People are embedded in webs of relationships which facilitate their access to niches in the urban informal economy, help them find a place to live, and sustain them through crises of various types.

The kind of informal relations and networks that characterise many urban neighbourhoods in Africa has not been sufficiently taken into consideration in urban development policies. This is due to a persistent obsession with visions of urban modernity, no matter how alien to local realities these may be. Current hegemonic approaches to urban governance and development tend to rest upon neo-liberal principles, emphasising economic competition and efficiency and individual performance based on "rational" choices and profit maximisation. Such approaches also assume that urbanisation will lead to economic individualisation and a homogeneous mass society.

We will argue that in their daily struggle for survival urban dwellers develop their own rationality and logic of behaviour, which often do not comply with externally imposed visions of the city. A variety of informal rights, i.e. rights that may not conform with market rationality and cannot be enforced in modern courts of law, seem to be playing a role in sustaining people's livelihoods in a context of widening material poverty. This paper addresses the role of such informal rights in alleviating increasing urban vulnerability. Several related points are also developed. Firstly, the differential ability of urban dwellers to exert such rights and to mobilise support is stressed as an important dimension of urban vulnerability. Secondly, assumptions that informal security systems are doomed to disappear in the face of urbanisation and economic crisis are questioned. Thirdly, the diversity of rules and motivations underlying support networks is highlighted by showing the coexistence of relations of co-operation and conflict in such networks, challenging common one-sided approaches to these issues. Field data from Bissau, the capital of Guinea-Bissau, are used in support of these propositions.

VULNERABILITY AND INFORMAL RIGHTS TO SUPPORT

The debate on vulnerability provides a good entry point into the discussion of access to support in situations of crisis.[1] The debate has accused conventional approaches of narrowly defining poverty in terms of income, attributing it to lack of employment, and of portraying the poor as a homogeneous and passive group fatally positioned under a defined poverty line. In its obsession with the measurable, local definitions and variations are erased and other dimensions (often qualitative and hence more difficult to measure) are neglected. Non-cash income is ignored, as is the great diversity of activities other than income-earning in which people engage in pursuit of their livelihoods. Critics have called for a deconstruction and disaggregation of the poverty concept, and have advanced alternative understandings. They propose the term *vulnerability* to reflect processes of change in human well being, as well as a variety of other dimensions that constitute deprivation in addition to income poverty. Chambers emphasises that the term should not be confused with poverty: vulnerability means "not lack or want, but defencelessness, insecurity, and exposure to risks" (1989:1). It is a multidimensional concept that includes a variety of aspects such as physical weakness, social inferiority, feeling of powerlessness and social isolation. Important implications of these statements are that the materially poor are not necessarily the only and most vulnerable group in a society, nor are they necessarily equally vulnerable.

Chambers identifies two aspects of vulnerability, "an external side of risks, shocks and stress to which an individual or household is subject; and an internal side which is defencelessness, meaning a lack of means to cope without damaging loss" (1989:1). Watts and Bohle (1993) further develop this idea by stating that the most vulnerable groups are those most exposed to

---

[1] For critical reviews and development of alternative notions of vulnerability, see Rakodi (1995) and Chambers (1995).

risks and shocks, with the least capacity to cope and the lowest potential to recover. Consequently, they argue, alleviating vulnerability implies reducing exposure and increasing in coping capacity and recovery potential, through public and/or private means. This, I will argue, is what urban dwellers do when they invest in webs of relationships and associations in the absence of functioning public security systems. Whether participation in such networks counters exposure and increases the potential for coping and recovering have to be tested empirically.

As argued above, access to support is not equal for everyone. The nature and extension of networks vary from one person to another, as does the ability to exercise claims for support. While the politics of state service provision has been a popular theme in urban research, the politics of support mobilisation at the micro-level has not been equally well documented. We need to address claims based on locally accepted notions of legitimacy and informal rights to support, which have their own systems of sanctions and rewards. Defended and fought over, these rights represent a coping resource for some and a particular kind of vulnerability for others, such as those who are isolated and marginalised in their own neighbourhood.

A brief review of relevant debates will aid us in our endeavour to see who are best equipped to obtain support and make informal claims. The debates relate to informal claims, informal security systems, gifts and the so-called "moral economy".

One approach emphasises sets of rules of behaviour that do not conform to those operating in the market. This is the case with research on cultural principles governing social interaction in general, and gift exchange in particular. Mauss's essay (1967) on gift practices in archaic societies is an important point of reference for such studies. One of his pioneering ideas was that gift transactions, or more precisely "the spirit of the gift", create enduring bonds between mutually dependent persons. The implied distinction between gift and commodity exchange (i.e. impersonal exchange between independent individuals) has been criticised and rational models of reciprocity have been advanced that focus on the material (rather than spiritual) motivations to return gifts (Appadurai, 1995; Sahlins, 1972).[2] Despite criticism, however, the basic idea about the link between personalised forms of exchange and long term social relationships has survived to this day. Werbner (1995), for example, emphasises the role of gifts in establishing links and alliances and in building morally binding relationships and describes how gifts objectify valued social relations.

Another approach is that of the "moral economy", most prominent in the study of precapitalist rural societies.[3] This approach assumes that such societies were geared to guarantee economic and social security for all their members, on the basis of socio-cultural rights to a minimum level of subsistence. It is argued that social arrangements and institutions developed in these societies to deal particularly with the threat of hunger and other risks (Scott, 1976;

---

[2] See also Yan (1996) for a discussion of the evolution of the anthropological discourse on the gift.

[3] See Scott (1976) for an important reference in this discourse.

Platteau, 1991). Mutual insurance relations and market relations (restricted to inter-village transactions and subordinated to control by socio-political mechanisms) are seen as exclusionary and even conflictual, in that the expansion of markets is interpreted as a threat to the reproduction of the value system that constitutes the moral economy. This approach has also generated considerable criticism. It is accused of a romanticised view of traditional norms, seen as "moral", welfarist and harmoniously working for the well being of all group members (Gore, 1993). Such idyllic interpretations of moral economies, which still pervade many statements about reciprocal support today, should be avoided because they foreclose the possibility of conflict and politics in informal security systems and networks of assistance. Nevertheless, the moral economy argument continues to be an important analytical tool for explaining human behaviour in contemporary societies that does not conform with market rationality (Platteau, 1991; Gregory, 1982).

A third set of approaches to informal rights and social networks downplays shared norms with respect to assistance and focuses instead on individual strategies and self-interested agents acting to maximise their returns. These approaches include research which adopts a rational model of reciprocity and assumes that economic rationality and careful calculation about return underlies all gift exchanges. Political economists in particular have been accused of trivialising gift practices in contemporary societies, by assuming that, with the expansion of the capitalist mode of production market exchange will replace gift exchange (Cheal, 1988; Platteau, 1991). Gift practices are seen as remnants of a precapitalist moral order, largely confined to the domestic sphere. These researchers have also tended to be sceptical about the notion of village-based collective insurance mechanisms, and have tended to see members of peasant societies as self-interested agents rather than individuals who are also altruistic or passively obedient to social or moral principles. The fact that social norms are negotiable and in continuous change prevents such efforts at collective insurance from succeeding, it is argued.

Relevant here is Jeremy Swift's (1989) discussion of the notion of *claims*. He argues for including claims on a variety of institutions (other households, patrons, the government, the international community etc.) in the list of assets a household has for coping with food crises. Tangible and intangible assets are created by the household during periods of surplus, which are invested in stores and claims of various types and then cashed in during a crisis. By assuming "no surplus, no claims", he equates the ability of households to activate community support with their capacity to generate a surplus. While Swift recognises that expectations of reciprocity may vary and that local systems of rights and obligations that do not conform with market principles of exchange may exist, such "deviations" do not influence his interpretation of how assets are generated. This suggests a utilitarian view of reciprocal support, resting upon careful calculations of the probability of equivalent returns.

Instrumental interpretations have also pervaded much social network analysis. One classical example is Kapferer's study of a conflict between two workers in a factory context (Kapferer, 1969). He concludes that the probability of an individual fulfilling the norms governing his relationship with another will depend on the extent of his social investment in this individual, as well as the expected returns on that investment. As a result of competitive mobilisation of colleagues during the conflict, he argues, some come out stronger with their authority confirmed while others come out weaker, isolated and marginalised. A similar view is held by Galaskiewicz (1979), who sees network formation as a result of the competition between actors in securing resources for survival and increased influence.

Both perspectives emphasising utility maximisation and individual strategies are clearly influenced by a neo-liberal view of the individual and of social exchange. This is, as we see it, too narrow a view to explain the patterns of assistance at work in African cities. They imply that those able to mobilise and claim support are exclusively those who are able to compete for it, and/or possess sufficient material resources to fulfil the expectations of their exchange partners. Werbner (1995) and Cheal (1988) have accused such approaches of ignoring both the cultural content and the role of sentiment in exchange relations. Others argue against reducing all transactions to "the depersonalised exchanges of neoclassical theory" (Rogers and Vertovec, 1995:18).

How then should we approach the issue of informal claims and mobilisation of support in urban Africa? An understanding of the alternative rationalities that pervade the webs of social ties operating in many urban communities, and of the kinds of claims that different categories of people can make on each other, will benefit from adopting perspectives that emphasise collective efforts and morally binding relationships between people. The urban social environment is not just one of fierce competition and high turnover in relationships. It also contains enduring social bonds that are continuously reproduced through the exchange of goods and favours. The long term sustainability of such bonds may be given priority over the satisfaction of one's immediate material needs. Bonds of this type may be voluntary and highly valued by those involved, nurtured by mutual affection. They may also constitute socially accepted and culturally determined sets of rights and duties and resilient customary obligations which are susceptible to sanctions if not fulfilled.

Such a nuanced perspective takes us beyond a moral economy conceived as self-contained, harmonious and equally beneficial to all actors involved. Perspectives focusing on conflict and competition in reciprocal support are useful in this context to uncover elements of instrumentality in "moral" economies, as well as those norms that work to benefit some and subordinate others. Thus, an analysis of informal security systems should draw on the strengths of both moral economy and political economy approaches, remaining in this way sensitive to both co-operation and conflict. Such a view will allow a better understanding of the politics of support mobilisation and the assertion of "claims" on other persons, and help shed light on issues of differential access to support.

Our review of the relevant debates shows that gift exchanges and informal systems of insurance have too often been assumed to be archaic, belonging in traditional precapitalist (rural) societies. The moral economy is often seen as doomed to disappear, whether under the impact of modernisation, urbanisation, the market, or the modern state (see for example Watts, 1984).

We have argued that such assumptions are too simplistic, and are of little use for understanding the current dynamics of support systems in the urban context. There is a rationality that does not conform to market principles, which exhibits a significant resilience under the pressures of the market or economic crisis. Gift exchange may have its roots in custom, but it adapts to change and has survived even in complex industrial societies (Cheal, 1988; Werbner, 1995; Otnes and Beltramini, 1996). A number of case studies have shown the existence of moral economies and "non-market" forms of exchange in urban environments in Africa.[4]

The effects of sudden crises and deteriorating economic conditions on informal security systems are far from clear. Such events are often seen as almost automatically leading to a breakdown of interhousehold exchange of support.[5] Although this might be so in many situations, there is scope for further probing into this issue. There are case-studies that point to an increase in the importance of social networks of assistance in conditions of hardship (Moser, 1996). Indeed, as Lomnitz writes in her study of networks of reciprocal exchange in an unplanned settlement of Mexico City, "those at the bottom of the social scale in society (...) have literally nothing. Their only resources are of a social nature" (1977:3). She even argues that such networks arise in conditions of economic necessity and structural insecurity.

Thus the available evidence seems contradictory: while economic crises and the spread of market relations exert pressure on informal mechanisms of assistance, the trend is far from being universal and uniform. Instead of asking whether informal relationships of assistance are disappearing, the question should be *how* support networks are adapting and changing in response to urbanisation and the current deterioration of living conditions in African cities. What types of networks and support relations are weakening, what types are being preserved and strengthened, and under what circumstances? The issue of the dynamics of urban social networks also needs further elaboration by relating it to both intra-network politics and wider processes in society, in order to deepen our understanding of why different groups and individuals in the city differ in their ability to exert informal rights and to mobilise support.

INFORMAL RIGHTS IN THE FOOD ECONOMY OF BISSAU

The propositions outlined above about informal rights and networks of assistance in the urban context find support in empirical material collected in Bissau, Guinea-Bissau. Data were collected as part of a study of household strategies for food provisioning, which included a range of social resources supporting consumption and food related activities.[6] Fieldwork was conducted in 1992 and 1995, using both qualitative and quantitative methods, and in-

---

[4] For example Tripp (1997) shows how social concerns may come before profit considerations among informal sector workers in Dar Es Salaam. Macharia (1997) affirms that social contacts are the secret behind the growth of the informal economy in Nairobi and Harare. Vaa et al. (1989) discuss the relevance of the exchange of gifts and services among women in Bamako.

[5] See e.g. Chambers (1989) and Swift (1989).

[6] See Lourenço-Lindell (1995) and (1996) for some of the published results.

cluding a survey of 340 households as well as interviews with households, food producers and traders.

Bissau's population has been going through a process similar to the one described in the introduction to this paper. A large proportion of residents are experiencing impoverishment, exacerbated by the effects of structural adjustment policies. The liberalisation of the economy initiated in 1987 has generally increased the availability of food, but access to food for the poorest sections of the population has deteriorated owing to declining purchasing power. People are surviving and adapting to these wider changes by growing food, increasing their engagement in informal trade, and participating in inter-household transfers of food and money. This section discusses the involvement in these activities, of residents in the district of Bandim in Bissau with a particular focus on the social resources supporting them.

Informal rights in urban food production

Bandim is a former village caught up by urban growth. It is an unplanned settlement, housing close to 30,000 people. Commercial activities constitute the main source of cash income in the area, with prominence for trade in foodstuffs and drinks. Self-employment predominates, but 30 per cent of the surveyed households rely on a mixture of self- and wage employment. Food production is also important for the Bandim population. About two thirds of the households practise agriculture (dominated by rice-farming), fishing or livestock production.

Rice fields in Bandim are held mainly by the Pepel, an ethnic group with ancient roots in the area. Their cultural heritage has been resilient in the urban context, owing to the strong opposition of this group to colonialism and their continued marginalisation from urban development after independence. Their cultural heritage is still traceable in their local political and social organisation, as well as in the organisation of rice farming activities and land tenure system.

Rice grown in Bandim does not reach the market. The harvest is used for the residents' own consumption, for feeding the workforce during agricultural seasons, for cultural ceremonies and as gifts to relatives and friends. Even when there is a surplus that could be sold, there is a deliberate decision not to sell: heads of compounds are expected to save surpluses to fulfil their obligations to assist others with rice or to help other farmers with seeds.

Land for farming in Bandim is normally allocated on the basis of traditional rights rather than through the market. The majority of rice plots has been distributed to the household by an elder, inherited or borrowed. Customary rules for land allocation are not easily tempered. However, the swamp areas where rice production is carried out are not immune to the pressures of urbanisation, as is evident from official town plans allocating rice land to purposes such as culture and sportsgrounds, high standard residential areas and industrial development.

The labour used in rice production is primarily from the farmer's own household or compound. But during periods of intensive work such as ploughing and harvesting other sources of labour have to be mobilised. Such labour is preferably recruited from the local compounds and age groups within the Pepel ethnic group, and their work is compensated by a good meal and wine. More recently, however, Pepel farmers have also recruited people from other ethnic groups and made small payments in cash in addition to food.

Rice production relies on social control of women and youth. Opportunities for making an income in the informal economy have expanded dramatically since 1987 in connection with the liberalisation of the economy. Some women and youngsters see in this an opportunity for evading the authority of the elders and traditional obligations in rice production. However, the low income and vulnerability of informal economic enterprises hold such a trend in check, in that the security offered by entering relations within the compound is considered vital.

In sum, the traditional social organisation of rice production is still largely in place, with some adaptations towards greater flexibility in terms of the types of labour recruited. Labour supply is still not at risk, as the current deterioration of living conditions ensures that there are people willing to work for a meal. The problem emerging is the tendency towards payment for labour and the lack of cash and material means for such a form of compensation among the farmers.

Subsistence rice farming in Bandim is thus not based on market principles, but rather on a set of cultural rights and obligations. The resilience of this system, which has survived centuries of commercialisation and decades of urbanisation, is remarkable.

Informal rights in fish marketing

While informal rights at work in subsistence rice production seem resilient in the face of pressures of urbanisation and commercialisation, others are changing and adapting to the new economic environment. This is particularly evident in the realm of food trade, an activity that has boomed in the last decade in the context of the liberalisation of the economy.

Selling fish is an important business opportunity for women. However, entry into fish trade is far from easy. It requires a vigorous body and spirit, sufficient start-up capital and, above all, relations of support with others. Some women generate their own start-up capital from other income earning activities, but many depend on relatives to lend them money. In such cases interest is not charged, and the repayment period is often long and flexible. Necessary marketing skills are acquired from other traders, sometimes by working for an older relative involved in the trade. Access to a good marketing site is sometimes attained through more official channels, but more often arranged through an older relative or a friend willing to share their marketing area. Finally, this activity often requires that women stay away from home for many hours. Help with taking care of children is necessary, and is obtained from other women (co-wives, sisters etc.), or from young girls.

The fish can be obtained from a variety of sources. The most important ones are the port in Bandim where canoes land catch; cold stores which sell frozen fish from industrial vessels to licensed intermediaries; and fish transported to Bissau by traders from the Bijagós archipelago outside Bissau and from the region surrounding the city. Some sellers tend to use one single source of supply, having an informal agreement with one particular supplier. However, many rotate between the different sources as a strategy to spread the risk. In this case, the daily decision about which source to use is dependent upon the information they get from other retailers. These informal channels of information keep the fishmongers informed about the supply and price of the fish at the different points where it can be purchased.

Secure access to merchandise is facilitated by establishing a personal relationship with suppliers. Let us illustrate with the two first mentioned supply sources. Obtaining fish at the cold stores requires close contact with one of the licensed intermediaries who in turn is connected to an employee at the store. This facilitates buying fish on credit and getting hold of supplies when the cold stores are short of fish. At the artisanal port, a number of informal arrangements for getting fish are also at work. While many women have to sleep at the port and run the risk of assault, others need not do this and are sure of getting supplies and even credit from the fishermen. The latter often become intermediaries and create their own clientele of retailers with whom they enter special arrangements.

The advantageous position of the intermediaries operating at the Bandim port and at the cold stores rests in many cases on kinship relations, but the use of sexual favours to seal informal agreements is also very common. The success of a business is thus often built upon relations of subordination between the sexes. Having said this, many women refuse to enter into such relations and agreements, retaining a space of relative autonomy, albeit often at a material cost. They use alternative strategies such as co-ordinating their actions in order to get better deals with the fishermen. These women rely more heavily on horizontal relations to sustain their businesses. They share their stock with their colleagues when fish is scarce; they help each other with selling and watch each others' merchandise; they agree on a single price to avoid disputes; they create savings groups which offer security etc. These ties of mutual assistance are often based on friendship or kinship, and sometimes on intra-clan ties. In short, both old and new types of relational categories, as well as relations both of an egalitarian and an exploitative nature, are at work in fish marketing in Bissau.

Participation in inter-household transfers

The household survey from Bandim mentioned above shows that most households rely on a combination of sources of food and income, and that inter-household transfers of food and money play a significant role. More than two-thirds of the households had received food from outsiders during the preceding twelve months. Such transfers primarily come from relatives and neighbours sharing a house or compound, but nearly one-fifth receive gifts from residents in other urban areas and one-tenth from people in rural areas. More than half of the households rely heavily on food transfers (i.e. receive gifts several times a month and/or monthly remittances). These households are often headed by women, have a very low level of food consumption, and have diversified livelihoods. Those least dependent on transfers are households with undiversified livelihoods, mainly depending on wage work.

Of those households who frequently find themselves without food or money to buy it, the majority state that they obtain assistance from households living in the same house or compound, neighbours, relatives or people attending the same church or workplace. The remainder argue that they do not eat sufficiently, beg in the market places, or eat whatever food they can get their hands on. This group thus seems to be isolated from networks of assistance. At the same time, the majority argue that they give food to people who ask for help, even if the remaining food is insufficient to meet the household's needs. This confirms the generally accepted rule of sharing with those in need. However, the 10 per cent that admitted not doing so are important, as they do not abide by the rules.

Who constitute this minority that refuses charity to others, and does not have people to turn to in times of crisis? What are the factors influencing participation or isolation from support systems? The answer requires qualitative analysis not yet concluded, but both personal and structural factors seem to be at work. In relation to the former, some people simply dislike the idea of having a wide range of contacts with whom to exchange material help, often for fear of gossip. Among structural factors, material necessity (as expressed in a low level of food consumption) seems to be a strong motivation for participating. Some poor people seem to be unable to get any kind of help while others can count on help at least in times of severe crisis. Here, household's type of livelihood seems to matter. Households involved in food production are in a position to give food to other households in times of surplus, and hence establish relations of "outstanding claims".

In sum, the preceding discussion of the role of social relations and networks among dwellers of Bissau illustrates some of the arguments of this paper. Firstly, a non-market rationality is evident in the urban context and important for sustaining people's livelihoods. Secondly, these forms of co-operation are not declining uniformly as a result of urbanisation and commercialisation. While some elements show signs of stress, others are clearly adapting to changes and emerging to cope with new conditions. Thirdly, the "moral economies" outlined contain elements of both co-operation and conflict. Finally, the involvement of urban dwellers in systems of non-market exchange differ between households and groups. More research is still needed for a deeper understanding of how informal rights and assistance networks operate during acute crises; of the ways in which such support systems are changing over time; and of the factors determining differential access to such networks.

Some initial reflections are advanced in the next section about the potential of networks as tools of analysis for further understanding of questions of urban vulnerability and support mobilisation in urban contexts.

NETWORKS AS TOOLS OF ANALYSIS

Clyde Mitchell, one of the early and most influential proponents of the network approach, defined social networks as a specific set of linkages among a defined set of persons, with the additional property that the characteristics of these linkages as a whole may be used to interpret the social behaviour of the persons involved (1969:2). He further states that a network can emerge from a set of consciously recognised rights and responsibilities between the persons involved. In addition to this, I suggest that we look at networks as an inventory of the range of social resources available to individuals or households.

Since emerging as an analytical tool in the mid-1950s in relation to studies of urban social conditions, social network analysis has been applied to a wide range of phenomena including mobilisation of support in situations of conflict, political competition, and personal crisis. By focusing on personal relationships, network analysis has also been useful for understanding the circulation of goods and information in seemingly "unstructured" social environments and for analysing patterns and principles of social interaction in the city. Network analysis also seems to be a promising avenue for approaching relationships of assistance and redistributive processes among urban dwellers.

Analysis of the structure and nature of relationships is usually subdivided into interactional aspects and structural characteristics.[7] Interactional variables consist of the *content* of the relationship (which basically means the purpose); the degree of *multiplexity (i.e.* the variety of purposes a relationship contains); and the *direction* of the interaction (meaning whether relations are reciprocal or asymmetrical). Structural or morphological characteristics of networks include the *size* of the network; the *density* of links in the network; the *intensity* of interaction (i.e. "the degree to which individuals are prepared to honour obligations, or feel free to exercise the rights implied in their link") (Mitchell, 1969:27); the *frequency* of interaction; the *reachability* (meaning the extent to which one can use personal relationships to contact people who are important); the *social range* or social field (which relates to the social heterogeneity contained in ego's network); and finally the *geographical range* of the network.[8]

Some studies[9] have related the capacity to mobilise support to the interactional and structural characteristics of networks. Mitchell (1969) also expresses the idea that "people who are bound together in many ways are more securely bound to each other" and asserts that this tends to affect the probability of support. He further relates *reachability* to norm enforcement and ability to exert pressure on others. Wheeldon (1969) shows how influential people had large and socially heterogeneous networks and how this influenced

---

[7] For discussions of network variables see Mitchell (1969); Barnes (1969); Bridge (1993).

[8] Bridge (1993) highlights the importance of space in the formation and maintenance of social networks, in his study of class reactions to gentrification in a neighbourhood of London. He shows how network analysis can be used for overcoming spatial formalism and demystifying certain geographical assumptions. Further problematisation and more research is needed on the geographical dimensions of networks.

[9] The few examples reported here pertain mainly to network studies conducted in Central African towns.

where they looked for help during a neighbourhood dispute. In a study of relationships between local organisations in a non-African context, Galaskiewicz (1979) sees centrality (i.e. the density of relational sets) as a pivotal factor determining an actor's level of participation and influence in community decision-making. He sees actors as embedded in relational systems where "some actors are able to raise more hell than others" (1979:156). He makes the point that status does not depend solely on material resources, but also on relational assets. In sum, persons with large, dense and highly reachable and heterogeneous networks have often been in a better position to exert influence and mobilise support than others.

The structure and content of social networks, as well as the relation between network characteristics and ability to mobilise support, will vary from one socio-economic and cultural context to another. However, the research tradition presented supplies us with some basic tools for classifying the range of social resources available to different categories of urban dwellers. From there, we can proceed by exploring beneath descriptive patterns of interaction into issues such as the diversity of motivations and meanings underlying personal relationships, intra-network divisions of rights and responsibilities, and relations of dependence and subordination.

Additional concepts useful when studying support mobilisation in conditions of crisis include the distinction between *effective* and *extended* networks, reflecting not only different degrees of acquaintance and multiplexity but also differences in terms of social range (Epstein, 1969; Wheeldon, 1969). Effective networks are those more immediately available, and thus particularly important in situations of sudden crises. But access to extended networks may become crucial during prolonged crises after effective links have been exhausted.[10] A similar distinction is that between *activated* and *potential* links, with the latter referring to dormant ties that can be activated when necessary, based on specific bonds or cultural norms.

Such a systematic analysis of networks equips us to ask how people strategise the use of their various kinds of social ties in times of crisis, what kinds of social ties are given priority and what links are the most resilient and reliable. Such questions are relevant for understanding who feels safe, and who feels insecure. Understanding long term changes in support systems is also facilitated. A network analysis prompts us to ask questions such as: Are social ties becoming more instrumental and short term, or are people concentrating their efforts on amore limited range of highly valued and reliable relationships? How do people select which ties to sacrifice and which to preserve in the short and long term? What are the strategies people use for establishing new links and claims and nurturing old ones, for building up a large network of contacts and for achieving a central position in it?

The shortcomings of formal network analysis, as well as the difficulties in applying its methods, are many and have been reviewed elsewhere.[11] Critical points relate to the fact that network analysis has been a historical, portraying

---

[10] See Granovetter (1982) for a discussion of the importance of "weak ties".

[11] For example Hannerz (1980).

networks as static.[12] Analyses of change in networks of assistance over time need to take account of both intra-network dynamics and the impact of wider changes. Many network studies have also depicted personal networks as being detached from their social context. Such narrow types of analysis should be avoided by relating instead to the numerous studies which link personal networks and wider social structures.[13] Indeed, the composition of a personal network reflects on individual's position in the social structure, his/her class, gender, ethnic and other positions, as well as wider social divisions and alliances (see Mitchell, 1969; Kapferer, 1969). Social position also affects an individual's ability to participate in support networks and to exercise claims.

Network analyses are also faced with problems of methodology. First, conventional network analysis has become rather rigid in its methods. An obsession with accuracy and rigor has led to an almost compulsory quantification and statistical manipulation of network ties. As Ottenberg (in Hannerz, 1980:185) puts it, "the individual as human being disappears in the network calculation". Hannerz defends a more flexible and humanist approach to network methods. The variables and procedures should be selected according to their relevance to the phenomenon being studied. Network ideas should be helpful in advancing understanding of how support is mobilised, not the other way around. Finally, delimiting networks for the purpose of analysis is a difficult task. The limits imposed are always arbitrary and do not necessarily reflect real-life situations. Delimiting networks for study should be guided by the purpose of the analysis. Having said this, one of the strengths of network analysis is that it does not have to comply with social or geographical boundaries, or with divisions between market and moral economies, and hence has the ability to capture highly complex and diverse patterns of exchange. This is useful for approaching the increasingly complex patterns of survival and coping in urban Africa. Networks allow us to approach this reality in all its inconsistency and fluidity, and still retain the ability to discern patterns of assistance.

CONCLUSIONS

The basic assumption in this paper has been that informal rights and networks of assistance play an important role in countering urban vulnerability, by sustaining the livelihood of urban dwellers during times of crisis. At the same

---

[12] See Anwar (1995) for an exception; it consists of a longitudinal study of the changes in the networks of Pakistanis in the United Kingdom over ten years.

[13] For example, Barnes, who introduced the network concept, used it to study conceptions of class in a Norwegian village in 1954 (Hannerz, 1980). Cochran et al. (1984) examine the effects of social class on the characteristics of parents' support networks. Bridge (1993) used network analysis to test assumptions about class responses to gentrification in London. He argues that network analysis can contribute to the structure/agency debate. The role of networks in shaping class and other perceptions, as well as in the formation of identity consciousness and social movements, has been discussed by both Bridge and Hannerz (1980). Galaskiewicz (1979) establishes a connection between the structure of (corporate) networks and the influence of actors on collective decision-making. He argues that a network approach can help bridge the gap between micro and macro levels of analysis of social organisation, and provides a resource network model of collective power.

time, it has been argued that the differential access to such networks and the varying capability of individuals to enforce informal rights and claims have not been sufficiently recognised in the literature. Empirical evidence from the capital of Guinea-Bissau indicates that the involvement of urban dwellers in exchange networks of assistance varies, as do their expectations of receiving help in critical periods. The factors underlying these variations deserve further research. A main objective should be to identify which social groups and categories are least endowed with social resources and hence are most vulnerable in the urban environment.

Approaches to informal systems of security provision and exchange of goods and services tend to give one-sided interpretations. The paper has drawn on perspectives usually seen as incompatible, in an attempt to bring forward the diversity of motives, norms and social relations that pervades such systems. Participation is motivated by a combination of shared norms and individual self-interest, of collective goals and instrumentality, of egalitarian and exploitative relationships, of conflictual and co-operative relationships.

The empirical material presented also suggests that informal rights and efforts of collective insurance are not simply deteriorating in the context of urbanisation, a market economy and economic crisis as is often assumed. Some informal rights seem to be under threat, but others show signs of vitality and capacity to adapt to changes.

A systematic network analysis can assist in exploring issues of differential access to assistance, intra-network divisions of labour, as well as the way networks operate in situations of acute crisis and adapt to longer-term socio-economic changes. A focus on networks may facilitate an analysis that goes beyond the traditional dualism between moral and political economy, and market and non-market forms of exchange. As Yan (1996) argues, in his study of social networks in a Chinese village, the cultivation of networks depends on "the combination of both interest and disinterest, expressivity and instrumentality, the voluntary and the constrained" (1996:210).

Referring to the key topic of this volume, social networks can be distinguished from associations, regarding their role and function in urban life. Networks seem more flexible and responsive to individual needs than most associations, because they operate on the basis of personal relationships and decisions. The fact that the poorest may not be able to afford participation in associations leaves them with personal networks as their only viable source of support.

Such informal networks may not have the political potential that some urban associations seem to have, but they are not without political implications. Epstein (1969) sees networks of social ties in the city as an area of autonomy in an urban environment dominated by economic and administrative institutions. Indeed, networks may nurture everyday forms of resistance and acts of non-compliance by urban dwellers dissatisfied with their own situation or with urban policies. This represents what James Scott (1986) has called "the weapons of the weak" which may[14] provide the popular basis for an alternative kind of urban development and governance.

References

Anwar, Muhammad, 1995, "Social Networks of Pakistanis in the UK: A Reevaluation", in Rogers, A. and S. Vertovec (eds), *The Urban Context: Ethnicity, Social Networks and Situational Analysis*. Oxford and Washington: Berg Publishers.

Appadurai, Arjun, 1995, "Introduction: Commodities and the Politics of Value", in Appadurai, A. (ed.), *The Social Life of Things: Commodities in Cultural Perspective*. Cambridge University Press.

Barnes, J., 1969, "Networks and Political Process", in Mitchell, J. Clyde (ed.), *Social Networks in Urban Situations: Analysis of Personal Relationships in Central African Towns*. Manchester University Press.

Bridge, Gary, 1993, *People, Places and Networks*. School for Advanced Urban Studies Publications, University of Bristol.

Castells, Manuel, 1977, *The Urban Question. A Marxist Approach*. London: Edward Arnold.

Chambers, Robert, 1989, "Editorial introduction: Vulnerability, coping and policy", *IDS Bulletin*, 20:2, pp. 1–7.

—, 1995, "Poverty and livelihoods: Whose reality counts?", *Environment and Urbanisation*, 7:1, pp. 173–204.

Cheal, David, 1988, *The Gift Economy*. London: Routledge.

Cochran, Moncrieff, et al., 1984, *The Social Support Networks of Mothers with Young Children: A Cross-National Comparison*. Department of Educational Research, University of Gothenburg.

Epstein, A., 1969, "The Network and Urban Social Organisation", in Mitchell, J. Clyde (ed.), *Social Networks in Urban Situations: Analysis of Personal Relationships in Central African Towns*. Manchester University Press.

Galaskiewicz, Joseph, 1979, *Exchange Networks and Community Politics*. Beverly Hills: Sage Publications, Inc.

Gore, Charles, 1993, "Entitlement relations and 'unruly' social practices: A comment on the work of Amartya Sen", *The Journal of Development Studies*, Vol. 29:3, pp. 429–60.

Granovetter, M., 1982, "The Strength of Weak Ties: A Network Theory Revisited", in Marshen, Peter V. and Nan Lin (eds), *Social Structure and Network Analysis*. Beverly Hills: Sage.

Gregory, C.A., 1982, *Gifts and Commodities*. London: Academic Press.

Hannerz, Ulf, 1980, *Exploring the City: Inquiries Toward an Urban Anthropology*. New York: Columbia University Press.

Kapferer, Bruce, 1969, "Norms and the Manipulation of Relationships in a Work Context", in Mitchell, J. Clyde (ed.), *Social Networks in Urban Situations: Analysis of Personal Relationships in Central African Towns*. Manchester University Press.

Lomnitz, Larissa A., 1977, *Networks and Marginality: Life in a Mexican Shantytown*. New York: Academic Press.

Lourenço-Lindell, Ilda, 1995, "The informal food economy in a peripheral urban district: The case of Bandim district, Bissau", *Habitat International*, 19:2, pp. 195–208.

—, 1996, "How do the urban poor stay alive? Food provision in a squatter settlement of Bissau, Guinea-Bissau", *African Urban Quarterly*, 11:2, 3, pp. 163–68.

Macharia, Kinuthia, 1997, *Social and Political Dynamics of the Informal Economy in African Cities*. Maryland and Oxford: University Press of America.

Mauss, Marcel, 1967, *The Gift*. New York: W W Norton & Company.

---

[14] See Tripp (1997) for an application of this argument to urban Tanzania, where informal sectors workers through non-compliance strategies pressed for a change in urban policies affecting their livelihoods.

Mitchell, J. Clyde ,1969, "The Concept and Use of Social Networks", in Mitchell, J. Clyde (ed.), *Social Networks in Urban Situations: Analysis of Personal Relationships in Central African Towns*. Manchester University Press.

Moser, Caroline, 1996, *Confronting Crisis: A Comparative Study of Household Responses to Poverty and Vulnerability in Four Poor Urban Communities*. Washington: The World Bank.

Otnes, Cele and Richard Beltramini (eds), 1996, *Gift Giving: A Research Anthology*. Bowling Green: Bowling Green State University Popular Press.

Platteau, Jean-Philippe, 1991, "Traditional Systems of Social Security and Hunger Insurance: Past Achievements and Modern Challenges", in Ahmad, E., *Social Security in Developing Countries*. Oxford: Clarendon Press.

Rakodi, Carole, 1995, "Poverty lines or household strategies? A review of conceptual issues in the study of urban poverty", *Habitat International*, 19:4, pp. 407–26.

Rogers, Alisdair and Steven Vertovec (eds),1995, "Introduction", in Rogers, A. and S. Vertovec (eds), *The Urban Context: Ethnicity, Social Networks and Situational Analysis*. Oxford and Washington: Berg Publishers.

Sahlins, Marshall, 1972, *Stone Age Economics*. New York: Aldine de Gruyter.

Scott, James, 1976, *The Moral Economy of the Peasant*. New Haven: Yale University Press.

—, 1986, "Everyday forms of peasant resistance in South-East Asia", *The Journal of Peasant Studies*, 13:2, pp. 5–35.

Swift, Jeremy, 1989, "Why are rural people vulnerable to famine?", *IDS Bulletin*, 20:2, pp. 8–15.

Tripp, Aili M., 1997, *Changing the Rules: The Politics of Liberalisation and the Urban Informal Economy in Tanzania*. Berkeley, Los Angeles and London: University of California Press.

Vaa, Mariken, Sally Findley and Assitan Diallo, 1989, "The Gift Economy: A Study of Women Migrant's Survival Strategies in a Low-Income Bamako Neighbourhood", *Labour, Capital and Society*, 22:2, pp. 234–60.

Watts, Michael, 1984, "The Demise of the Moral Economy: Food and Famine on a Sudano-Sahelian Region in Historical Perspective", in Scott, Earl (ed.), *Life Before the Drought*. London: George Allen and Unwin.

Watts, Michael and Hans Bohle, 1993, "The space of vulnerability: the causal structure of hunger and famine", *Progress in Human Geography*, 17:1, pp. 43–67.

Werbner, Pnina, 1995, "From Commodities to Gifts: Pakistani Migrant Workers in Manchester", in Rogers, A. and S. Vertovec (eds), *The Urban Context: Ethnicity, Social Networks and Situational Analysis*. Oxford and Washington: Berg Publishers.

Wheeldon, P., 1969, "The Operation of Voluntary Associations and Personal Networks in the Political Processes of an Inter-Ethnic Community", in Mitchell, J. Clyde (ed.), *Social Networks in Urban Situations: Analysis of Personal Relationships in Central African Towns*. Manchester University Press.

Yan, Yunxiang, 1996, *The Flow of Gifts: Reciprocity and Social Networks in a Chinese Village*. Stanford: Stanford University Press.

CHAPTER 3

Between Ghetto and Globe:
Remaking Urban Life in Africa

AbdouMaliq Simone

INTRODUCTION: BETWEEN INSIDE AND OUTSIDE

The forces impacting on the shape of urban economies, politics and cultures
are constituted along distinct trajectories: localised constellations of interests
and urban practices are proving progressively resilient *vis-à-vis* municipal and
national governments. More than ever before, the city is an arena for particu-
laristic and contested modes of living. As a result, urban spaces embody highly
specialised interests, often relatively autonomous of the dynamics prevailing in
the rest of the urban system.

The globalisation of economic transactions, on the other hand, creates
new urban arrangements, which compels cities to consider their prospects,
complementary to those of urban entities in other countries, rather than securing their development within national space. Erstwhile connections between physical and social spaces are progressively disjoined, as identity formation, belonging and social allegiance are less rooted in specific localities than
spread across multiple territories, sectors and nations (Amin and Graham,
1997).

Within this global urban context, the move toward "normalisation" of
governance and economic management in most African cities opens up spaces
where efforts to remake everyday life—households, schooling, religious devotion, morality, practices of accumulation, etc.—become increasingly significant
(Diouf, 1996; Mbembe and Roitman 1996; Watts 1996; Chabal and Daloz,
1998; Moore, 1998). None of these "re-makings" have crystal-clear trajectories. At times, the efforts communities make to compensate for the absence of
effective urban government converge, and at times they conflict, with new
forms of social action made possible through broadened local democracies.
The relationship of these "re-makings" with the new regulatory environments
is uneasy, often volatile, resulting in a wide range of tensions.

At the same time, as conceptualisations of urban poverty broaden to include vulnerability and risk, as well as social capital, increased emphasis has
been placed on understanding the role of local institutions and organisations
in remaking everyday life. Can they be mobilised for poverty reduction work
(Johnson 1997; Kanbur, 1999)? But if a renewed approach to local processes
seeks to find greater coherence of social life at this narrower scale, it is bound
to misunderstand what the local really means and how it is situated in a
broader framework. For the "local" can comprise the various ways in which a
specific population organises its survival; a domain of administration defined
by the state; a framework of norms and behaviours which continues over time

to reinforce common objectives; and an arena for engagement with a larger world (Cox, 1998). These aspects may or may not operate in a co-ordinated fashion.

Additionally, the local is increasingly characterised by actions which seek to forge links between particular economies, aspirations, cultural practices and larger global processes in ways that often "by-pass", yet impact on, the national state or local urban system—through migration, smuggling, social movements, and transnational cultural communities (Portes 1995; Appadurai, 1996a; Dey and Westendorff 1996; Swyngedoux, 1996). As Appadurai (1996b) points out, locality is also an act of imagination, defining locality by negotiation of links between sites of agency and multiple imagined worlds, as these worlds are constituted by historically situated groups across the world. Hence, the ability of a locality to exist with a measure of coherence derives from its position in a larger world in which it is operating, and from which it is able to set itself off as identifiably but never comprehensively distinct.

Accordingly, examinations of urban associational life have come to the fore as vehicles through which specific domains of action are constituted. How do diverse urban communities understand their situation and life chances? What is expected from them? What is the nature of opportunities they try to create for themselves? How should they deal with each other? How are memories and events concerning past actions to be used? How do communities legitimate these practices? How and under what circumstances should all of these assumptions change (Webster, 1998)? These questions have become important for assessing how different urban populations in Africa mobilise themselves or can be mobilised within specific settings, i.e. to what extent actions should be taken at individual, household or higher collective levels. For example, several experiences in Africa suggest that collective organisation against poverty at neighbourhood levels, while resulting in better service delivery, consciousness-raising and self-sufficiency, fragments the ability of poor urban communities to work together at the level of the broader metropolis (Sandbrook, 1993; African NGO Habitat II Caucus, 1996; Edwards and Hulme, 1996).

In other situations, collective organising is not able to make the transition from demanding attention from the state to using such organising as a tool for exploring alternative self-provisioning or empowerment opportunities (Fowler 1993; Sondberg 1994; Monga 1996). At other times, proficient and extensive networks of social support and mutual aid cannot be mobilised for larger social or political objectives—especially when vulnerable communities place great value on the continuity of local support networks. Additionally, communities make their own assessments as to how participation in formal institutions can best be achieved and at what price—especially when efforts to foster inclusion are perceived as a mechanism for maintaining a *status quo* of power relations (Bayat 1997; Marsden, 1997).

Ways of organising survival, economy and politics outside formal institutions are conventionally seen as either compensations for inefficiency and exclusion, instruments for circumventing the "rules," or necessary but "hidden" domains so that formal institutions can "really" function (Peters-Berries,

1993; Sanyal, 1996; van Dijk, 1996; Rogerson, 1997). Rarely are such ways of organising viewed as historical "outgrowths" in their own right, which defy "formalisation" either because it is perceived as disadvantageous or because existing formal institutions have largely served to repress them.

Decentralisation provides greater political manoeuvrability for urban governments. But at the same time, these governments face shortages of funds, which render their manoeuvrability largely fictitious. The combination of these factors has produced greater diversity of organisational practices at the local level (Lambooy and Moulaert, 1996; Varet, 1996; Clarke and Bradford, 1998). The institutional boundaries between religion, politics, culture, and social economy have become increasingly blurred, giving rise to a proliferation of *ad hoc* initiatives. Often, formally organised civil society organisations (CSOs) are either out of touch with such initiatives or attempt to control them. This does not mean that CSOs are not playing important roles, but their emphasis on targeting specific populations, identities, sectors or themes often means that they cannot extend themselves to work among other actors or relate to different processes (Paerregaard, 1998). Given these dynamics and the proliferation of ways of organising at local levels, urban development work must critically assess what various ways of organising might be able to achieve and how different forms can be articulated into complementary instruments of action (Simon, 1998).

TALES OF TWO CITIES: DAKAR AND JOHANNESBURG

The discussion in this chapter focuses on two disparate forms of urban associational life in Dakar and Johannesburg. By focusing on diffuse and largely "invisible" ways in which participation and collaboration are mobilised, it is possible to discern tensions and contested development trajectories of the urban arena.

The discussion is based on an ethnographic and comparative community dynamics assessment undertaken as part of a project managed by the African NGO Habitat Caucus. The Caucus, made up of urban development NGOs in fifteen major African cities, worked collectively to establish context-specific platforms of dialogue between local community associations and municipal governments within selected neighbourhoods in each city. These platforms served as a basis for negotiating specific partnership arrangements in terms of local planning, administration and service delivery. As a senior researcher for the Caucus, I managed the assessment process, and was directly involved in co-ordinating a series of focus groups and informant networks in the neighbourhoods examined in Dakar and Johannesburg. Additionally, I have worked for almost five years with African immigrant communities in the inner city of Johannesburg. This work centres on operationalising the ways in which these communities can deal more effectively with a broad range of local institutions, and "regularise" their presence in terms of housing rights, minimising harassment by the police, and incorporating consideration of many of their economic practices and livelihoods into economic planning fora.

Additionally, this work is an extension of long-term research I have undertaken on networks of cross-border unconventional trade in various parts of

Africa. This has been a highly precarious engagement, as clandestinity and dissimulation are crucial elements in the conduct of this trade, and the knowledge generated about it requires many years of careful cultivation of personal relationships and involvement in people's lives. It also means that the records and accounts usually relied upon to constitute "empirical evidence" are usually absent, and the researcher is left with piecing together larger pictures on the basis of cross-referencing scores of sketchy accounts. Nevertheless, in dogged journalistic fashion, it is possible to generate a reliable sense of what is taking place. One either identifies various and legal opportunities to directly witness the transactions referred to or ensures that accounts of such transactions are verified by multiple sets of unrelated actors assuming various positions in relation to such transactions.

In Dakar and Johannesburg, as well as in most African cities, population shifts resulting from migration, demographic change, dispersion of economic resources, and relocation of growth mean that localities encounter instability. This instability is exacerbated by the proliferation of survival strategies pursued by local residents forced into opportunistic and *ad hoc* behaviour. The adherence of African states to prevailing economic wisdom—the need to create an entrepreneurial class, small businesses, commercial agriculture, etc.—has provided opportunities for land appropriation, circumvention of rules regarding the hiring of labour, proliferation of political clientelism into the provision of social welfare and technical assistance, and hiding assets from the state (Bayart et al., 1999). For the most part, such informalisation stems from opportunities for individuals to access multiple sources of income by securing niches in various sectors. These multiple positions are then used to cover up, divert, or circumvent scrutiny by regulatory agencies. In most of the developing world, no household is fixed in any single economic position, but is rather operating in-between several. This operation "in-between" changes the ways in which economic positions are linked, constituted and remade as they evolve or dissipate over time (de Soto, 1989).

Increased diversity within communities provides different links and modalities of engagement with the larger world. Sites of opportunity and resources are thus maximised. But such heterogeneity can also connote a falling away of the need for common practices of civility and a shared sense of belonging. For, as links to the outside world are diversified, so are the range and kinds of inequities within communities, with ensuing disruption in the way localities once understood, and perhaps tolerated, internal disparities in wealth and power. Sudden and inexplicable accumulations, opportunities or losses generate additional confusion as to who is doing what to whom, who has access to what, and to what extent these changes are attributable to things not being what they appear to be (Appadurai, 1998). Households, extended families, social networks or neighbourhoods are increasingly uncertain as to what is constraining their life chances, and, as a result, they must pay attention to other realities, with which they once co-existed only at a "distance". But as these realities are increasingly viewed as salient there may be concomitant narrowing of the field of social affiliation, loyalty, trust and co-operation. Different groups operating in close proximity are often forced to become competitors in what are, for the most part, shrinking economies and public domains.

Consequently, groups have to make continuous adjustments in how they deal with each other. At times, such adjustment is best accomplished by neither making things too clear, nor by assigning different groups to specific roles and rights *vis-à-vis* each other (Smith and Blanc, 1997). At best, such informal regulation gives rise to a "common sense"—a pool of local knowledge open to contribution and use by all groups. At worst, it simply does not exist as a result of any form of human agency or with any validity.

These processes tend to promote a notion that all aspects of everyday life can be negotiated. Instead of adhering to an unequivocal set of rules and procedures, anything and everything is negotiable. Such negotiability introduces greater flexibility and potential for problem-solving, but also raises the question as to when negotiations end and how many different actors can be negotiating partners. If everything can be negotiated, then predicting the outcomes of any given transaction is uncertain. It is thus difficult for individuals to assess what implications their actions will have for others or to ascertain what it is feasible for them to do. Uncertainty is also increased by a tendency either to limit the range of social exchanges and reduce the number of those with whom one negotiates, or to constantly change "negotiating partners".

Since some local groupings are often precluded from collaborating with each other in the formal public sphere, but cannot ignore each other, a series of informal processes comes into being to regulate exchanges. Given the diminution of authority in local public institutions—in part occasioned by an inability to comprehend the social changes under way, as well as their lack of capacity and resources—these informal processes increasingly take precedence. As localities are reasserted as a collection of parochial identities and lifestyles, often marked by extreme disparities in terms of access to opportunities and resources, there is also an intensifying sense of cosmopolitanism, especially in the larger African cities. In a globalised world, inter-penetration of all kinds across economic, cultural and political terrains throws into question the integrity of any identity. Any effort to achieve unequivocal clarity with regard to identities of race, religion, gender, nation, or ethnicity finds itself "interrupted" and intersected with influences, "pollution", and exceptions beyond its control. In a world of incessant mobility, travel, communication, and exposure, any culture or grouping has little choice but to take a vast range of "others" into consideration. By doing so, that culture or grouping implicitly becomes some of what those "others" are. Investments in association, then, must attempt to both bridge the need to maximise the opportunities involved in crossing borders of all kinds, and to solidify often highly localised arrangements of social support and solidarity.

SOIREE IN SOUMBEDIOUNE

Soumbedioune is a historic Lebu fishing village, incorporated as an extension of the Greater Medina in Dakar. Although the quarter still provides residence for scores of individuals involved in the fishing trade and is the site of a key fish market, its proximity to the city centre has resulted in great diversification of its inhabitants and economic activities. Soumbedioune has become a dense quarter containing a diversity of people: those who continue to inhabit one of the first public low-cost housing schemes in the city; conventional compounds which include self-constructed wooden barracks; privately constructed apartment buildings providing both low and middle-income residences; student dormitories; and several large residences occupied by politicians. Its abutment to the coast and its woodworking and artisan shops have brought a modest infusion of tourist money. The diversity of residential opportunities and its physical location have also combined to make the quarter historically available for occupation by large numbers of "foreign" residents, mostly originating from other Francophone countries, particularly Congo, Cameroon, Guinea and Mali.

In addition to activities surrounding the fish market, the bulk of the local economy centres on small artisan workshops, tailoring, furniture making, vulcanising, car repair, used clothing, telecentres and hawkers, which line the length of one of the city's primary sewage canals. There are also large numbers of residents who work in the public bureaucracy and central city businesses. A multiplicity of guild organisations operates, and the area is an important site of political contestation in the ongoing struggle for influence, waged primarily between the Socialist Party, ruling until 2000, and the Democratic Socialist Party. While community fora around issue-specific initiatives have been maintained, allowing representation from various ethnic, guild, gender, age and religious-based organisations, both major political parties have impeded the effective establishment of open-ended community associations.

Common to the political, economic, and social lives of most Dakaroise neighbourhoods is the importance of the *turuq*—Islamic Sufi-based brotherhoods which constitute a powerful linchpin in the cohesion of Senegalese national identity. Perhaps the most important of these groupings is the *Mouriddiya*, which operates as the focal point for the elaboration of an urban popular culture intersecting Islam, home-grown Rastafarianism, self-help, political resistance and multinational corporatism. Dakar is increasingly rife with a certain volatility stemming from and, conversely, being held in check by this reinvented sense of cultural heritage.

The *Mouriddiya* commits itself to salvation through diligent work. It specifies a moral ethos that combines the rigour of Islamic discipline with an almost messianic vision of individuals transcending their material and social conditions. Its centre, the city of Touba, is, for all practical purposes, a sovereign state unto itself. Only recently have Senegalese state authorities been allowed access without permission. The deceased spiritual leader, Shayk Amadou Bamba, acts as the guarantor of Senegalese identity, and his picture proliferates in every Dakar neighbourhood. The suspension of prayer and encouragement of forbidden activities for a "warrior class" have marginalised the Mourides from the conventional Islamic world. Yet, the *Mouriddiya* has turned its traditional organisation of groundnut production into a world-wide network of traders in watches, Gucci bags, and brass ornaments in every large city of the world. Income derived from these activities has been invested in real estate in New York, Paris, Dakar, and more recently, in Southeast Asia.

On several occasions the state has attempted to reduce the power of the Mourides, but to no avail. Even when state marketing boards offered significantly higher prices to groundnut farmers, they continued to place their harvests in traditional marketing systems controlled by Mouride networks. The *Mouriddiya* currently controls large swaths of commerce in the central city and has made major inroads into traditional Lebanese domination of this sector. Loyalty is in part cultivated by using the religious context for individuals to avail themselves of business opportunities and to institutionalise a practice of sharing resources.

Senegal is also the centre for the *Tijanniya*—the largest Sufi organisation in Africa—which uses extensive networks to control much of the mercantile sector of the Sahel and more recently, the highly lucrative trade in consumables and electronics from Asia. While the dominant Socialist Party has been secular in organisation and personnel (the first President, Leopold Senghor, was a Christian in a predominantly Muslim country), each election victory has been secured by courting the rural base controlled by the religious leaders of these two *turuq*. Their influence has been strengthened by their domination of the transport sector, their hold on petty commerce and large-scale entrepreneurship—positions enabling them to take advantage of employment opportunities in an overall climate of public sector shrinkage. In addition, a largely Lebu and urban-based Islamic reform movement, popularly known as "the Lion," is on the ascendancy and draws increasing support from residents in Soumbedioune.

All of the modalities of social, political and religious organisation command strong loyalties. For the *turuq*, an oath, "wird", is taken; but the strength of loyalty does not preclude participation in a broad range of other secular forms of associational life—something the *turuq* actually encourages. At times, the value of being a Mouride rests not in having a self-contained identity, but rather to be a Mouride within a particular business or sector, within politics, etc. Since individuals are likely to have multiple memberships across different organisations, there is a continuous process of contestation about how possible amalgamations of different associations might take place.

For example, occupational groupings, such as tailors, will coalesce around specific issues. Sometimes, this consolidation will result in affiliation to certain political parties or *turuq* that are then institutionalised. At other times, the alliances are more fleeting, even if, for example, everyone within the tailor grouping may belong to the same *tariqa*. At other times, there may be a hedging of bets, where various social organisations—be they guilds, women's, community, professional or youth associations—may engineer an implicit division of labour. Some members will affiliate with certain political parties or religious organisations, whereas other members will be "encouraged" to affiliate with others, and in various combinations. The basis for such combinations is continuously re-negotiated, as individuals act as "barometers" for exploring what kinds of countervailing identities, expectations and responsibilities can be functionally put together. What is produced is a complex topography of intersecting social networks, which simultaneously "dissolve" into each other but also often maintain rigid operational hierarchies, norms and criteria for participation. On top of such institutional affiliations are strong personal, street, and face-to-face networks, which are important in residential areas of great density.

Given the past opportunities available to Senegalese for educating themselves abroad, the opportunities to travel organised by Mouride and Tijani networks and the growth of expatriate communities in places such as Paris, Rome and New York, local organisational dynamics are increasingly influenced by social practices and money derived from outside the city. Investments in local residential and commercial structures come primarily from repatriated earnings. Popular urban styles in thinking, attitude and appearance are also influenced from the outside. The intersection of competing identifications and practices, the dissatisfaction with some of the anachronisms of historical social and religious organisations, and external influences combine to elaborate new styles of affiliation and co-ordination.

Currently, being *thiof* is increasingly important. Appropriating the word for the fish which is a staple of the daily diet, the concept refers to a set of unwritten rules for how individuals can be opportunistic in rapidly shifting circumstances, or at least appear to be. While most of these "rules" specify the contents of one's lifestyle, they also deal with how one is supposed to behave, talk and, importantly, how one is to get others to do one's bidding and circumvent the wide range of constrictions imposed by local cultural norms, social organisations and politics. Not only is "thiofness" a practice incorporated into various aspects of the public realm, but it implicitly reinforces the salience and reinvigoration of "traditional" family and religious ties for those who fail in their "thiofness."

There are thus residues of ambiguity everywhere in the quarter, and any clear sense of what makes Soumbedioune tick remains elusive. Yet, the ambiguities in the organisation of social life contribute to enhancing the speed and mobility of transactions, resources and alliances. For, if no clear roles and channels of exchange are institutionalised people are forced to be as opportunistic as possible, and almost everyone is available to do something out of the ordinary, things can happen very fast, if not necessarily efficiently. It is a process of keeping communities on their toes, but in which they are also vulnerable to implosive disruptions—where solidarity, coherence, functionality must be re-pieced together almost on a day-to-day basis.

In Soumbedioune, whom one goes to see to straighten out small disputes with neighbours or matters of cleanliness on the street, or organising social events varies, depending on whom amongst one's neighbours has acquired newly important connections, whether elections or religious events are upcoming, or on what kinds of deals have been made between particular actors and networks at any given time. In fact, there seems to be an incessant precipitation of problems, in excess of those usually associated with people living in dense quarters, simply to find out just who has what status and to ascertain what opportunities present themselves at any given time. Such processes give rise to a sense of fluidity about how local power is organised and deployed. Because this process can be tedious, many people end up doing what they want to do, while others end up seldom doing anything different at all.

One recent example of these dynamics concerns a situation where a project to manage the completion of a large housing estate was being put out to tender by one of Dakar's top companies. The company was obligated to invite tenders, even though it clearly preferred and had every intention of keeping the entire project "in-house". An architectural firm was to be hired, as well as a general contractor to secure materials and labour. In a cursory gesture, to abide by the rules, an announcement was issued to a nearly empty conference centre on a Thursday evening to the effect that tenders would close at seven the next morning. The selection of this particular weekday was significant because Thursday evening is a time when many people participate in special worship in the mosques.

Nevertheless, and subsequent to this announcement, the night was busy with a proliferation of visits among architects, engineers, labourers, politicians, deal-makers, *marabouts*, soccer clubs, youth organisations, artisan guilds, and scores of their relatives who all thought they could discover pathways of influence to the person who was to award the contract. Although the official who was to award the contract no longer resides in Soumbedioune, a sister occupies the family compound. While she received many visits, most of the activity pervaded the surrounding area, as neighbours, friends and purported social connections were sought out and discussions held. Hundreds of thousands of CFA, the local currency, changed hands, sexual scenarios were played out, as were prayers, family injunctions, pleas, reiterated obligations, and "chance" encounters. A broad array of rhetorical strategies was involved: memories of past infractions and promises, personal knowledge, cultural etiquette, political procedure, technical know-how, sorcery—all circulating in various constellations marking gaps and hybrid conjunctures.

While professional firms unofficially joined the fray, there were also people looking for any opportunity to affiliate with the project. Even if they could not design, build, or supply relevant inputs, they knew others who could and thus hoped for possible in-kind "finder's fees" or opportunities to parlay information into other opportunities.

By morning, there were no official submissions of tenders but it had become clear to the company that there were hundreds of options to choose from, and theoretically, hundreds of different housing estates could have been built from this nocturnal deliberation. Dakar has roughly 100 architects to choose from and a lesser number of contracting firms capable of handling a project of this size. The political and religious loyalties of these players are commonly known. But with a flurry of activity crossing boundaries of all kinds and producing various constellations of alliances, workforce compositions, inputs, and cash flows, it was not clear what the possible implications of any particular choice might have been. People known to be unwilling to work together expressed their willingness, best friends parted company for the moment to broaden their chances. There was a sudden opportunism and a proficiency for cutting across social divides, networks and alliances that could not be absorbed by any formal representation. The company asked for more time to weigh the decision that probably had already been made a long time ago.

ON THE OUTSIDE IN THE JOHANNESBURG INNER CITY

Johannesburg has long been Africa's most developed city. Its status was acquired through an oppressive political system, which rigidly regulated access to urban space and services and imposed two distinct development trajectories: a city with all the Western amenities for whites, and impoverished peri-urban labour reserves for blacks. The race-based zoning of urban residential communities kept blacks out of the inner city for several decades. Accelerating white movement to the suburban areas, coupled with economic recession, pushed up vacancy rates in the neighbourhoods of Hillbrow, Bertrams, Joubert Park, Berea and Yeoville. Although officially illegal until 1991, blacks had begun moving to what was known as "grey areas" in the mid-1980s (Tomlinson et al., 1995).

The accelerated turnover of populations has itself provided a feasible cover, if not necessarily a major motivation, for the sizeable immigration of foreign Africans to Johannesburg. This migration, in turn, has substantially shaped the nature of inner-city life and commerce, further contributing to a process of internationalisation. Because the inner city is one of the most circumscribed and densely populated urban spaces on the continent, with neighbourhoods such as Hillbrow made up of row after row of high-rise apartment blocks, this socio-cultural reconfiguration has taken place with a large measure of invisibility.

Because the overwhelming majority of South African black inhabitants of the inner city are recent arrivals to Greater Johannesburg, conditions are wide open for intersection of many groupings. Long displaced to the periphery of the city, the absence of stable black institutions within the inner city also contributes to the perception that it is becoming an increasingly desperate place, living on an edge without a strong core of cohesiveness.

What is perhaps most significant about the transformation of the inner city is not so much its character but the speed with which it has occurred. The sheer rapidity of demographic and economic change has created uncertainty as to what it is possible to plan for and do. The uncertainty has caused sudden and substantial divestitures of all types. These divestitures further impede adequate monitoring by adding a large volume of transactions to the quick pace of change. Insecurity has intensified and, with it, the practice of getting rid of property and position at a cheap price.

In response to these changes, a large measure of xenophobia prevails, where foreign Africans are blamed for an overcrowded informal trading sector, the growth of the narcotics trade and general deterioration of the inner city. Many South African residents believe that it is because of such a foreign presence that government authorities and the private sector are unwilling to make investments in upgrading and service provision (Mattes et al., 2000).

Although migrant labour from the sub-region had played a major historical role in the South African economy, the nature of migration radically changed once conduits of transport and a context suitable for individualised exchange of labour and pursuit of entrepreneurship were opened up. While the bulk of migration continues to originate in Southern African states, the inner city has become a staging area for individuals from Francophone countries, Ethiopia, Somalia, Nigeria, Ghana and Kenya (Crush, 2000).

Much of the initial African migration corresponded to shifting policies pursued by the South African state. Political favours offered by African states, as well as their co-operation in circumventing sanctions and creating trade opportunities and havens for capital flight, were often rewarded with relaxed entry and stay requirements. At different times, visas were waived for Congolese, Ivorians, Malians and Senegalese. Changing circumstances for potential migrants in other countries also contributed to a move southwards (Reitzes, 1999). For example, interviews with long-term Malian residents indicate that the bulk of the early Malian community was largely derived from diamond smuggling syndicates in Zambia, which faced crackdowns during the early days of the Chiluba regime. In another instance, long-term co-operation between South African multinationals and the Congolese ruling hierarchy produced an almost wholesale transfer of much of Zaire's ruling elite to South Africa, following the advent of a protracted political crisis (Kadima, 1999).

Because economic survival in much of the continent depends on the constant search for new opportunities, borders, and markets, the exchange of information about the relative advantages of particular destinations is a constant topic of conversation. The relatively well developed infrastructure of South Africa, coupled with its ignorance of how migration-based economies work throughout most of the continent, quickly made Johannesburg a desired destination. Both large and small merchants in the franc zone, sensing the imminence of devaluation and the possibilities for profit-taking, rushed to take advantage of highly disparate currency values to buy large amounts of non-perishable commodities (Bouillon, 1999).

Any businessperson knows that financial transfers and payment for commodities can become a nightmare in Africa. At the same time, at medium and small scales, there appears to be an abundance of trade. While conventional trade still "hobbles" along at the macro-level, an economy less dependent on money and credit, especially hard currency transactions, proliferates in various forms of barter arrangements. Because depreciated commodity prices, balance of payments difficulties and devalued local currencies have severely tightened access to hard currency, a wide range of alternative methods for acquiring and distributing goods has developed (Egg and Herera, 1998).

Because these arrangements circumvent bank guarantees, pre-payments, and letters of credit (financed trade), alternative structures have been set up to ensure the trustworthiness of transactions. These often take the form of family and kinship arrangements where individual or groups of family members are placed in different locations to handle the acquisition and transfer of goods (Bredeloup, 1999). These arrangements are often conducted in association with a syndicate of merchants, fellow nationals, or ethnic or political associations (MacGaffey and Banguissa-Ganga, 2000).

Consider one example of how this process works, taken from an actual transaction that I tracked for three months based on leads provided by several informants involved in it. A bureaucrat in the Ministry of Public Works in Dar es Salaam over-invoices for an order of spark plugs from Taiwan for government vehicles. The bulk of the shipment is diverted to associates on the private market. The plugs could be sold on the local market or constitute a piece in a counter-trade agreement, say, for shipment of canned goods from South Africa, which in turn are acquired with the collateral of gemstones smuggled into the country from Congo. A Tanzanian colleague of the merchant grouping in Johannesburg is informed when the plugs have been shipped from Dar, heading for Durban, and the shipment of canned goods is timed to coincide with that from Dar. When "steerers" in Dar and Johannesburg confirm the arrival of the shipments, the collateral is withdrawn and applied to other transactions. Usually the collateral consists of manageable commodities of high value, e.g., diamonds, gold, gems, as well as a cash reserve moving from deal to deal.

There are many variations of these arrangements, as well as varying complexity and complicity among public officials and large and small entrepreneurs. But in almost every case they require a tightly co-ordinated group of associates who opportunistically cultivate contacts in various locations, and assiduously contribute to a comparison of regulations, prices, and procedures regarding trade in various goods.

Additionally, the ability to "move people around" is the key to entrepreneurial success—i.e., the cultivation of patronage, whereby an entrepreneur commands the loyalty of a group of related or unrelated individuals, many of whom are engaged in petty tasks the entrepreneur could well do him/herself but add to the general impression of success or importance. For example, Congolese with professional positions in South African multinationals dominating mineral production in the Democratic Republic of Congo may receive high salaries, allowing them to live in the middle and upper class northern suburbs. Interviews I conducted with several Congolese professionals in their plush offices in the corporate centre, Sandton, seem to confirm the official financial capacity of many of them. Some will acquire property there, yet continue to live in dense inner city apartment blocks in Yeoville, where they stay close to the scene of less privileged compatriots and cultivate a following among them. Young men are frequently "assigned" various tasks, from arranging sexual favours to delivering goods to the professional's relatives back home.

On the other hand, many small traders with limited resources and manoeuvrability actively create the impression of success based only on their presentation of the conventional signs of it. For example, investment is often in expensive clothes and accessories with designer labels in order to "prove" their business prowess and connections. The idea is that if people believe they are dealing with "up and coming" entrepreneurs, they will deal with them. As a result, a rampant ambiguity is produced as to who is who—who is one really dealing with and what are their capabilities and connections? Although this ambiguity may seemingly distract from the process of creating reliable partnerships, the tactic employed by many entrepreneurs is to use this ambiguous "front" as a way of forcing their potential customers and suppliers into revealing more about their respective abilities, knowledge, styles—so as to better manipulate them. At the same time, if everyone knows this to be the game, investment is also made into more intricate means of defence against such manipulation, and therefore actors in this process must balance between opportunism and securing tighter and more confident networks of operation.

If one observes, for example, the informational economy, which prevails in the Johannesburg inner city, information regarding new acquisitions and opportunities is closely guarded. Such information becomes the primary instrument in a parasitic economy where social ties—between neighbours, co-workers, affiliates and even family members—are manipulated so that one person may take advantage of an other. Although increasingly susceptible to such tendencies, immigrant communities, however, remain committed to sharing information as a vehicle for expanding the capacities of the larger group with which a person identifies.

Such sharing is based on several prerequisites. No matter how close social, national, family and religious ties might be, one rarely inquires into the precise nature of someone else's activities—thus giving them the operational space to function in a climate of great uncertainty. The common assumption is that overly intrusive scrutiny or even curiosity constrains the possibility of enjoining others to any given activity. While a sense of obligation persists, in terms of the support immigrants provide for each other, this obligation can be functional only if it works in ways that are distinct from the mores which prevail in the contexts immigrants have left. For many migrants that I have interviewed, acquiring the space necessary to build-up some savings outside of the tightly knit family networks that can quickly eat up any earnings made at home is a major motivating factor for migration. Accordingly, individuals must insist upon some flexibility in how they manage their income generation, social lives and movements through the city. The prevailing "common sense" is that groups can only provide support as long as individual migrants have some flexibility to pursue various alliances, contacts and activities—as long as they do not add undue vulnerability to their associates.

Such flexibility adds a comparative advantage. New and unconventional forms of articulation can be made among different sorts of activities. In other words, opportunities are expanded by finding ways of putting together disparate activities within the overall framework of trust and solidarity which prevails among immigrant groups. I have followed various networks of Soninke entrepreneurs, who originate in Mali and Senegal, for nearly three decades. Relying upon the trust established over those years, I have cultivated three generations of informants, and been particularly interested in how the Soninke have plied their historic availability as cheap and mobile labourers into an expanding capacity to cultivate the political favour and business acumen enabling them to operate at increasingly larger scales (Manchuelle, 1998). Soninke entrepreneurs were among the first "pioneers" in the inner city, and have linked distinct specialities built up over the years (Bouillon, 1998).

By virtue of their long presence in Brazzaville, and their networks with different Angolan political factions—which have acted as a nexus between Anglophone West Africa and Angola—the Soninke were able to dominate a lucrative trade in supplying different regions of Angola with a wide range of consumables originating in South Africa (Bayart, Ellis, Hibou, 1999). Soninke traders originally based in Dakar and Conakry have also cultivated a wide range of activities in Southeast Asia, particularly in importing of textiles, clothing and electronics. Soninke traders I interviewed over ten years ago in Bangkok had built up substantial contacts in the port of Cape Town. They told me that they were often able to circumvent custom controls under simulated re-packaging deals where containers are supposedly destined elsewhere, most particularly Luanda. By converging these formerly distinct networks, a great deal of functional ambiguity is created which allows the Soninke entrepreneurs to manipulate loading and off-loading of goods, depending on relative prices and market opportunities.

Although the overall fluidity of the inner city provides an opportunity for putting in motion or improvising upon many of the standard practices of African entrepreneurship, conflicts between local South African small entrepreneurs and foreign Africans have bubbled to the surface. Because South Africans have not participated substantially in the circuits of movement and exchange dominating the rest of the continent, they know little about other African cultures and practices. Local South Africans frequently conclude that the success of foreign hawkers and well-heeled businessmen is at their expense. Foreign Africans, long accustomed to the relative domesticity of public space, have become easy targets for muggers and con-men. Frequent assaults, coupled with cultural misunderstandings and disputes over space and access, have produced an increased defensiveness among the diffuse foreign African communities (Peberdy, 1997).

Since there are few occasions when foreign Africans of different nationalities align against local Africans—due to the absence of explicit common objectives—locals often provoke disputes between groups of foreigners. The rapidity of social and demographic changes, coupled with a lack of entrenched black institutions and a protracted search for appropriate local political forms, turn being foreign and anti-foreign into key reference points for organising.

Local South Africans at times attribute an almost monolithic solidity to particular foreign national groupings, such as being "Nigerian" or "Senegalese"—characteristics in contradistinction to which they rally, due to their own lack of history in and relative newness to the city. Just as Mozambicans, for example, may have their special hang-outs, some local South Africans claim buildings, streets or certain bars as "their places," as a means of adding consistency to their social affiliations and movements. A frequent invocation by South Africans is that the French-speaking Africans never deal with their English-speaking counterparts, that Nigerians never deal with Cameroonians, etc., so why should they be compelled to deal with any of them.

At the same time, foreign Africans try to up-end these assumptions with moves to "Africanise" their associations in the widest sense, i.e. attempting to build their personal networks from many different national communities. While ethnic and national groupings are maintained, many traders, hawkers and businesspeople are beginning to elaborate collaborations that cut across these divides, from acquisition of buildings, coalescence of hawking and service groups, to cross-border trade. Once "business discussions" in the bars of the renown immigrant hotels, e.g. the Mariston, Protea Gardens, the Mark, and the Sands, were strictly between those of common national identity. But in recent years I have observed Ethiopians, Congolese, Mozambicans, and Zambians, for example, talking about ways to consolidate their individual agendas and networks to provide greater scope and flexibility. Thus, local pressures, which act to "ghettoise" and constrict the operations of foreign migrants, are also prompting new forms of organisation, which enable individuals of distinct nationalities to maximise their manoeuvrability and reach outside the confines of the Johannesburg inner city.

CONCLUSION: GOING FORTH INTO THE WORLD

This chapter does not address viability or sustainability. It is not clear what is likely to happen in cities such as Dakar and Johannesburg, if adequate forms of governance fail to emerge. While such considerations are important in terms of what happens to the lives of individuals who are "condemned" to remain in cities unable to provide employment, legality, shelter, etc., the urbanites retain the possibility of circumventing such considerations.

In Dakar, it has been demonstrated how a neighbourhood is capable of enormous resilience and determination to use the symbolic, material and social resources at its disposal to enhance overall resourcefulness and flexibility. It has acted on the basis of a sense that it is always possible to make something happen. Thus to de-link the religious from the political, the political from the entrepreneurial, the familial from the public, etc., as a step towards consolidating effective urban governance and regulatory environments, may weaken the very mechanisms through which African urban neighbourhoods manage to retain a foothold in a rapidly changing global economy. On the other hand, the proximity of these "ways of life" may not create sufficient space for changes within individual domains to take hold, so as to generate new forms of independent action and innovation that could be brought into the public sphere. The interdependencies among religion, government, politics, family life and business also mean that the stakes are high for any shift in the internal dynamics of any one sector. Again, the locus of independent action is constrained, at the same time as the resolution of any particular difficulty within one sector is potentially availing itself of the resources of another.

In Johannesburg, the use of the city to consolidate co-operative arrangements among various ways of organising "unconventional" economic activities on the continent is becoming a major arena of contest in terms of the city's future. While most foreign Africans do not like the place and do not recognise anything like "home" in it, they see it as allowing them new ways of interacting with each other and of better "plying their wares in the funny business which is all business," according to Ali Isong from Calabar.

If cities are increasingly characterised by parallel realities, Johannesburg harbours chasms in-between them, which, in turn, are being shaped as conduits that in small but significant ways contribute to a re-spatialisation of intra-continental contact. The recent history of urban governance in Johannesburg has been an uneasy mixture of institutional and policy innovation and stringent structural adjustment in the fiscal domain; a mixture of drawing upon a wide range of actors and sectors to form an integrated urban system but an almost in-built inability to "recognise" where the city is located within a global urban system and within Africa itself. Johannesburg as an urban system seems to act like an "immigrant" in its "own" continent.

As the city has been "opened up" to a full range of diverse uses and inhabitants in the aftermath of apartheid, autonomy from administrative impositions has also been enjoyed. This autonomy stems from both the full complement of market forces and increasingly individualised aspirations accompanied by differentiated practices of "being" in the city. These forces and aspirations both break down barriers and resurrect barriers between national and racial groupings; defend the "proper" uses of space, commerce and facilities and disrupt them as well.

Based on these stories from Dakar and Johannesburg, a critical future area of research would be to follow the trajectories and movements of informal and provisional associational dynamics as they intersect with the functioning and reach of specific institutions, politics and economic activities. If the city is characterised by increasing segregation and fragmentation, it may be important to chart the complicity, co-operation, boundary-crossing, interpenetration, affiliation and divergence which "come and go" across the city, its neighbourhoods and its facets.

In a fundamental way the question of where African cities are going could be addressed by assessing—in a broader sense—where African urban residents are going, within their different time frames and in terms of their respective objectives. While urban poverty is indeed growing worse, as is a concomitant disarticulation among urban social spheres and a narrowing in the terms of belonging (Zeleza and Kalipeni, 1999), urban residents are not standing still. There is something going on, efforts are being made to come up with new ways of earning a living, of helping others out, and of trying to create interesting cities. An awesome sense of responsibility is being displayed, as well as an awesome sense of irresponsibility shown by the rest of the world to the future of African cities.

References

African NGO Habitat II Caucus ,1996, *Citizenship and Urban Development in Africa: Popular Cities for Their Inhabitants*. Dakar: Enda Tiers Monde.

Amin, Ash and Stephen Graham, 1997, "The Ordinary City", *Transactions of the Institute of British Geography*, 22, pp. 411–29.

Appadurai, Arjun, 1996a, *Modernity at Large: Cultural Dimensions of Globalisation*. Minneapolis: University of Minnesota Press.

—, 1996b, "Sovereignty Without Territory," in Yaegar, Patricia (ed.), *The Geography of Identity*. Ann Arbor: University of Michigan Press, pp. 41–58.

—, 1998, "Dead Certainty: Ethnic Violence in the Era of Globalisation", *Public Culture*, 10, pp. 225–47.

Bayart, Jean-Françoise, Stephen Ellis and B. Hibou, 1999, *The Criminalisation of the State in Africa*. Bloomington: Indiana University Press.

Bayat, Asef, 1997, "Uncivil Society: The Politics of 'Informal People'", *Third World Quarterly*, 18, pp. 53–72.

Bouillon, Antoine, (ed.), 1998, *Immigration africaine en Afrique du Sud: Les Migrants francophones des anneès, 90*. Paris: Karthala.

—, 1999, "Transition et logiques territoriales en Afrique du Sud: 'races', (im)migration, territoires et réseaux", *L'Espace Geographique*, 2.

Bredeloup, Sylvie, 1999, "Le migrant africaine et le ville étrangère", paper presented at the conference *Etre Étranger et Migrant en Afrique au Xxème Siecle*, sponsored by the Sociétés Développement dans l'Espace et dans le Temps, Université Paris 7, 9–11 December 1999.

Chabal, Patrick, and Jean-Pascal Daloz, 1999, *Africa Works: Disorder as a Political Instrument*. The International African Institute in association with James Currey, Oxford and Indiana University Press, Bloomington.

Clarke, David and Michael Bradford, 1998, "Public and Private Consumption and the City", *Urban Studies*, 35, pp. 865–88.

Cox, Kevin, 1998, "Spaces of Dependence, Spaces of Engagement and the Politics of Scale, or: Looking for Local Politics", *Political Geography*, 17, pp. 1–23.

Crush, Jonathan, 2000, "Migrations Past: An Historical Overview of Cross-Border Movement in Southern Africa", in McDonald, David (ed.), *On Borders: Perspectives on Cross-Border Migration in Southern Africa*. Cape Town and New York: St. Martins Press.

de Soto, H., 1989, *The Other Path: The Invisible Revolution in the Third World*. New York: Harper and Row.

Dey, Krishno and David Westendorff (eds), 1996, *Their Choice or Yours: Global Forces or Local Voices*. Geneva: United Nations Research Institute on Social Development.

Diouf, M., 1996, "Urban Youth and Senegalese Politics: Dakar 1988–1994", *Public Culture*, 8, 225–49.

Edwards, Michael and David Hulme, 1996, "Too Close for Comfort? The Impact of Official Aid on Nongovernmental Organisations", *World Development*, 24, pp. 961–73.

Egg, Johnny and Javier Herera (eds), 1998, *Echanges Transfrontaliers et Integration Regional en Afrique Subsaharienne*. Paris: ORSTOM.

Fowler, Alan, 1993, "NGOs as Agents of Democratisation: An African Perspective", *Journal of International Development*, 5, pp. 325–39.

Johnson, Craig, 1997, "Rules, Norms and the Pursuit of Sustainable Livelihoods." Institute for Development Studies Working Paper 52. Brighton: University of Sussex.

Kadima, Denis, 1999, "Congolese Immigrants in South Africa", *Codesria Bulletin*, 1–2, pp. 35–39.

Kanbur, Ravi, 1999, "Attacking Poverty, World Development Report 2000/1, Chapter Outline". Presented at a World Bank Consultation on "Values, Norms and Poverty" Johannesburg, 12–14 January 1999.

Lambooy, J.G. and Frank Moulaert, 1996, "The Economic Organisation of Cities: An Institutional Perspective", *International Journal of Urban and Regional Research*, 20, pp. 217–37.

MacGaffey, Janet and Remy Banguissa-Ganga, 2000, *Congo-Paris: Transnational Traders on the Margins of the Law*. International African Institute in association with James Currey, London and Indiana University Press, Bloomington.

Manchuelle, François, 1998, *Willing Migrants: Soninke Labor Diasporas 1848–1960*. Athens, Ohio: Ohio University Press and London: James Currey.

Marsden, Peter, 1997, "Geographies of Dissent: Globalisation, Identity and the Nation", *Political Geography*, 16, pp. 37–64.

Mattes, Robert, Donald Taylor, David McDonald, Abigail Poore and Wayne Richmond, 2000, "Still Waiting for the Barbarians: South Africa's Attitudes to Immigrants and Immigration", in McDonald, David (ed.), *On Borders: Perspectives on Cross-Border Migration in Southern Africa*. Cape Town and New York: St. Martins Press.

Mbembe, Achille and Janet Roitman, 1996, "Figures of the Subject in Times of Crisis, in Yaegar, Patricia (ed.), *The Gegraphy of Identity*. Ann Arbor: University of Michigan Press.

Monga, Celestin, 1996, *The Anthropology of Anger: Civil Society and Democracy in Africa*. Boulder, CO: Lynne Rienner.

Moore, Donald, 1998, "Subaltern Struggles and the Politics of Place: Remapping Resistance in Zimbabwe's Eastern Highlands", *Cultural Anthropology*, 13, pp. 344–81.

Paerregaard, Karsten, 1998, "Alleviating Poverty in Latin America: Can Local Organisations be of any Help?", in Webster, Neil (ed.), *In Search of Alternatives: Poverty, the Poor and Local Organisations*. Copenhagen: Centre for Development Research.

Perbedy, Sally, 1997, "The Participation of Non-South Africans in Street Trading in South Africa and In Regional Cross-Border Trade", in Crush, Jonathan and F. Veriava (eds), *Transforming South African Migration and Immigration Policy*. Cape Town and Kingston: South Africa Migration Project.

Peters-Berries, Christian, 1993, *Putting Development Policies into Practice: The Problems of Implementing Policy Reforms in Africa*. WEP 2–19/Wp. 63. Geneva: International Labour Organisation.

Portes, Alejandro, 1995, "Transnational Communities: Their Emergence and Significance in the Contemporary World System", paper delivered at *The Conference on the Political Economy of the World System*, North-South Center, University of Miami, April 21, 1995.

Reitzes, Maxine, 1999, *Patching the Fence: The White Paper on International Migration*. Johannesburg: Centre for Policy Studies.

Rogerson, Chris, 1997, "Globalisation or Informalisation: African Urban Economies in the 1990s", in Rakodi, Carole (ed.), *The Urban Challenge in African Cities*. Tokyo, New York and Paris: United Nations University Press.

Sandbrook, Richard (ed.), 1993, *Empowering People: Building Community, Civil Associations and Legality in Africa*. Toronto: Centre for Urban and Community Studies, University of Toronto.

Sanyal, Bishwapriya, 1996, "Intention and Outcome: Formalisation and Its Consequences", *Regional Development Dialogue*, 17, pp. 161–78.

Simon, David, 1998, "Rethinking (Post)Modernism, Postcolonialism and Posttraditionalism: South-North Perspectives", *Environment and Planning D: Society and Space*, 16.

Smith, David and Maurice Blanc, 1997, "Grassroots Democracy and Participation: A New Analytical and Practical Approach", *Environment and Planning D: Society and Space*, 15, pp. 281–303.

Sondberg, Edith (ed.), 1994, *The Changing Politics of Non-Governmental Organisations and African States*. New York: Praeger.

Swyngedoux, Erik, 1996, "The City as Hybrid—On Nature, Society and Cyborg Urbanisation, *Capitalism, Nature, Socialism*, 7, pp. 65–80.

Tomlinson, Richard, Roland Hunter, M. Jonker, Chris Rogerson and J. Rogerson, 1995, *Johannesburg Inner-City Strategic Development Framework: Economic Analysis*. Greater Johannesburg Transitional Metropolitan Council.

van Dijk, Meine Pieter, 1996, "The Urban Informal Sector as New Engine for Development: Theoretical Developments Since 1972", *Asien Afrika Lateinamerika*, 24, pp. 177–92.

Varet, L. Gerard, 1996, "Decentralising Public Action", *Courrier du CNRS*, Special Issue for Habitat II. Paris: Centre National de la Recherche Scientifique, pp. 177–80.

Watts, Michael, 1996, "Mapping Identities: Place, Space and Community in an African City", in Yaegar, Patricia (ed.), *The Geography of Identity*. Ann Arbor: University of Michigan Press.

Webster, Neal (ed.), 1998, *In Search of Alternatives: Poverty, the Poor and Local Organisations*. Copenhagen: Centre for Development Research.

Zeleza, Paul and Ezekiel Kalipeni, 1999, "Rethinking Space, Politics and Society in Africa", in Zeleza, Paul and Ezekiel Kalipeni (eds), *Sacred Space and Public Quarrels: African Cultural and Economic Landscapes*. Trenton, NJ: Africa World Press.

CHAPTER 4

Women's Groups and Urban Poverty: The Swaziland Experience

Miranda Miles

INTRODUCTION

Sustainable development is development that not only generates economic growth, but distributes its benefits equitably; that regenerates the environment rather than destroying it; that empowers people rather than marginalising them. It is development that gives priority to the poor, enlarging their choices and opportunities and providing for their participation in decisions that affect their lives. It is development that is pro-people, pro-jobs and pro-women (UNDP, 1994).

One of the primary objectives of the post-colonial Swaziland Government has been to achieve sustainable development (Government of Swaziland, 1995). Whether or not one goes by UNDP's definition of sustainable human development, after three decades of independent rule the success of the country's efforts at human development remains modest.

Like many African countries, Swaziland's independence from British rule came with much optimism in the 1960s. In adopting and inheriting the development strategy of the colonial administration, the new Government placed emphasis on rapid industrialisation, to be realised mainly through foreign investment and resulting in spatial patterns of post-colonial development with a bias towards a few urban centres. Rapid annual rates of growth in these centres have posed a challenge to urban administrations and have had a marked effect on the Government's ability to provide adequate housing, health and education for the Swazi population.

To achieve sustainable human development and to overcome and alleviate some of the urban problems that low-income groups face, the Government of Swaziland has pledged a commitment to provide a modicum of social and public services. Yet the omission of women's needs in the planning process and the persistent adherence to traditional norms that deny them access to resources have placed women in a precarious position. As growing numbers of women move to the city, insecure employment, low wages, poverty, housing shortages and lack of access to credit and to land are only some of the challenges they face.

By examining women's responses to Swaziland's changing geography in the nineties, this paper explores the efforts of low-income women to pick up the slack created by Government's inability to alleviate urban poverty. Against a backdrop of unfulfilled development goals, the paper looks at how women overcome the dimensions of urban poverty that threaten their livelihood and increase their vulnerability. The paper also draws attention to the need to incorporate the situation of women in Government planning, with the aim of complementing and strengthening their own forms of survival rather than substituting or preventing them. This entails an investigation of how women attempt to reduce their vulnerability in an urban environment, and how they create coping mechanisms in which they mobilise their assets as a form of collective action in the face of urban crisis. Various types of associations and networks are central to these endeavours.

VULNERABILITY AND WOMEN'S COPING STRATEGIES

For Swazi women, poverty has always been a significant feature of their lives. The period 1930–1963 marked an era of irrational control over their exodus out of rural Swaziland to the urban centres of Swaziland and neighbouring South Africa. Rather than address the problems of rural poverty that women were facing, and that were causing them to leave for town in search of employment, drastic measures were taken to curb women's migration, which was seen as a serious threat to social order and patriarchy (Miles, 1996a).

The seriousness with which poverty has affected women's lives and opportunity-situations is still being downplayed. Drawing on the work of Caroline Moser (1989, 1993, 1996), women's vulnerability as urban residents is investigated within the broader context of rural-urban migration and urban development. Focusing on a group of migrant women occupying the lower rungs of the employment ladder, particular attention is paid to domestic workers, who represent a substantial proportion of the women who migrate to the urban areas of Swaziland. It is argued that these women are confronted with harsh conditions, exacerbated by economic fluctuations, job scarcity, housing shortages and social and cultural factors that have historically marginalised them in society. Rather than migrate back to the rural areas, they adopt strategies to cope with the day-to-day problems.

Moser (1996) uses the concept of *vulnerability* to describe the insecurity of individuals, households or communities in the face of a changing environment. Ecological, economic, social and political change can increase an individual's risk, uncertainty and self-respect. To resist and recover from the effects of these changes, individuals, households or communities mobilise their assets in the face of hardship. Moser further argues that women's ability to avoid or reduce their vulnerability and to increase their economic productivity depends not only on their initial assets, but also on their ability to effectively transform those assets into income, food and other basic necessities. Therefore, the more assets people have, the less vulnerable they are, and the greater the erosion of their assets, the greater their insecurity.

As Swazi women have been migrating to the urban areas in search of employment because of various adversities in the rural areas, how have they responded to low and stagnant incomes, harsh working conditions, increasing inflation and increased expenditure on food, health, education and services in their new urban lives? Our main argument is that women's resilience has culminated in the creation, adoption and reinforcement of networking and in joining formal and informal associations and that this is a dimension of the analysis of urban poverty that deserves increased attention.

COPING IN THE CITY: WOMEN'S NETWORKS OF RECIPROCITY

Women in Africa have a long history of organising themselves, formally or informally, in order to overcome the problems they face (Malombe, 1996). In Swaziland this is a practice set within the age-old tradition of communal work parties (*lilima*) amongst neighbours to help each other in a number of activities (Armstrong and Russell, 1985). Through such initiatives, women have helped each other to meet family welfare needs and to give each other advice and moral support (Malombe, 1996). There are many registered women's groups in Swaziland, and Armstrong and Russell (1985) show that Swazi women have a great desire and ability to organise themselves into groups when they can do so on their own terms. These include savings groups, burial societies, wedding groups, and land and housing acquisition groups. These groups are not necessarily formal, but may be informal reciprocity networks based on kinship, friendship or organised around their home areas of origin. The primary purpose of the groups is to support one another financially and materially.

However, other forms of non-material support are becoming increasingly relevant for migrant women in the city. The lives of domestic workers represent a good opportunity to review some of the coping strategies that urban women adopt. First, their migrant status, and the strength and intensity of their rural-urban linkages, determine the strategies they adopt. Second, their role as poorly paid domestic servants offers no security and is on the bottom rung of Swaziland's economy. And third, the nexus of their roles as migrants, mothers and workers creates a necessity for a variety of coping strategies.

Becoming domestic workers has been made imperative by the need to provide for their families. Their jobs offer no future and their socio-economic status as migrants renders them helpless. Yet their role as mothers inspires them to adapt to harsh conditions in the workplace and in the city, for the sake of their children. As workers they may be regarded as passive because of an "undeveloped consciousness" (Bozzoli, 1985), yet their stories reveal that they have not been passive in their attempts to take advantage of their job situation to negotiate control and to reap what benefits they can. Social networks and support systems common to rural communities in Swaziland are re-created in the city and form a basis of survival and acquisition of resources within the urban setting.

Three important coping strategies may be identified, in which women have mobilised themselves into support groups to provide tangible and intangible support to one another in the face of the adversities of urban poverty. These are burial and church societies, rotating credit systems, and land and housing acquisition strategies. Going beyond the prescribed expectations of the support groups, they have also been instrumental in supporting women in finding employment and providing other basic needs.

Burial and church societies

Burial societies (*masingcwabisane*) are an important mainstay of black urban populations in the Southern African region. Commonly referred to as "societies", membership is seen as extremely important, particularly amongst women. In principle, these societies are formed to function as a financial, emotional and spiritual support structure in the event of a death in the family of one of its members. The principal activities of the burial society involve bi-monthly meetings to discuss financial matters and problems that might have arisen in the lives and families of its members. Meetings are held at the homes of different members, on a rotation system. The hostess is expected to provide food and drinks for the society members after the meeting. Members pay a fixed monthly subscription (see also Bozzoli, 1991) and membership is restricted exclusively to women. In the event of death in the family of one of its members, a society provides funds for a coffin or casket, for food and transportation, as well as spiritual support to the bereaved family.

However, in the absence of a social welfare system and with weakening rural-urban linkages, burial-societies have gone beyond their formal functions to provide a broader support structure for women in the urban environment. For domestic workers, who are non-unionised and technically unprotected by any labour legislation in Swaziland, societies form an integral part of their urban lives and are a source also of moral support. They provide a platform for airing grievances and giving advice to each other on marital disputes, harsh work conditions, bringing up children and coping with "wayward" children in the city. Societies have also helped women to form networks through which they find jobs within domestic service or placements in school for their children, through which they pass on more mundane information, such as knowing where to buy cheaper soap or how to cook in town. Women's support groups form a very vital part of the lives of domestic workers, migrants and mothers amidst the failure of kin, community and the State to provide for their well-being in the city.

Women's groups in also include prayer groups, through which women give and receive financial, spiritual and emotional support. Their involvement in Christian prayer groups is an important support structure, involving mutual exchange of food and shelter in times of need (Gaitskell, 1982; Bozzoli, 1991). Through the network of Christian women that the various groups expose their members to, homelessness can be warded off. Economic development in Swaziland has also brought with it rising inflation, which has made it more difficult for domestic workers to make ends meet. Christian associations and networks are particularly important to alleviate immediate crises.

The gap created between Government's ability to provide social services and enhance human development on the one hand, and the reality of Swazi women's everyday experiences on the other, has increasingly been filled by women's own initiatives. Their initiatives speak to a need to address their problems and to incorporate them and their strategies into the planning process. Their strategies can be seen clearly in their ability to secure land and shelter, credit and social support in the city through their own social networks and

support systems based on kinship, friendship and a common cause: to overcome poverty and to provide for their children.

Rotating credit systems

In a study of migrant women employed as domestic workers in Manzini, an
analysis of their household budgets reveals that over 50 per cent of their
monthly wages of US$ 50 is used for rent and transport to and from work
(Miles, 1996b). Other demands placed on their earnings included food, school
fees, fuel for cooking, clothing and monthly subscriptions to the various societies and associations they join for social support. Because their earnings were
so low, monthly groceries tended to comprise only maize-meal, some soap,
candles and fuel for cooking. A lot of sacrifices were made for the sake of their
children: for example, some women reported having gone without a much-
needed pair of shoes for up to four years. None of them had savings account,
because, as one woman remarked, "... after paying for everything there is
nothing left to save". Neither could they approach banking institutions for
loans because their earnings were below the $2,000 mark demanded by most
financial institutions. Moreover, they usually lacked collateral or their hus-
band's permission to obtain a loan. Budgetary stress demanded that they devise a strategy that would ensure a cash flow to meet overhead costs that their
monthly wages could not meet. The most common strategy, that was adopted
almost universally by domestic workers, was an informal credit system called
luholiswane ("paying each other"). This helped them build and/or roof their
houses, pay their children's school fees, buy much needed furniture and buy
seed and fertiliser for planting maize.

Rotating credit systems and other forms of reciprocity networks are not
unique to Swaziland, and are becoming a common strategy of women to improve their daily lives in both First and Third World countries. Rowbotham
and Mitter (1994) refer to women's efforts to organise themselves as "new
forms of economic organising" in the face of global economic hardship. A
rotating credit association is organised among groups of women where two or
three agree to pay a defined sum of money (usually $5–$20) into a common
fund every month (see also Hansen, 1989). The funds rotate among members
of the group so that if four women pay $10 every month, each woman gets
$40 every four month. The women interviewed preferred to join *luholiswane*
with their friends because it is flexible and based on trust and empathy, and it
also compels them to pay into the fund every month. *Luholiswane* generally
helps them to supplement their incomes and to make ends meet.

Accessing work

Changes in Swaziland's labour market since the early colonial period have
been a major source of vulnerability for the large majority of the Swazi population. Women's response to declining incomes and a stagnant rural economy
has been to join the labour force in increasing numbers. The absence of any
significant economic growth nodes in the rural areas has forced rural women
in large numbers to migrate to the urban centres, mainly to the capital city of
Mbabane and to Manzini. The fact that Swazi women have increasingly joined

the labour market does not mean that fewer men are working, but rather that many households have multiple earners. The hardships of working in competitive, dead-end occupations with long work hours and low pay is vividly portrayed through the lives of women employed in Manzini as domestic workers.

A major reason for the vulnerability of women in the urban areas has been their marginal role in the labour market (Moser, 1996). Swazi migrant women have been confronted with the challenges of poverty, unemployment, low-incomes, inadequate services and infrastructure and limited access to land. To keep their households out of poverty and to reduce their vulnerability, they have mobilised their own labour as well as that of other household members. Migrant women who come to the city of Manzini to eke out a living for themselves and their children, with no education or marketable skills have few chances in the formal labour market (Russell, 1986). With a generally high level of unemployment in the country (Government of Swaziland, 1995), domestic service has been their only option. Not only has it functioned as an entry point into the urban economy, but there has been increasing demand for cheap domestic labour as more Swazi women move into the formal labour market.

Informal sector activities also provide an avenue for income generation for urban women. However, prohibitions on street vending by the City Council of Manzini, tight control over the distribution of stalls at the city marketplace, and high levels of competition within the informal sector, has made informal activities less of an option.

Domestic work has provided a foothold into the urban economy, particularly for younger women who have moved to the city with aspirations of entering more lucrative forms of employment such as factory work. It can also be effectively used as a strategy to feed and clothe their children. A frequent response was that "... I am doing it for the sake of the children." Their ambitions are simple: to obtain a good education for their children, and to establish a path of upward social mobility for them. In this way, by investing in their children's education at all costs, women try to prevent the perpetuation of poverty from one generation to the next.

Domestic work is also attractive to migrant women, as it provides accommodation and a measure of safety and security that informal housing does not offer, given the high rates of crime in Swaziland's informal housing settlements. Domestic workers who use domestic work as a strategy to obtain a roof over their heads do so also to save on food, rent and transportation costs.

The migration literature points to a very important factor in the ability of a new migrant to find a job in the city or in town, namely a trusting reliance on the "homegirl network" (cf. Vaa et al., 1989; Bozzoli, 1991; Trager, 1995).

> The only way to get a job is to ask women you know if they have heard anything. And if they have, you wake up early in the morning to go and try your luck.[1]

---

[1] Interview with Tryphinah Bhembe in Manzini June 20, 1995.

69

Unless women know somebody in the city, who knows somebody else who needs a domestic worker, it is difficult to get a job. Without contacts, the search for employment will mean going from door to door with limited chances of success. A network made up of friends, acquaintances and homegirls is part of the coping strategy of women, based on a mutual understanding of the need to secure employment "for the sake of the children". It is also a way of helping each other maintain their dignity in the midst of the pressures of both rural and urban poverty. The absence of domestic work employment agencies has been an impetus for women to help each other find jobs in the city. The willingness of women to find employment for one another, particularly in the realm of domestic service, is another effort by women fill a gap created by the Government's inability to keep pace with growing rural-urban migration and unemployment in the urban areas.

A home in the city

Housing is an important productive asset that can cushion households against severe poverty, and land market regulation can either create opportunities to diversify its use or foreclose them (Moser, 1996:7).

Swazi women's traditionally limited rights to land have had serious implications for their access to land in urban areas. Land in urban areas is title deed land and in principle open to ownership even by women, but the rapid growth of the urban population in relation to the relatively small size of the country has resulted in an encroaching of the urban area onto communal Swazi Nation Land. This has created a multitude of problems for the local urban authorities, in terms of provision and management of urban areas. Even more significant for the urban residents in these areas is that the housing insecurity which is characteristic of urban informal settlements increases their vulnerability (cf. Moser, 1996). A large proportion of the urban population is housed in the informal settlements that have mushroomed on communal land in peri-urban areas (Hoek-Smit, 1998; LHMS, 1993; Government of Swaziland, 1995).

Yet notwithstanding the hurdles women face with respect to land acquisition in the city, some women have been able to build their own houses, largely depending on their marital status and the structure of their households. Only a married woman, a woman who lives with a man, or a woman with sons (even an infant son) are able to obtain land. For female headed households, women's social networks have been significant in helping to provide shelter.

Ownership opportunities for the urban poor in Swaziland are very limited, particularly for women, who are faced with financial, legal and cultural constraints on home ownership. At the same time, women are increasingly realising the significance of the role of housing in reducing their vulnerability. For women with weak or no links with the rural areas, housing is an effective strategy for being urban, not least because it offers prospects of generating income by letting out rooms. The opportunities that housing provides for home-based enterprises and other income-generating activities are equally important for women. A third and more sombre reason is that, according to

Swazi custom and tradition, it is important to have a home for oneself and one's children because it is regarded also as one's final resting place. Culturally, a deceased family member is never buried in a cemetery but rather in the family homestead, even if the deceased is an urban dweller. It is therefore considered shameful to have no home to be buried in.

How then does woman's social networks in Swaziland assist her in securing a home of her own? To evade the social processes and power relations that reinforce gender inequalities in land and housing acquisition, women have sought homeownership in other ways, albeit ways that accentuate their vulnerability. Perhaps the most common strategy is to rely on the goodwill of a friend who already has land. This is usually an informal agreement in which a woman is given permission to erect a house on the friend's land free of charge. An alternative strategy is to squat or erect an illegal dwelling, but this is normally a short-lived strategy with potentially serious repercussions. Finally, some women use various types of relations with men as a means to obtain shelter, but this also often turns out to be a short-lived strategy.

For those women who have secured a home of their own in and around the city of Manzini, through marriage, through their sons, or through women-centred networks, housing becomes an effective tool for generating additional household income, extending personal relationships and accessing social capital (Moser, 1996). Housing is thus used as an asset on which they can capitalise, particularly when other sources of income fail to meet the needs of the household.

CONCLUSION

Development in Swaziland has been typified by many contradictions. In common with other African countries, the Government of Swaziland is faced with an urban crisis. It is a crisis exacerbated by legacies from the colonial administration, and that continues to marginalise large sectors of society. The phenomenon of rural-urban migration has had serious effects on urban development and has led to growing urban poverty. For domestic workers living below the poverty line, the situation has been particularly serious. Their vulnerability has been increased by the fact that the Swaziland Government continues to treat domestic work as an "invisible" occupation. Even the legal system protects them only in theory.

The obstacles facing migrant women coming to the city have not changed much since the colonial era. They include the absence of a social welfare system, inflated health, education and housing costs, limited rights to land and a lack of financial resources. Yet this has not hindered them from adopting strategies to overcome these obstacles and to pursue their ambitions. For the sake of their children, domestic workers have devised coping strategies compensate for Government's failure to adequately ensure sustainable development in Swaziland.

Faced with severe difficulties, including marginalisation as women, domestic servants rarely convey a sense of despair. This paper has referred to the importance of their collective action as women in reducing their vulnerability

71

in the urban environment. The paper also points to the need for recognition of domestic work as a legitimate employment sector for women.

The growth and development of the Swaziland labour market has resulted in gendered patterns of employment that have not been in women's favour. Women have had to move into the realm of domestic work as part of their labour strategy, not only to earn an income but in order to feed and clothe their children. The significance of social and homegirl networks in securing employment and shelter in the city cannot be over-emphasised.

Unless the land question is resolved, women will continue to be denied the right to homes of their own. For them, the chance of owning a dwelling unit in the formal housing market is only remotely possible. This has called for alternative housing strategies. The desire for a home of one's own is deeply influenced by their need to mobilise housing as an asset, to reduce vulnerability in a society riddled with social, economic and gender inequalities, and to provide a home for their children.

Women's coping strategies in the city are central to a discussion that brings out the gap between Government development policy and a general failure to equitably implement this. They are coping strategies that demand attention, as increasing numbers of Swazi women join the ranks of the urban poor. Women and their coping mechanisms need to be assimilated into gender planning. Women in Swaziland play a significant role in managing households. Yet economic decline and the development policies adopted after independence seriously threaten their well-being and that of their families, leading to the adoption of a variety of coping strategies that draw attention to the need to understand urban women's actions, needs and visions in creating gender sensitive approaches to planning in Swaziland.

References

Armstrong, A. and M. Russell, 1985, *A Situation Analysis of Women in Swaziland*. Kwaluseni: SSRU/UNICEF.

Bozzoli, B., 1985, "Migrant Women and South African Social Change: Biographical Approaches to Social Analysis", *African Studies*, 44, pp. 87–96

—, 1991, *Women in Phokeng*. Johannesburg: Ravan.

Gaitskell, D., 1982, "Wailing for Purity: Prayer Unions, African Mothers and Adolescent Daughters, 1912–1940", in Marks, S. and R. Rathbone (eds), *Industrialisation and Social Change in South Africa*. London: Longman.

Government of Swaziland, 1995, *Habitat II: Swaziland Draft National Report prepared for the "City Summit" United Nations Conference on Human Settlements*. Instanbul and Mbabane: Ministry of Housing and Urban Development.

Hansen, K.T., 1989, "The Black Market and Women Traders in Lusaka, Zambia", in J.L. Parpart and K. Staudt (eds), Women in the State in Africa. Boulder, CO: Lynne Rienner Publishers.

Hansen, K.T., 1996, "Gender, Generation and Access to Housing in Zambia", in Schlyter, A. (ed.) 1996.

Hoek-Smit, M., 1998, *Low-Income Housing in Swaziland*. Mbabane: Government Printers.

LHMS, 1993, *Swaziland Land and Housing Market Survey*. Mbabane: Government Printers.

Malombe, J., 1996, "Women's Groups and Shelter Improvement in Kenya", in Schlyter, A. (ed.) 1996.

Miles, M., 1996a, "Controlling Swazi Female Migration in Colonial Swaziland", paper presented at *The 28th International Geographical Congress*, The Hague, The Netherlands, 4–10 August.

—, 1996b, "Housing for Domestic Workers in Swaziland", in Schlyter, A. (ed.) 1996.

Moser, C., 1989, "Gender Planning in the Third World: Meeting Practical and Strategic Gender Needs", *World Development*, 17, 11, pp. 1799–1825

—, 1993, *Gender Planning and Development: Theory, Practice and Training*. London: Routledge.

—, 1996, *Confronting Crisis: A Comparative Study of Household Responses to Poverty and Vulnerability in Four Poor Urban Communities*. Environmentally Sustainable Development Studies Monographs Series No. 8. Washington, DC: The World Bank.

Rowbotham, S. and S. Mitter, 1994, *Dignity and Daily Bread*. London: Routledge.

Russell, M., 1986, "High Status, Low Pay: Anomalies in the Position of Women in Employment in Swaziland", *Journal of Southern African Studies*, 12, 2, pp. 293–307.

Schlyter, Ann (ed.), *A Place to Live: Gender Research on Housing in Africa*. Uppsala: Nordiska Afrikainstitutet.

Trager, L., 1995, "Women Migrants and Rural-Urban Linkages in South Western Nigeria", in Baker, J. and T. Akin Aina (eds), *The Migration Experience in Africa*. Uppsala: Nordiska Afrikainstitutet.

UNDP, 1994, *Human Development Report*. Oxford: Oxford University Press.

Vaa, M., S. Findley and A. Diallo, 1989, "The Gift Economy: A Study of Women Migrants' Survival Strategies in a Low-Income Bamako Neighbourhood", *Labour and Capital and Society*, 22, 2, pp. 234–60.

SECTION II

RELIGION AND IDENTITY

The question of rootlessness or integration has been a recurring theme from the earliest studies of African urban society. The assumption that urban life is characterised by a lack of meaningful personal and social relationships has not been borne out by empirical research. On the contrary, numerous empirical studies have demonstrated that continuity and integration through the formation of new of social links is typical of African cities. In the absence of the ideal-type close-knit network of the rural village, urban residents have formed associations for recreation or mutual aid based on one or several shared characteristics, such as neighbourhood, common area of origin or ethnic background.

Religious groupings have been found to play an important integrative role. The three contributions presented in this section shed light on the relationship between religion, identity and integration in three different institutional settings: the church-affiliated township association, the urban congregation and the holy city.

Harri Englund presents the case of a home-villagers' association in a peri-urban township in Lilongwe, Malawi. The association was established as a welfare and recreational body for migrants from a rural area some 50 miles from Lilongwe. It gave the "home" a particular definition, where specific ethnic and religious practices were highlighted, and others ignored. The home area becomes an "virtual" village, which the actual residents of the area would probably not have recognised as theirs.

The association was founded by an experienced urbanite with distinctive entrepreneurial qualities. A devout Catholic, he had built a Catholic Church in the township and it was here that the founding meeting took place. Pains were taken to include not only Catholics, but also Presbyterians, but the association did not acknowledge the fact that an African Church was also important in the home area and among the out-migrants. The association emerged at the interface of national and local politics, and represents only a narrow range of its members' active social ties. Among its most important features is a fund to assist villagers in town in the event of illness or funerals. Assistance serves to ease the existential and material burden of funerals, while stressing the moral obligations embedded in cultural notions of personal growth and authority. Through active manipulation, the association fosters an identity based on the urban experience of particular migrants. The chapter is thus a contribution to the critique of ethnicity as the ultimate source of identity in post-colonial Africa.

In her study of two New Generation Churches in Port Harcourt, Nigeria, Yomi Oruwari raises the question whether these institutions play a role in providing welfare and services, and the extent to which they are a source of political empowerment and democratic experience for their members. The new generation churches have grown rapidly over the last two decades, and among their new members, youngsters, women and the poor are over-represented. Membership in the congregations is not based on locality and cuts across ethnic affiliation and class.

The principal finding is that the churches still see the spiritual development of their members as their primary role, but that this is gradually changing. They take on more and more welfare activities as they realise that poverty and lack of services negatively affect the spiritual growth of their members. The two churches investigated are not training grounds for democracy: spiritual guidance rather than members' influence informs decisions. They divorce themselves from the state and from partisan politics, which hardly serves to empower their members. Women are discriminated against. In biblical activities, they are relegated to the background, their participation in social affairs is limited and they do not take part in the management of the congregation.

The new generation churches are getting more and more involved with the socio-economic circumstances of their members through assistance to individuals and their families. However, provision of services such as health, education and housing is still in its infancy. The churches have yet to define their role *vis-à-vis* local and state authorities and financial institutions. It is likely that for a long time to come, their prime importance will continue to be in offering new social identities to their "born-again" followers, through inclusion, guidance and visions of a brighter tomorrow.

In the third article in this section, Cheikh Gueye takes us to the city of Touba in Senegal, headquarters of the Muslim brotherhood of Mourides. The city is devoted to the memory of the brotherhood's founder. The article is a study of how one particular association of disciples has grown into a considerable force when it comes to channelling resources from the Mouride diaspora to Touba, and in claiming ideological leadership through zeal, rigorous discipline and ostentatious devotion to the religious authorities.

The association was started by a group of students who sought each other out for mutual support and to further a Mouride identity in a university setting. Till then, Mouridism had been seen primarily as a movement with rural roots, with few adherents among educated urbanites. After some years, the association allowed non-students to become members, but it continues to define itself as an organisation of intellectuals, mastering the teaching of the French school system but rejecting cultural assimilation.

Touba celebrates a yearly festival, the *Magal*, in commemoration of the founder's banishment into exile by the colonial authorities. It is an occasion for which Mourides from all over the country and abroad congregate. The activities of this particular association of disciples have become more and more centred on this event. From one year to another, considerable sums are mobilised from its members and supporters, to provide shelter and food for the pilgrims. The association also gets revenue from business and agriculture. Lately, it has established a permanent centre in Touba as a base for its continued demonstration of zeal, faith and innovative actions. From being a marginal association of university students, it has evolved into a contender for influence in the central affairs of an important religious movement.

CHAPTER 5

New Generation Churches and the Provision of Welfare: A Gender Study from Port Harcourt, Nigeria

Yomi Oruwari

Nigeria, like other countries in Africa, is currently facing an urban crisis manifest in the gross lack of basic services. Those that remain are not only expensive, they are nearing total collapse. Meanwhile, the urban population is growing rapidly, promoted by federal policies of state creation, with state capitals being the pivots of physical development. However, cities in Nigeria have become cities of the poor, and it is becoming increasingly difficult to sustain economic growth in them. This puts great stress on the quantity and quality of resources produced and managed there.

That the state has failed in the provision of basic urban services is gradually being accepted in Nigeria. Recently, many community based organisations (CBOs) and non-governmental organisations (NGOs) have been assisting with and gradually taking over the provision of urban services hitherto provided by the state.

THE BASIS FOR THE CREATION OF NGOs IN NIGERIA

NGOs are not a new feature of African societies. According to Mulyungi (1990), before organised state structures were put in place by the colonialists, self-help efforts by groups were a cultural fact. They continue to play important roles in rural development and presently in urban development, especially in the economic sector outside government structures. However, the recent upsurge of the NGO phenomenon in Africa has Northern origins and depends in large measure upon funding from Northern agencies. Thus, it is not surprising that the field of African NGO work is in a state of revolution. NGOs operate with different levels of performance, in facilitating and supporting grassroots development projects, awareness raising and development education.

An NGO has been defined as:

> Any voluntary grouping of people, whether physical or moral, constituted with the unique aim of promoting development by, with and for a target population, so that the latter master its living conditions at the economic and socio-economic levels. Kabarhuza (1990:xx)

In Nigeria, people have been responding to the multiple problems caused by the economic situation resulting in part from Structural Adjustment Programmes (SAPs) and the failure of the state to look after its people. People have been coming together to pool forces and resources and to organise their own survival. Initially, the efforts by urban residents were directed at improving their areas of origin (villages), since they have great affinity to these areas and according to the Nigerian constitution, claims to citizenship are based on one's area of origin (even if not born or living there). Of note is that, in the recent past and present, the failure of many formal financial institutions both as savings and lending establishments has induced many people to loose confidence in them. People therefore depend more and more on the NGOs and CBOs that are located in the urban areas for their economic survival. Also of note is the fact that it is the inability of government agencies to provide essential services that has made residents provide them on a communal basis e.g. provision of security for life and property, or repair of access roads to residences. These associations have withstood the test of time, since they are based on shared interests and geographic, tribal and social proximity. NGOs are not a new phenomenon in Nigeria; it is the involvement of Northern NGOs including their financial assistance and their relationship with existing CBOs and other voluntary associations that is new. What is also new is the involvement of urban residents in providing services hitherto provided by public agencies through their communities and associations, not on tribal lines. These associations include churches and organisations like Rotary or Lion's Clubs.

The emergence in the past two decades of new generation churches and their followers, especially in urban areas, is of particular interest. Earlier research into these organisations (Kemdirim, 1996; Isaacson, 1990) has been in terms of their religious significance rather than their involvement in urban development. Lately, these churches have generated much controversy with respect to their importance and role in urban communities. Public officers and better off urban residents seem to question the relevance of these churches in urban areas. Despite this observation, there is continued interest in them and an astronomic growth in the congregations. This growth is made up of mostly women, youth and the poor.

In this study, the activities of two churches are investigated, i.e. the Deeper Life Bible Church and the Celestial Church of Christ. Both are national churches founded by individuals. The purpose is to look at their changing role, from purely spiritual development to socio-economic development, and their political significance (if any) to their followers. Hence, the welfare activities of the churches, their impact on the neighbourhoods where they are located, and the involvement of the congregation in the decision-making process within each church are examined, in order to determine the degree to which the churches are a source of political empowerment and democratic experience for their members. As a majority of members are women, the involvement of members in the decision-making, management and implementation of programmes is analysed on gender lines.

The new generation churches have become involved in socio-economic development through provision of urban services at a level that surpasses government welfare facilities and accomplishments. To highlight this shift in emphasis, the study addresses the following questions:

(i)   What is the relationship between public authorities and religious organisations in Nigeria?

(ii) While the churches can be seen as fostering participation within the congregation, of what does it consist and can it be understood as empowerment?

(iii) Do the churches perform any role in training their members in democratic decision-making?

(iv) What has been the level of their involvement in provision of services, e.g. housing, health and education, and how has this involvement affected their following and original purpose?

METHODOLOGY

The information for the study was obtained largely through a qualitative approach. During a period of two months (February and March, 1998) open-ended interviews were conducted with officials in the following ministries: Finance, Health, Education and Housing, to find out the relationship of NGOs (especially the churches) with public establishments with respect to provision of services. Focussed group discussions were held with five men and five women in each of the two churches. The discussions centred around members' perceptions of the role of the churches in their lives and the effects of their activities in the communities and the country. The pastors in charge of these churches were also interviewed, using a semi-structured interview guide. This strategy was adopted in order to gather a rich variety of data to provide as full and vivid a picture as possible of the problem under inquiry.

THE CASE STUDY

The Deeper Life Bible Church, Port Harcourt

The Deeper Life Bible Church was founded in 1973 by a mathematics lecturer at the University of Lagos, Pastor Kumuyi. It started as a Bible studies class of 15 members who met in his flat. This became a church in 1982, with more than 10,000 members. Presently it is a national church. The church is not a cult. If a person no longer wishes to be a member, he or she just stops attending the church. To be a member you must be ready to share your experiences, learn the Bible teachings and abide by the doctrines of the church. Initially female members were identified by the lack of use of ornaments on their persons and the way in which they always cover their heads. Presently, with the emergence of other psychedelic and charismatic churches, this dogmatic adherence to the teachings of the Old Testament is changing and women now have a more cheerful appearance.

The church is engaged in a variety of welfare activities:

(a)   Economic: Training of women for economic improvement—home science.

(b)   Health: Provision of health facilities—maternity and ante-natal services.

(c) Education: Early childhood training—nursery schools, which are still in the planning stage because finance and available land are lacking.

(d) Housing: Housing for staff, guest houses for members in transit, hostel rooms for just transferred members who have still to obtain their own accommodation, and most importantly, provision of lodging when members are on retreat or attending "crusades", which are rallies to win souls for Christ.

Administration

The smallest unit within the church is the home caring fellowship, which consists of 10–15 members. The group's leader reports any problem to the zonal co-ordinator, who reports to the pastor of the local church. The affected member is then interviewed by the local pastor, who then identifies and defines the problem from the member's narrative.

The church operates a unitary system of government. Although, the complaints, suggestions etc. of members are listened to, a final ruling comes from the General overseer and founder—Pastor Kumuyi. Spiritual leading is highly emphasised in all their deliberations and decisions. Officers (leaders) are therefore chosen on the basis of their spiritual merit.

When social problems are identified (mostly through suggestions of members), solutions are sought by divine means, through prayer and fasting and these are disseminated to the members through seminars and workshops. Thus, members are not subjected to democratic experiences. They believe that Nigeria's political problems can be solved only by divine intervention.

Provision of welfare

It is expected that the church's role in welfare provision will be on the increase as the state is becoming more and more incompetent in providing essential services. Since the ultimate concern of the church is with the spiritual life of its members, it is believed that only when members are satisfied with their socio-economic lives can their spiritual lives be fulfilling. As the majority of the members are booth poor and women or children, reaching these categories is a must for the church. However, all activities are directed solely at its members. So for a person to enjoy most of the facilities he or she has to become a member.

Relationship with the neighbourhood

Initially there was no relationship between the church and its surrounding neighbourhood although it is believed that the church provides spiritual protection. Presently, members believe that the church is sited where it is for them to try to win local residents for Christ. Non-member residents have mixed opinions. Some complain vehemently about the inconvenience of noise and traffic pollution caused by the church in their neighbourhood, but they agree that, with the siting of the church, the neighbourhood is protected from robbers.

Gender and welfare

Since "women are the weaker vessels" according to the scriptures, the church takes note of the disadvantaged positions of women, widows etc. in the congregation. It is believed that a woman is the root of a stable family and therefore by reaching her, the family is reached. "The Woman Mirror", a monthly magazine published by the church, is very popular. Although there is a counterpart for men, more emphasis is placed on "The Woman Mirror". The founder's wife (Mrs Kumuyi) as the leader of the women's ministry frequently organises both national and local workshops and seminars for members on gender issues.

Political leanings

As a member of the Christian Association of Nigeria, the Deeper Life Bible Church abides by the decisions of the association. The church does not encourage partisan politics, although it recognises the place of government in society. At the same time, it does not place any sanction on members who wish to go into politics.

The disencouragement of members taking part in partisan politics, according to the church, is because it believes that the process of choosing rulers in Nigeria is fraught with cheating, corruption and hooliganism. This situation is seen as being against the teachings of the Bible.

Association with the State

It was mooted recently by a Federal Minister of State that, with the astronomic increase in the membership of the new generation churches, and the changing role of churches as money-making ventures, the churches in Nigeria must pay taxes. When the general overseer and founder of Deeper Life Bible Church, Pastor Kumuyi, was interviewed by one of the national media organisations, he agreed that new generation churches should pay taxes, as long as the law includes the mosques and traditional religious bodies (i.e. all religious organisations operating in Nigeria). Due to the controversial nature of his response, the issue was dropped by the federal government. Pastor Kumuyi also stated that the Deeper Life Bible Church is willing to go into partnership with the federal, state and local governments to provide services, as long as they affect the welfare of the members of the church.

The Celestial Church of Christ, Rumuola, Port Harcourt

The Celestial Church was started in 1947, by Pastor Osuolale B. Oshoffa, a child of a Methodist wood-trader, who later also became a wood-trader. A native of a neighbouring country, Benin Republic, Oshoffa was said to have been lost in the forest when he was on an ebony wood buying trip. When he resurfaced three months later, he had been transformed into a preacher and a healer. Since he was persecuted and ridiculed in his own country, Benin Republic, he moved to Lagos, Nigeria, where he established a church that later became both a national and an international church. Although the church is not a cult (in the sense that members are free to leave it without sanctions), its mode of worship incorporates many traditional ways of worship.

The members wear white flowing gowns and are barefooted. The Church has a constitution that states clearly the mode of worship. However, involvement of the church in the community is not mentioned in the constitution.

Welfare activities are varied:

(a) Economic: During the Sunday service, alms are given, through a special collection by the congregation, to members or non-members who need help in their businesses or just for survival. Those in need are first screened by the resident Pastor before being announced to the congregation. This exercise is taken as an important function of the Sunday service, as the members of the church believe that they will receive special blessing by God for alms giving. Since they do not know when the angels (whose duty it is to give such a blessing) will do so, it is necessary to give alms regularly.

(b) Health: The members believe strongly in faith healing (through prayers and visions). In fact, these aspects of the church's teachings rule their lives. Special services are held to cater for members' needs and faith clinics are held for pregnant women.

(c) Education: Some branches that can afford to have opened nursery schools open to everyone. School fees cover running costs and no profit is made.

(d) Housing

- Housing is provided for staff.
- Lodging is provided for members in transit.
- Rooms are provided for members who have just been transferred to town and do not have accommodation.
  Protection rooms are provided for females and males during special prayers that may last for days.

Administration

Church administration is handled by a parochial committee consisting of thirty-three (33) members (male and female) elected by members for a two-year term. Of a higher rank are the elders (who attain the position through spiritual ranking), who advise the shepherd (Pastor) spiritually on the day-to-day management of the church. Thus, the Celestial Church teaches democracy and elected officers are chosen based on the need of the church, interest in its activities and members' assessment of the capabilities of the person. More importantly, the process of choosing leaders is first of all subjected to prayers and fasting to ensure spiritual intervention. However, once in a while, the system has led to disagreements and disturbances when the police have temporarily entered the premises to keep the peace. These disagreements have always been resolved by members themselves.

Provision of welfare

Members and the shepherds alike feel that there has been an increase in the number of people needing assistance from the church. They know that the church will have to get more involved with provision of services, as the state has failed. The members believe strongly that the more assistance given to those in need, the more grace received from God.

Relationship with the neighbourhood

Presently, the church does not have any relationship with the residents in the neighbourhood in which it is situated. The church sees urban problems in terms of demonic attack from witches and wizards and the only solution divine intervention. Thus it is believed that building the church in a particular neighbourhood, with its doors wide open to accept visitors, will entice people with problems to seek assistance. In some cases, assisting visitors to solve their problems may result in them becoming members.

Gender and welfare

The church discriminates against women. Women are not allowed to preach the sermon, read the lesson or make announcements during church devotional services. In fact they are not allowed to perform any spiritual functions connected with church services other than saying the prayers when asked and reading portions of the bible chosen by the preacher. All these restrictions are clearly stated in the constitution of the church. Observation, however, shows that women are more numerous than men in the congregation.

Political leanings

The Celestial Church has never been interested in or encouraged its members to be interested in partisan politics. They see their empowerment in spiritual terms, based on studying the Bible.

Association with the State

Informants mentioned the proposed tax, and that the proposal was withdrawn.

Findings

(i)   The primary role of both churches is to develop members spiritually. This role is gradually changing and extending to socio-economic activities, because of the inability of the state to provide services that have always been its traditional role. This has been encouraged by the churches' realisation that lack of services is negatively affecting the spiritual growth of their members.

Thus the churches are gradually being reorganised, so that they can be involved with development of a target population (i.e. the members of their congregations) and therefore are changing from purely religious bodies to organisations engaged in NGO activities. This trend is expected to continue in Nigeria, and church groups are expected to seek affiliation to national NGOs, e.g. NGO for the Improvement of Women Agricultural Co-operatives.

(ii) The provision of services (economic, health, education and housing) is still in its infancy and as yet is not well developed by the new generation churches. But the intention is to improve with time rather than stop providing such services.

Of note is the fact that non-governmental development efforts took place specifically under the banner of the orthodox churches, Moslem organisations and progressive communities during the colonial period. These efforts included educational institutions, health facilities and staff housing. The state intervened and took these facilities over by the early 1970s. Presently, these institutions have been grossly mismanaged and the churches are being asked to take over such establishments again. Most of the churches are reluctant to do so as they no longer have the resources to restore the facilities to the standard they had before the state took them over, in terms of provision of services and the management of materials, personnel and students. Meanwhile private organisations are providing these facilities at exorbitant prices that are way beyond what poor people can afford.

(iii) The two churches investigated have different forms of government. However, in both cases spiritual guidance rather than notions of democracy influences the running of their affairs. Both churches are passive or negative about partisan politics. They divorce themselves from the state. They do not encourage their members to be politically active, nor do they discourage them. Even at the national level, it is only when government policy directly impacts on the activities of churches that the Christian Association of Nigeria voices an opinion in the national newspapers.

(iv) Generally the churches are not concerned with the neighbourhoods in which they operates. The community of each church is its congregation. This includes members from different tribes and classes, although the majority of members are poor. The members see themselves as belonging to one family—The family of Jesus Christ.

(v) In terms of gender, the Christian churches in general are highly discriminatory. This is more so with the new generation churches that combine traditional activities with Western religion. For example, the issue of women being ordained as priests is still very controversial. Amongst the orthodox Christian churches, the Presbyterian Church of Nigeria is the only church that views the ordination of women as one of the great issues in ensuring Christian justice for women (Kemdirim, 1996).

Traditionally the roles of women were strictly restricted to the domestic domain. However, there was an apparent recognition and respect for the dignity of womanhood in traditional religion, regarded not as a matter for the individual but as a concern for the entire group. Thus, the involvement of women in religious ceremonies is common in many African cultures. In the two churches studied here, women are seen as "weaker vessels" that should be protected and, in the Celestial Church especially, should be kept in the background.

(vi) The state does not see the new generation churches in terms of their assistance in providing services for the poor. What concerns the responsible public officers is the potential of the churches' astronomic growth on taxes that would increase the revenue base of different local governments. However, any policy on generating taxes from churches must be handled with caution, as the issue of religion in the country is a volatile one, which can easily lead to a national crisis, since the country has three principal religions: Christianity, Islam and traditional religions.

(vii) Some negative effects of the role of the churches in the neighbourhoods in which they are located were observed. The indiscriminate location of these churches close to residences makes them a nuisance, in terms of noise and traffic congestion, since they operate every day and for long hours. The dependence of some members on faith healing has in some instances, led to avoidable deaths. Most importantly, a lot of people, especially women, spend valuable time in the churches receiving "visions", experiencing "miracles" and conducting prayers.

DISCUSSION AND RECOMMENDATIONS
The changing role of churches
The Church and stress

In South Africa, charismatic religious sects have been and continue to be the focus of Africanist writing on social organisation, cultural resistance, political mobilisation etc. The situation is different in West Africa and especially in Nigeria, where the rise and popularity of such churches have been characterised as a palliative for the individual's inability to cope with the demands of an impersonal, modernist urban society. These movements are attractive to young adults because they fill the gap created by the removal of strong and extensive religious instruction in school curricula. They are also seen as responses to the stresses arising from modernisation, which in turn has created religious institutions that mix Western and traditional (African) elements. Their ability to reclaim "lost" souls (individuals) and to renew social identity that was assumed to have weakened in the often overly emphasised confusion (both material and spiritual) of urban life were said to explain their attraction. We should not forget that these churches offer visions that promise their congregations a brighter tomorrow. It is this hope that gives urban dwellers the courage to persevere despite their deplorable existence. Thus in the long run such churches may assist in reducing the number of poor patients both in psychiatric hospitals and in the homes of the cities.

The Church and provision of services

The new generation churches are getting more and more involved with the socio-economic circumstances of their congregations instead of their souls alone, resulting in entry into the provision of services.

In the case of housing, the time is ripe for religious organisations to be directly involved. The state as obvious from studies of public housing policy has not been able to provide housing for the poor.

Presently, the churches studied assist their members financially on request. With the poor economic situation and the inability of commercial banks to assist poor informal entrepreneurs, there might be a role for the new generation churches to set up finance sections to make available soft loans to members to assist them in their businesses instead of encouraging them to beg for alms.

The Church and the State

The churches investigated have little political significance in their neighbourhoods. The only significant involvement of the state in their affairs is the controversial issue of paying tax which was later dropped as it is extremely sensitive and could lead to a national crisis.

It is necessary for the state to provide an enabling environment that will assist the churches in providing the much needed urban services—education, health, housing and finance. Even if finally they have to pay tax, they can be given incentives for providing the services. But the question remains—should they provide the services for their members alone or for the entire neighbourhood in which they are located?

Gender and the New Generation Churches

This study has shown that the churches are discriminatory. In the organisation of biblical activities, women are relegated to the background. This ultimately affects their participation in social activities at the managerial level. As women form the majority of members in the churches, it is necessary for them to assume more managerial positions so that they can directly voice their contribution to the running of the organisations and especially in the provision of services that affect the members.

Finance

The churches advocate solidarity and the desirability of helping each other. This is also fuelled by the problem of visible absolute poverty, with children dying due to lack of essential health facilities, families suffering because the state does not address their basic needs etc. And, most importantly, both churches have created trust and gained credibility over the years, because their congregations see them as being sensitive to their needs.

Most of the new generation churches in Nigeria were given seed money to start their ministries by affiliated churches, mostly in the United States (through special offerings for evangelisation), and, as they get better organised, the churches have access to these funds for their work. The churches therefore strive to develop credibility with their donors. In addition, their ability to work with their congregations has given their members confidence and the courage needed to undertake projects independently.

Tithes are strongly encouraged and as the congregations consist of both the poor and the well-off, it is relatively easy to get funds for developmental projects through pledges and donations by members. Members are encouraged to donate generously by the use of such quotes from the Holy Bible as "God loves a cheerful giver".

Also of importance is the churches' growing ability to reward a person for every good gesture in terms of assistance. This is common to all cultures and traditions in Nigeria. Since Christians believe in divine intervention, members of these churches automatically return thanks to God for every prayer answered. A lot of resources are generated through this practice. Throughout Nigeria, there is a widespread belief that church business is the most lucrative segment of the informal economy.

Empowerment

Poverty and marginalisation do not arise in a vacuum. To recognise injustice is to see that it is maintained by a distribution of power that perpetuates social and economic exclusion. Addressing poverty means attacking its causes, bearing in mind that development is about giving poor people access to the tools to change their situations and empowerment implies the power to bring about change (Thompson, 1996).

Although education may confer some power, which changes the status-quo, it does not in itself allow people to challenge the injustice which causes their marginalisation. This is possible only if the balance of power which maintains injustice can be changed. This argument leads to another area of discussion, the power to choose who should be a leader. Presently, the democratic way of choosing leaders as obtaining in Western countries, has not worked well in most of Africa. Leaders cling to power ruthlessly, even to the economic detriment of their countries. The insincerity of politicians is contrary to the teachings of the Bible or the Koran. The present attitude of non-involvement in politics of new generation churches will not solve the problem of unscrupulous politicians. The religious bodies have to get involved, and by example, change the attitudes of Nigerian politicians.

The non-involvement of churches in the political life of their members and even the non-democratic decision-making processes in the new generation churches show the deficiency of such churches as a source of political empowerment and democratic experience for their members. For example, the supremacy of the founders is never questioned by members. With hindsight, maybe, the time has come for us to question whether democracy as obtaining in the Western world is the form of government that will save Africa, as both old and new leaders have exhibited unwillingness to abide by the decisions of the electorate.

Churches and urban planning

In the past decade, there has been an upsurge in the formation of new generation churches. In the case of the orthodox churches, the architecture of centres of worship is very elaborate and with monumental church buildings a lot of attention paid to details of columns, openings, etc. These architectural symbols are intended to generate the reverence of worshippers in the presence of God and consequently result in their spiritual upliftment. The changing role of churches in Nigerian society has affected the architectural forms and icons used in the design of present day churches in the country. Attention has been shifted from the form and scale of the buildings to the quality and well being of church members. The implication of this observation is that any available space is converted into a church.

Thus, churches are located in residential neighbourhoods where they disturb non-members. It is necessary, therefore, for the urban planning division to set down criteria in respect of location of religious establishments, so that they can blend with the urban setting. However, enforcement of development control by the government planning officials is necessary to make sure the churches comply.

CONCLUSION

A new trend in development policies is the focus on civil society and the related issues of urban governance and community involvement in provision of services. It has been asserted that CBOs are best situated to determine the needs of their own communities and therefore initiate and manage the projects. It may be useful to see the new generation churches as a form of CBO groups that is gradually getting involved in provision of urban services. The churches' role is expanding from the purely spiritual to that of including welfare of their members.

In this paper an attempt has been made to study the changing role of the new generation churches. It was found that:

(i) Presently, the public authorities have no relationship with these churches, in terms of the provision of services. However, it would be possible to develop a relationship that will make it possible for the religious organisations to provide urban services.

(ii) The participation fostered by the churches is limited and does not empower their members. Participation is also discriminatory and women are relegated to the background.

(iii) The churches do not expose their members to democratic decision-making or teach civics.

(iv) The churches have the potential for being more involved in the provision of urban services. In the long run, this would greatly improve their relevance in their communities.

The contention here is not that, since the state has failed in the provision of urban services, NGOs and CBOs should take over this task. What is being envisaged is that while the state is grappling with the process of developing sustainable urban management policies and programmes, NGOs and in this specific case, the new generation churches, should be fully involved in such provision, as it is not possible to develop and improve the spiritual life of their members, if their socio-economic lives are neglected. The churches have begun to realise this.

References

Celestial Church of Christ, 1980, *The Constitution.* Lagos: Celestial Church of Christ (Nigeria Diocese).

Isaacson, Alan, 1990, *Deeper Life: The Extraordinary Growth of the Deeper Life Bible Church.* Toronto: Hodder and Stoughton Publishers.

Kabarhuza, Hamuli, 1990, "Development NGOs in Zaire: Experiences and Challenges", *Voices from Africa: NGOs and Grassroots Development,* Issue No. 2. Geneva: UN-NGLS.

Kemdrim, Protus O., 1996, "Towards Women Inclusiveness in Nigeria Churches", in Oruwari, Yomi (ed.), *Women, Development and the Nigerian Environment.* Ibadan: Vantage Publishers (Int.) Ltd.

Mulyungi, Josephat, 1990, "On the Role of African NGOs", *Voice from Africa: NGOs and Grassroots Development,* Issue No. 2. Geneva: UN-NGLS.

Thompson, Martha, 1996, "Empowerment and Survival: Humanitarian Work in Civil Conflict", *Development and Practice,* Vol. 6, No. 4.

The article also draws on the following works

Scarnecchia, Timothy, 1997, "Mai Chaza's Guta re Johova (City of God): Gender, Healing and Urban Identity in an African Independent Church", *Journal of South African Studies,* Vol. 23, No. 1, March.

Schlyter, Ann (ed.), 1996, *A Place to Live: Gender Research on Housing in Africa.* Uppsala: Nordiska Afrikainstitutet.

Wellard, Kate and James Copestake (eds), 1993, *Non-Governmental Organisations and the State in Africa.* London: Routledge Publishing Co.

Westergaard, Kirsten, 1992, "NGOs, Empowerment and the State in Bangladesh", CDR Working Paper 92.2. Copenhagen.

Whitaker, Jennifer Seymour, 1988, *How Can Africa Survive?* New York: Harper and Row Publishers.

CHAPTER 6

The Politics of Multiple Identities: The Making of a Home Villagers' Association in Lilongwe, Malawi

Harri Englund

INTRODUCTION

Current perspectives on urban governance in Africa put emphasis on the "local" whilst often leaving it under-theorised. Associational life, with its characteristics of voluntarism and spontaneity, is understood by policy-makers and scholars to constitute one of the most vital aspects of the "local" in contemporary urban Africa. Among scholars, caution against romanticising associational life is usually well-taken, but the two observations that are often made in this regard hardly contribute to a more nuanced understanding of the "local". On the one hand, it is argued that local associations often emerge to provide services out of necessity, indicating the extent of suffering, especially among poor households; on the other, it is noted that such initiatives may also lead to fragmentation which undermines the long-term governability of cities (see e.g. McCarney, 1996:12).

Both observations, while valid, arise more from policy considerations than from a proper discussion of the assumptions that guide analysis. Two bodies of scholarly literature, in particular, can be brought to bear on the study of associational life. One questions the applicability of the concept of "civil society" in many African contexts and thereby brings the boundaries between "local" institutions and the state into critical focus (see e.g. Lemarchand, 1992; Robinson, 1994). A good example comes from post-war Mozambique (see Alexander, 1997). Far from being constituted by intrinsically democratic relationships, local communities bear all the traces of colonial and postcolonial interventions. Their positions of authority have been moulded by a history that transcends the confines of the "local". As a consequence, and in contrast to the tenets of the decentralised mode of governance, there are no pristine "communities" which local authorities might represent.

This chapter focuses on another current debate which may benefit the study of associational life. "Identity is the key concept in this debate. For current urban policy-making in Africa, the appeal of the "local" partly lies in the recognition it seems to give to personal and collective identities. This interest is a part of a world-wide movement in which a "politics of recognition" (Taylor, 1994) appears to have replaced the great ideological dispute between capitalism and socialism. Critical social scientists cannot, however, avoid the task of interrogating the apparent naturalism of identities. There are, for example, convincing studies of the creation and consolidation of ethnic or "tribal" identities during colonialism in Africa (see Vail, 1989). Although such studies may fail to convey the extent to which those identities are experienced as compelling facts of life, their greatest achievement is to substitute historicity for primordialism in analysis. The persuasive naturalism of identities can otherwise circumscribe the scope of political analysis and treat as given something that should be investigated (Rouse, 1995; Hobsbawm, 1996; Ortner, 1998). More specifically, this chapter subscribes to the view that the nature of the modern state, including to the colonial period, is crucial to understanding contemporary identity politics (Asad, 1992; Mamdani, 1996). Enormous differences between actual states notwithstanding, the modern state places a distinct bureaucratic significance on social categories. In this regard, personal and collective identities are not only thoroughly contemporary phenomena but also are conditioned by the state formation in which the "local" is embedded.

A key aspect of these conditions is that resistance against the state's bureaucratic practices also takes place in a social field that already presumes the existence of those bureaucratic practices (Asad, 1992:335). One example of this dynamic in an urban African context is given in Bruce Kapferer's (1995) reinterpretation of J. Clyde Mitchell's classic study The Kalela Dance (1956). Mitchell analysed *kalela*, a popular "tribal" dance in the Copperbelt towns of colonial Zambia, not simply within a framework of discrete ethnic groups, but within the structure of black-white relations that underlay the colonial labour market. Because employers provided Africans with housing, migrants' social ties often spread across several urban locations. *Kalela* brought together young men, smartly dressed in the "European" way, to express in song and in attire their own desirability, the delights of their home areas and the general backwardness of other "tribes". The tribal definitions in this context were very broad, subsuming narrower categories, but the ensuing relations among the Africans of the Copperbelt were not simply antagonistic. Mitchell (1956:35–42) argued that the exchange of insults between different tribal categories was a modern and urban version of joking relationships among specific relatives and clans who also performed certain duties for one another, particularly in funerals. Kapferer extended Mitchell's insights by arguing that, while *kalela* was "not an overt act of political resistance" (1995:63), it was "critical of the techno-rational and bureaucratic world in which it was performed" (1995:61). Migrants to Copperbelt towns, in other words, resisted the colonial bureaucratic order by devising their own system of social categories. Identities were not transplanted from rural areas to town—they assumed a specific form under the colonial state formation.

This chapter seeks to question identities as keys to unlock the "local" in contemporary African urban governance. It explores—in the context of an expanding peri-urban township in Lilongwe, Malawi's capital—a process by which multiple identities were circumscribed to give way to a neat, bureaucratic identity. The focus is on a home villagers' association which was established in 1997 as a welfare and recreational body for migrants from a rural area in Dedza District, some 50 miles from Lilongwe. I was conducting fieldwork in this township in 1996–97, and was able to follow the founding of the association at close hand. Despite being a setting for various ethnicities, Christian denominations and political allegiances, the "home" area received a particular definition in the township. In this definition, specific ethnic and Christian practices came to be highlighted, while others were ignored. This chapter shows the intricately political nature of the process and, as such, contributes to the critique of ethnicity as a primordial and ultimate source of identity in postcolonial Africa (cf. Mbembe, 1992; Werbner, 1996). The home villagers' association was a thoroughly urban phenomenon; it emerged in a social field constituted within a postcolonial state formation. By disclosing the contrast between township residents' plural arenas and the bureaucratic nature of their association, this chapter throws the complexity of the "local" into starker relief.

LILONGWE AND CHINSAPO TOWNSHIP

"Urbanisation" has long remained a misnomer for migration within Malawi. The country's population has been very mobile, both within and across international boundaries, from the early colonial, if not pre-colonial, past, but migration has only marginally contributed to the growth of Malawi's urban areas. In some rural districts, international labour migration took the majority of men to mines and plantations in southern Africa from the turn of the twentieth century until the early 1970s (see e.g. Crush et al., 1991). A massive return of migrant labour occurred during the 1970s, after the Malawi government had imposed an embargo on labour recruitment by South African companies (Chirwa, 1996). A plane crash was the official reason for this action, but many observers have also noted the need of Malawi's growing plantation economy for cheap labour during that period (e.g. Kydd and Christiansen, 1982; Mhone, 1992). Many of the return migrants, as well as younger men who had never had the opportunity to go abroad, remained mobile in a rural-rural pattern of migration between villages and plantations. The return migrants from South Africa did not contribute to urbanisation in significant numbers (Christiansen and Kydd, 1983). According to the 1987 population census, *urban to rural* migration was by far more common among urban dwellers than rural to urban migration among the rural population (Malawi Government, 1994:xxiv).[1] Even after political change in the early 1990s, which has encouraged free economic enterprise, urban growth remains relatively modest at the national level.

The 1966 population census put the size of the urban population at 200,000—5 per cent of the population of four million (Malawi Government, 1966). Blantyre, the oldest commercial centre, accounted for 54 per cent of the urban population, and the four main towns (Blantyre, Lilongwe, Mzuzu and Zomba) for 78 per cent (Potts, 1986:106). The same pattern of urban concentration has remained in place ever since. The 1977 census recorded an urban population of 8,5 per cent, while in 1987 the proportion was 11 per

---

[1] Among those in rural areas whose places of birth and enumeration were different, rural to rural migration accounted for 3 per cent and rural to urban for 9 per cent of the discrepancies; the same figures among urban dwellers were 11 per cent for urban to urban and 38 per cent for urban to rural migration (Malawi Government, 1994:xxiv). The figures for those who had migrated 12 months before the 1987 census were, among the rural population, 1 per cent for rural to rural migration and 9 per cent for rural to urban migration; and, among urban dwellers, 6 per cent for urban to urban migration and 28 per cent for urban to rural migration (Malawi Government, 1994:xxvii).

cent (Malawi Government, 1987:x). The urban growth rate is, however, difficult to establish, because considerable changes both in the criteria by which urban and rural centres have been distinguished and in the demarcation of urban boundaries have taken place between the censuses (see Potts, 1986:107). The preliminary results of the 1998 census indicated that still only 14 per cent lived in urban areas, again the vast majority of them in the four centres (Malawi Government, 1998:iii). At the district level, Lilongwe had overtaken Blantyre with 13,6 per cent as against 8 per cent of the national population.

The establishment of Lilongwe as the new capital in the early 1970s has sometimes been seen as a ploy to enhance socio-economic development in the Central Region, the apparent "power base" of Kamuzu Banda's autocratic regime of 1964–94 (Lwanda, 1993:153). However, if seen more positively, the aim of the project was to address regional imbalances which had concentrated much of industry and commerce in Blantryre, while the university and parliament continued to keep Zomba, the colonial capital, as an urban centre. Both of these centres are in the Southern Region. Faced with a lukewarm response from the British government, the Banda regime entered into a highly controversial agreement whereby the planning, financing and building of Lilongwe's new city centre were largely given to South Africans. The "Garden City" concept that was adopted bore resemblance to urban planning in apartheid South Africa, with very strict zoning between land-use types. Residential areas, in many cases far apart from one another, came to have a clear class character.

The move of most ministries and government departments to Lilongwe immediately made it the fastest growing city in Malawi, and its intercensal annual growth in 1966–77 was anything between 7 and 16 per cent, depending on which boundary changes are taken into account (Potts, 1986:279). By the 1990s, the spatial expansion of unplanned settlements indicated population growth in the poorest areas of the city. Their annual growth may well be more than the 7 per cent which the Lilongwe City Council has posited for the city as a whole during the 1990s (see Kawonga, 1997). However, as is discussed below, the growth of the unplanned areas may indicate both congestion in older townships and the lure which economic and political liberalisation has represented to smallholders in the countryside, in many areas grappling with the consequences of land shortages.

Chinsapo township, the site of my fieldwork in 1996–97, is a fast-growing unplanned settlement in Lilongwe, with an estimated population of 30,000 in the mid-1990s. Situated some three miles from the Old Town and eight miles from the New City Centre, it has grown on the site of old Chewa villages where local chiefs and headmen still demand a recognition of their authority in the governance of the township. As such, residents are "squatters" only for the City Council and aid agencies, whereas in practice they depend on a complex local housing and land market for their accommodation. Despite being overwhelmed by strangers from all the districts of Malawi and even abroad, headmen in Chinsapo strive to maintain control over land acquisition by selling unoccupied land and by requiring a token payment every time land is resold or a new tenant moves in. Township residents make a distinction between the "born" (*obadwa* in Chichewa) and the "arrived" (*obwera*) residents, and "making someone to pay a chicken" (*kulipiritsa nkhuku*), an idiom from village courts, is the monetary penalty headmen impose on the "arrived" who fail to comply with their rulings. This has created much tension between the two social categories in the township, because most migrants acknowledge the need to comply with such rulings only in their villages of origin. Chinsapo, they say, is "in town" (*ku tawuni*), where such obligations do not apply.

A survey in 1992 found that Chinsapo was "growing at an alarming pace" (Roe, 1992:58), with urban facilities lagging far behind the actual population growth. Soon thereafter the township was included in Lilongwe Urban rather than Lilongwe Rural, thereby coming under the City Council. Although many houses gained access to electricity after 1996, Chinsapo, one of the poorest townships in Lilongwe, continues to retain a rural character in its housing standards. Towards the end of the 1990s, the vast majority of houses did not have piped water, and communal water-points were established as recently as the early 1990s. Industrial labourers, watchmen, artisans and low-ranking civil servants such as drivers and clerks form the bulk of the employed population, but few are able to support themselves without additional income from petty trading and cultivation. In fact, self-employed entrepreneurs are more common than persons in formal employment, although it is common to move between the two sources of income, as it is also common to try different businesses in the course of time.

Chinsapo's growing popularity indicates not only improved amenities and continuing rural-urban migration but also congestion in Lilongwe's older townships, with Kawale, situated closer to the Old Town, having an average of 23 persons per plot in the early 1990s (Roe, 1992:64). Despite the improved access to electricity and water, however, Chinsapo's housing standards and rents remain at a level where the township caters, on the whole, for an even poorer populace than the older townships. This can also be seen in the fact that Chinsapo's residents maintain close links to their villages of origin and thereby remain, to the irritation of Chinsapo's headmen, somewhat detached from the township. Obvious material reasons account for this pattern. As mentioned, meagre salaries and profits make cultivation necessary for many township residents, and it is usually women who spend a part of the year in the village cultivating and harvesting. Those whose villages are too far away often rent land in nearby villages in Lilongwe District.

More than mere material want underlies this engagement with the village of origin, and *mudzi*, meaning both "home" and "village", is a deeply moral notion. For most residents in the township—both women and men—permanent urbanisation is not an option. Most migrants to cities invest not only in cultivation but also in houses and various ceremonies in their villages of origin.[2] Semi-skilled and unskilled migrants, in particular, often see their stay in

---

[2] Permanent urbanisation as a postulate of "modernist narratives" has been debated by Ferguson (1990, 1996 and 1999) and Macmillan (1993 and 1996). For comparative perspectives into rural-urban ties and identity in contemporary Africa see Gugler (1996) and Geschiere and Gugler (1998).

the city as a means of acquiring capital to commence a business in the countryside. In many cases, their capital is not enough to sustain a commercial enterprise for long, and a temporary return to the city is often inevitable in order to regain the capital they have lost. Especially among the residents of Chinsapo township, rural-urban migration is, therefore, circular in character.

ASSOCIATIONAL LIFE: THE NATIONAL AND LOCAL CONTEXT

The home villagers' association described in this chapter is an example of the many voluntary organisations that have emerged after Malawi's transition to multi-party politics in the early 1990s. After thirty years of autocratic rule, Kamuzu Banda's regime was ousted from power in the 1994 general elections, following the 1993 referendum in which the majority registered a preference for multi-partyism over one-party rule (see e.g. van Donge, 1995). The election results showed a clear regional pattern, each of the three main parties winning one of Malawi's three regions. Malawi Congress Party (MCP), the ruling party during Banda's regime, emerged victorious in the Central Region, the populous Southern Region made Bakili Muluzi the new president and his United Democratic Front (UDF) the new ruling party, whereas the sparsely populated Northern Region provided a power base for the Alliance for Democracy (Aford). Even though each of the three regions is ethnically diverse (Kaspin, 1995), ethnic stereotypes are easily asserted in the current pluralist political order. Whatever the truth about Banda's origins as a Christian Chewa, his long stay abroad gave him a cosmopolitan identity which encompassed the various ethnic identities within Malawi. By contrast, Muluzi's identity as a Yao and a Muslim was widely seen to be inimical to establishing country-wide authority, a predicament that bred counter-assertions of other ethnic, regional and religious identities.

Seen from another perspective, the difference between the old and new regimes lies less in the contrast between an encompassing national identity and ethnic parochialism than in coercion and self-help. Banda's frequent appeals to "his" people to "work hard in the fields" indicated his understanding of "individualism" as the basis of rural Malawi's economy (see Pryor, 1991:7; Davison, 1993:415). In contrast to the neighbouring countries, communalism and co-operatives were condemned in official rhetoric. Outside the churches, repression discouraged active associational life, and the development projects that mobilised entire communities often took place during "Youth Weeks", introduced to maintain communal spaces such as roads and closely supervised by party and "traditional" authorities. For the UDF government, such projects represented *thangata*, a notion with deep historical resonances of forced labour (see Kandawire, 1979). The new government introduced, with funding from the World Bank, the Malawi Social Action Fund (Masaf) to encourage project proposals from local communities themselves. Numerous schools have been built or extended with the help of Masaf, with the community usually providing labour or basic materials such as bricks.

The difficulties faced by Masaf and other participatory development projects in Chinsapo township indicate the other facet of the new pluralism in

Malawi. The self-conscious assertion of contrasting identities is sometimes seen to arise from incommensurate interests which undermine the pursuit of the common good. Chinsapo's Development Committee consists of party leaders, "traditional" authorities, representatives of religious denominations and City Council officials, but its meetings rarely achieve much. They are often adjourned, because some participants fail to appear, and when they do take place, intense bickering prevents decision-making. As a consequence, not only Masaf but also other organisations often fail to elicit labour and other contributions from the township's residents. UNICEF, for example, has provided the township with piped water and new school buildings. At an early stage of improvements to existing school buildings, UNICEF's expatriate representative announced that local residents would be paid for their work. When no payment was forthcoming, residents stopped working, amidst rumours that their leaders were pocketing the money. A food-for-work programme led to a temporary resumption of residents' participation, but UNICEF has subsequently relied upon contracts with private companies in its work.

The home villagers' association emerged in this context of pluralist politics. Whatever its founders' views of the UDF government, the new political order had revitalised associational life and intensified identity politics. Whatever, also, the bureaucratic categories the founders introduced in their definition of the home village (*mudzi*), their action emerged from the material and moral conditions of migrants' lives in Chinsapo township. For the founders themselves, moral considerations appeared more important than transformations in government. They did not establish the association in order to negotiate with the state; nor were there obvious ways in which the state could support their association—despite the rhetoric of self-help in promoting Masaf. The state and aid agencies had not begun to recognise such associations at the grassroots level. However, far from being an example of primordial loyalties in a democratic "civil society", the association emerged at the interface of national and local politics. The intensifying tension between the "born" and the "arrived" undermined participatory development projects in Chinsapo township and contributed to the migrants' view that only a home villagers' association could properly take care of residents' interests. The perceived need to assert a distinctive identity was consistent with the bureaucratic practices of the modern state.

COLLECTIVE IDENTITIES AND PERSONAL PROMINENCE

The founders' aspiration was to establish "the association of the people from Bembeke" (*bungwe la anthu a ku Bembeke*). Bembeke, the site of my initial fieldwork in 1992–93, is an area on the southern margin of Dedza District in the Central Region some 50 miles from Lilongwe. It falls under the orbit of Kamenyagwaza, a Sub-Traditional Authority in the Malawian hierarchy of "traditional" authorities. This authority is, in turn, encompassed by the progressively wider orbits of Kachindamoto, Traditional Authority, and Gomani, Paramount Chief. They are all Ngoni chiefs who descend from the Maseko faction that arrived in the area in the late 19th century, capturing populations they encountered (Linden, 1972). Bembeke is on the margin of the Maseko Ngoni's territory and is bordered by the territory of Kasumbo, a Chewa chief. It also shares a boundary with Mozambique's Angónia District, where more descendants of the Maseko Ngoni live, albeit under different chiefs from their ethnic compatriots on the Malawian side of the border.

The Ngoni identity of many Bembeke villagers is complicated by frequent crossings of these boundaries. The Malawian and Mozambican national identities sometimes undermine, and are sometimes undermined by, ethnic solidarity. The international border has nearly always stood unguarded, and in 1986–93 thousands of refugees fled the FRELIMO–RENAMO war in Angónia to villages in Bembeke. Some refugees were received as relatives, others remained strangers, but, on the whole, this displacement was only a dramatic addition to the long-term pattern of cross-border moves. On the other hand, some villages are seen to have more Chewa than Ngoni. In the absence of clear social or linguistic differences, Chewa and Ngoni identities are distinguished above all by the performance of *nyau* (also known as *gule wamkulu*, the big dance) and *ngoma*, respectively. The latter, usually performed at beer parties, is a recreational dance in which the old Ngoni military reputation is recounted. *Nyau* is a male secret society into which Chewa boys are customarily initiated and which parades its masked dancers especially during funerals and Chewa girls' initiation ceremonies (see Yoshida, 1992). In Bembeke, even men who in other contexts see themselves as Ngoni belong to *nyau*, thereby blurring the distinction between Chewa and Ngoni identities. Such identifications are largely situational and part of local politics where, for example, *nyau* is condemned as "pagan" by Christian churches and, by the same token, represents a source of authority distinct from these churches (for more discussion, see Englund, 1996a).

An imposing Roman Catholic cathedral near Bembeke's small trading centre is an index of widespread Catholicism in the area's villages. The vast majority of the population are Catholics, following the opening of the first mission school in the area in 1907 and Bembeke's status as a mission centre from 1910. Likewise, Angónia District on the Mozambican side of the border is also a Catholic stronghold. A Dutch Reformed Church mission from South Africa later led to the establishment of the Church of Central African Presbyterian (CCAP), but its influence has extended only to one large village and to scattered members elsewhere in Bembeke. The third major church in the area, an independent church known as the African Church, has no obvious base in any one village, but has branches in another trading centre near the main highway and in some villages. It is distinguished from the mainstream churches mainly through its liberal attitude to the "African" customs of polygamy and beer-drinking. All three churches formally oppose *nyau*, and those who attend its performances may be excommunicated by the Catholic and Presbyterian churches. As mentioned, this has had consequences for identity politics in which initiation into *nyau* bestows authority distinct from that which is acquired in the Christian churches. However, there are also men who covertly attend both church and *nyau* ceremonies; the difference between the two does not lie in incompatible cosmologies.

These multiple ethnic, national and religious identities received a specific interpretation when Bembeke villagers' association was established in Chinsapo township in early 1997. The founders themselves were by no means recent migrants to town, and the association was not, therefore, a sudden invention by anxious newcomers. Gama (pseudonym), who first conceived the idea of an association, had talked about it to his fellow migrants from Bembeke for almost a year before the launching took place. The variety of Gama's own pursuits, rather than the reluctance of other migrants from Bembeke, accounted for this time-lag. In effect, Gama's multiple identities are one example of the many social networks of which residents are part, whereas the association represented only a very narrow range of its members' active social ties. Such networks indicate diverse personal pasts and present circumstances, whereas the association necessarily delineated only one aspect of its members' relationships. Moreover, it was created in its founders' image, themselves relatively well-established urban dwellers with power to mould collective definitions of a rural "home" in the city.

Despite his humble beginnings and continued residence in Chinsapo township, Gama had so much grown in prominence by the mid-1990s that his idea of a home villagers' welfare association was not based on personal material want. Indeed, a welfare association would have been more essential in 1978 when he first moved to Lilongwe. Chinsapo, then sparsely populated, became his and his young family's home in the city the same year. Gama did not arrive in Lilongwe from Bembeke but from Zambia, where he had lived with his sister for two years. He married a Zambian woman who has remained with him throughout the years in Chinsapo. In Bembeke, the families of Gama's father's siblings had long cultivated on the Mozambican side of the border and were forced to move there in 1950 by an ordinance from the Portuguese authorities. Gama has, however, maintained close links to his classificatory brothers in a Mozambican border village. Gama himself was born and bred in one of the villages renowned for their supply of relatively successful labour migrants—earlier generations to South Africa and their descendants as professionals to Malawian towns. A visitor to their villages in Bembeke will notice a preponderance of spacious, iron-roofed houses, tangible signs of successful migrants' investment in their home villages.

Unlike some of his fellow villagers, Gama was endowed with little material support to pursue formal education. After his move from Zambia to Lilongwe, he first worked as a watchman and, in 1979, became a civil servant as a pavement sweeper. With his relatives' support and with considerable personal investment, he obtained a driving-licence and was, in 1984, employed as a driver by the government, a post he has retained ever since. It involves irregular working-hours and prolonged absences during travels elsewhere in Malawi. He has the air of an important and busy man, an image which is reinforced when he visits Chinsapo in the government's four-wheel drive Mitsubishi Pajero. His absences bring unusual material benefits in the form of allowances which he uses for investment in both the city and the village. By the late 1980s, he had built several houses in Chinsapo to provide the increasing numbers in the township with accommodation they could rent. He is also heavily involved in cultivation, especially of maize, both in Lilongwe and Bembeke. In Lilongwe, he has long rented gardens in nearby villages, cultivated by his wife and children; in Bembeke, he lets his sisters cultivate his gardens and provides them with chemical fertiliser. As a consequence, his family does not have to buy maize and, on the contrary, often has a surplus to sell. During bad seasons, he gives maize as a gift to both those who have rented him gardens in Lilongwe and to relatives in Bembeke.

A devout Catholic, Gama has also built a Catholic church directly opposite his house in Chinsapo. He had argued that the couple of miles' distance to the nearby Likuni mission was too long for women and children, especially for attending late-evening masses. He therefore received permission to build a church in Chinsapo, a modest grass-roofed building made of earth, and to conduct services there. However, it gathers its congregation mainly from the immediate neighbourhood, and, significantly, those who come from elsewhere are usually long-time friends, including Bembeke villagers in the city. Most Catholics in Chinsapo, by contrast, continue to attend church services in Likuni.

Gama gradually became prominent in the township less as a consequence of a conscious strategy than as a concomitant of his own growth as an influential person, facilitated by success in formal employment and investments. The notion of "growth" (kukula) is crucial to understanding the process by which the association was established. In the Chichewa idiom, "growth" is a continuous process by which persons ideally consolidate their moral standing in the course of their life cycles. Crucially, the process is less a matter of individual virtues than of being able to "care for" (kusamala) many dependants.[3] In Gama's case, therefore, material success did not entail individualism but was compatible with, and indeed gave resources to engage in, moral personhood in which prominence only became visible through wide sets of relationships (cf. Englund, 1996b and 1999). The home villagers' association was a further proof of Gama's prominence, along with, among others, the church and the people he supported in villages both in Lilongwe and in Bembeke. The association was, in this sense, possible only after some twenty years in the city. A recent migrant, scraping a living through petty business or underpaid employment, could hardly have acted as a convincing founder.

This profoundly moral dimension of the association was consistent with the fact that its members viewed assistance during funerals as its most important task. In Bembeke, as elsewhere in Malawi, funerals are the most inclusive communal events. They mobilise not only the immediate relatives of the deceased but also their own relatives, affines and friends. It is firmly held that, the deceased ought to be buried in his or her "home" which is, in this predominantly rural country, most often the village even among urban dwellers. Mudzi, as mentioned, is the term for both village and home.

For the migrants in Chinsapo township, funerals are particularly distressing for both moral and material reasons. Any funeral that is not con-

---

[3] The ways in which persons are expected to "care for" their dependants varies between men and women, but the general idea of a "moral being" applies to both.

ducted in a proper manner may provoke the ire of the deceased's spirit (*mzimu*) and lead to illness or further deaths (Englund, 1998). When a death occurs, the impoverished township dwellers find themselves under the obligation to arrange at least transport to their rural home, where they are likely to be received as townspeople with easy access to urban goods and services. In some cases burials do take place in the graveyards of the township, but they are spaces jealously guarded by Chinsapo's headmen, themselves criticised by the Council City for selling land without taking into account the need to expand the graveyards. In this sense, the home villagers' association was crucial to creating a sense of home, precisely by easing the existential and material burden of funerals in Chinsapo.

Despite these important moral and material considerations, however, its members continue to have multiple identities and contrasting interests. For example, although the association ostensibly underlined Gama's commitment to his rural home, his and his wife's private reflections often indicated more ambiguity. Gama was concerned about rumours that the new government would begin retrenchment, which could also result in him being made redundant himself. He said, therefore, that "we take care of the place" (*timasunga malo*) in the village, in both material and moral senses. Yet, he had also bought a plot in Area 25, a new residential area far from both Chinsapo and Lilongwe's city centre, although he had not yet started to develop it. He and his wife were harbouring thoughts of staying in the city and of engaging in commercial farming elsewhere in the Central Region after Gama's retirement. One reason behind these thoughts was her own network of active social ties which had never extended to Bembeke. She felt comfortable in the city, where she knew many others from Zambia. Her interests, in other words, were one factor which complicated Gama's commitment to his rural home, despite his prominence as a "Bembeke villager" in the township.

THE FIRST MEETING AND BEYOND

The association came to be dominated by migrants from the same cluster of villages where Gama himself originated. Since he was the pioneering Bembeke villager in Chinsapo, Gama was seen as a benefactor by most persons in the founders' group, although they had themselves lived for several years in town. During the early stage of their migration, Gama had provided them with information on land and livelihoods and, over the years, had even given them material support. Some had become veritable henchmen, such as Mbewe, a childhood friend from the same village, who built his house near Gama's in the early 1980s. Mbewe had remained a self-employed entrepreneur, and when the association was founded, he was, among other ventures, the owner of a grocery store in Chinsapo. He was more often present in the township than Gama, who often entrusted him with making announcements and managing the church while he was away. Two of Gama's sister's sons had also long lived in the township; young men to whom Gama was in the category of *malume*, mother's brother and the customary guardian figure in the matrilateral extended family.

It was through such immediate ties that Gama's idea of a Bembeke villagers' association was first publicised. Even though only Mbewe lived in Gama's neighbourhood, he and Gama had received and assisted numerous others from their cluster of villages in Bembeke and had active ties spread over several neighbourhoods in this vast township. The express intent was to make the association as encompassing as possible, but the first meeting disclosed whom the founders knew among the migrants from Bembeke. Many from other parts of Bembeke had not heard about the idea before the first meeting. It did not occur to the founders to inquire about Bembeke villagers in the city from headmen in Chinsapo and in Bembeke. The founders presumed, in effect, that their cluster of villages, the conspicuous source of successful labour migrants, had the largest number of Bembeke villagers in Chinsapo. This presumption ignored the fact that, on the contrary, migrants from the poorer villages in Bembeke were precisely more likely to settle in the impoverished township of Chinsapo than in other areas of Lilongwe.

For the first meeting, some thirty persons, of whom about as many were women as men, gathered in Gama's church building. The main objectives of the meeting were to discuss the tasks of the association, to select its officers and to establish a fund for it. The meeting took place on a Sunday afternoon, Chinsapo residents' popular time for leisure activities. This could be experienced in the atmosphere of the meeting which was convivial, towards the end jubilant, further eased by the intoxication of some participants. Disagreements were voiced in an outspoken, and yet humorous, manner, the very fact of felt commonality inviting free expression of difference. At the centre of all debate was Gama, apparently detached, refusing to chair the meeting and also declining to be an officer because of his busy schedule as a driver, and yet his opinion was always sought before final decisions. Chairman, Vice-Chairman, Secretary and Treasurer were selected, the first two also in the women's group. The wealthiest, most established township residents from the wealthiest Bembeke villages acquired the positions. The fund was established to provide resources to assist Bembeke villagers in the township during funerals and illness. Everyone was asked to contribute 10 kwacha (US$ 0.65) to the initial capital, and a smaller monthly fee was introduced to maintain the fund subsequently. However, some participants failed to contribute even to the first payment. The officers seemed to take no offence, although they wrote down the names of those who did contribute.

Unity, and the acceptance of differences within that unity, were major preoccupations during the meeting. In the speeches, "the village of Bembeke" (*mudzi wa Bembeke*), non-existent in reality, was a recurring theme, and people were urged not to ask which specific village anyone was from. Nor were ethnic differences recognised. Differences were acknowledged not only in gender but also between Catholicism and Presbyterianism. As mentioned, the meeting took place in a Catholic church and it opened with a prayer conducted according to the Catholic routine. At the end of the meeting, however, Gama intervened to reject a suggestion that was going to let another Catholic lead the closing prayer. Instead, he announced that the association was not for Catholics only and that Presbyterians should also feel at home in it; he therefore invited a Presbyterian to lead the prayer. After the somewhat sober agenda of selecting officers, establishing the fund and discussing the need for assistance during funerals, one male participant observed that the association should also give opportunities for social events where free beer would be consumed, *ngoma* danced and "our Ngoni way of life" (*chingoni chathu*) displayed. The observation was received with enthusiasm, prompting two women to stand up and begin an *ngoma* while singing *tadziwana* (we know each other). More women and men joined them to underline the utmost gaiety of the occasion.

During the first six months after the meeting, the association organised a social event of the kind that the speaker in the first meeting had outlined. This also took place by the church near Gama's house, as did the association officers' meetings at irregular intervals. The contributions to the fund appeared to be somewhat uneven, but the association did provide support for hiring transport to take the bereaved and their deceased relatives from Chinsapo to Bembeke. The activists in the association were aware that its reach among the township's Bembeke villagers was by no means complete, and they often made calls to enlarge the membership base. No concentrated efforts to break the confines of the existing networks took place, however. In fact, I had, as a fieldworker, the opportunity to meet a wider range of Bembeke villagers in Chinsapo than the activists themselves. Many non-members heard about the association for the first time from me and were seldom acquainted with its activists. The latter's origins in a specific cluster of villages often prompted the comment that perhaps the association was less for all migrants from Bembeke than for those from that cluster.

Some recent migrants' attitudes were particularly revealing. They seemed reluctant to invest in a home villagers' association in the city, because the act would have indicated undue commitment to a particular township in a situation where it was not clear in which part of the city they would live, or whether they would soon return to the village. More broadly, however, recent migrants' attitudes, not unlike those of more established residents in the township, were largely a function of whom they knew in Chinsapo, and participation in the association precisely reinforced an existing relationship. It was not, in other words, an act of a primordial and categorical loyalty in a supposedly alienating urban context. The founders had already established *themselves* as central figures in the township before they established the association. Others' participation in that association arose more from specific relations of debt and dependency than from a categorical allegiance to the abstract "village of Bembeke".

CONCLUSION

Two observations have been crucial to the analysis of associational life in this chapter. On the one hand, whatever its founders' views of their Bembeke identity, the association circumscribed only one aspect of their and other members' multiple identities. On the other, the founders and members were mobilised less by parochial ethnic sentiments than by moral obligations which were integral to the cultural notions of personal "growth" and authority. Important was the fact that the founders had demonstrated their capacities for patronage already before the association existed.[4] The "individual", in other words, was not a value, and this apparent "voluntary association" was not best understood as a contract between mutually independent subjects.

The home villagers' association was a thoroughly urban phenomenon, not a nostalgic enactment of village life in the city. The association was based on an abstraction which would not have made sense in its activists' villages of origin. "The village of Bembeke" delineated one field of relationships against several others which impinged upon the founders' lives in the city. Their immediate neighbours were often strangers, and in their economic activities they constantly encountered the searing inequalities which had pushed them to live in one of the capital's poorest townships. The association was, therefore, one attempt to generate social value and meaning in a setting that in itself seemed to promise little for them. In understanding the experiential dimension of the association, its activists' preoccupation with the *ngoma* dance must be seen as more than a mere quest to attach an ethnic marker to their association. In politico-economic contexts which foster anonymity or oppression, dance has often been a medium of resistance (see e.g. Ranger, 1975). It engages senses and emotions in a vivid bodily expression of another sociality (cf. Kapferer, 1995:66).

The ethnography of Bembeke migrants' association in Chinsapo township has, however, also indicated how their abstraction resisted the modern state's bureaucratic order with another bureaucratic operation. The identity category that came to define "Bembeke villagers" both excluded similar migrants from the association and codified a highly circumscribed set of the founders' own multiple identities. On the one hand, the association made no acknowledgement of those Bembeke villagers who considered themselves as Chewa, were initiated into *nyau* or belonged to the African Church. The founders' acknowledgement of differences amongst themselves—in gender and between the mainstream churches—was inevitable in the current pluralist setting of Malawian politics, but it avoided those contentious differences that could have subverted their own authority. On the other hand, by ignoring the plural arenas of their lives, the association made its activists themselves into abstract "Bembeke villagers". Gama's multiple identities were one striking, albeit not uncommon, example. The plural arenas of his life-world ranged from his work as a civil servant to villages in both Bembeke and Lilongwe, to the Catholic church, to his status as a prominent landlord in the township and to transnational connections in Zambia and Mozambique. The home villagers' association delineated only one aspect of his relationships, although the activists were, in certain situations, keen to represent it as the most important, if not the only, aspect.

---

[4] This mode of authority might be defined as "patrimonialism", but it is important to be clear about the multiple identities and contrasting interests that underlie widely shared moral ideals. A recent overview of African politics makes this mode of authority a function of an essentialized "culture" and fails to appreciate how subjects in different positions may have different interests (see Chabal and Daloz, 1999).

As mentioned, however, the association indicated a certain notion of morality which precisely mitigated its codification of social boundaries. It presupposed "growth" in moral being, already made visible by the founders' capacity to assist others in various contexts in the city and villages. In this sense, the association was a logical addition to personal prominence in plural arenas. "Local" studies remain, therefore, important for understanding such dynamics of morality and identity, despite the fact that the "local" itself is constituted within the power relations and bureaucratic practices of the modern state. Such studies can also address the question of the extent to which the home villagers' association, with its stress on a certain ethnicity, will remain only one of the many arenas where its activists operate. Although associational life has taken many forms in Africa's towns and cities, through burial societies for example, the current pluralism, as mentioned, often places a special emphasis on ethnicity. In some countries, various élite associations emerge as counter-forces to political parties (see Eyoh, 1998; Nyamnjoh and Rowlands, 1998), while it is also perfectly conceivable that the association described here may adopt an overtly party political agenda if regionalism continues to gather momentum in Malawian politics. A parallel would emerge with the welfare associations that gave way to clearly politicised trade unions during the rise of nationalism in urban south-central Africa (see Epstein, 1992:46–47). However, the post-nationalist politicisation of associational life is likely to result in parochialism. The manipulation of the home villagers' association as a party political base would conflate its definition of "Bembeke village" with party political allegiance and thereby confine further the scope of the identity category. With the force of a party machinery, moreover, the association could also engage in patronage independently of the moral standing of its founders.

It would not, of course, be a matter of party politics suddenly threatening the purity of a pristine association. The burden of this chapter has been to show how the association, as an example of a burgeoning "civil society" in "democratic" Malawi, was consistent with the bureaucratic significance which the modern state places on social identities. The identity on which the association was based was a product of an urban experience among particular migrants, not a corollary of a "natural" social group that existed without active manipulation. As objects of conscious representation and even without the direct involvement of central and local governments, identities are constructed. The very preoccupation with identity politics arises from political and bureaucratic processes which transcend the confines of the "local".

References

Alexander, Jocelyn, 1997, "The Local State in Post-war Mozambique: Political Practice and Ideas about Authority", *Africa*, 67, pp. 1–26.
Asad, Talal, 1992, "Conscripts of Western Civilisation", in Gailey, Christine Ward (ed.), *Civilisation in Crisis: Anthropological Perspectives*. Gainesville: University Press of Florida.

Chabal, Patrick, and Jean-Pascal Daloz, 1999, *Africa Works: Disorder as a Political Instrument*. The International African Institute in association with James Currey, Oxford and Indiana University Press, Bloomington.

Chirwa, Wiseman Chijere, 1996, "The Malawi Government and the South African Labour Recruiters, 1974–1992", *Journal of Modern African Studies*, 34, pp. 623–42.

Christiansen, Robert and Jonathan Kydd, 1983, "The Return of Malawian Labour from South Africa and Zimbabwe", *Journal of Modern African Studies*, 21, pp.311–26.

Crush, Jonathan, Alan Jeeves and David Yudelman, 1991, *South Africa's Labour Empire: A History of Black Migrancy to the Gold Mines*. Boulder, CO: Westview.

Davison, Jean, 1993, "Tenacious Women: Clinging to Banja Household Production in the Face of Changing Gender Relations in Malawi", *Journal of Southern African Studies*, 19, pp. 405–21.

Englund, Harri, 1996a, "Between God and Kamuzu: The Transition to Multi-party Politics in Central Malawi", in Werbner, Richard and Terence Ranger (eds), *Postcolonial Identities in Africa*. London: Zed Books.

—, 1996b, "Witchcraft, Modernity and the Person: The Morality of Accumulation in Central Malawi", *Critique of Anthropology*, 16, pp. 257–79.

—, 1998, "Death, Trauma and Ritual: Mozambican Refugees in Malawi", *Social Science and Medicine*, 46, pp. 1165–74.

—, 1999, "The Self in Self-Interest: Land, Labour and Temporalities in Malawi's Agrarian Change", *Africa*, 69, pp. 139–59.

Epstein, A.L., 1992, *Scenes from African Urban Life: Collected Copperbelt Papers*. Edinburgh: Edinburgh University Press.

Eyoh, Dickson, 1998, "Through the Prism of a Local Tragedy: Political Liberalisation, Regionalism and Elite Struggles for Power in Cameroon", *Africa*, 68, pp. 338–59.

Ferguson, James, 1990, "Mobile Workers, Modernist Narratives: A Critique of the Historiography of Transition on the Zambian Copperbelt", *Journal of Southern African Studies*, 16, pp. 385–411 and 603–21.

—, 1996, "Urban Trends on the Zambian Copperbelt: A Short Bibliographic Note", *Journal of Southern African Studies*, 22, p. 313.

—, 1999, *Expections of Modernity: Myths and Meanings of Urban Life on the Zambian Copperbelt*. Berkeley: University of California Press.

Geschiere, Peter, and Josef Gugler, 1998, "The Rural-Urban Connection: Changing Issues of Belonging and Identification", *Africa*, 68, pp. 309–19.

Gugler, Josef, 1996, "Urbanisation in Africa South of the Sahara: New Identities in Conflict", in Gugler, Josef (ed.), *The Urban Transformation of the Developing World*. Oxford: Oxford University Press.

Hobsbawm, Eric, 1996, "Identity Politics and the Left", *New Left Review*, 217, pp. 38–47.

Kandawire, J.A. Kamchitete, 1979, *Thangata: Forced Labour or Reciprocal Assistance?* Zomba: University of Malawi.

Kapferer, Bruce, 1995, "The Performance of Categories: Plays of Identity in Africa and Australia", in Rogers, Alisdair and Steven Vertovec (eds), *The Urban Context: Ethnicity, Social Networks and Situational Analysis*. Oxford: Berg.

Kaspin, Deborah, 1995, "The Politics of Ethnicity in Malawi's Democratic Transition", *Journal of Modern African Studies*, 33, pp. 595–620.

Kawonga, A.J.C., 1997, "Population Projection and an Assessment of Development Status of Peri-urban Squatter Settlements of Mtandile and Chinsapo". Report for Plan International Malawi.

Kydd, Jonathan and Robert Christiansen, 1982, "Structural Change in Malawi since Independence: Consequences of a Development Strategy Based on Large-Scale Agriculture", *World Development*, 10, pp. 355–75.

Lemarchand, René, 1992, "Uncivil States and Civil Societies: How Illusion Became Reality", *Journal of Modern African Studies*, 30, pp. 177–91.

Linden, Ian, 1972, "The Maseko Ngoni at Domwe: 1870–1900", in Pachai, B. (ed.), *The Early History of Malawi*. London: Longman.

Lwanda, John Lloyd, 1993, *Kamuzu Banda of Malawi: A Study in Promise, Power and Paralysis*. Glasgow: Dudu Nsomba.

Malawi Government, 1966, *Malawi Population Census 1966: Preliminary Report*. Zomba: Government Printer.

—, 1993, *Population and Housing Census 1987, Volume II: Population Charecteristics*. Zomba: Government Printer.

—, 1994, *Population and Housing Census 1987, Volume IV: Migration*. Zomba: Government Printer.

—, 1998, *Population and Housing Census 1998: Report of Preliminary Results*. Zomba: Government Printer.

Mamdani, Mahmood, 1996, *Citizen and Subject: Contemporary Africa and the Legacy of Late Colonialism*. Princeton, NJ: Princeton University Press.

Mbembe, Achille, 1992, "Provisional Notes on the Postcolony", *Africa*, 62, pp. 3–37.

McCarney, Patricia L. (ed.), 1996, "Considerations on the Notion of 'Governance'—New Directions for Cities in the Developing World", in McCarney, Patricia L. (ed.), *Cities and Governance: New Directions in Latin America, Asia and Africa*. Toronto: Centre for Urban and Community Studies.

Mhone, G.C.Z (ed.), 1992, "The Political Economy of Malawi: An Overview", in Mhone, G.C.Z (ed.), *Malawi at the Crossroads: The Post-Colonial Political Economy*. Harare: Sapes.

Mitchell, J. Clyde, 1956, *The Kalela Dance: Aspects of Social Relationships among Urban Africans in Northern Rhodesia*. Rhodes-Livingstone Paper No. 27. Manchester: Manchester University Press.

Nyamnjoh, Francis, and Michael Rowlands, 1998, "Elite Associations and the Politics of Belonging in Cameroon", *Africa*, 68, pp. 320–37.

Ortner, Sherry B., 1998, "Identities: The Hidden Life of Class", *Journal of Anthropological Research*, 54, pp. 1–17.

Potts, Deborah, 1986, "Urbanisation in Africa with Special Reference to the New Capital City of Lilongwe". Unpublished Ph.D. dissertation, University of London.

Pryor, F., 1991, *The Political Economy of Poverty, Equity and Growth: A World Bank Comparative Study of Malawi and Madagascar*. Oxford: Oxford University Press.

Ranger, Terence O., 1975, *Dance and Society in Eastern Africa, 1890–1970: The Beni Ngoma*. London: Heinemann.

Robinson, Pearl T., 1994, "Democratisation: Understanding the Relationship between Regime Change and the Culture of Politics", *African Studies Review*, 37, pp. 39–67.

Roe, Gillian, 1992, *The Hidden Economy: An Exploration of the Income Generation and Survival Strategies of the Urban Poor*. Zomba: University of Malawi.

Rouse, Roger, 1995, "Questions of Identity: Personhood and Collectivity in Transnational Migration to the United States", *Critique of Anthropology*, 15, pp. 351–80.

Taylor, Charles, 1994, "The Politics of Recognition", in Gutmann, Amy (ed.), *Multiculturalism: Examining the Politics of Recognition*, Princeton. NJ: Princeton University Press.

Vail, Leroy H. (ed.), 1989, *The Creation of Tribalism in Southern Africa*. London: James Currey.

van Donge, Jan Kees, 1995, "Kamuzu's Legacy: The Democratisation of Malawi", *African Affairs*, 94, pp. 227–57.

Werbner, Richard, 1996, "Introduction", in Werbner, Richard and Terence Ranger (eds), *Postcolonial Identities in Africa*. London: Zed Books.

Yoshida, Kenji, 1992, "Masks and Transformation among the Chewa of Eastern Zambia", *Senri Ethnological Studies*, 31, pp. 203–73.

CHAPTER 7

Touba: The New *Dairas* and the Urban Dream

Cheikh Gueye

INTRODUCTION

With its approximately 300,000 inhabitants, Touba has, in the 1990s, become the second largest city of Senegal. Only Dakar, the capital is larger. Touba's growth shows no signs of declining. Between 1988 and 1998, the annual growth rate was over 19 per cent. In 1973, its population was estimated to be only 16,000; it has thus grown almost twentyfold in less than thirty years (Gueye, 1997). Its spatial expansion is considerable: the built-up areas of the city, which increased from 575 to 3,900 hectares between 1970 and 1990, have since 1997 spread beyond 12,000 hectares.

Senegalese urban growth is characterised by the disproportionate swelling of Dakar and the relative stagnation of secondary cities,. The state has played an active role in urban development. In this pattern, Touba is a case apart. Moreover, unlike other Senegalese cities of a certain size, it is not governed as a municipality, but still has the status of a village. The urban structure of Senegal, essentially oriented towards the coast, is thus enriched by a large interior agglomeration, reducing the dominance of the capital.

Yet Touba is equally a conglomerate of paradoxes that spell out the complexity of the relationship between the state and a Muslim brotherhood. The Mouride brotherhood is a powerful element of Senegalese society, whose support to the state has long guaranteed its stability (Villalón, 1995). The "social contract" (Cruise O'Brien, 1992) which has bound them to each other for several decades has been manifested by a strong commitment from the state to building up the city. Roads, water supply and health institutions have often been financed by the Senegalese government to secure the Mouride vote. The Mourides are strongly identified with Touba. However, it is the special status granted to the city by the state that best expresses the strength of this bond. Those land concessions accorded to the brotherhood by the colonial state have been confirmed and subsequently reinforced by the independent Senegalese state, thus making Touba an exception in terms of territorial control (Cruise O'brien, 1971). The sovereignty of the state is circumscribed. Thus the police, the national constabulary and customs officers are not allowed to enter. In a speech in the early 1990s, the *khalifa general* (chief administrator of the city and its religious leader) proposed also outlawing national political demonstrations, the vote, building "French" schools, the consumption of tobacco and alcohol, gambling, football, the cinema, etc. This status of "free zone" has allowed the city to grow rich through smuggling with Gambia, and the money accrued through several years of this activity has been channelled into other activities.

Touba has become an important market for rural produce and a commercial centre of some standing, competing with Dakar in certain fields. Above all, Touba has become both for the Senegalese in general and for the Mourides in particular an attractive residential alternative, a social and economic refuge existing artificially on the considerable sums of money remitted by the Mouride diaspora. The town has grown through massive in-migration, mainly from rural areas, but also from other towns. Its population is still highly dependent on agriculture, and many from Touba return seasonally to their villages of origin. In other respects this city, the focus of the dynamic and nostalgic diaspora of all the Mourides scattered throughout the world, has become an important financial centre, where billions of CFA francs[1] are sent by disciples.

The founding of Touba in 1888 represented the realisation of the dream of an ascetic who had a vision of a city of paradise, built around a mosque, and a spiritual and religious centre, a symbol of mystical power. His name was Amadou Bamba (1853–27), who is regarded as the founder of the Mouride brotherhood (Cruise O'Brien, 1971). The city represents one of the stages in the creation of this brotherhood. The Sufic brotherhoods have ancient origins, going back to a "parallel Islam", still springing from the original and individual experience of a believer. With the evolution of the mystic strain in Islam the brotherhoods represent a totality of prescriptions and rites by which a spiritual guide enables the disciples he initiates to achieve a mystical experience. The group of disciples in one path forms a *tariqa* (a path or order). At their head is the *shaykh* (or *khalifa*), successor to the first religious leader from whom emanates a spiritual link and from whom he has inherited the power to perform miracles (Diop, 1980, 1981).

The first brotherhoods emerged in the Middle East and from there they have progressively gained important Muslim enclaves through conquests and trade. They are to be found today throughout the Muslim world, in various local or transnational forms (Popovic and Veinstein, 1985). The penetration of Islam into West Africa has been brought about through the proselytising of religious bodies eager not only to spread Islam, but also to promote the various Sufi religious orders that prospered in the Maghrib. This expansion is essentially due to the *Qâddiriyya,* the Sufi order founded in the twelfth century by Shaykh Abdal-Khadir Djeylani (1077–1166) in Bagdad, and which has subsequently spread out globally, above all in Asia and Africa. The Mouride order, the brotherhood that has most influenced the religious and political landscape of Senegal, has long been regarded as a local branch of the *Qâddiriyya,* which was a brotherhood introduced to Africa by Fez in Morocco (Cruise O'Brien, 1971).

The Mouride brotherhood inherited the dream that became the vision of a city and then the city itself in all its reality. The religious authority in charge of realising the urban dream of its founder is equally in charge of the administration of the city. This is the task of the *khalifa general*, the supreme head

---

[1] The CFA franc was the currency of the ECOWAS (Economic Community of West African States) of which Senegal is a member. In January 1994 it was devalued by 50 per cent. From then on 1 French Franc was worth 100 CFA.

and successor of the founder. The first *khalifa general* was the oldest of Shaykh Amadou Bamba's sons. The *khalifa* finances acquisition of land, heads the distribution of plots, and tries to respond to the multiple demands of an increasingly diverse and complex urban society. The city is the result of a variety of actors appropriating space, including the religious authorities, the State and a host of other collectivities. Among them are the *dairas,* originally associations of newly urbanised Mourides who were anxious to build up their bonds of mutual help. (Diop, 1980). The *dairas,* which since then have become widespread wherever the Mourides have moved, have assumed functions, and above all new ambitions, linked to the development of the city of Touba. They have thus evolved into mass movements, using Touba as a symbol to mobilise both disciples and their considerable financial resources. How can this development be explained? Which actors have taken part in this dynamic? What was their justification and what was their incentive? And what have been the consequences for the brotherhood? Answers to these questions through a study of one particular *daira* are sought. The principal sources of information are various archives, interviews with former and present leaders and members, and participation in meetings and manifestations.

THE EMERGENCE OF ASSOCIATIONS OF DISCIPLES

The Mouride brotherhood is a religious movement born in the last quarter of the nineteenth century in response to the disintegration of Wolof society owing several centuries of slavery and dynastic wars, and to the pressure of French colonisation. The Wolof are the ethnic majority in Senegal, with approximately 45per cent of the total population. A brotherhood emanates from a path of spiritual ascent and mysticism laid down by one saint, in this case Shaykh Amadou Bamba. With its hundreds of thousands of disciples, all devoted to the religious authorities, it constitutes a political force that has been present in all the electoral contests that have taken place in Senegal for over a hundred years. Yet the hallmark of the Mouride brotherhood is equally linked to a crop that Senegal has made its speciality: groundnuts. The cultivation of groundnuts has allowed the Mourides to take possession of the rural areas of the central west and the east of the country, while contributing to the wealth of the brotherhood. The formal Mouride structure catering for the rural elements of the brotherhood is the *dara.* This was originally a Koranic school where the pupils worked the land in order to feed themselves. It is only later that this has changed into a maraboutic farm where the education of a disciple is based more on work than on instruction. This also served to bring about the pioneering land conquests of the Mourides in Senegal. In addition, the Mourides have become a significant financial power since their entrance in 1945 into the economic affairs of Senegalese cities, where they now dominate informal trade and transport. In the 1980s and 90s there was considerable emigration to European and American cities (mainly France, Italy, Spain and USA), forming an active and homesick diaspora (Ebin, 1992).

The *daira* is an institution which has helped successive waves of migrants settle in the cities. Its functions, analysed by Diop (1980), are multiple. For the disciples from rural areas it provided, above all, a bulwark of solidarity and togetherness in the face of the disruption, anonymity and hostility encountered in the urban environment. It allowed them to come together at regular intervals to chant or recite the poems of the founder of the path, to have discussions to boost and renew their faith, and to receive orders and precepts from the *marabouts*. Equally, the *daira* played an important part in proselytising and organising the celebrations that popularised the thinking and retold the "miracles" of Amadou Bamba. In the 1980s these events assumed dimensions that at times were to make the whole of Dakar hold its breath. For the *marabout* leadership, the *daira* is above all a means towards financial and political mobilisation. It has demonstrated the flexibility of the Mouride brotherhood. The charisma of the *marabout*, based on a special relationship between *marabout* and disciple, has through the *dairas* shown itself adaptable to distance. This relationship is not confined to the agricultural work groups, the *daras*, where the leaders have direct control over the clientele and their activities through physical proximity.

Within the Mouride system and in the political system of Senegal, it is a double advantage for a *marabout* to control a large number of believers. Firstly, it allows him to benefit each year from the financial resources generated, which will vary according to the number of followers. Secondly, the numbers of followers allow him to negotiate with the State that can provide access to credit "rarely reimbursed and always renewed." (Diop, 1980:184). The number and diversity of *dairas* controlled by one *marabout* indicate his charisma and reflect his political and economic stature. These are of several types, according to the context of the grouping of its members, and a Mouride disciple can be a member of several *dairas* at the same time. There may be the neighbourhood *daira*, the *daira* set up by a *marabout* or particularly attached to his charisma or his memory, the *daira* of the workplace, the professional *daira*, the overseas *daira*, the *daira* according to citizenship, the *daira* affiliated to a particular religious celebration of the brotherhood, national or international groups organised according to place of origin and distribution. They are frequently organised "on the blueprint of secular organisations, notably those of the Western administration" (Diop, 1980:138). But they are not subject to the 1901 law on associations in Senegal, which stipulated registration with the authorities. Officers are elected, in principle to be regularly replaced. The names in themselves often indicate such factors as the occupation of its members, where they have come from and the *marabout* to whom they adhere.

In the 1950s the first *dairas* set about renewing the site for the great mosque of Touba and contributed to the organisation of the great *magal*, or pilgrimage. A *magal* is a celebration of the memory of a Mouride saint or of an important event in the history of the brotherhood. In this case the date of departure into exile of the founder of the brotherhood is the occasion for a pilgrimage of Mouride disciples to the city of Touba. With the rapid growth of the city, several *dairas*, both from Dakar and elsewhere, continue to play a role in the life of Touba. Yet a recent tendency is the formation of large-scale organisations, counting several thousand members and constituting a real social project. These movements have developed a strategy of autonomy by which they aspire to take charge of all the needs of each disciple. Seen in this light, Touba becomes the ideal place for aspirations towards a perfect society. The new *dairas* are making the dream of the town more and more their own, and they are involved in building up the city through investing considerable funds towards the organisation of the great pilgrimage that the town hosts annually, constructing dwellings, health centres, sanitation and other urban facilities. The city and its needs have become the means of mobilisation for the *dairas* who see their actions as part of their support for the *khalifa*. This fund-raising strategy has rapidly led to the channelling of all the financial benefits from the Mouride diaspora to Touba. The case of *Hizbut Tarkhiyya* sheds light on the role of a disciples organisation in the accelerated urbanisation of the capital of the Mourides.

HIZBUT TARKHIYYA, A *DAIRA* IN CHARGE OF THE PILGRIMAGE TO TOUBA

Hizbut Tarkhiyya, which in Arabian means "The Party of Ascent" is the new name for the Mouride student *daira* (DEM—Dahira des Etudiants Mourides) in Dakar. According to Momar Coumba Diop (1980), DEM was founded at the University of Dakar during the academic year 1975–1976, comprising a dozen or so young men who had just finished secondary school and who had met on the university campus. They sought each other out in need of mutual support and to further a Mouride identity in a university setting. Their association was facilitated by a shared experience of attending Mouride schools (*dara*) where they had been exposed to the thoughts of the founder of the brotherhood, in an orthodox mode, and to an in-depth study of his writings. Their activity thus deviated from the popular notion of Mouridism as backward, full of myths, legends and epic accounts of the founder. The representation of Mourides as ignorant, reinforced by the rural roots of the brotherhood, is essentially an urban and intellectual phenomenon. Both in Saint-Louis and in Dakar a vague disdain and hostility were also nourished by the rivalling presence of the numerically superior Tijan brotherhood, more entrenched in the cities. In this context, the urban and the academic origin of the DEM thus was a major departure.

The DEM, like other *dairas* at the time, had an organisational structure modelled on that of secular bodies, with a board, consisting of a chairman, a secretary general, a treasurer and several secretaries in charge of specific activities, such as communication, organisation, and cultural affairs. This organisational matrix, copied from earlier *dairas*, was well suited to a modern, university-based structure with students as capable participants.

The change in DEM from 1978

The DEM was originally a student association, but from 1978 the organisation was expanded to include non-students. One reason was that, in the space of four years, the founding members had had the time to complete their studies and hence lose their student status. They had to find a new justification for continuing their activities within the framework they had created, and which in a way signified for them a path towards finding a meaning in life. Another reason was that their activism and the innovative nature of their approach attracted non-students, even illiterates. These two significant factors determined the first great change in the *daira*. The first principle that was jettisoned after this change was the stipulation that only students could be elected to the board. This basic rule, which had determined earlier appointments continued for many years despite the growing number of non-students and their increased weight in the organisation. In the end this rule became a front which allowed the *daira* to benefit from the advantages of being a student body. In particular it made it possible to hire coaches from a university facility centre (COUD, Centre des Oeuvres Universitaires de Dakar) for convoys on the pilgrimage or the *ziyara* (devotional visits) to Touba. The student status also ensured that they could rent halls for lectures, film shows and exhibitions on the life and works of Amadou Bamba.

Behind this facade of university status was concealed a more widespread and comprehensive organisation of students, to a lesser degree school pupils, and in particular sympathisers who were former students. They were no longer able to take office but continued to be extremely active in their new status, be it as merchants, civil servants or various kinds of employees. Organised in an association of former students and sympathisers (Regroupement des Anciens Etudiants et Sympathisants, RAES), they formed the first elements of permanence in the *daira*; they financed events, paid the rent of the venue, and bills for water, telephone and electricity. Some who had become important personalities or *marabouts* acquired the status of honorary members. The RAES had a treasurer who was essentially the financial director of the movement. The membership fees and other contributions were graduated according to the means of each: students on grants, students not on grants, sympathisers, *daanou kat* (those who stripped themselves of all or who donated almost their entire salary). In 1980 the number of students and sympathisers had, according to Momar Coumba Diop, risen to 300–400 members. An indication of the financial power and dynamism of the *daira* at the time was the sum remitted to the *khalifa general* on the occasion of the devotional visit organised each year at Touba. The amount was 600,000 CFA francs the first year, and 3 million CFA francs from the next year onwards (100 CFA=1FFr). The expenditure of the *daira* between 1980 and 1985 was of the order of a dozen million CFA francs. If at first, the most important benefactors were civil servants, undoubtedly merchants have since taken the lead. Their large contributions can be explained by their commitment but above all through their feeling of inferiority compared to academics. They made money their chief means of ensuring their status in an intellectual to which context they otherwise would not have had access. The competition among members was kept up by publicising the amount of each contribution. Some individuals or groups took it upon themselves to finance particular events or projects.

The board was supposed to function according to basic democratic tenets, including debates on decisions and ideological direction, and some turnover of its members. However, practice was somewhat different. A member of the board was replaced only when he lost his student status through passing or failing his exams or through personal choice. These changes were mainly made by nomination: "Those who have proved themselves or who are capable in one area and recognised by all of us".[2] There would be no opposing candidates, no debate, nor any vote on the choice of a candidate. No one remained president for very long. Despite its origins and membership, the *daira* never made its headquarters on the university campus. It always sought to be accessible to non-students without departing too far from its original base. At this time *dairas* were beginning to emerge in high schools, modelled on the DEM The confluence between these two movements was not problematic, not least because many former members of the DEM were now teachers in the secondary schools where they could organise proselytising meetings. Shortly after its establishment the DEM was recruiting from among high school students.

The need to keep separate from the campus was also dictated by the activity of the *daira*. Members did not take turns to host events, as is normally the case in other *dairas*. One day—Friday—was chosen for the weekly meetings. They always took place in one particular building, initially in a house lent by an elder—a teacher—then in another house which belonged to a member of a *marabout* family settled in Dakar. The success of a *daira* that emphasises the profound study of the founder's texts depends upon a good knowledge of Arabic. The majority of the members who came from Diourbel or Saint-Louis had learned the Koran and could read Arabic, but others needed intensive tutoring to become literate in Arabic. Therefore a teacher was appointed. Teaching materials and texts collected for various cultural activities had, little by little, accumulated into a documentary base consisting mainly of the writings of Shaykh Amadou Bamba and some modest publications produced by the *daira*. This heritage was kept in the form of a library in the garage of a house rented in Grand-Dakar. It was in the courtyard of this house that a shelter was built to accommodate the Koranic school, which also accepted children from the neighbourhood. The library, the Koranic school and the rented house may be seen as elements of permanence. Yet at the board level, there could be no permanence, as long as the principle that students alone were eligible for office was maintained.

The change in the *daira* in the 1980s bears the stamp of one man. This was Atou Diagne who, being in charge of cultural affairs, progressively attained a status that was to be yet another element of permanence. Having left the university after taking a degree in geography, he suddenly decided to settle in Touba near the *khalifa*, the supreme head of the brotherhood, thereby renouncing an academic future his family had hoped would be brilliant. In a way he thus presented the gift of his person, a deep and significant gesture creating a special bond between him and the *khalifa*: the latter in return giving him in marriage the daughter of the principal *marabout* family, the Mbacké. After returning from his stay in Touba, he stayed with members of the association of former students (RAES), and demonstrated activism and zeal in the service of the *daira*, devoting all his time to its service. He thus gained the esteem and respect of all, and gradually became indispensable to the daily

---

[2] Interview with Atou Diagne, president of the *Hizbut Tarkhiyya*.

running of the *daira*, the success of major celebrations, and the custody of its assets. Brimful of initiative and tireless in advancing ideas to strengthen the progress of the *daira*, his position became assured.

Above all it was the rehabilitation of the ancient holy well that had been dug when the city was founded and which supposedly had special qualities, that made Atou Diagne the most charismatic personality in the *daira*, at the expense of the president, who was still a student. Titulated *diawrigne* (leader) of the site by the *marabout* in 1985, he yet again demonstrated his efficiency and spirit of self-sacrifice. It was essentially after this performance that he received the accolades that were to keep him at the head of the *daira* after 1985. His numerous initiatives reinforced the title of *diawrigne* that had emerged from his work on the well. His influence extended to other fields of activities in the *daira* and his position was formalised. The force of his personality gradually influenced all its members: decisions and initiatives that were previously discussed were from now on entirely left to his discretion. He ended up by convincing the members, of whom an increasing proportion was illiterate, that a Mouride organisation could not work on democratic lines with interminable debates, and that these, moreover, could not be reconciled with the Mouride conception of authority. Thus disputes and disagreements which could no longer be aired were henceforth clandestinely expressed in the corridors. Even General Assemblies were denounced as secular institutions. Only the financial accounts were publicly declared in order to solicit confidence. Ideological direction and important decisions were given by a group faithful to Atou Diagne, whose hold on the system makes him resemble a guru of certain sects swarming in Europe and in some African countries.

Having totally succumbed to the charm of the students, and transferring to the entire *daira* the deep affection he had always declared for Atou Diagne, the third *Khalifa General* gave way to all their demands. Thus the DEM reaped the full benefit of attention from the *Khalifate*. Its members were employed in printing the works of Amadou Bamba that were kept in the library. They also decorated the well and put it in working order. A memorial was erected and inscribed with the sayings of the *Shaykh* concerning the well, translated into French and English. These improvements indisputably cemented the relationship between the *daira* and the *khalifa*, the former being seen by the latter as a spearhead of modernity and a showpiece. And the members of the *daira* equally basked in the protection of the supreme authority of the brotherhood, who took pains to appear in person every day to make sure that the work was progressing correctly. In addition, the quality of the improvements increased the admiration of others for the *daira* whose numbers rose dramatically. In this same period the *khalifa* put them in touch with several important people, so that these in turn could impart their admiration. The scope of the *daira* has thus been much expanded in the course of a few years. More than a *daira*, one can see the emergence of a movement of a significant scale, diversifying its resources through expanding its recruitment base, and extending its operations into numerous spheres.

The death of the third *khalifa general* in 1989 was another decisive turning point. His relations with the DEM had been affectionate, almost "umbilical". The "students" swore exclusive devotion to him, even as their movement augmented in size and attracted covetous feelings from most of the great *marabout* families of Touba. In their view, the *daira* belonged to the whole brotherhood, and they wanted it be equally attentive to themselves. In answer to this, the DEM turned in on itself, which increased the *marabout* families' feelings of rejection and defiance. The influence of the third *khalifa* in national politics and his authority so strongly consolidated in the brotherhood by his active participation in the construction of Touba, all benefited the *daira*. The association now began to dream of a role in national politics, finding support in an utterance attributed to Shaykh Amadou Bamba. He is held to have said that sooner or later the whole country would be ruled by the brotherhood.

The third *khalifa general's* death, however, left the *daira* without protection, and led to internal discord. It became urgent to find legitimate expressions of change: from now on, the relationship with the *khalifate* would hinge on personal and emotional bonds with the *khalifa*. But the relationship between the *daira* and the new *khalifa* were not of the warmest. He and his family had for several years frequently been "ignored" by the "students", except for some rare visits—only once a year, in stark contrast to the all-pervading presence of the *daira* in the compound of the previous *khalifa*. Then the members had had buildings reserved for them near the living quarters of the *marabout*.

The decease of the fourth *khalifa* after a short reign of eleven months only served as an interruption in the process of rapprochement. A new approach was initiated with the fifth *khalifa* (Serigne Saliou), who was somewhat closer to the *daira* thanks to his habit of taking part in the celebrations the *daira* organised to commemorate the birth of the prophet Muhammed. Although relations between the *daira* and the son of the new *khalifa* were strained; contact was made. The most visible sign of this new rapport was undoubtedly changing the name "Student *Daira*" to "*dara Hizbut Tarkhiyya*". This notion of the *dara* was not new to the DEM It was linked to the first years of the *daira* in its earlier stages of training and combating illiteracy. Above all, it indicates a large-scale movement seeing itself first and foremost as an educational force imparting the cultural values attributed to Mouridism. The *khalifa* had earlier chosen the designation "*Hizbollah*", but fearing negative reactions and unfortunate associations with the South Lebanese "Islamic" group bearing the same name, he made an alternative suggestion with which the whole *daira* could agree.

It was the great *ziyara* or devotional visit that played a large part in sealing the new rapport with the *khalifa general*. The *daira* had decided to demonstrate their goodwill by furnishing the new palace just built by the third *khalifa*. For several months, luxury articles in keeping with their ambitions were patiently made and stored. Some members were in charge of furnishing the bedrooms, others were responsible for the reception rooms. The *daira* took upon itself the purchase of materials needed to furnish the main reception hall, leaving the assignment to one member, a cabinetmaker by trade. In addition to the furniture and a sum of fifteen million CFA francs, innumerable products, commodities and objects were presented to the *khalifa* as gifts. Lorry-loads of salt and sugar, cattle, roasted lambs, two horses, carved chests, electric fans, watches, thermos flasks etc. made up a spectacular convoy stretching for over a kilometre. This fashion of giving the *marabout* an *adiyya* or devotional gift, with no thought of amount or expense, was a tradition revived from that of the peasants at the time of Shaykh Amadou Bamba. Several initiatives of this sort were set in motion, masterminded by Atou Diagne to stimulate the generosity of the members.

Ideological base: Elitism and legitimate fervour

The process of change had started in 1978 with the abandonment of segregation between students and sympathisers. This was when the formulation of the movement's ideological base truly began. Thus, according to Momar Coumba Diop (1980), the drive for orthodoxy that sustained the "cultural celebrations" and the other activities of the *daira* gave prominence to an archetypal model, that of the educated "Arab", in which only those who could read and write Arabic were considered suited to exercise power. But how was this model superimposed on the French, or at least Francophone, scholarly and academic orientation that the *daira* could not escape, and that Momar Coumba Diop never evoked? The latter element was constantly present, justified as a means of first suppressing western values, then surpassing them and finally combating them. Superimposing models or combining them would have implied that only those who could fit into the two moulds should be in power. The DEM could only function well through this type of member, both intellectually resourceful and aware. Thus the board was exclusively composed of students and former students.

There was as yet no opening in the office for sympathisers without proficiency in French. The *daira* had a standard to maintain, as well as its own image and that of Shaykh Amadou Bamba. It "decided not to deal with themes with a popular appeal" (Diop, 1980:178), but rather devote to itself to the editing and translation into French of the thoughts of the founder, in particular those of his works that clarified Sufi thinking and his orthodox bent. Regarding themselves as the cream and the showpiece of Mouridism, the students wanted to distinguish themselves from the masses that were looked down on in the cities and by intellectuals, both Francophone and those working in Arabic. For the same reason, they also chose to take a collective part in the *magal*, the great annual pilgrimage where all the days of celebration are used to manifest the faith, as well as the number and the immortality of the works of the founder. Gradually this became their calling and their sole justification.

The DEM had also reflected on its ideological direction. First of all they chose to register outside the framework of secular structures by not declaring themselves as an association to the Minister of the Interior. Their project relied essentially on their will to serve the Islamic cause, according to the founder of Mouridism whose "elect" they considered themselves. Despite the considerable presence of non-students, they defined themselves as an organisation of intellectuals, imbued with the knowledge of ancient power, defending at all costs the values laid down by the Mouride brotherhood. The DEM thus stood out as the proof incarnate of the victory of Shaykh Amadou Bamba over the cultural assimilation that was the French colonial power's oppressive weapon of subjugation. This image of the resistance of the *marabout* which served Senegalese nationalism in the throes of the country's independence is thus reiterated in the ideological foundations of the *daira*: "We are the ones: This is the way we shall move! We will master all that the French school can teach us, but wherever we are to be found, it will be clear that Serigne Bamba[3] is our leader and guide."

However, the most vital ideological pillar is another dimension of the *jebbelu*, the fundamental action whereby a Mouride disciple declares allegiance to his *marabout*, accompanied by extensive studies as to the political, economic and social implications of this alliance. This is the *diayanté*, a sacred pact or contract, the total gift of his person and his worldly goods to be devoted to the cause of Shaykh Amadou Bamba. The disciple is constantly reminded and rekindled by the evocation of the example of the Prophet Mohammed's companions who, after the battle of Badar (Bedr),[4] pledged themselves to die for the new faith and the furthering of Islam in exchange for the highest favours of Paradise. In order to exhort the members, they are often reminded of the exploits of Shaykh Ibra, Amadou Bamba's second in command, who is seen as the epitome of the perfect disciple. The principle of "doing the impossible" or "nothing is too difficult" also underlies all the actions of the *daira* whose members claim to be soldiers in the service of Shaykh Amadou Bamba.

The striving and the competition between the members is often extreme, and those who grumble at a task or who question orders are discredited or disqualified, even expelled. Along these lines, the DEM does not accept that its members define themselves as ordinary men. They consider themselves an elite, singled out by a fervour expressed in the magnitude and the quality of their service. They thus stand in opposition to the common people, who resent this, seeing it as implying rejection and ostracism. This defiant stand serves to construct an elitist and special image of the *daira* and has found its outward expression in the *baay laat*, their own robes, consisting of a long tunic with wide sleeves and embroidered neckline. As a mark of affection and respect for his standing, the *baay laat* bears the name of the *khalifa* who gave the disciples approval within the brotherhood and in the city. There are also various insignia, such as the *makhtoum* which is a sort of hip-length or thigh-length hanging leather pouch, slippers, and the *kaala*, a long scarf which can be tied round the waist for working. To complete this picture are the shaved head, the small

---

[3] Another name for the founder. This quotation is from the introductory speech of Atou Diagne to the General Assembly of 11 May 1996.

[4] The progress of Islam occurred despite the hostility of Arab tribes who adhered to animism. The evocation of the Battle of Bedr is for Muslims hagiographic, both in its praise of the courage of the prophet's companions and as a reminder of the miracles wrought by God on their behalf. According to Islamic tradition the battle took place in the month of Ramadan between 313 muslims practically without arms or horses and thousands of infidels armed to the teeth and mounted on more than 700 horses.

beard and the bare feet that in Touba signify the sacred nature of the city, its very ground and its holy sites.

The magal

Above all the *Hizbut Tarkhiyya* has for several years totally identified itself with the pilgrimage to Touba. This takes place on the 18th Safar, the second lunar month in the Muslim calendar, which corresponds to the anniversary of the exile of Shaykh Amadou Bamba and also, according to Atou Diagne, to the end of his trials. With this commemoration, Amadou Bamba reversed the colonial idea of "exile". To be exiled and have to hold meetings in a house under surveillance were described by him as trials that allowed him to proceed to the highest state of grace. Thus the *magal* is a festive event with religious chanting, recitals of the holy Koran, and visits to holy sites and to the *marabouts*. It is also "the occasion to commemorate and to relive intensely the glorious cultural victory brought about by the Great Shaykh in his battle against all the forces of assimilation and alienation of our own values".[5] Diagne here attributes to the founder a symbolic significance with a nationalist flavour. The pilgrimage attracts up to two million disciples, who come to Touba from all parts of the country and from the diaspora settled abroad. The city has largely been built around this event, and the life of the town falls into its rhythm.

Convoys to Touba paid for by members' dues have been arranged since the foundation of the *daira*. It was not only the students who organised their travel in this way. It was important for all members of the *daira* to share the ups and downs of the journey to Touba, to share sleeping quarters and visits to holy sites and have communal meals. This is a time that is anticipated all through the year, and no efforts are spared in preparing for it. For the *magal* of 1995, the DEM set up a large convoy and were granted accommodation for the three days in a building facing the entrance of the great mosque. This building, lent by a descendant of the founder (Serigne Abdou Aziz Bara), has for several years housed a large exhibition during the *magal*. It shows the life and works of Shaykh Amadou Bamba, based on the holdings in the library and the educational material used at the lectures held in Dakar. This exhibition was chiefly internal but represented a new approach which further underlined the particular quality of the *daira* with regard to the rest of the brotherhood. The exhibition also appealed to intellectuals, demonstrating that the Mouride culture could find modern expression. It was shown in the open air with large display boards with captioned photographs and texts retelling the story of the relations between the brotherhood and the colonial authorities.

The importance of the *magal* was also described in the texts. The exhibition was an innovation which steadily grew in importance. It was moved out of the building where the *daira* was lodged and put on display in public spaces, at the place of prayer at the end of Ramadan and at the great library of Touba. The main roads were festooned with banners bearing the slogans of

---

[5] Interview with Atou Diagne published in *SUD Quotidien*, Number 928, Saturday 11 May 1996.

the brotherhood. This conquering of public space indicates a new dimension of the presence of the *daira* in the city brought about by the pilgrimage. It took a lot of effort to get the exhibition mounted and to satisfy all the demands of the *daira* during the great celebration. There was, in turn, considerable appreciation of this contribution by the students who had previously been regarded as intellectuals, disdainful, arrogant and above all a product of colonial schools. Their contribution was seen as something to be proud of, because of its intellectual and modernising aspect, and was brandished to show the power of the works of the founder, he who had ended up by "conquering all hearts", even the most stubborn, those of the intellectuals.

The work on the sacred well also became a turning point for the *daira* and its relations with the *magal*. In anticipation of the pilgrimage, the "students" received from the *khalifa* a sum of money that was generous, and to them charged with mystic significance. It was partly seen as remuneration, and they also received food supplies. The surplus of that year and the optimistic predictions of the *khalifa* ("this will just go from strength to strength each year" he is said to have commented) have been the determining factor and the starting point for a *diayanté* (pledge) to continually do more and better to make this great show of strength of the Mouride brotherhood and the city of Touba a success. No sacrifice was seen as too great, so as not to do less than in this pivotal year. This pledge has been progressively worked out and elaborated, so as to become the mainstay of *Hizbut Tarkhiyya*, as well as its means of positioning itself in the Mouride brotherhood and in Touba. The celebration was the springboard for its ideological foundation and its organisation. The celebration provided an occasion to demonstrate the permanent force of the *daira*, and can be seen as the yardstick of its fierce commitment and fidelity. This principle carries to extremes the recommendation of Shaykh Amadou Bamba to render grace to God by any possible means.

In the General Assembly of 11 May 1996 the operational structure of the *daira* was made public, as well as the techniques for mobilisation and motivation in regard to the great *magal*. The object of this meeting was by no means to bring about change, the whole organisation being at the time in charge of the *diawrigne* which picked out trusty men and set down lines of command. The computerising of the membership lists and detailed administrative procedures were the chief means of keeping a tight control on its men. To motivate and mobilise members, a communication policy was adopted. It gave priority to dynamic productions such as audio-visual representations giving the impression of a go-ahead and high-powered organisation. Yet inside the *daira*, information remained closely guarded, restricted and given out sparsely. Only those in power might give and receive information.

From now on the whole organisation was centred on the yearly *magal*. The decision to prepare for the next event immediately after the preceding one is an indication of this choice. A review of the balance sheets for one year (1995–1996) provides insight into the systems of mobilisation and the extent of the funds set aside for investment. From the month of July 1995 the *daira* had three major tasks in preparation for the 1996 *magal*. The first was to secure accommodation and lodging to shelter hundreds of thousands of members and other pilgrims. This involved all the work carried out in the construction of an immense secluded camp for the *daira* and its immediate neighbourhood, as well as the construction works carried out in the compound of the *khalifa general*. This extensive work, stretching over 11 months, also entailed certain administrative and other expenses, some in connection with other celebrations of the brotherhood. In total, up to the time of the General Assembly, 322 740 000 CFA francs, or more than 3 million FFr were spent for this purpose.[6]

The second objective of the *daira* was to have sufficient foodstuffs ready to feed the members of the *daira* and some of the pilgrims. On this account a "property" campaign was solemnly launched concurrently with the shelter project. Cattle, sheep, millet, oil and sugar to the value of 35 305 860 CFA francs were collected between September and November 1995. In the following two months commodities as diverse as tomatoes, mustard, olives, pepper, flour and vinegar were collected for the sum total of 28 530 840 CFA francs. The next four months were devoted to sanitation arrangements, water supply, medical and other provisions, raising the sum of 35 683 570 CFA francs. The fund-raising "One member—one sheep" project was launched, bringing in the sum of 41 750 405 CFA francs. Finally a need for 11,000 chickens was announced, and the sum of 8 millions CFA was raised in four months. The third task was the contribution from the *daira* to the mosque, following an appeal for its renovation from the *khalifa* to the entire brotherhood. In this connection 33 millions CFA were raised.

All these contributions stem from members who vie with each other in generosity. The detailed information which the *daira* possesses on each of its members makes it possible to identify the most willing, and their respective monetary value. Thus the *daira* is proving a real financial drain on its members. In addition to the regular and compulsory dues, the *sas*, which are contributions regulated by the *daira*, are graduated according to the means of each member and in accordance with the projects to be undertaken in readiness for the *magal*. A member of the *Hizbut Tarkhiyya* is thus at all times under pressure. Some run into debt, others stake their businesses or give up the profits they could gain from their enterprises. The demands are often the root cause of family dramas, with parents feeling abandoned by their sons who are weighed down by membership dues and who under such pressure prefer to deprive their parents of the help they otherwise could give them. Equally, several initiatives have been criticised by the rest of the Mouride and Islamic community because of the extremism they encourage. One example is the decision of the *daira* to forbid its members to celebrate the Tabaski and carry out the sacrifice to Abraham, one of the most sacred rites of Islam, in order to reserve all the sheep for the *magal*.

In addition to the funds provided by members, the *daira* has innumerable other financial sources through its "telecentres", shops, and above all the irri-

---

[6] From September to November 1995, preparations for accommodation raised the sum of 60 373 880 CFA francs; between November 1995 and January 1996: 72 750 125 CFA francs; between January and March 1996: 77 460 245 CFA francs; from March to May 1996: 112 155 545 CFA francs.

gated areas in the Senegal River valley, extending for hundreds of hectares. The irrigation techniques are advanced, and 30 205 905 CFA francs were spent in 1996 on maintenance, seed and other inputs.

The financial resources of the *daira* are particularly impressive seen against the backcloth of misery and poverty prevailing in Senegal. In 1996, two months ahead of the *Magal*, more than 6.5 million FFr had already been invested in its preparation. Yet these figures do not convey the quality of human resources and their level of involvement. These are incalculable. The *daira* engenders a spirit of independence and autonomy necessary for the ideological thrust to promote the heritage and "the cultural values that Mouridism entails." "This is the guiding principle around which the whole educational system of the *Hizbut Tarkhiyya* is run".[7] Chemists, physicians, engineers, administrators, communication experts, members of the *daira* are all imbued with this spirit of autonomy, although their ambitions are in reality more modest than those vehemently proclaimed by Atou Diagne. What the *daira* does is to profit on the one hand from the methods and technologies of an occidental society that it rejects with the other hand.

Atou Diagne is the leader of the Steering Committee which directs both the permanent secretariat and the secretariat of the board. He co-ordinates all the local member organisations in Senegal and abroad. The Steering Committee is responsible for the mobilisation and morale of its members through its theoretical discourse on the involvement of the movement and its plans for action and investment. The Committee also directs all financial operations and imposes a veritable veil of silence towards the outside world. The source of wealth and the labyrinths of the organisation are considered part of its "mysteries", as is the number of members and of chapters.

The "students" create their own centre

Hizbut Tarkhiyya has made the *magal* its means of positioning itself within the brotherhood, and has moved its headquarters to the city of Touba. From then on, this movement of national and international proportions has aspired to increase its influence on the brotherhood and its power struggles. It was in this spirit that the *daira* built its own seat in Touba. Since 1992, this centre has developed in a spectacular fashion, demonstrating that the movement has appropriated the dream of the founder of Mouridism and made it a city project.

Yet, more than a single building, the *Hizbut Tarkhiyya* built up a whole part of the city. The nerve centre of this is a wide, walled-in compound. A large entrance opens up onto a green space dividing the area in two. To the east and at ground level are the offices and rooms reserved for the Touba chapter, as well as an adjacent building housing the kitchen quarters. To the north-east is an enclosed area reserved for the women of the movement, who play an important part in the *magal*. The west wing contains the offices of the Steering Committee, a sick bay, as well as two enormous lecture halls that are

---

[7] Interview with Atou Diagne of 11 May 1996.

sumptuously decorated and furnished. These impressively luxurious structures have been erected to receive the thousands of members of the movement during the pilgrimage. Yet the centre functions all year round and gives the impression of an entrenched camp where the "representatives" imperturbably go about their own business. Outside the wall, well-equipped workshops (metalwork and wood) spend all year constructing the shelters for the *magal*, while a shopping centre catering for the needs of the *daira* gets more and more business. Opposite the great portal, with its gate-keeper, there is a petrol station run by the *daira's* men. This compound was established in 1992 and formed the first stage of *Hizbut Tarkhiyya's* settling in Touba. That the organisation is still gaining ground can be seen in the construction of a mosque dedicated to the *khalifa general*, and above all by the acquisition of hundreds of plots of land close to the headquarters. This is the embryo of an all-year life, with functions addressed to the needs of its members. It is of much concern to other citizens of Touba that the rules imposed in the *daira* may eventually also apply to them: bare feet, proper dress etc.

Since 1992 it has been the aim of the *daira* to establish its own neighbourhood. This decision is linked to its leaders' awareness of the new possibilities inherent in the city. It is an expression of their new relationship with the *khalifate*, which has become increasingly close since 1992. The centre they have built is part of their total strategy of asserting themselves in the brotherhood by locating in its city. It allows them to draw nearer to the affairs of the *khalifa general*, who has found the movement more and more to his liking. Thus the members have played an increasingly important part in the running of the compound of the *khalifa general* and its ceremonial. The *daira* recognises no authority but that of the *khalifa general*, and has put this into practice. They will not serve other members of the brotherhood, not even the grandsons of the founder, who consider themselves the bearers of the charisma of Shaykh Amadou Bamba, whom the students claim to serve. This group of grandsons resents their attitude and sees it as one of defiance and scorn.

Setting up the headquarters of the *Hizbut Tarkhiyya* on the outskirts of the city has also been seen by some as a literal acknowledgement of their marginalisation. The site chosen in 1992 was at the time of little interest. It was situated in a part of the city which was outside the control of the different important religious families on whom the movement turned its back. The movement used the ill-will of other citizens of Touba to better mobilise its members, and saw the establishment of its own centre as an act of defiance in the face of the citizens of Touba. "We are the orphans and the exiles who have found refuge with Shaykh Amadou Bamba; he who will neither turn us away, nor chase us. We are here, and we shall never leave the city. We have taken root" proclaimed Atou Diagne at the General Assembly in May 1996. This was his answer to the many threats, obstructions and constraints which the movement had encountered from those who wanted to expel it from the city.

Dakar remains nonetheless a strategic chapter, proving the attachment of the *daira* to its university roots and its great interest in the economic and political pole that the city represents. Other important cities in the country and particularly dynamic sections of the movement also have their own chapters.

For some years the strong migratory dynamic of the Senegalese brought about a rapid spread of the movement through chapters established in large African, European and American cities, such as New York, Washington, Bergamo, Paris, Madrid, Tenerife, Las Palmas and Abidjan (Ebin, 1992).

CONCLUSION

To sum up; *Hizbut Tarkhiyya* represents a break with the traditional *daira*, as studied by Momar Coumba Diop. This is due partly to its academic origins and partly to the strategy of making the city of Touba its base through zealous and innovative actions. In time, it turned into a mass movement because of the great pressure from non-academics who gained influence thanks to the enormous financial benefits they brought to the *daira*. Its organisation and doctrine responded to the needs of the Mourides when they had to confront the social and economic crisis of Senegal. But above all, the carefully nurtured image of an ardent faith and rigorous discipline have attracted hundreds of thousands of Mouride disciples. *Hizbut Tarkhiyya* is a movement that has found its particular identity and evolution through its ideological direction and its mode of operation. In a city where the path to promotion is through immoderation and zeal, the movement has ended up by appropriating the urban dream and conquering elements of power, to the point where the bastions of the brotherhood's religious authorities tremble. *Dairas* such as *Hizbut Tarkhiyya* will probably continue to contribute to the expansion of religious urban centres such as Touba economically, socially as well as ideologically.

References

Cruise O'Brien, D., 1992, "Le 'contrat social' sénégalais à l'épreuve", *Politique Africaine*, No. 45, pp. 21–38.
—, 1971, *The Mourides of Senegal*. Oxford: Clarendon Press.
Diop, Momar Coumba, 1980, *La confrérie mouride: organisation politique et mode d'implantation urbaine*. Thèse de doctorat de troisième cycle de l'Université de Lyon.
—, 1981, "Fonction et activités des *dairas* mourides urbains (Sénégal)", *Cahiers d'études Africaines*, XX, (1–3) 1981, pp. 79–91.
Ebin, Victoria, 1992, "A la recherche de nouveaux 'poissons'. Stratégies commerciales mourides par temps de crise", *Politique Africaine*, No. 45, pp. 86–99.
Gueye, Cheikh, 1997, "Touba: Les marabous urbanisants", in Bertrand, Monique et Alain Dubresson (eds), *Petites et moyennes villes d'Afrique noire*. Paris: Karthala.
Popovic, Alexandre et Gilles Veinstein, 1985, *Les ordres mystiques de l'islam. Cheminements et situation actuelle*. Paris: Editions de l'EHESS.
SUD Quotidien, No. 928 du Samedi 11 mai 1996.
Villalón, Leonardo A., 1995, *Islamic Society and State Power in Sénégal. Disciples and Citizens in Fatick*. African Studies. Cambridge University Press.

SECTION III

LAND AND HOUSING

As a basic human right, shelter is a central concern in all the cities of Africa. In-migration and the natural growth of urban areas have created a great demand for housing. However, urban authorities and private developers have not been able to meet the increasing demand. Consequently, informal settlements have emerged and appear to be sprawling unchecked. Not only do such settlements contain sub-standard dwellings, the overcrowding also causes severe problems of sanitation and solid waste disposal.

In the face of defaulting urban authorities, urban residents have taken initiatives themselves, with a view to solving their shelter problems. The three contributions in this section discuss various ways in which people try to address this problem, including the acquisition of urban land for building purposes. The empirical cases are drawn from Accra, the capital city of Ghana, the secondary city of Eldoret in Kenya, and Zimbabwe.

In Ghana, the responsibility for urban management has been devolved to decentralised district assemblies, which have become the basic units for political decision-making, administration, planning and implementation of urban programmes, including revenue-raising. However, Katherine Gough and Paul Yankson show that the efficiency of these district assemblies has not improved significantly after the introduction of decentralised structures—mainly due to inadequate revenues, interference from the central level and local level patronage relations. In response to persistent urban problems organisations of civil society have taken up the challenges that the district assemblies have failed to meet. The relationship between the state and civil society has remained an uneasy one.

In their contribution Gough and Yankson analyse various civil society initiatives in the Ga and Tema Districts of the Greater Accra Metropolitan Area, focusing on the relations between three main actors: NGOs/CBOs, customary authorities (chiefs) and the decentralised state organs. The role of the chiefs is particularly important in the conversion of agricultural land under communal ownership to housing purposes. Even so, the land tenure system is changing and a quasi-market in land is emerging. The chiefs' and residents' associations as well as other NGOs, are involved in urban infrastructure development (roads, water supplies, waste disposal, etc.). The NGOs are partly dependent on external funding sources.

Sarah Gitau's contribution addresses the problems poor people face when acquiring land for housing purposes. Throughout the history of Kenya, struggles over land ownership, have been fierce which is seen as a manifestation of power and wealth. In the scramble for land the poor have tended to become marginalised. Not only are they generally short of money to buy at the going market rates, the legal framework is also so complex that many additional hurdles are put in the way of the poorer echelons. Altogether thirty pieces of legislation have a bearing on the land question in Kenya, causing great confusion and inefficient management. The complexity of the allocation procedures also gives rise to irregularities based on nepotism and politicised clientelism.

In the face of severe housing shortages, the urban authorities have not been able to provide adequate housing or serviced building plots. As a result, individuals and groups have had no option but to face the challenge on their own. After independence, the formation of land-buying companies became a vehicle for the poor to acquire land for any purpose—whether for farming purposes or housing development in urban areas. Typically, a group of prospective buyers would form a land-buying company to pool the necessary funds for purchasing a farm near an urban centre. After acquisition it would be sub-divided and the company dissolved.

Gitau makes an empirical examination of two land-buying companies in Eldoret, a fast-growing secondary town in Kenya—focusing on their achievements for the benefit of the members, and their internal management problems. The latter derive largely from the lack of skills and experience on the part of the leaders as well as from political interference. The political dimensions can only be appreciated within the context of the contemporary ethnic constellations in Eldoret; the membership of both these land-buying companies is exclusively Kikuyu, whereas the predominant ethnic group in Eldoret is Kalenjin—the core constituency of the incumbent central government.

Amin Kamete's contribution documents the proportions of the housing problem in Zimbabwe, i.e. the severe shortage of housing units at affordable prices for the low-income strata of the urban population. Towards ameliorating the crisis, caused by the inability of the state to meet the growing demand, there has been an expansion in the number of co-operatives, albeit not confined to the housing sector. Their membership is drawn from the official housing waiting lists kept by local authorities. They may be either community based or work-based. As popular associations the housing co-operatives have a dual objective: (a) acquisition of urban land for housing purposes; and (b) financing and construction of dwellings.

Governed by the Co-operative Societies Act these co-operatives have acquired a status as legal persons in their own right, capable of entering into contracts, taking up loans, suing and being sued. This is a major operational advantage. On the other hand, since housing is such a hot political issue the incumbent political party has taken a keen interest in them, arguably affecting their mode of operation.

Significant achievements have been made in redressing the housing problem but Kamete points out that expectations on the part of the co-operative members have been too high, and management practices have not been up to par, leading, in turn, to inefficiency and in some cases to indebtedness. Also, affordability remains a problem for most low-income members. Overall, therefore, progress has not matched the initial expectations.

CHAPTER 8

The Role of Civil Society in Urban Management in Accra, Ghana

Katherine V. Gough and Paul W.K. Yankson

INTRODUCTION

It is estimated that over half of the developing world will be urban by the year 2010, and that the majority of the world's largest cities will soon be found in the developing world (UNCHS, 1996). Although Africa is the least urbanised continent, many of its cities are experiencing the highest growth rates in the world. As levels of urbanisation rise, the successful management of urban development processes becomes of increasing importance. Many cities have expanded without formal planning and there is a severe lack of services, resulting in a common reference to the "urban crisis" in Africa (Stren and White, 1989). The current urban management paradigm, as promoted by the World Bank and other lending agencies, extols the virtues of decentralisation of government agencies. Formal government institutions, however, are not the only forces managing the urban environment, and it is increasingly being recognised that a range of civil society organisations also play a pivotal role in many African cities (McCarney et al., 1995).

In Ghana, the responsibility for urban management has officially been devolved to decentralised district assemblies. The ability of the district assemblies to adequately plan and manage the urban environment, however, is very limited, hence a range of civil society organisations also play an important role. This paper analyses the role of civil society in urban management in Accra. By focusing on three very different parts of the city, it is shown how important, but also how complex and diverse, the involvement of civil society in urban management has become. The paper is divided into three parts. First, the concepts of decentralisation and civil society are discussed, particularly in relation to Ghana. Second, after outlining the operation of the district assemblies in Accra, three case studies are used to illustrate differing aspects of the role of civil society in urban management: a peri-urban settlement where the customary authorities still play an important role; a newly developing area where a community based organisation (CBO) has been established by the new residents; and an inner-city settlement where a non-governmental organisation (NGO) plays a leading role. In the conclusion, the problems and prospects for the role of civil society in urban management are discussed.

Acknowledgements
The fieldwork on which this paper is based was funded by the Danish Council for Development Research and the Faculty of Natural Sciences, University of Ghana.

URBAN MANAGEMENT IN GHANA

The concept urban management can "convey an objective, identify a process or describe a structure" (Stren, 1992:538), hence definitions vary widely and the elusiveness of the concept is widely acknowledged (Stren, 1993; Mattingly, 1994). The focus of the urban management paradigm promoted by the World Bank has changed over time from projects in housing and infrastructure in the 1970s, to city-wide urban management activities in the 1980s, to decentralisation and good governance in the 1990s (McCarney, 1996). Correspondingly, the responsibility for managing the urban environment has shifted from being considered primarily a task for central and municipal governments, to a recognition of the role played by civil society, including NGOs, CBOs, interest groups and the private sector (Wekwete, 1997). The urban management approach of the World Bank, however, is still being criticised for being too state-centred, too top-down, and too narrow, formalised and technocratic (Aina, 1997). It has been claimed that there is still a need to "respect and incorporate the wide range of human practices and actions utilised by the poorer sectors or communities of African cities in providing themselves with urban services" (Aina, 1997:421). This paper considers a range of ways in which the inhabitants of Accra try to gain access to services. First, however, two aspects of urban management, namely decentralisation and civil society, will be discussed in relation to Ghana.

Decentralisation

Decentralisation is generally seen as a way of improving urban management by reducing the size and power of the central state and improving the accountability of development planning and participation at the local level (Crook, 1994). It has long been a topic of discussion in African politics. In the late 1950s and early 1960s, the discussion of decentralisation was associated with the concern to create democratic structures after the imposition of colonial rule. During the 1970s, as the ineffectiveness of continued centralised planning became increasingly clear, decentralisation was advocated as a way out (Cheema and Rondinelli, 1983). During the 1990s, decentralisation has become increasingly in vogue with its adoption by the World Bank and other lending agencies as a policy towards achieving good governance.

In Ghana, attempts to establish a decentralised local government system date back to the middle of the 19th century when municipal and town councils were set up in the major cities. They proved to be relatively ineffective, though, and Ghana emerged from the period of colonial rule with a centralised political system characterised by a strong central government and a weak local government system. The post-independence modernisation and national development strategies further strengthened central government, resulting in a lack of effective administrative machinery at the local level and the marginalisation of communities and individuals in the decision-making process. Since the 1970s, there have been several attempts to reform the local government system and make planning and the administrative system more responsive to development needs at the grassroots. However, it was not until 1988, when the PNDC government of President Rawlings increased the number of districts from 65 to 110 and set up assemblies to administer the district's affairs, that a decentralised system of planning and administration became firmly established.[1] The introduction of the decentralised district assemblies has been attributed to a range of factors, including the macro-economic policies pursued under structural adjustment programmes; the international funding agencies' desire to establish democratic structures, strengthen local government and instigate bottom-up decision-making to achieve greater participation in the development process; the demand (internal and external) for a devolution of power to ensure efficient mobilisation and utilisation of local resources on a sustainable basis; the weaknesses and shortcomings of both pre- and post-independence local government systems; and the government's genuine commitment to decentralisation and grassroots participation in development activities (Republic of Ghana et al., n.d.).

The district assemblies have become the basic administrative, political and planning units of the country, incorporating typical local government functions and powers, including revenue raising (Crook and Manor, 1995). The primary role of the district assemblies is responsibility for the overall development of the district, including the formulation of a development plan and budget. Many of the assemblies' functions are related to the provision of services at the local level (Mohan, 1996a; Ayee, 1997). The main sources of funding for the district assemblies are: local taxes including general rates, special rates, fees and licenses; commission from customarily controlled land; and grants from central government (Oquaye, 1995; Mohan, 1996b).[2] At least two-thirds of assembly members are elected by their constituencies on a non-partisan basis and the other third is appointed by the central government, as is the District Chief Executive who heads the assembly (Shillington, 1992). The first assembly elections were held in late 1988/early1989. Below the assemblies are three further tiers with no independent financing or functions of their own. These are the sub-metropolitan area, the town or area councils and the grassroots unit committees set up in 1991 (Crook and Manor, 1995). It is through the devolution of power to the district assemblies that the government is seeking to achieve its visions of democratisation, transparency and public accountability, participation of the majority of the people in decision-making, effective policy and development planning, resource mobilisation and allocation, and day-to-day administration of the country (Zanu, n.d.).

Despite the high ideals of decentralisation, the co-ordination of planning and enforcement of development control have not become more effective in the urban areas of Ghana. The planning aspect of the decentralisation programme is very weak and the programme for administrative decentralisation has not been fully implemented; the sub-metropolitan structures, as well as the town councils and unit committee system have not yet been fully established.

---

[1] The role of the District Assemblies is outlined in PNDC Law 207, and updated in the 1992 constitution of Ghana, as well as in the 1993 Local Government Act 462.

[2] The District Assembly Common Fund (DACF), a constitutional provision that a minimum of 5 per cent of the national income be distributed to the assemblies on the basis of a formula prepared by the administrator of the fund and approved by parliament, has been implemented since 1994.

The poor performance of the district assemblies has become a source of deep frustration for many Ghanaians, as the high expectations that were aroused have not been fulfilled (Gough, 1999). The district assemblies have ended up in a vicious circle in which they are unable to carry out development projects because they have little revenue, resulting in the local population losing interest and refusing to pay their local taxes (Crook, 1994; Ayee, 1995). The central government has not provided the district assemblies with sufficient funding partly due to pressure from the World Bank, through the Ministry of Finance, to keep down government expenditure as part of the structural adjustment programmes. Some district assemblies have been able to make some improvements in their areas, particularly in the education and health sectors, but they have not had the resources to improve infrastructure and services. As the level of services has declined, elements of civil society have become increasingly involved in urban management.

Civil society

The concept of civil society has been widely debated to the extent that "notions of civil society are as varied and contested as those of the state" (Aina, 1997:417).[3] Following Aina (1997:418), civil society can be defined as "the sphere of social interaction that comprises the intimate sphere (family), associational life, social movements, and forms of public communication operating in the arena of the organised non-state, non-market sector with origins in both the modern and traditional bases of society." Both the nature and overall intensity of civil society vary over time. With increasing urbanisation, civil society has evolved a range of mechanisms for solving daily problems (Walton, 1998).

The relevance of the term civil society in relation to African society has been a subject of debate and it has been argued that many attempts to apply civil society in the African context have been either ethnocentric or historically insensitive in their analysis (Mamdani and Wamba-dia-Wamba, 1995; Mamdani, 1996). Civil society has long existed in Africa but became dormant or was stifled during the early post-colonial phase. In the 1980s, associations of many different types proliferated in most African countries (Widner, 1997). Contemporary civil society is primarily urban-based and consists of a large body of associations and civic institutions, including trade unions, religious associations, women's organisations, youth groups, ethnic associations, professional associations, and NGOs including community and neighbourhood groups (Aina, 1997). There are, however, very significant differences between African states in the extent to which they have a functioning civil society (Clapham and Wiseman, 1995).

Throughout Ghana's political history, there has been an uneasy relationship between civil society and the state (Chazan, 1983; Gyimah-Boadi, 1994; Nugent, 1996). Since the late 1960s, Ghana has been characterised as having "a cycle of short-lived democratic republics being overthrown by the military,

---

[3] See McIllwaine (1998) and Sjögren (1998) for outlines of the discussion of civil society.

leading to state repression of civil society, and years later a resurgence of civil society leading to the reinstitution of democratic rule" (Snook et al., 1998:19). Today, Ghana has many civil society organisations including trade unions, professional body associations, religious organisations, youth groups, trade and artisanal associations, and social, ethnic and home-town associations. These organisations are mainly urban based and most are formally structured, with their own constitutions and officers. Members of the associations usually pay monthly or annual dues and, in turn, they derive certain benefits, mainly social but sometimes material. These organisations usually function independently of the government. However, the relationship between most civil society organisations and district assemblies has been found to be good in terms of their degree of consultation and co-operation (Snook et al., 1998). Several aspects of associational life in Ghana will be outlined below, both customary authorities and newly established NGOs.

Prior to colonial rule, traditional rulers, usually chiefs, exercised great powers within their jurisdictional areas. The functions of the chiefs were religious, administrative, judicial, legislative, military, trusteeship and cultural. The chiefs were assisted by elders who were appointed on the basis of lineage or personal achievements. One of their main roles was the maintenance of peaceful relations within the community and its defence from external attack. During the period of colonial rule, the British colonial government involved the native political and social institutions in the administration of the country. Eminent chiefs were recruited and assigned responsibility for maintaining law and order, collecting taxes, settling disputes and managing essential socio-economic services (Asibuo, 1992). From 1951 to 1982, chiefs were represented on all local councils (except for a brief period during the regime of the Convention Peoples Party (CPP) of the late Kwame Nkrumah) but since 1982 this role has been removed. The political authority of chiefs today is almost entirely confined to traditional matters such as arbitration in local disputes. Chiefs are elected to serve on national bodies, such as the Judicial Council, but are forbidden from taking part in party politics and can only serve on district assemblies if they are included among the assembly members appointed by the President. The chieftancy system is very closely linked with the family system and ownership of land (Harvey, 1966). Prior to colonial rule and government intervention in the administration of land, all land was customarily controlled; ownership was corporate and vested in the stool or skin represented by a chief, or in a family (Aidoo, 1996). British colonial land policies resulted in a complex tenurial system shaped by both customary land laws and the British conveyancing system (Larbi, 1995). Control over land is still one of the most important roles of the chiefs today and has gained increasing significance as the land has increased in value (Gough and Yankson, 2000).[4] Chiefs also still have roles as religious and spiritual leaders and perform customary rites, but

---

[4] According to the Ghanaian constitution, stool lands cannot be sold freehold, however, lease-holds may be sold. The sale of stool land is managed by the chiefs and elders, though the Town and Country Planning Department (TCPD) is charged with developing land-use plans and plot layouts. However, as land is being sold at a far faster rate than the TCPD can produce plans, they are often prepared by a surveyor employed by a chief.

these roles have been greatly undermined by the spread of Christianity. The chiefs, though, remain important agents in the development of their areas, as they are the foci for the mobilisation of their people for community action.

A more recent element of civil society is NGOs, which are often viewed as being the primary agents of civil society today (Clark, 1997). NGOs have been the subject of much definitional scrutiny, with a wide range of organisations being defined as NGOs, including social and cultural groups, religious groups and other more specific task-related groups (Lee, 1994). A distinction is now often drawn between NGOs and CBOs with the latter being more firmly based in a community, whereas the former are often led by outsiders who obtain external funding. In many developing countries, NGOs and CBOs have been instrumental in improving the access of urban communities, particularly the urban poor, to essential environmental resources and services such as water, sanitation and drainage (Hardoy et al., 1990). Although the activities of foreign NGOs in the Third World have been widely documented, the contributions of indigenous NGOs and CBOs in development have not been studied so extensively. Many such organisations make positive contributions within their respective neighbourhoods, cities and countries but are not known beyond their borders (Badu and Parker, 1992). In the late 1970s, a few NGOs were established in Accra, but many more have emerged in recent years. The NGOs have varied orientations, but are mostly externally funded. Most of the NGOs operate nationally, usually working either in rural areas or in inner-city areas; few have chosen to operate in peri-urban areas, which is lamented by officials of Ga District Assembly. The CBOs operating in Accra focus mainly on environmental and waste management issues and on the provision of basic services. They have emerged not only in low-income areas but also in high-income areas, where the inhabitants have formed residents' associations in an attempt to meet some of their most pressing needs.

MANAGING THE URBAN ENVIRONMENT OF ACCRA

Accra is the capital city and the largest urban centre of Ghana. In 1984 Accra had a population of almost one million; today the population of Greater Accra Metropolitan Area (GAMA) is estimated to be over 2 million. This rapid growth has resulted in Accra, like many other sub-Saharan cities, facing severe environmental problems due to the shortage of infrastructure and services (Benneh et al., 1993). GAMA consists of Accra Metropolitan Area (AMA), Ga District and Tema District. The rate of population growth in GAMA has been very rapid, with all three districts experiencing average annual growth rates of more than 3 per cent since 1960. Although approximately three-quarters of the population of GAMA is located in AMA, Ga and Tema Districts have experienced higher growth rates (Table 8:1). Ga District has had the highest population growth rate of the three, due to the development of new housing in the peri-urban area and the movement of tenants from the inner-city areas to the old settlements in the periphery to escape overcrowding and high rents.

Accra Metropolitan Assembly has been concerned mainly with stimulating the economic growth of the central business district through a programme of redevelopment and upgrading of communities in central Accra. In Ga District Assembly, there is currently no master development plan for the whole district and urban development is taking place at a faster pace than they can produce the plans. Ga District Assembly does not have the necessary resources to provide services such as electricity, water, roads, waste disposal, telephones and drainage to the communities in the district. Waste management is particularly weak; there are no authorised refuse dumps in the district (though one of AMA's two waste disposal sites is located in Ga District near Gbawe) and there is only one vehicle for emptying septic tanks, which most of the time is on loan to Tema. The provision of services within the district is supposed to be partly funded by development fees that all land acquirers are required to pay to the district assembly. However, many of the land acquirers do not pay these fees and the limited finance raised is used on recurrent expenditure rather than capital expenditure. Moreover, Ga District Assembly has not been able to reach an agreement concerning the collection of development levies from stools and families who sell plots in the district, which could provide an important source of funding for service provision. The district assembly expects central government to help with service provision, but the responsible national agencies are unable to meet the demand in GAMA.

Table 8:1. *Population Trends in Greater Accra Metropolitan Area, 1969–1984*

District	Population			Annual growth rate	
	1960	1970	1984	1960–70	1970–84
Accra	388,396	636,667	969,195	5.1	3.1
Tema	27,127	102,431	190,917	14.2	4.5
Ga	33,907	66,336	132,786	6.9	5.3
Total GAMA	449,430	805,434	1,292,898	6.0	3.5

Source: Ghana Population Census 1984 (latest available census)

Different elements of civil society have adopted the role of urban managers and service providers in the absence of adequate provision by the state. Three different examples are presented below covering both a range of differing geographical locations and inhabitants with differing socio-economic resources. The specific examples have been chosen as they represent relative success stories as to how civil society can participate in urban management.

Gbawe—An indigenous peri-urban settlement

The peri-urban area of Accra is experiencing rapid transformation. Originally the land was covered by forest, but this has been cleared over the years by members of the indigenous communities to facilitate farming. Only a decade ago, the area still consisted of dispersed rural settlements where subsistence agriculture was practised. This agricultural land is now rapidly being transformed into a residential area. Although land on the urban fringe is still owned on a communal basis and dealings in land are founded on the principles of customary land ownership and tenure, a land market has emerged in which outsiders purchase plots (Kasanga et al., 1996). Peri-urban Accra is now characterised by a wide area of land scattered with large, single family villas at various stages of completion, in the midst of which are fairly compact indigenous villages consisting of compound earth houses (Gough and Yankson, 1997).

Gbawe is an old farming village situated approximately 10 kilometres west of the centre of Accra.[5] According to oral tradition, a hunter migrated from among people who had settled on the coast in Ga Mashi (now Accra). He used to hunt in a large, uninhabited area and finally settled with his family at the present site, which was referred to as Gbalowe meaning hunter's village. The residents of Gbawe were traditionally farmers. Although farming still provides an occupation for a number of residents, it is declining in importance as the land is increasingly being sold for residential purposes. Sand and stone winning provide alternative employment for some of the residents, though most of the women work in food preparation and trading. Very few of the inhabitants have been educated beyond middle/junior school and over a third of the women have had no education at all. The population is predominantly young with almost 40 per cent under the age of 15 and only about 10 per cent over the age of 50 (Gough and Yankson, 1997). Most of the inhabitants have grown up within the settlement or within the region. Many are indigenous Ga, but strangers have also moved into the area to rent rooms.[6] As in other indigenous villages, the chiefs and elders have traditionally been the leaders and main decision-makers. Service provision used to be no problem for the inhabitants as they could generally rely on natural resources. However, as Gbawe has now been more or less surrounded by newly built houses, the traditional sources of water, modes of waste and garbage disposal, as well as the "free-range" toilet method, are no longer sustainable (Yankson and Gough, 1999).

In Gbawe, the chief and elders are directly involved in urban management and have become the main actors in improving the level of services. The chief and elders have direct control over a considerable area of land, part of which has been sold to individuals for building purposes. As the planning authorities have not yet drawn up a development plan for the area, the chief and elders have employed surveyors themselves to plan the plot layout. This can lead to problems, as the surveyors used are not always very accurate, leading to disputes between new land acquirers, and as the space allocated to communal activities is often inadequate, if existing at all. However, unlike in many other indigenous settlements, the chief and elders have set aside a large portion of land for the indigenous population, to ensure that they will not be landless in the future.

Since the new land acquirers only pay "drink money" for the plot leaseholds, the payments are not officially recorded, but the amount paid approaches the market value of the land. As the demand for land has increased,

---

[5] A census survey was conducted by the authors of all households in Gbawe from which a 15 per cent random sample was taken for a questionnaire survey. Seven in-depth interviews were also held as well as focus group discussions with the chief and elders, the women's group and the youth group.

[6] A stranger is a non-subject of a clan, tribe, skin or stool, hence the term stranger is used to refer to migrants in the host communities. As regards access to land, indigenes and strangers are not on an equal footing and strangers do not have a communal right to land.

the money raised from the sale of the leaseholds is a not inconsiderable amount. The chief and elders of Gbawe have the right to dispose of the profits from the land sales themselves. They have used some of the proceeds for infra- structural development including extending electricity to the village, providing public toilets and baths, bringing in piped water, and improving the access road. A new palace has also been built for the chief. Ironically, considerable sums of money have also been spent on court cases to settle land disputes with neighbouring stools. The chief and elders of Gbawe are proud of the way in which they are managing their urban environment, and they are praised by the youth and women's groups.

Gbawe is often cited within Accra as an example of how customary land tenure can work to the benefit of the indigenous people (Kasanga et al., 1996). It is important to recognise, though, that not all the chiefs and elders in the peri-urban area have been equally successful in their urban management prac- tices. There are many instances of the money raised from land transactions being misused, and if the chief or land-owning family is resident outside of an indigenous village, the money is rarely invested there. In many indigenous villages, the inhabitants are thus increasingly looking towards their assembly member to solve their practical problems (Gough and Yankson, 1997). As- sembly members, however, cannot hold a meeting in a settlement without first contacting the chief who may also be highly influential in their election. Hence, the nature of the relationship between the chief and the assembly member can be of crucial importance. In Gbawe, the chief and assemblyman co-operated closely and the assemblyman was involved in organising commu- nal labour to maintain a clean environment in the village. In other settlements, the chief and assemblyman scarcely communicate, thus restricting the chances of improving the level of services.

East Legon—A newly developing area

East Legon is located approximately 13 kilometres north east of central Accra just off the Accra-Aburi road near the University of Ghana and is a newly developing high-class residential area. In 1944, the government acquired a large tract of land (approximately 1,500 hectares) belonging to the people of La Bawaleshie, Shiashie and other communities in the area, purportedly to extend the airport. This land has subsequently been demarcated and lease- holds allocated to individuals, many of whom are, or have connections to, influential public figures (Kufogbe, 1996). In the part known as East Legon Extension, house owners bought their plot leaseholds either through the La Bawaleshie chief or directly from the land-owning chief in Labadi.[7] Most of the new house owners acquired the land during the past 20 years, and espe- cially during the past 10 years. The houses that are being built are mainly large, prestigious, single-family villas, but as access to finance for building is very limited, many of the houses remain empty at various stages of comple-

---

[7] In East Legon Extension a questionnaire was conducted by the authors with 20 house owners and a focus group discussion was held with committee members of the residents' association.

tion. Those who have completed their dwellings and are now resident in the area are mainly well educated, middle-class public servants and business executives, most of whom originate from outside Greater Accra Region. Many of the new owners have funded the building of their houses through savings earned abroad. Most of them are male, married and many are over 50 years of age. The area is inhabited mainly by property owners, few are tenants.

The vast majority of plots in East Legon were not serviced when purchased and some were not even accessible by a dirt track. East Legon is within the jurisdiction of Accra Metropolitan Authority (AMA). AMA, however, does not even have any plans for developing the area, as it has deemed the needs of the high-density, inner-city areas to be far greater and, hence, has directed its limited resources elsewhere. The national service agencies also claim not to have sufficient resources to invest in infrastructure in the area. Government officials maintain that the chiefs have a responsibility to channel some of their profit from land sales into improving the level of services in the area. The chiefs, though, claim that the provision of services is the responsibility of the government. Since the chief who sold the plots in East Legon Extension is not resident in the area but is based in Labadi, there is little chance of any money being invested in improvements to the area. Meanwhile, the inhabitants of the newly developing area are left with grossly inadequate, if any, services. Although many of the new land acquirers have had contact with the local chief during negotiations on the purchase of the land, none of them believe he will come to their aid in the provision of services. Likewise, there is widespread disillusionment amongst the inhabitants with the district assembly system and the ability of assembly members to improve conditions in the area. Many of the inhabitants did not vote in the most recent district assembly elections and few of them even know who their assembly member is. The new land acquirers, therefore, have formed their own action groups called residents' associations to try to improve the standard of infrastructure in the area.

Within East Legon, there are several residents' associations operating. One of these is East Legon Extension Residents' Association, which was formed in the early 1990s by a few residents who were particularly concerned to liaise with the authorities over service provision in the area. The association has grown to have about 80 members, of whom about 20 regularly attend monthly meetings. There is an executive committee that makes plans to put before the members for discussion, and decisions are taken on a consensus basis by all members present at a meeting. Working committees are set up when necessary to take responsibility for specific projects. The association outlined its two main objectives as improved fellowship and services in the area. The first project undertaken was to improve the roads. The Department of Feeder Roads provided machines to do the work but the residents had to pay for the fuel and a small fee plus small payments to the workers. They paid for the gravel themselves and have subsequently used communal labour to make small repairs. Their second project was to improve the electricity supply. The main lines were provided by the Ghana Electricity Company while the association had to pay for wires and poles and give "tips" here and there. The third major project was to improve the water supply. The Ghana Water and Sewage Company installed a six-inch water pipe along the roads in the area from which residents had to make their own connections. The success of the association in gaining these services probably has much to do with the high level of education of many of the residents and their influential contacts in various government offices.

The residents' association has also adopted a town planning role to ensure that the zoning regulations and development control system are observed by both the original land owners and the new land acquirers. More specifically, it attempts to ensure that no-one builds in spaces earmarked for roads or communal areas, and that the chief does not sell plots designated for these uses. The association also has a social role in facilitating contact between new residents and arranging social functions. In fact, despite all the material improvements the association had made, the members said that its biggest achievement had been in bringing people together. By working together residents had been able to improve security in the area by establishing a watchdog society and by mobilising the police to check their problems.

The role of the residents' associations should not be romanticised, though, and they operate out of necessity under far from ideal conditions. One of their major problems is that people move into an area at different times and it can be very difficult to get those who have not yet moved in to contribute, either financially or manually to communal work. They have very limited resources and are constrained by lack of finance. This often results in solutions which may be adequate for the present, but which in the future, when the area is more densely populated, will no longer be sufficient. Officers of the East Legon Extension Residents' Association claimed that their greatest frustration was that the government had not come to their aid. They complained that whenever the association tried to meet the relevant officials in AMA they were never available, hence, they were unable to find out about AMA's plans for the area. Their hope for the future was to get everyone who has a property or is building in the area to join the association and to liaise more with other residents' associations to ensure better co-ordination between areas. This highlights the additional problem of the lack of co-ordination between service provision in adjacent areas that arises when residents' associations are responsible for installing services.

Nima—An inner-city immigrant area

Nima lies just north of the centre of Accra. It is a densely populated low-income settlement inhabited primarily by Muslims from the north. The area consists of largely unplanned compound houses narrowly separated from one another by narrow paths and smelling drains, and has been described as being a "haphazard mish-mash of noise and people" (Brydon and Legge, 1996:29). Nima was founded in 1931, when the Odoi Kwao family granted right of settlement to Mallam Futa who was a Muslim cattle dealer. Nima grew steadily during the 1930s and 1940s, attracting mainly northerners. During the second World War, the establishment of an American military base not far from Nima caused an upsurge in the population of the area, due to the job opportunities which the base offered. After the war, many of the ex-servicemen settled in Nima because rents were low and there was plenty of land available for building. Until the mid-1950s, Nima was outside the Accra city boundary was and thus not subject to planning regulations. Pipe-borne water first arrived in the 1950s and public latrines and electricity in the 1960s (Brydon and Legge, 1996). Nima developed a reputation for having cheap accommodation and continued to grow rapidly, housing an ethnically diverse population. Houses were built in a haphazard manner and the area soon became overcrowded. By 1984, the population density of Nima had reached 335 people per hectare. The level of services continues to be very poor: there are only a few public water taps in the area, the number of public latrines is hopelessly inadequate, there are very few drains, and waste management facilities are grossly inadequate resulting in the streams which cross the area being full of garbage. The health and education facilities are also totally inadequate.

Each ethnic group within Nima has its own chief or leader. There are also a range of self-help groups or clubs that perform largely social functions, such as assisting their members in times of bereavement, sickness or other times of difficulty. Brydon and Legge (1996) claim, though, that the inhabitants of Nima have had little experience of bottom-up community development, and the little that has taken place has been ethnically fragmented and episodic. However, in recent years, several NGOs and CBOs have emerged in Nima, formed mainly in order to confront the problems of sanitation and waste management. One such organisation is the Ayawaso Committee for a Clean Environment (ACCEN), which was established in 1997 following a visit of the President of Ghana, J.J. Rawlings, to a Muslim festival in Nima, during which he expressed concern about the poor sanitation in the area. Local leaders, tribal chiefs, opinion leaders and politicians took up his challenge to do something about the problem.[8] With initial support of five million cedis (approximately 2,700 US$) from the Nation of Islam (a Muslim organisation based in the US) and some funds generated from within the area and elsewhere, a planning committee was set up to create an organisational structure for the association. ACCEN has an executive council, a general council, and five sub-committees of the general council. The executive committee makes proposals that are presented for discussion and ratified by the general council. All the assemblymen and women of the area are ex-officio members of the executive committee. The chiefs attend meetings and offer advice and suggestions. ACCEN started with 20 core members, half of whom were chiefs and half opinion leaders, but it now has approximately 500 registered members, mainly local residents.

ACCEN aims to assist the community in mobilising human and material resources to confront the problem of poor environmental sanitation. It organises communal labour to desilt gutters and carry out clean-up campaigns. Those who participate in the activities receive either a small cash payment or

---

[8] The information on ACCEN was collected by the second author and is based on an interview held with the chairman, a focus group discussion held with key members of the organisation, and an analysis of their official records.

refreshments after the campaign. In the short time since its establishment, ACCEN has made an important impact on the sanitation of the area. Thus ACCEN is providing real support to AMA and the sub-metropolitan area office in discharging their sanitation and waste management functions. ACCEN also has more long-term aims to tackle the root causes of environmental degradation by tackling the problems of high population density and poverty. ACCEN, therefore, intends to assist the community in the future in a range of ways: through income-generating activities; by the provision of community facilities such as schools; by fighting social vices and problems such as drug abuse, teenage pregnancies and crime; and in bringing about social cohesion within the community. To date, however, ACCEN has been entirely preoccupied with sanitation. ACCEN's success so far in this respect has been due to a range of factors, including the dedicated leadership provided by its current executive, especially its chairman, who is also a chief; the involvement of tribal chiefs and opinion leaders who are highly respected in the community; and the relative homogeneity of the community in terms of residents' migrant status as well as the dominance of Muslims, for whom their religion acts as a rallying point for community action. The traditional as well as religious leaders and the mosques are used as points of contact and media for disseminating information about the activities of ACCEN. They are also used for settling disputes among its members.

ACCEN is registered with AMA and the Ayawaso sub-metropolitan area office in Nima. AMA has provided ACCEN with some tools for its work and has promised cash and other logistical help in the future. ACCEN has established a fairly strong working relationship with some government departments and agencies but claimed that this relationship is not entirely unproblematic, since it is sometimes seen as a competitor rather than a partner to the government in its development efforts. Although ACCEN has forged some links with other CBOs and NGOs, it is difficult for them to co-ordinate their activities. The traditional respect accorded the chiefs, however, has without doubt been a major factor in the mobilisation of the people and their enthusiastic response to the clean-up campaigns and hence the level of success of ACCEN's activities.

CONCLUSIONS

Elements of civil society are increasingly becoming involved in urban management in Africa (Wekwete, 1997). Ghana is no exception to this trend. Despite the introduction of decentralised district assemblies, the standard of urban planning and management by the state is very low. Consequently the level of services in Accra, as in many African cities, is very poor. Neither the national service agencies nor the district assemblies have the resources to install the infrastructure required by the city's inhabitants. It is not only the urban poor who are affected but, as Peil (1994) has claimed, environmental problems are part of the everyday experience of most urban dwellers in sub-Saharan Africa. This paper has shown how, in three different areas of Accra, differing elements in civil society are involved in urban management, in particular in attempting to solve the problem of lack of services. These different solutions have arisen due to the differing socio-economic level and ethnic composition of the residents, and the differing locations of the settlements within the city. The implications of these differences will be summarised here and the need for greater co-operation between the different organisations stressed.

The three settlements discussed in this chapter are: Gbawe, an old settlement located in the peri-urban area and inhabited mainly by low-income indigenous Ga; Nima, a densely populated inner city area facing severe environmental problems and inhabited mainly by low-income northerners; and East Legon, a newly developing area where middle- and high-income earners are building large villas. The decentralised state, represented by the assembly members, does play a role in urban management in Accra, though not the major role it has been assigned. In Nima, assembly members have been involved in the work of the NGO ACCEN, and in Gbawe the assemblyman works closely with the chief, whereas in East Legon the residents are totally disillusioned with the entire district assembly system. In all of these areas, elements of civil society have assumed an important role in urban management.

In the low-income areas of Nima and Gbawe, the role of the traditional authorities, especially the chiefs, is still very important. In Gbawe, the money gained from the selling of plot leaseholds has been re-invested in the community and hence the level of services has been improved. As the inhabitants of Nima are from the north, their chiefs do not own any land in the area and as a result do not have a source of funds that can be invested. The chiefs, though, have been instrumental in rallying the people and involving them in the work of the NGO ACCEN. In East Legon, however, the new residents have little contact with the chief; although they have obtained their plot leaseholds from him, they feel little allegiance to him as they are from many different ethnic groups. They have no faith in the chief investing in improving the services in the area, as chiefs generally consider the installation of services in newly developing areas to be the responsibility of the state. Even the indigenous settlement of La Bawaleshie, located within East Legon, has not benefited from the land sales, as the La Bawaleshie chief is only a caretaker chief; the land-owning chief lives in Labadi and is not interested in investing in improvements in La Bawaleshie. Hence, in contrast to the situation in Gbawe, the level of services in La Bawaleshie remains very low. This indicates that it is not possible to generalise about, nor rely on, traditional authorities in indigenous settlements providing services.

Although the chiefs play an important role in Nima, the leading actors are various NGOs. The NGO ACCEN was established with outside money and has managed to improve the standard of the urban environment in the area. Nima has managed to attract NGOs for a range of reasons: it suffers from a severe lack of services; it is highly visible, being located in the inner city; the inhabitants have low incomes; and the predominance of Muslim northerners has attracted funding from the world-wide Muslim community. Their common religion seems to have served as a rallying point for the inhabitants of Nima, which, combined with the close involvement of both their chiefs and assembly members, has led to ACCEN's success. Neither Gbawe nor East Legon are attractive to NGOs in the same way.

In East Legon, most of the new home-owners belong to the upper- and middle-income brackets who are conscious of their investments and wish to protect them by ensuring that the area where they have bought a plot does not deteriorate into a slum. As they receive minimal support from the chiefs or assembly members they have formed their own associations to tackle the problems they face, especially lack of services. By lobbying the service agencies through contacts and by contributing both financially and manually they have managed to improve the level of services, as well as the safety and social cohesiveness of the area. The fact that they have been able to achieve so much through their CBO lies in their relatively high education and resource levels, which increase their bargaining power with the service agencies and their ability to contribute financially (though this remains limited). Areas inhabited by lower-income groups are much more restricted in their ability to establish self-financed and self-organised CBOs.

This study of three areas of Accra has shown that a range of groups within civil society is involved in urban management, the nature of their specific roles being both complex and interdependent at times. However, despite the success of civil society in the sphere of urban management, one of the main disadvantages is the piecemeal nature of the resultant service provision. There is a clear problem of lack of co-ordination both between the various elements of civil society and between civil society and the state. Although the state is beginning to acknowledge the role of civil society in urban management, there are no formal structures to incorporate the organisations in the decision-making process, nor to co-ordinate the activities taking place. Formal relationships need to be established between the elected local governments and civil society so that the former can be more demand-responsive and the latter better co-ordinated (Wekwete, 1997). As the work of most civil society organisations complements that of the state, the state has everything to gain by supporting their activities. Urban governments need to have allies in the community to enable them to mobilise the necessary resources for sustained urban development (Swilling, 1996). If no action is taken and they fail, civil society may start to challenge rather than co-operate with the state.

References

Aidoo, J.B., 1996, "Tenancy and the land reform debate in Ghana", *Our Common Estate*. Royal Institute of Chartered Surveyors, London.

Aina, T.A., 1997, "The State and Civil Society: Politics, Government, and Social Organisation in African Cities, in Rakodi, C. (ed.), *The Urban Challenge in Africa: Growth and Management of Its Large Cities*". Tokyo: United Nations University Press.

Asibuo, S.K., 1992, Decentralisation in Ghana—Myth or Reality, *Journal of Management Studies*, 8:63–74.

Ayee, J.A.R., 1995, "Financing Sub-national Governments in Ghana: The District Assemblies' Common Fund", *Regional and Federal Studies*, 5(3):292–306.

—, 1997, "The Adjustment of Central Bodies to Decentralisation: The Case of the Ghanaian Bureaucracy, *African Studies Review*, 40(2):37–57.

Badu, Y.A. and A. Parker, 1992, "The Role of Non-Governmental Organisation in Rural Development: The Case of Voluntary Workcamp Association of Ghana, *Research Review*, 8(1&2):28–35.

Benneh, G., J. Songsore, J.S. Nabila, A.T. Amuzu, K.A. Tutu, Y. Yangyouru and G. McGranahan, 1993, *Environmental Problems and the Urban Household in the Greater Accra Metropolitan Area (GAMA), Ghana* Stockholm: Stockholm Environment Institute.

Brydon, L. and K. Legge, 1996, *Adjusting Society: The World Bank, the IMF and Ghana*. London: Tauris Academic Studies.

Chazan, N., 1983, *An Anatomy of Ghanaian Politics: Managing Political Recession 1969–1982*. Boulder, CO: Westview Press.

Cheema, G.S. and D.A. Rondinelli (eds), 1983, *Decentralisation and Development: Policy Implementation in Developing Countries*. London: Sage.

Clapham, C and J.A. Wiseman,1995, "Conclusion: Assessing the Prospects for the Consolidation of Democracy in Africa", in Wiseman. J.A. (ed.), *Democracy and Political Change in Sub-Saharan Africa*. London and New York: Routledge.

Clark, J., 1997, The State, Popular Participation and the Voluntary Sector, in Hulmes, D. and M. Edwards (eds), *NGOs, States and Donors: Too Close for Comfort?* Basingstoke: Macmillan.

Crook, R.C., 1994, "Four Years of the Ghana District Assemblies in Operation: Decentralisation, Democratisation and Administrative Performance", *Public Administration and Development*, 14:339–64.

Crook, R.C and J. Manor, 1995, "Democratic Decentralisation and Institutional Performance: Four Asian and African Experiences Compared, *Journal of Commonwealth and Comparative Politics*, 33(3):309–34.

Gough, K.V., 1999, "The Changing Role of Urban Governance in Accra, Ghana", *Third World Planning Review*, 21(4):397–414.

Gough, K.V. and P.W.K. Yankson, 1997, *Continuity and Change in Peri-urban Accra: Socio-economic and Environmental Consequences of Urbanisation*. Final report to the Danish Council for Development Research (copy available from authors).

—, 2000, "Land Markets in African Cities: The Case of Peri-urban Accra, Ghana", *Urban Studies*, 37(13).

Gyimah-Boadi, E., 1994, "Associational Life, Civil Society and Democratisation in Ghana", in Harbeson, John W. et al. (eds), *Civil Society and the State in Africa*. Boulder, CO: Lynne Reinner.

Hardoy, J.E., S. Cairncross and D. Satterthwaite (eds), 1990, *The Poor Die Young: Housing and Health in Third World Cities*. London: Earthscan.

Harvey, W.B., 1966, *Law and Social Change in Ghana*. Princeton, NJ: Princeton University Press.

Kasanga, R.K., J. Cochrane, R. King and M. Roth, 1996, *Land Market and Legal Contradictions in the Peri-Urban Areas of Accra, Ghana: Informant Interviews and Secondary Data Investigations*. Land Tenure Centre, University of Wisconsin-Madison, USA / LARC, U.S.T., Ghana.

Kufogbe, S.K., 1996, "Urbanisation and Changing Patterns of Land Use in the Peri-urban Zone along the Airport-Ayimensah Transect of Accra, Ghana", *Our Common Estate*. Royal Institute of Chartered Surveyors, London.

Larbi, W.O., 1995, "The Urban Land Development Process and Urban Land Policies in Ghana", *Our Common Estate*. The Royal Institute of Chartered Surveyors, London.

Lee, Y.S.F., 1994, "Community Based Urban Environmental Management: Local NGOs as Catalysts, *Regional Development Dialogue*, 15(2):158–79.

Mamdani, M. and E. Wamba-dia-Wamba (eds), 1995, *African Studies in Social Movements and Democracy*. Dakar: CODESRIA Books.

Mamdani, M., 1996, *Citizen and Subject: Contemporary Africa and the Legacy of Late Colonialism*. Princeton, NJ: Princeton University Press.

Mattingly, M., 1994, "Meaning of Urban Management", *Cities*, 11(3):201–05.

McCarney, P.L., 1996, "Considerations on the Notion of 'Governance'—New Directions for Cities in the Developing World", in McCarney, P.L. (ed.), *Cities and Governance: New Directions in Latin America, Asia and Africa*. Toronto: Centre for Urban and Community Studies, University of Toronto.

McCarney, P., M. Halfani and A. Rodriquez, 1995, "Towards an Understanding of Governance: The Emergence of an Idea and Its Implications for Urban Research", in Stren, R. and J.K. Bell (eds), *Perspectives on the City*. Toronto: Centre for Urban and Community Studies, University of Toronto.

McIllwaine, C., 1998, "Civil Society and Development Geography", *Progress in Human Geography*, 22(3):415–24.

Mohan, G., 1996a, "Neoliberalism and Decentralised Development Planning in Ghana", *Third World Planning Review*, 18(4):433–54.

—, 1996b, "Adjustment and Decentralisation in Ghana: A Case of Diminished Sovereignty", *Political Geography*, 15(1):75–94.

Nugent, P., 1996, *Big Men, Small Boys, and Politics in Ghana*. Accra: Asempa Publishers.

Oquaye, M., 1995, "Decentralisation and Development: The Ghanaian Case Under the Provisional National Defence Council (PNDC)", *Journal of Commonwealth and Comparative Politics*, 33:209–39.

Peil, M., 1994, "Urban Housing and Services in Anglophone West Africa: Coping with an Inadequate Environment", in Main, H. and S.W. Williams (eds), *Environment and Housing in Third World Cities*. Chichester: John Wiley.

Republic of Ghana, MLGTD and GTZ, n.d., "Decentralisation and Local Government in Ghana". Report prepared by Aforo PAB Consultants for Rural Action.

Shillington, K., 1992, *Ghana and the Rawlings Factor*. London and Basingstoke: Macmillan Press.

Sjögren, A., 1998, *Civil Society and Governance in Africa—An Outline of the Debates*. Working paper No. 1, Research Programme on Cities, Governance and Civil Society in Africa. Uppsala: Nordic Africa Institute.

Snook, S.L., J.R.A. Ayee, K. Boafo-Arthur and E. Aryeetey, 1998, *Civil Society and Local Government in Twenty Districts in Ghana: Surprises, Problems and Opportunities*. Accra IFES Project ECSELL Baseline Assessment.

Stren, R.E., 1992, "African Urban Research since the Late 1980s: Responses to Poverty and Urban Growth", *Urban Studies*, 29(3/4):533–55.

—, 1993, "Urban Management in Development Assistance", *Cities*, 10(2):125–38.

Stren, R.E. and R.R. White (eds), 1989, *African Cities in Crisis: Managing Rapid Urban Growth*. Boulder, CO: Westview Press.

Swilling, M., 1996, "Building Democratic Local Urban Governance in Southern Africa: A Review of the Key Trends", in McCarney, P.L. (ed.), *Cities and Governance: New Directions in Latin America, Asia and Africa*. Toronto: Centre for Urban and Community Studies, University of Toronto.

UNCHS 1996, *An Urbanizing World: Global Report on Human Settlements, 1996*. Oxford: Oxford University Press.

Walton, J., 1998, Urban Conflict and Social Movements in Poor Countries: Theory and Evidence of Collective Action, *International Journal of Urban and Regional Research*, 22:460–81.

Wekwete, K.H., 1997, "Urban Management: The Recent Experience", in Rakodi, C. (ed.), *The Urban Challenge in Africa: Growth and Management of Its Large Cities*. Tokyo: United Nations University Press.

Widner, J.A., 1997, "Political Parties and Civil Societies in Sub-Saharan Africa", in Ottaway, M. (ed.), *Democracy in Africa: The Hard Road Ahead*. Boulder and London: Lynne Rienner.

Yankson, P.W.K. and K.V. Gough, 1999, "The Environmental Impact of Rapid Urbanization in the Peri-urban Area of Accra, Ghana, *Danish Journal of Geography*, 99:89–100.

Zanu, S.Y.M., n.d., *Poverty Reduction in Ghana: Governance and Decentralisation*. Accra: Ministry of Local Government and Rural Development.

CHAPTER 9

Land-Buying Companies for Urban Housing in Eldoret, Kenya

Sarah Karirah Gitau

INTRODUCTION

The institution of private property is firmly entrenched in the constitution of Kenya (Section 75). In this regard, in order to demonstrate its commitment to a sound urbanisation policy, the government, has since independence in 1963, assumed the obligatory role of providing serviced land for building purposes (Republic of Kenya, 1986). This was feasible when government-owned land was plentiful. However, in the last fifteen years, land has been in short supply. Kenya's land policy has consistently championed particular interests. Under colonialism, land policy was determined by the colonial administration, resulting in the White Highlands being set aside for the European settlers. In post-independence Kenya, it is the interests of public officials, influential politicians and the rich who determine land policy (Olima, 1997). For these groups land ownership is a true manifestation of power and wealth, to the extent that they are willing to do almost anything to influence the allocation process. In the scramble for land, the interests of the urban poor are marginalised.

The overwhelming desire to own land has given rise to corruption, favouritism, nepotism, land grabbing and hoarding, and blatant discrimination in land allocation practices. As a result, the urban land administration has become inefficient, especially in the application of public land allocation procedures, causing double and multiple plot allocations and land grabbing.

The disposal of unalienated central government land and land in the custody of local authorities is being undertaken through inappropriate practices by a bloated, corrupt bureaucracy. Thus, ownership and control of land is a very political and sensitive issue in Kenya. The loopholes in the existing land laws give room for serious irregularities. Furthermore, there is widespread land speculation due to inflation and lack of other profitable investment opportunities; land is considered the safest of all domestic investments. Consequently, a lot of urban land is withheld in anticipation of its value appreciation. The above are the main factors which reduce the supply of serviced land. In addition, although the state can invoke compulsory acquisition procedures when land is required for public use, the procedures are slow and the land has to be paid for at market prices (Syagga, 1994). Compulsory acquisition, as set out in the Land Acquisition Act (1968), empowers the government to expropriate private property for public use without the consent of the owner, albeit subject to payment of just compensation. The government acknowledges the existing difficulties in the supply of serviced land. It is cited in the current

National Development Plan as the main constraint in the expansion of both existing and established housing projects, urban services and infrastructure (Republic of Kenya, 1997).

The land delivery system in Kenya has profound effects on land tenure and ownership patterns. The allocation procedures and other land transactions are the very reasons why a majority of the urban population is denied access to serviced land. This paper seeks to examine the urban land management practices and policies that create room for the development of informal land development. A brief description of the government land allocation procedures and requirements to be met in subdivisions is given. The informal land development practices are briefly discussed illustrating how they occur and the official view regarding informal land development. Before embarking on an in-depth comparison of the land buying companies, the paper gives a brief background of Eldoret town.

METHODOLOGY

The data are drawn both from field studies undertaken in Eldoret town in April and May 1998 and a review of documented cases. The field survey comprised interviews with the committee members of the two land buying companies discussed in this paper. The original initiators of the two land buying companies were also interviewed with the aim of ascertaining the historical development of the two companies, the participants behind the companies' formation and their motives. Additional information was collected when the author attended the annual general meeting for one of the land buying companies. The above information was supplemented with findings from an earlier study (Gitau, 1996) of other land buying companies in Eldoret.

LAND POLICY

Kenya has no comprehensive, coherent land policy, which inevitably leads to developments without adequate provision of basic infrastructure. There are thirty pieces of legislation that have a bearing on the land question in Kenya. This complex situation causes confusion and impacts negatively on the supply of land. The politicisation and red tape are evident in the procedures for legal transactions and development of land, and fail to consider the real costs to landowners and land developers. Indeed, politics often triumph over law. Moreover, the legal framework for controlling dealings in land found in the Land Control Act creates room for informal sub-division. The act provides for the establishment of Land Control Boards whose duties involve control of sales, transfers, mortgages and sub-divisions of land registered in terms of the Registered Land Act. However, land transactions are merely rubberstamped by the Board; deals are made, in effect, before consent is granted. The principal legislation concerned with the control of land development in urban areas is not only outmoded and impractical, but also non-supportive of the welfare of the urban poor. It does not facilitate meaningful and effective local level participation, especially in the formal/legal land and housing development processes.

Olima (1995:95) distinguishes the following three main types of policy measures in Kenya:

- Legal measures influencing private land use decisions (land use planning, zoning, forms of tenure, development control and compulsory acquisition);
- Taxation measures, including property taxes, capital gains taxes, estate duty and site rates;
- Direct action by public authorities, e.g. preparing land for development, laying of infrastructure, direct government investment, land acquisition for planning purposes or for the creation of reserves.

The above factors make the majority of the urban poor resort to land acquisition through land-buying companies, which are exempt from the legal requirements for planning, sub-division and eventual housing development. The section below outlines briefly the roles of the government in land allocation as stipulated in various laws.

THE ROLE OF THE GOVERNMENT IN LAND ALLOCATION

In Kenya's urban areas, the public land allocation and tenure system introduced by the colonial administration is cumbersome and bureaucratic (Olima, 1997). Depending on the type of development proposed, three different procedures are to be followed in allocation of both government and trust land:

Advertisement in the Kenya Gazette when plots are ready for allocation. The required information for inclusion in the advertisement covers the closing date for applications, payment of a refundable deposit and other relevant information. Prior to the advertisement, the Commissioner of Lands must ensure that:

- The surveying of the parcel in question has been completed in the correct manner;
- The use to which the plot is intended is as specified in the appropriate land use zone;
- A valuation of the plot has been undertaken and registration details ascertained.

Direct applications or special requests sent to the Commissioner of Lands. All applications normally have to be channelled through the respective District Development Committees (DDSs) or Investment Promotion Centre (IPC);

Reservations, i.e. direct allocation of government or trust land by the Commissioner of Lands to a public agency (ministry, department), a local authority, or a parastatal;

Government and trust land plots allocated to individuals and/or organisations through issuance of letters of allotment, which indicate the names of the allottees, the land/plot being allocated, area, location, terms and conditions of allocation.

Once allotted—when the terms and conditions of allotment have been received and fulfilled—the preparation and registration of the title commences
in the prescribed manner (Republic of Kenya, 1991). The government is responsible for overall land management, determining who gets or enjoys what,
where and how with respect to public land. However, double, triple and multiple allocations are common, due to inefficiencies in the public land allocation
procedures. The contributing factors include a complex legal framework, poor
record keeping and incomplete noting of files in the office of the Commissioner of Lands (Olima, 1997). This situation is exacerbated by the representation of the Provincial Administration in the land allocation committees since
1990, and the involvement of the council of elders in the arbitration over disputes, all of which resulting in further confusion, uncertainty and corruption.

   The allocation committees are composed of government officials at the
district level. The district commissioner representing the provincial administration is automatically a member. The other members include the local authority
officials i.e. the town clerk and other officials of the council, district planners
and any other government officers at the district level. Prior to 1990, it was
not mandatory that the district commissioners be members. The council of
elders is selected by the people mobilised by the provincial administration for
resolution of land disputes. These are usually mature persons who have resided in the area much longer than most other residents.

Table 9:1. *Basic categories of land in Kenya*

Land Category	Ownership	Type	User	Government Legislation
Government Land	Government on behalf of the public	Utilised Unutilised Unalienated (Reserved)	Government use General public uses	Government Lands Act Cap 280 Administered by Commissioner of Lands
Trustland (Communal)	Trusteeship under local authorities, County Councils (Customary laws and and rights)	Utilised Unutilised	Local Residents, Various uses mainly agriculture	Trustlands Act Cap 288 Constitution of Kenya Administered by the Commissioner of Lands
Private Land	Private individuals	Freehold and Leasehold Tenure	Registered individuals, organisations	Registered Lands Act Cap 300

Source: Republic of Kenya, 1991

REQUIREMENTS FOR LAND DEVELOPMENT AND SUB-DIVISION

In Kenya, stringent and restrictive requirements apply to land development
and land use approvals. Hence, unregistered land-buying companies and other
land associations are considered informal/illegal because they do not abide by
these requirements. Generally, the consent for development depends on land
tenure, location and an application conforming to the requirements prescribed
by the relevant authority (Gitau, 1996). Failure to comply results in non-
approval. This is irrespective of the land tenure. No formal registration is
allowed after unapproved subdivisions.

   A private developer or landowner wishing to sub-divide his or her land
located in a peri-urban area for sale or residential development is required to

apply for "change of use" from agricultural to urban use before sub-division can be approved. Furthermore, even in areas zoned for urban uses, the process is lengthy and does not guarantee approval. Non-approval may occur when the local authority has put a proviso that sub-division may only be approved after it has installed the trunk infrastructure (due to the weak financial status of most local authorities this may take 10–15 years). This procedure induces private developers to sub-divide without approval (ODA, 1995). In brief, legal/formal sub-division requires that:

- The resultant sub-plots are accessible and adequately served with open spaces and infrastructure;
- The proposed density is in accordance with the available services e.g. water supply, sewerage, drainage, etc.;
- Development is planned and co-ordinated in order to avoid uncontrolled and isolated residential areas;
- Central and local governments share in the enhanced value arising from the sub-division;
- Qualified surveyors and planners undertake the sub-division. These professionals often charge exorbitant fees, which the urban poor are unable to meet, opting instead to engage unqualified planners or retired land adjucators, if any at all, which means that the sub-division remains unapproved.

INFORMAL LAND DEVELOPMENT

Informal land development results from non-approval of sub-division. The erected structures usually do not meet the stipulated requirements of building standards, materials and workmanship, which, in turn, give the area an informal appearance. Since the formal land allocation processes depend on economic rather than social factors, informal land allocation processes have become increasingly more important for the poor segments of the urban population, operating on the fringes of institutional legality. The informal allocation process takes account of socio-economic factors, for instance the ability of the members of the land-buying companies to pay for the plots. Through informal sub-division and the resultant price reduction, as well as flexible payment methods the poor are able to mobilise their scarce resources. Covering the up-front costs is made feasible by reversing the development process from Planning-Servicing-Building-Occupation (PSBO) to Occupation-Building-Servicing-Planning (OBSP). Informal land allocation processes have been realised through self-help groups, land-buying companies and other informal associations, as expressions of voluntary, collective efforts in land development. They offer new possibilities for mobilising popular resources for land acquisition, preparation, servicing and development (Olima, 1995).

Most land buying companies started immediately after independence in Kenya's urban areas. The large number of people who migrated to urban areas where they did not own any land mainly occasioned this. Others had migrated from the native reserves that had been created by the colonial government. They no longer owned any land in the rural areas (Jackson, 1987).

Most companies that emerged in the early 1960s were organised along ethnic lines as will be evident in the discussion of the two land buying companies analysed here. Women could become members as long as they were able to pay. A land-buying company is a vehicle for mobilising members' resources towards realising a common good, generally following the pattern below.

A landowner may encourage individuals to form a company for the purpose of buying his/her land (farm). The motivation to do so lies in the added value the land would fetch when developed with services and infrastructure. Moreover, if the land were sold as a whole it fetches a lower value per acre. The larger the area, the lower the price/value per acre/unit. Indeed, if the owner harbours political ambitions, selling the land to a company consisting of many members would guarantee him or his political allies a fair number of future votes. Such a strategy would be more effective if he sells part of the land, and becomes an official of the company or a trustee. For example, the owner of Munyaka in Eldoret approached a few individuals, with a view to selling his land on a commission basis. The prospective buyers started the Munyaka-Muitirithia land-buying company. In this case, the individuals in question became the company's directors and the former owner a trustee. A landowner may also encourage friends, relatives and tribesmen to form a company to buy his land, with the aim of ensuring that it is purchased by them, and not by others (Gitau, 1996).

In other cases individuals buy land by negotiating directly with the owner. Later, they may join forces and form a company to enable them protect their interests by relying on "strength in numbers". This may be an advantage when land and housing developments are progressing informally, or when pooling of resources is necessary in order to acquire services and infrastructure.

In Kenya, the majority of land-buying companies are formed after a few individuals have conceived the idea of mobilising people to form a company. They may be motivated by a desire to acquire land for monetary gain or other purposes, which would otherwise be impossible on their own. The precondition would be land being offered for sale.

In all the above ways, witnesses or legal firms are engaged during the various transactions. In some cases the block title deed is used as collateral for loan procurement to offset the bulk of the purchase price. Land acquisition through land-buying companies is an increasingly used mode not only in rural but also in urban areas. Moreover, this is not only limited to the urban poor but also applies to middle-income groups.

THE OFFICIAL VIEW OF LAND BUYING COMPANIES BY CENTRAL AND LOCAL GOVERNMENT

Although the community development field in general is well established in Kenya there is no supportive policy framework for the many local voluntary associations of which land-buying companies are an example. This is due to the prevalent top-down development approach. The central and local governments support local initiatives, but do very little to ensure that conducive policies are in place, which may facilitate and buttress community action through land-buying companies. The first policy document that indirectly referred to community organisations was Sessional Paper No. 5 of 1966. It emphasised the need for development through co-operative self-help (*harambee*) efforts (Republic of Kenya, 1966). Twenty years later, Sessional Paper No. 1 of 1986 underscored the need for increased participation in service delivery (Republic of Kenya, 1986). In addition, the various National Development Plans mention the importance of community action in various development strategies. However, no institutions or mechanisms have been created for effective community involvement by local voluntary associations. Indeed, the policies relating to community development through associations are vaguely formulated, scattered in multiple policy documents, poorly implemented and lacking in determination (Gitau, 1996).

The government has, in some cases, exploited the formation, operation, growth and/or dissolution of land-buying companies for political expediency. For instance, it is required by government that any public meeting of a group of people must obtain a permit from the Provincial Administration (District Commissioner, District Officer or the Chief) of that area. This is stipulated in the Preservation of Public Order Act. Indeed, the Provincial Administration is required to send a representative to such meetings and to approve the agenda before issuance of the permit. The chiefs hold the lowest position in the provincial administration structure. They are not traditional chiefs but appointed by the government. Through its local officers, the state can keep land-buying companies under surveillance, making it possible to intimidate or harass any such company if so wished.

The large land-buying companies (in terms of membership and holding size) have been used for political gains in election campaigns. This is particularly prevalent in the capital city, Nairobi (Jorgensen, 1987; Gatabaki-Kamau, 1995). The extension of power to such companies carries with it considerable political clout. Those vying for political posts with a desire to garner votes from the inhabitants of informal settlements acquired through land-buying companies, tend to extend political protection to such areas. If the incumbent government is opposed to a politician affiliated to a certain company or the company's settlement is situated in his constituency, action may be taken to undermine his position, including refusal to extend urban services or grant title deeds, or outright demolition. However, this practice is not widespread in Eldoret—one of the secondary towns in Kenya.

As from 1990 the government has required the Provincial Administration to supervise the election of settlement committees at district, divisional and locational levels (Kiamba, 1992). The incorporation of these committees in the broader political process enables the government to exercise control over land-buying companies. In a move to strengthen its control over these companies, the incumbent head of state issued a decree granting blanket approval to illegally/informally sub-divided land acquired through land-buying companies or co-operatives. The purpose was to demonstrate political patronage of settlements formed through such associations, or to discredit or destroy the political base of opposition politicians (Gitau, 1996).

Furthermore, in response to the increasing number of settlements created by land-buying companies, it has become a requirement that Area Development Committees be set up to oversee the sub-division of company and co-operative land. These are committees comprising of representatives of land-owners of a particular area, local authority officials and representatives of any Non-Governmental Organisation (NGO) operating in the area. The effectiveness of these committees is questionable. They do not meet regularly, nor are they composed of the appropriate professionals such as surveyors, planners, land registrars or municipal engineers (Mwanzia, 1994).

Land-buying companies are a means for the poor to acquire urban land. Before describing two land-buying companies, a brief background will be given on Eldoret town. This is important in order to highlight some of the peculiar characteristics of this town, which have made it an area in which such companies thrive.

BACKGROUND ON ELDORET TOWN

Eldoret is the fifth largest town in Kenya, with a population of 211,335 and an annual growth rate of 8 per cent. By the year 2001 Eldoret is expected to account for 4 per cent of the urban population of the country (Republic of Kenya, 1997). After independence in 1963, the land market in Eldoret and its environs became very active in response to the following factors:

First, with independence, the urban population grew rapidly due to the fact that the new government no longer discouraged rural-urban migration. Second, there was spatial expansion of the town, which brought privately owned agricultural land (freehold) under municipal jurisdiction. Specifically, in 1911 the town had an area of 11 sq. km; by 1963 it had expanded to 26 sq. km; by 1974 to 59 sq. km and by 1988 to 147.9 sq. km (Gitau, 1996). Privately orientated land tenure systems in urban areas are directly and positively related to the problem of rapidly escalating land prices for all types of land use (Kiamba, 1989). Third, most of the land brought within the municipal boundaries had been used for agriculture on large-scale farms (80 per cent) owned by white settlers. This area had been attractive to the settlers due to its location in the high-potential agro-ecological zones of the highland plateau. Land-buying companies had been known to flourish in the Central and Rift Valley Provinces where white settlers had once owned large farms. Finally, Eldoret is located in an area characterised by a number of physical constraints that affect the pattern of urban development (the north escarpment and the Sosiani river cutting across the town, which makes it difficult to service and subjected to periodic floods). Consequently, coupled with rising demand, land is at a premium in Eldoret, reflected in rising land values. This makes compulsory acquisition for public development very expensive and a protracted, politically difficult process seriously delaying development programmes, e.g. the Third Urban Project funded by the World Bank (Kiamba, 1989). Hence, rapid urban population growth, the nature of land ownership, land use and the physical development constraints have created conditions which have spurred the formation of informal land-buying companies and associations.

Land buying companies in Eldoret

The settlement pattern of Eldoret town has been maintained more or less as it was in the days of the white settlers. Within the municipal jurisdiction, substantial areas were privately owned agricultural land under freehold titles. The advent of independence and the ensuing pressures of Africanisation after 1963 (and the creation of the Land Board) resulted in migration of many people to Eldoret, especially from the Central Province. This was occasioned by the fact that the indigenous peoples of the area—the Kalenjin, the Sirikwa and the Maasai—were pastoralists. Therefore, the large settler holdings of sedentary agriculture offered a large number of employment opportunities, especially for the agricultural Kikuyu. In addition, since the first President of independent Kenya was a Kikuyu, many land-buying companies of the 1960s had a predominantly Kikuyu membership under Kikuyu leadership.

The first land-buying companies in Eldoret were formed in the early 1960s. They provided tremendous opportunities for radicalisation of organisational practices and serviced many needs arising from rapid urbanisation. New social networks of alternative grassroots associations emerged; whose collective action was made possible through mutual assistance and solidarity, based mainly on organisational principles derived from tribal, rural-based associations. From time immemorial, different African peoples had engaged in community self-help activities (harvesting, planting, and welfare schemes) organised by the elders. Therefore, the land buying companies that were formed adopted and adapted strategies that had been applied previously in a rural setting.

The main objective of the majority of the land-buying companies is basically the identification of land for acquisition, organisation of its purchase, sub-division and allocation to the shareholders. The member's interest in land is for any one or a combination of the following purposes:

(a) Acquisition for owner occupation;

(b) Acquisition for commercial exploitation;

(c) Acquisition for the provision of services.

The number of shares a member holds determines his or her plot size. Some land-buying companies dissolve unofficially or become dormant after plot allocation, leaving members to develop their plots individually. A few land-buying companies have registered under the Registration of Societies Act, most of them after their formation, others during sub-division, allocation or housing development. Registration legalises the company and institutionalises its operation (Gitau, 1996).

By 1998, there were twelve land-buying companies in Eldoret. The location of the land bought by the companies indicates the age of the company and the likely ethnic composition of its membership. The older companies are located nearer the central business district (the former town boundaries before the 1979 and 1988 extensions). The number of the members is determined by the agenda/motives of the initiators, the extent of their network of relationships and the size of the land purchased. The few companies that were formed in the 1970s are composed of people of ethnic backgrounds different from the older companies of the 1960s. The Uasin Gishu Land-Buying Company (UGLBC) and the Mwenderi Land-Buying Company (MLC) were selected for closer analysis in this paper. Both companies were registered in terms of the Registration of Societies Act, but only long after the companies had been formed, acquired and subdivided the land. Over 95 per cent of the members have already developed their houses.

THE UASIN GISHU
AND THE MWEYENDERI LAND-BUYING COMPANIES

The comparison of the UGLBC and the MLC is based on data gathered from field visits. This section describes the process of formation, growth, achievements, leadership, political influence, and problems encountered by members of these two companies.

Membership composition

The members of both companies were new immigrants to the town and others who had worked there during the colonial period. They were mainly Kikuyu from the Central Province of Kenya, who were well integrated into the Eldoret local community. They had relations and networks with fellow Kikuyu, who had migrated to Eldoret during the colonial period to work on the settler farms. The sociability that evolved was based mainly on common ethnic origins and similar work places. These people were able to come together in a network of support, communication and interaction, to devise their own self-governance structures to meet some of their basic needs—in this case land for housing purposes. In both companies, women constitute only 15 per cent of the membership. Knowledge of and the choice to join the company depended on social networks and the ability to pay the required down payment and subsequent payment in monthly instalments. The payments are made to the company treasurer who banks the money. The deposited money plus accrued interest is used to offset the outstanding purchase amount. Once this is cleared, the money may be used for other investments. The MLC used the balance to develop a nursery school. UGBLC purchased more land. By 1990 all the members of both companies had completed their payments.

Formation

The *Uasin Gishu Company* was started in 1964, and is the oldest and largest land-buying company in Eldoret. Three individuals who had resided in the town for over ten years conceived the idea. They had worked on settler farms and originated from the Central Province. The limited supply of town council housing and the appalling conditions of their own houses motivated them to take action. Many former farm workers had been laid off after the settlers left. A few worked in Asian-owned businesses in town. As newcomers in Eldoret, they owned no land within the district, unlike people belonging to the indigenous groups. At the formation stage the leaders played a critical role in mobilisation, actual recruitment and in stimulating co-operation among members. Member participation in the initial phases is an important factor explaining the success of land-buying companies, i.e. the degree to which they mobilise their resources and contribute towards the achievement of a common good. At its formation the company consisted of 100 members. Over time 100 more joined and had to pay defence funds (K.shs. 2,000) to the company in order to be recognised by the original members. The company acquired its first parcel of land in 1964: 585 acres at Kamukunji (outside the then Eldoret boundaries), a 2,000-acre farm on the plateau in 1966 (which is still outside the Eldoret boundaries) and a 50-acre farm at Gatonye (within the present town boundaries). The Kamukunji purchase included a number of assets other than land (cattle dip, tractors and fencing materials).

Mweyenderi Company was formed in 1970, and is a small company with 37 members. Unlike the UGLBC no new members have joined since its formation. A 25-acre farm with a farmhouse was purchased. Five people motivated by the successes and achievements of other land-buying companies in the town initiated the MLC. In all stages of the company's growth, the leaders have played critical roles, especially at the beginning (land identification, acquisition, sub-division, and allocation). The good leadership was attributed to transparency, accountability and the full participation of all members in decision-making processes during the annual general meetings. The leaders discuss the emerging issues, suggest strategies to be adopted and report on the progress of various activities. Debating and voting has been the common mode of reaching decisions and solving problems.

Leadership

The clout and power of the leaders determine a company's success. However, the Uasin Gishu Company differed in its organisational and managerial style from the Mweyenderi Company. A professional lawyer, who also offered legal guidance at different times, drew up the company constitution of the former. The Mweyenderi Company did not have a constitution at all and most of the decisions were reached at the annual general meetings. The law requires companies to have constitutions before registration. However, the Mweyenderi did not comply even after it was registered (when housing development had started). The Uasin Gishu Company was able to elicit views and involve its members in grassroots decision-making for the first twenty years. The company leadership avoided clientelist relationships inside and outside the company by formal distribution of functions. For the different properties owned, the members selected different individuals to form sub-committees. The management style and selection of leaders of the Uasin Gishu Company was based on the traditional mode used by welfare and social groups in the rural areas. The important considerations were age, commitment and trustworthiness. The chairman was usually a person who was respected by the members. For a UGLBC member to qualify as a representative on the sub-committees, he or she had to devote time to the project and have leadership qualities. The subcommittee members were selected at the annual general meetings, where all members had to be present. The election procedures exemplified the principles of self-determination, autonomy and grassroots democracy.

This was possible in the early formative stages of the 1960s, when the social relations among the members were close. However, since the mid-1980s, this has changed considerably. The decisions of earlier meetings on what the company was to undertake expressed group solidarity. This was felt to be strong and evident when the Uasin Gishu Company made decisions regarding the selection and acquisition of other properties in addition to Kamukunji. Indeed, Uasin Gishu Company has come up with many innovative ideas which have been copied by other land buying companies in the town. However, some leaders and members of the two companies have been recruited into committees of the ruling political party, which is not appreciated by the rest of the members.

Land acquisition, sub-division and allocation

Land-buying companies play a significant role during the pre-development phases. For instance, in site selection the leaders are active in location analysis, regarding price, accessibility and the characteristics of the land itself (soil type and topography). The poor wish to participate and because of their strong desire to improve their lives are able to do so because of the flexible payment schedules (instalments over time). The Uasin Gishu Company used the block title deed for Kamukunji as collateral when borrowing from financial institutions for other investments. This was in addition to savings from the proceeds of sales of the farm products (milk and wheat). A committee selected by the members managed the farm on behalf of the company.

The sub-division of the land purchased by the two companies was not approved initially due to non-compliance with the sub-division requirements referred to above. The Uasin Gishu Company used a private surveyor, while the Mweyenderi Company enlisted the services of a retired land adjudicator. In both cases beacons were positioned, and planners and surveyors later reconfirmed these when, in 1983, the government, in conjunction with the World Bank, set out to upgrade the resultant settlements under the Third Urban Project. Both companies allocated the plots through secret balloting. The Uasin Gishu Company set aside land for public utilities (graveyard, market, dispensaries, churches, nursery and primary school). The Mweyenderi Company set aside only one acre for a nursery school. Once the plots had been allocated, the activities of both companies were reduced. The Uasin Gishu Company has been inactive since 1983 (the time of upgrading). Indeed, over the past fifteen years no annual general meeting had been convened until April 1998. The companies had been formed for the sole purpose of land acquisition, sub-division and allocation. Once these goals had been realised, there was no urgent need to meet annually. It is at this stage that some companies in Kenya are dissolved. Housing development on land purchased through land-buying companies adopts a flexible approach allowing members to decide on when and how they will invest in house construction. Ownership of a plot provides economic security, not only because rent no longer needs to be paid, but also from sub-letting or sale.

After allocation of the plots, the habitat has evolved and improved, as individuals and households obtain more resources. The land-buying companies sometimes create avenues for the formation of smaller self-help groups, especially for income-generating purposes. Members of both companies later initiated other land-buying companies and/or joined new ones purely for economic reasons (speculation, development, sale or rent).

Achievements of the Uasin Gishu Company

After the Uasin Gishu Company had bought the land at Kamukunji, 100 plots were allocated to members. The remaining acreage was set aside for farming (wheat and maize). The company charged a fee for the use of the cattle dip and hired out the tractors. For the first two years it sold the milk to Kenya Co-operative Creameries and the maize and wheat to Unga Limited. The members kept contributing more money to purchase two additional farms: Plateau of 2,000 acres, and Gatonye of 50 acres. Once sub-divided, the Plateau farm was used mainly for farming, while Gatonye was designated for housing development (rental). These two farms generated some income for the company and the profits were distributed to the members annually in proportion to their shares.

The Uasin Gishu Company members initially agreed on most issues regarding their assets. Half an acre of land was set aside for each of the four churches, five acres for the graveyard for members and their families, and a one-acre plot for the market. The remaining plots were left as a reserve pool belonging to the company. The company received assistance from the Municipal Council in grading the main roads. Savings enabled them to install a water point for their common use (later, in the 1980s the water was sold to all residents). Two company members manned this water point for a modest remuneration paid after the water costs had been met. The farmhouse was converted into a nursery school. The school fees meet the teacher's salaries and the balance is saved. A primary school was constructed in 1985 with the assistance of a donor (World Vision). The Uasin Gishu Company built the foundation, while the donor constructed four classrooms. A church, under the guidance of a school committee, runs this primary school. Two of the committee members are Uasin Gishu Company directors. A market built in Kamukunji in 1970 was supposed to provide each member with a stall.

Achievements of the Mweyenderi Company

Apart from the land, the company acquired the farmhouse, which was converted into a nursery school. Six members, elected annually by the 37 members, run this school. The company still retains a joint account where the fees collected are deposited. Some of the money is utilised for the teacher's salary and the maintenance of the farmhouse building. At the end of each year, the amount saved is shared equally among the members. The nursery school is the only ongoing common project of the 37 company members. The members, therefore, meet only once a year to elect the nursery school committee and to divide the savings accruing from the nursery school fees. The directors are still active in the issuance of title deeds, which has been delayed by the boundary and plot disputes discussed below.

PROBLEMS ENCOUNTERED

The two companies encountered problems of mismanagement of funds and land disputes. From informal interviews with members of both companies, and observations from the April 1998 annual general meeting of the Uasin Gishu Company, it emerged that the problems stem from the leaders' limited financial and managerial skills and lack of capacity to cope with critical issues.

In both companies, it was established that, since the upgrading of roads in the early 1980s by the government and the World Bank, the leadership had neglected to inform the members about certain activities. In fact, since plot allocation, there had been limited interaction, co-ordination and sharing of information between the members and the leaders within both companies. Moreover, the leaders made major decisions without consulting the members. This resulted from the inadequate oral communication in both directions between leaders and rank and file members. Another palpable reason was the increase in number of new members in the UGLBC. Those 100 who joined after the company's formation in 1964 and heirs of the founder members had changed the membership composition drastically; the newcomers accounted for 75 per cent of the total. Their commitment and dedication to the company was not the same as those of the founder members.

The presence of representatives of the Provincial Administration in the annual general meetings inhibits open and free debate, especially on issues relating to the government. Indeed, the Provincial Administration infringes on the organisational freedom of the company by requiring the agenda to be approved before a license to hold an annual general meeting is granted. Also, agenda items that are sensitive to the government may be removed from the agenda before a license is granted.

The leaders do not share power amongst themselves; instead they converge into a single hierarchy exercising power in all segments and levels of the company. Although leaders responded to the sentiments of the members at the UGLBC 1998 annual general meeting, fifteen years had elapsed since the previous meeting. Some issues were debated and voted upon. The members felt that they no longer had a forum where they could meet to be kept informed of company progress, air their views and learn what the leaders were doing. This general feeling was significant, because the annual general meetings are the only fora through which members can exercise direct influence over the leaders.

The problems with the nursery school were related to the dilapidation of the building. Although the farmhouse had been used as a nursery school for the past fifteen years, the committee in charge had not accumulated savings from school fees for maintenance purposes. Hence, the building had fallen into disrepair. The three teachers were paid from the school fees, but at the 1998 annual general meeting, it was alleged that the treasurer had spent the balance without the school committee's consent.

Other problems concerned disputes over plot boundaries, which have led to up to three readjustments of Kamukunji plots. Furthermore, although the mode of allocation was through secret balloting, some members who got plots that were waterlogged in the rainy season had refused to accept them.

A dispute arising over the funds collected from water supplied to Kamukunji plot owners remained unresolved due to lack of recorded sales. The members demanded to know the status of the title deeds for the public utilities and the reserved plots. Although the leaders tried to avoid the question, many members insisted on being informed about the fate of their title deeds. It transpired that the company secretary had kept them. It was resolved, however, that in the future a lawyer should keep them. The Uasin Gishu directors had secretly allocated some of the reserved plots to themselves. Not all the original members had been allocated a stall in the market. Instead, new members, with close ties to the company directors, were allocated stalls. Moreover, inadequate information was given by the leaders on the fate of the moveable assets that once belonged to the company. These assets were no longer found within the settlement.

The land set aside for the graveyard was four acres. However, only two and a half acres remained by 1998. The chairman had grabbed the rest for a quarry, while the company treasurer had built a residential unit on half an acre of land set aside for a church. Another member of the company committee had taken possession of one of the two acres set aside for the nursery school. The above conflicts are pending in court after 30 members sued the directors and the committee members.

The Mweyenderi Company faces similar problems. The main issues relate to improper sale of plots to close relatives and friends of the company directors. Five cases are currently before the courts, after some members who discovered that their neighbours were unable to develop their plots, either sold the plots or claimed them—especially if their own plots were on the flood plain. This phenomenon is peculiar to the Mweyenderi Company, because each member was allocated plots in three phases after sub-division of the farm. It is possible, therefore, to develop one plot and leave the others undeveloped. Although the Mweyenderi Company members meet annually, they complain that the leaders sometimes withhold vital information.

The externally induced problems facing the members of both the Uasin Gishu and the Mweyenderi Companies have affected community cohesiveness and ability to take action. The political climate has created difficulties because both companies are made up of people of the same ethnic group, which is currently not favoured by the ruling party. Indeed, this is one of the ethnic groups affected by the "tribal" clashes that erupted over land in the Rift Valley Province (1991–97). Even with the advent of multi-partyism, ethnicity largely determines the degree of public support extended to different community or local voluntary associations.

CONCLUSION

This paper has discussed the critical role land-buying companies play in the initial land acquisition and conversion processes. They are the main vehicles for the poor to acquire land. The leaders of land-buying companies have been able to mobilise people to find realistic and practical solutions, on a collective basis, to their land and housing problems. This avenue has been sought due to the inability of the urban poor to afford serviced land. Moreover, land-buying companies have been able to capitalise on the shortcomings of both public and private developers by exerting influence on urban land development. For instance, the Uasin Gishu Company owns a lot of assets, which, in turn, enhances the members' socio-economic status. Land-buying companies with political connections and protection manage to obtain title deeds after a short time.

Those in positions of political authority in Kenya, have been found to interfere in the allocation of urban land, and even grab public utility land. The sum total effect of all these malpractices is to reduce the supply of serviced land. Moreover, the beneficiaries are often those with a lot of land. It is these that leave the poor with only one option—to become members of land buying companies accessing land that is informally acquired. The formation of land-buying companies and subsequent developments are linked to the political and economic growth of urban areas. With the advent of independence and free movement to urban areas, the majority of the migrants realised they could only access land by pooling their resources together.

The leadership exercises tremendous control over the resources at the disposal of land-buying companies and over the outcome of key decisions. The majority of members lack skills and tools to perform the necessary tasks, especially the management of funds and company resources. Those land-buying companies with capable leaders who act in a transparent manner can achieve a lot for their members. However, there is need for targeted skills development of the leaders. Proper training would ensure effective management of funds and help to reduce conflict (Gitau, 1998).

The land-buying companies will continue to increase in number and persist in non-compliance with the sub-division and use requirements unless the existing land regulation bottlenecks are removed. The two land-buying companies discussed in this paper sub-divided their land by engaging retired land adjudicators and private surveyors, in flagrant violation of laws and regulations. To address the pervasive practice of such "illegal" behaviour, the government should revise the existing complex rules and regulations, and institute, instead, realistic and minimal land development requirements—without necessarily lowering standards. For instance, allowing unserviced but planned layouts to be provided would be feasible if the existing land sub-division rules were amended to facilitate land development by informal land associations. Moreover, the government needs to come up with workable instrumental arrangements for allocating land to meet urban developmental needs. In reality, some government officials perpetuate the prevailing discriminatory practices.

Positive responses by central and local government to popular collective action in land development and management is a prerequisite, if development control in urban areas is to be achieved. This entails adopting policies that promote co-operation between relevant public sector agencies and informal land developers. Such policies do not exist at present. There is a need to strengthen the existing development committees at various levels on sub-division of company and co-operative farms. This would ensure that land for the necessary public facilities is reserved and that planning standards are followed. The committees should meet frequently and include relevant professionals.

Legitimacy, success and effectiveness of leaders of land-buying companies is only achievable through regular annual general meetings and by eliciting support and community action. In such meetings the members are able to exert direct influence on company decisions by electing representatives, by debating and voting, and through involvement in negotiations and exchanges in problem-solving. However, as demonstrated by the case of the Uasin Gishu Company, once land is sub-divided and allocated, membership involvement wanes. For fifteen years the constitution and the organisational policies of the Uasin Gishu Company were not adhered to. If land-buying companies are to be successful, a proper constitution needs to be drawn up from the very beginning, stipulating what needs to be observed in all activities, composition and characteristics of the leaders, tenure, powers, and how decisions are to be reached. This constitution should be easily accessible to all members.

The central and local government officials can learn much from the experiences of land-buying companies in land development, and incorporate them in their formulation of urban development policies and strategies.

References

Gatabaki-Kamau, R., 1995, "The Politics of an Expanding Informal Housing Sub-market in Nairobi, Kenya The Informal Development of a Middle-Income Settlement, 1961–1993". Unpublished Ph.D. Thesis, University of Birmingham.

Gitau, S.K., 1998, "Important Considerations for Sustainable Community Development Projects". Institut für Raumplanung, Universität Dortmund.

—, 1996, "Community Participation in Informal Settlements Development in Kenya". Unpublished Ph.D. Thesis, University of Central England, Birmingham.

Jackson, Tudor, 1987, *The Law of Kenya*. Third edition. Nairobi Kenya Literature Bureau.

Jorgensen, N.O. et al., 1987, "Informal Sector Housing Finance: A Survey of Two Informal Settlements Combined with a Review of Literature". Nairobi: USAID/RHUDO.

Kiamba, C.M. et al., 1992, "Urban Management Instruments for Neighbourhood Development in Selected African Cities: The Case of Kenya". Nairobi

—, 1989, "Urban Land Tenure System, Land Use Planning and Development Strategies in Eldoret". First National Workshop on Planning and Development of Eldoret and its Environs, Eldoret.

Mwanzia, A.M., 1994, "Issues in Urban Planning—Land Tenure, Land Title Identification and Property Rights in Sustainable Planning in Uasin Gishu District". Eldoret.

ODA, 1995, "Urban Poverty in Kenya Situation Analysis and Options for ODA Assistance". Nairobi: Matrix Consultants.

Olima, W.A, 1995, "The Land Use Planning in Provincial Towns of Kenya A Case Study of Kisumu and Eldoret". Unpublished Ph.D. Thesis, Universität Dortmund.

—, 1997, "The Conflicts, Shortcomings, and Implications of the Urban Land Management System in Kenya", *Habitat International*, Vol. 2, No. 3, pp. 319–31.

Republic of Kenya 1966, *Sessional Paper No. 5*. Nairobi Government Printer.

—, 1986, *Sessional Paper No. 1*. Nairobi: Government Printer.

—, 1991, *Handbook on Land Use Planning, Administration and Development Procedures*. Ministry of Lands and Housing. Nairobi Government Printer.

—, 1997, *National Development Plan 1997–2001*. Nairobi: Government Printer.

Syagga, P.M., 1994, "Human Settlements Development and Management in the African Region". Background paper for High-Level Meeting of African Experts on Human Settlements, UNCHS and ECA, Nairobi

CHAPTER 10

Civil Society, Housing and Urban Governance: The Case of Urban Housing Co-operatives in Zimbabwe

Amin Y. Kamete II

INTRODUCTION

Urban areas in Zimbabwe are deep in the throes of a housing problem. The most noticeable aspect of this problem—and the one that has received the greatest attention—is the quantitative dimension (Okpala, 1992:9). It is estimated that the national housing shortage is around two million units (Zimbabwe, 1995). About 80 per cent of the shortage is in the urban low-income category (MPCNH, 1991:8). To overcome this deficit by the year 2010, about Z$8 billion would be needed annually (Nkomo, 1997:7). This comes to about a quarter of the annual national budget. In the period 1991–95, the public and private sectors invested an annual average of only Z$100 million and Z$480 million, respectively, in housing.

The housing problem has been attributed to several factors. Among these are (NHC, 1997):

- Inappropriate housing policies
- Legislation and bureaucracy
- Land delivery and planning bottlenecks
- Lack of capacity in the construction industry
- Lack of finance
- Increasing unaffordability

In turn, all the above are symptoms of the macro-economic adversities dogging Zimbabwe. These are characterised by unemployment, high inflation, soaring interest rates and a continuously rising cost of living in the face of dwindling incomes (Kamete, 1998b). Some critics have also pointed fingers at government, accusing it of having its priorities wrong in terms of expenditure and economic behaviour (Payne, 1997).

There have been laudable official attempts to deal with the urban housing crisis in Zimbabwe. Local government became involved in housing delivery as early as the late 19th century—a period that coincided with the beginning of urbanisation in the country (Ashton, 1969:29ff). By the end of the 1930s, central government was complementing the efforts of urban local governments (Mafico, 1991; Kamete, 1998a). State efforts continued right into the 1990s (Zimbabwe, 1995).

Apart from being directly involved in the provision of housing, the state took other measures to contain the housing crisis. These include:

- A review of standards to make housing affordable (Chikowore, 1993; Van der Linden, 1986:57–60)
- Financial measures to ensure availability of adequate and affordable finance (MPCNH, 1991:3,4)
- Allowing and facilitating private sector participation in the various stages of housing development (Zimbabwe, 1995)
- Adopting new strategies of housing delivery such as sites and services and pay schemes[1] (Zimbabwe, 1995; see also Rakodi and Withers, 1995:374).

The private sector has only periodically been interested in housing in general and never in low-income housing in particular. This has been attributed to an over-regulated housing sector that has made it unprofitable and cumbersome to do business in housing (Galante, 1996:2; Okpala, 1992). The sole contribution of the private sector prior to the 1990s was limited to contracts in certain aspects of the housing process like engineering and materials provision.

By the late 1980s it was becoming increasingly obvious that the efforts of the state, and to some extent the private sector, were not doing much to solve the quantitative urban housing crisis. As indicated above, the problem for the low-income groups was essentially twofold:

- A huge quantitative deficit, due to mismatch between supply and demand
- Inaccessibility, mainly caused by low incomes and unaffordable housing

It was during this period that a new housing production system came into existence. This is the housing co-operative movement. This paper examines urban housing co-operatives as an effort by civil society to provide housing. The discussion is undertaken within the context of urban governance. The next section will provide an overview of co-operatives in general before focusing on housing co-operatives. The Zimbabwean experience with housing co-operatives will then follow, after which the case study, Kugarika Kushinga Housing Co-operative (KKHC) will be introduced and discussed. The paper will conclude by looking at government responses to housing co-operatives

HOUSING CO-OPERATIVES: AN OVERVIEW

Co-operatives have the potential of making significant contributions to the improvement of the socio-economic fabric in developing countries. In general, a typical co-operative has the following features (ILO, 1971):

- A group of people who coalesce voluntarily
- Focus on a common end
- Self-help

---

[1] Pay schemes, popularly known as "Pay for House Schemes" were public sector housing strategies where prospective homeowners were required to contribute fixed monthly amounts into the National Housing Fund. After their deposits reached a specified minimum, they would be allocated houses. The schemes were discontinued after massive fraud was unearthed.

- Democratic control
- Corporate entity with the right to sue and be sued
- Member contributions which are equitable
- Acceptance by members to shoulder a share of the risks and benefits

Co-operatives signify the desire of the members to improve their lot. Taimni, (1978:1) maintains that co-operatives are "... totally committed towards the uplift of the weak, the poor, the exploited and the needy". This explains why they continue to be prevalent in socio-economic sectors like agriculture, transport, marketing, finance and housing. They can be taken as a representation of the realisation that the government can not satisfy all the needs of its subjects; hence they represent a move towards self-help and self-reliance.

Co-operatives are associations in the sense that they incorporate a group of people who intend to promote certain common goals and aspirations. Like most associations, co-operatives have members who have a stake in the form of subscriptions or membership fees. The difference compared to most associations is that co-operatives are more formal, an aspect which results from their being governed by government regulations or statutes. They thus have formalised structures and procedures, like management committees, constitutions and accounting systems. This may suggest that co-operatives are a special kind of association. It should be noted, however, that associations also have procedures and structures in place, although they may not be as formalised as those in co-operatives. Like all associations, co-operatives signal a desire by sections of the community to help themselves.

The co-operative movement in Zimbabwe predates the independence period. As early as the 1950s, the Co-operative Societies Act (Chapter 193, 1956) was passed. The purpose of the Act was to establish "a legal basis for the formation and registration of co-operatives" (Butcher, 1990:2). The post-independence period saw an expansion in the number of co-operatives in all sectors of the Zimbabwean economy. By the beginning of the 1990s the number of co-operatives exceeded 1,100 (Butcher, 1990). By the second half of the decade, the co-operatives had more than quadrupled numerically, despite the demise of a large number of co-operatives and the socialist stigma attached to them.

Urban housing co-operatives grew out of the need to house low-income people, a need that both the public and private sectors had clearly failed to satisfy. Fologwe notes,

> Once the homeless people realised the inability of council to provide them with houses, they decided to come together as organised groups to solve their housing problem (1997:3).

Butcher (1990) expands this notion to include the failure of both local authorities and central government to provide housing against a backdrop of a large housing deficit. The Executive Director of the National Housing Construction Trust (NHCT), one of the giant housing co-operatives in Zimbabwe, attributes the setting up of the NHCT to the agreement by members that "government alone could not provide for our housing needs" (Socks, 1997:2). So, the *raison d'être* for housing co-operatives lies in the perceived failure by government at its various levels to deliver houses to the homeless sections of the low-income groups.

The first housing co-operative was formed in Bulawayo—Zimbabwe's second largest city—in 1986. This was followed by the formation of one in Harare a year later. By the end of the 1980s there were 12 registered urban housing co-operatives—just over one per cent of the total number of co-operatives in the country. At the end of 1997 there were over 180 housing co-operatives in the urban areas of Zimbabwe (Munzwa, 1997). This figure represented about five per cent of the total number of co-operatives in all sectors. The number of urban housing co-operatives has thus grown both in absolute and relative terms.

Housing co-operatives draw their membership from official housing waiting lists kept by local authorities. By far the most predominant group on these lists is the low-income group currently living in high-density areas. For example, 80 per cent of the people on Harare's housing waiting list are in the low-income category (Fologwe, 1997:2). It is hardly surprising then that the majority of co-operative members are from this group.

Table 10:1 is an income profile of members of three of the most popular housing co-operatives in Harare (see Mudonhi, 1998). More than a third of the members have incomes of Z$1,000 or less. In two of the co-operatives, a majority of their members are in this income category. It should be noted, however, that one in five of the combined membership has an income of over Z$4,000. This is above the officially stipulated maximum income of low-income groups, which in 1998 was put at Z$1,200. Interestingly, using the more recent official maximum income demarcation for the low-income group (about Z$3,000) the proportion of this group in the housing co-operatives swells to 74 per cent of the sample.

Table 10:1. *Income profiles of members of three housing co-operatives in Harare in the first half of 1998*

N=50

Name	Salaries Z$				
	Up to 1,000	1,001–2,000	2,001–3,000	3,001–4,000	4,001+
Highfields	10	5	1	1	3
Zvakatanga Sekuseka	5	1	1	0	3
Kugarika Kushinga	4	7	3	2	4
Totals	19	13	5	3	10
Total sample (%)	38	26	10	6	20

Source: adapted from Mudonhi (1998:50). In 1998, 1 UD$=182Z$.

While one can point out that the low-income group dominates housing co-operatives, it should be stressed that middle-income earners are increasingly becoming interested in housing co-operatives. This is perhaps a result of the absence of an official government strategy for middle income housing in the face of a segmented housing market (Rakodi, 1992).

Urban Zimbabwe has two types of housing co-operatives, namely community based and work-based. The very first housing co-operative to be formed was Cotton Printers, a work-based co-operative (UNCHS, 1989:107). In fact the most aggressive co-operative in the country—the National Housing Construction Trust—is an offshoot of a government employees' trade union. In a work-based housing co-operative a group of employees comes together, usually with the blessings of the employers. However, community based housing co-operatives are by far the most numerous. These are made up of groups of homeless people whose major unifying link is that they are homeless, in the sense of not being house owners. Other characteristics may include living in the same neighbourhood, having a similar profession (such as domestic workers), and living in the same political-electoral constituency (i.e. having the same political representative in the urban council and/or national parliament). The main operational characteristics of housing co-operatives—be they community or work-based—have to do with motivation, mobilisation of resources, administration, and duration.

The reasons for the establishment of any co-operative revolve around a common socio-economic goal that forms the basis for co-operative efforts. Housing co-operatives in Zimbabwe are virtually mono-purpose entities. They are established as instruments for meeting a common need—housing—by joint action based on mutual assistance (see Mapedza, 1996). As argued earlier on, it was the failure of government (national and local) to provide housing to the lower sections of the urban income groups that led to the formation of housing co-operatives (UNCHS, 1989:1,3). The single most important driving force behind urban housing co-operative is thus the satisfaction of members' housing needs. The success or failure of any housing co-operative is based on the number and quality of housing it delivers to its members, and how quickly this can be done (see below).

One commentator describes co-operatives as the "poor peoples' joint stock companies" (Watzlawick, 1978:13). With some important qualifications that we will return to, this applies to the Zimbabwean situation. Urban housing co-operatives get their resources from compulsory subscriptions by voluntary members (UNCHS: 27–31). The subscription is fixed and is payable every month. Some financial resources accrue as interest is earned from savings deposited in financial institutions. Income-generating projects can also be used to boost a co-operative's financial resources. Members who have been allocated co-operative houses pay rent in addition to their monthly subscriptions.

Because housing co-operatives draw their subscriptions from the hard-earned money of the urban poor (see Table 10:1), the issue of the mobilisation and use of resources always generates controversy among members and interference from influential outsiders. Facts and rumours about corruption and incompetence are often at the top of the agenda.

In Zimbabwe, co-operatives are legally recognised. They have a legal status that is separate from that of the co-operators, and can enter into contracts, acquire loans, sue and be sued. However, there are some traits that make them different from private companies.

Members own the co-operatives, and democratic management is important. In Zimbabwe each member, regardless of the date at which they joined and their financial stake, has one vote. In this way management, control and decision-making are all democratised. Regular meetings are the main administrative instruments. Elected committees may be in charge of everyday affairs, but their activities are subject to approval and scrutiny by the general membership. Some big co-operatives have employed full-time administrative staff who are again answerable to the members.

This democratic management tends to make housing co-operatives recruit officers on the basis of influence, charisma and power rather than performance, skill or experience. With such people elected into positions of leadership, there is little managerial capacity in the running of co-operatives. Over time the leaders tend to get further and further away from the general membership, as they use power and political clout to violate rules or co-opt their "followers". As will be demonstrated later, the mixing of politics and co-operative business has done a lot of administrative harm to housing co-operatives.

The recently introduced legal requirement for full time employees to manage the daily affairs of housing co-operatives in Zimbabwe is an attempt to redress what may be termed the administrative weaknesses of democratic management. Despite this, leaders in some co-operatives have made this provision ineffective by interfering in the day to day administration of co-operatives' affairs or by appointing their henchman as full time employees.

Housing co-operatives in urban Zimbabwe use private and/or public contractors to erect housing units. In fact all professional services in the acquisition and development of land are subcontracted to experts. By their very nature, co-operatives are politically attractive. It is not surprising therefore that they use and are used by key national and local politicians. Land and loan acquisition, planning servicing, as well as surveying of plots are all bureaucratic and cumbersome processes in Zimbabwe (Thema, 1997). Co-operatives often need politicians and the ruling party to smooth their way through the system. At the same time, the party and politicians also use the co-operatives to further their interests (see below).

A host of non-governmental organisations (NGOs) has sprung up since the 1980s to offer technical services to housing co-operatives. Leading the way is Housing People of Zimbabwe (HPZ) and the Civic Forum for Housing (CFH). These NGOs offer invaluable assistance in areas that the co-operators would be at a loss to perform. These include administration, financial management, investment, negotiations and the whole housing development process. Additionally, housing co-operatives deal with different donors, bankers (including commercial banks) and lenders, principally in the form of building societies.

Allocation of houses is done mainly on a first-come-first-served basis. This may be qualified by an individual's record of subscriptions or other contributions to the group. As noted above, those who have had houses allocated to them have to pay rent in addition to their subscriptions. The question of allocation is often conflictual. Sometimes a member can get a house ahead of members who have been in the co-operative for years. The reason may be that the newcomer has a better record of subscriptions—in terms of regularity and amount. Whatever the reasons for allowing somebody to "jump the queue", the action always raises emotive accusations of favouritism, interference and corruption.

Individual members can withdraw at any time, subject to the rules governing the co-operative. The resigning members are entitled to get their contributions back, sometimes with interest. The constitution or other relevant regulations govern reimbursement. The life span of the co-operative itself will depend on its initial aims. In most cases, the mono-purpose co-operative ceases to exist as soon as all its members are housed and the co-operative's financial obligations are satisfied.

THE CASE OF THE KUGARIKA KUSHINGA CO-OPERATIVE IN HARARE

To date there are around 200 urban housing co-operatives in Zimbabwe. Harare alone has about 80. The achievements of the co-operatives in Harare are summed up in Table 10:2. The table refers to 33 housing co-operatives with a total membership of 4 682.[2]

Table 10:2. *The achievements of housing co-operatives in Harare by mid-1997*

Aspect	Achievement
Serviced plots	
Number of co-ops allocated serviced land	22
Total number of plots	694
Development	
a. four-roomed units	414
b. Two-roomed wet cores	32
Unserviced plots	
Number of co-ops allocated unserviced land	11
Number of plots	1,903
Number developed	
a. four-roomed houses[3]	1,095
Total units built	1,541
Total asset value of houses built	Z$107.31 million[4]
Work in progress	
1. Under construction	280 units
2. Being serviced	808 stands
3. Value of work	Z$20 million

Source: Author's analysis based on data by Fologwe (1997) and City of Harare (1997)

[2] Not reflected in the table are 47 housing co-operatives with a total of 4 609 members. These had been registered but at the time of writing they were still awaiting allocation of land (City of Harare, 1997:11)

[3] The four-roomed house was then the standard. It comprises two bedrooms, a kitchen, living room and combined toilet and shower all on 300m².

[4] At the time of writing the exchange rate was Z$18 to US$1. By the end of 2000 the rate had changed to Z$55 to US$1.

Of the 2,597 plots allocated to housing co-operatives in Harare, almost three-quarters were virgin land. This means that the co-operatives had to do the on-site servicing themselves. Their performance is reflected in the fact that over 57 per cent of the unserviced stands had been fully developed by mid-1997. The remaining 808 were in the process of being serviced. It can be seen from the table that about three in five of the combined plots allocated had been fully developed, just under 98 per cent of them being used for standard four-roomed extendable units. The total amount of work done by the same period was valued at about Z$130 million. It should be pointed out that at this time government had abandoned its massive housing construction drive because it had run out of money. Save for occasional joint-venture schemes, housing co-operatives were virtually the only actors in the low-income housing delivery system in Harare.

Useful insight into the co-operative movement can be obtained by examining the first and biggest housing co-operative in Harare, namely the Kugarika Kushinga Housing Co-operative (KKHC). KKHC provides an informative study of housing co-operatives in Zimbabwe by virtue of it being the first community based housing co-operative. Because of its enormous size and its location in Harare, it reflects most issues concerning housing co-operatives in the country. The next section is devoted to an examination of this huge housing co-operative, one of the pioneers in the movement.

Motivation, mobilisation of resources and administration

Based in the high-density low-income suburb of Mabvuku in Harare, Kugarika Kushinga Housing Co-operative (KKHC) was established in 1986. Formally formed in 1988, it was registered two years later. Most of the 1,600 founding members were in the low-income category, comprising lowly paid domestic workers and fruit and vegetable vendors. The chief motivation was what were perceived to be the woes of lodgers (renters of rooms), which included exorbitant rentals; unsuitable, inadequate and dangerous accommodation sometimes in fire-prone single-roomed wooden-shacks; and "friction with landlords who sometimes came up with tough lease regulations" (Mapedza, 1996:30).

The ruling party—ZANU-PF—was instrumental in the formation of the co-operative. This was the time when the party perceived it as its right and duty to run all community organisations. Since the original members were all ZANU-PF members, the idea of establishing a co-operative was approved by the party leadership.

Upon registration, member contributions for KKHC were set at Z$100 per month. The amount of the subscription proved to be a burden. Before the end of the year, the monthly contributions were reduced to Z$50. By 1996, in line with improved member incomes and escalating costs of land and building materials, the amount had been restored to the former level plus a Z$2 administration levy. Payments are made directly into the KKHC account at a commercial bank. The co-operative also has two other accounts with building societies. Currently the co-operative receives over Z$2 million dollars per month in member subscriptions. Some more funds are obtained through an income generating project (see below) and rentals from co-operative houses allocated to members.

KKHC employs five full-time employees comprising an administrative officer, an accountant, a bookkeeper, a receptionist and a security guard. The administrative officer is also the chairman of the co-operative. He receives a monthly salary, despite legal stipulations to the contrary (see below).

The co-operative has built houses in two phases. Details are given in Table 10:3, which shows that by 1996, the co-operative had built 361 houses on donated land. The first phase was marked by optimism and confidence. Twenty six-room houses were built using a private contractor at a total cost of Z$1,000,000. The aspirations were adjusted downwards in the second phase, which saw the delivery of 341 four-roomed houses at a total cost of Z$15,686 million.

In contrast to the self-reliance shown in the first two phases, phase 3 is to be financed by a building society loan. According to the co-operative project proposal, the loan sought amounts to Z$11 million. It is also envisaged that the co-operative will set up its own construction company (KKHC, 1996). The land for phase 3 is a 32-hectare unserviced stretch to be purchased from Harare City Council. At the time of the proposal the co-operative had Z$4 million in its coffers.

Table 10:3. *Details of phases 1 and 2 of housing development by KKHC (1988–96)*

Detail	Phase 1	Phase 2
Land		
1. Source	Donated by the State President	As in Phase 1
2. Nature	Unserviced	As in Phase 1
Houses		
Number of units	20	341
Type	6-roomed	4-roomed
Cost per unit	Z$50,000	Z$46,000
Construction	Private sector	Government ministry
Beneficiary rentals		
Per month	Z$380	Z$200
Source of funds	Own	Own

Source: Author's analysis based on Mapedza (1996)

Ethics and conduct

This section tries to peer into the operational conduct of KKHC. The preceding section has already raised a few of the critical issues. Below are some of the questionable areas.

Section 68 of the Co-operative Societies Act (Chapter 167) stipulates that the chairperson of any co-operative is not entitled to a salary. As seen above, the chairperson of KKHC is also the administrative officer. He gets a monthly salary despite the legal stipulation to the contrary.

The co-operative went outside the legal boundaries of the Act in buying and operating a commuter omnibus. The 76-seater bus, which is intended to supplement member contributions, was the result of a "unilateral decision made without consulting the stakeholders" (Mapedza, 1996:34). In the first five months of its operation, the bus made a net profit of Z$30,049. Interestingly, the Registrar of Co-operatives does not allow housing co-operatives to go into activities that are not complementary to house construction.

Mapedza (1996) asserts that KKHC does not have an accurate up-to-date record of its membership. While the register kept by the Registrar of Co-operatives at the Ministry of National Affairs, Employment Creation and Co-operatives (MNAECC) showed a membership of 1,600 at that time, the chairman of KKHC gave a tentative figure of 2,000 but hastened to point out that a definite figure would be known after the records had been updated. Three years later, Mubvami and Kamete noted the same inconsistencies (Mubvami and Kamete, 1999).

The preceding section and Table 10:3 reveals misplaced optimism, over-confidence and miscalculated investments. Over Z$16 million had been spent on building houses for 361 members. At current figures this is equivalent to around ten years' contributions. The co-operative still owes over Z$5 million to the Ministry of Local Government and National Housing for construction services undertaken by the then Ministry of Public Construction and National Housing in Phase Two. At current contributions alone (Z$2,000,000 per annum), it will take almost half a century for the last member to obtain a house.

There are also problems of affordability. With the average income at Z$648.00 per month, a member would have had to pay 48 per cent of his or her monthly income to be able to stay in the cheaper four-roomed houses (rent $200 per month) and still pay the Z$102 subscription and administration fees to the co-operative in 1996. This proportion does not include monthly rates and electricity charges (Mapedza, 1996).

In addition to affordability the co-operative also has an inefficient cost-recovery method. At Z$200 per month for four rooms and less than Z$400 for six rooms, the rentals paid are definitely too low compared to current the mortgage rates which are more than eight times the KKHC rentals. A proposal to double the rent was rejected. This is hardly surprising considering that in mid-1996 arrears in rentals and contributions were Z$3 million—equivalent to 18 months' subscriptions. The management committee thus finds itself with two problems, namely uneconomic rents and member defaults. Partly as a result of this, resignations are beginning to take their toll.

Housing people of Zimbabwe (HPZ), an NGO that offers technical assistance to housing co-operatives, came up with a minimalist strategy that would have enabled all the 2,000 members of the co-operative to be housed on the 32 hectares of land earmarked for Phase Three. This was a toned-down strategy involving 500 cluster houses, comprising one room and a wet core per unit. If this approach had been adopted, the building society loan would have been paid by the year 2004. The rentals were to be set at Z$80. The co-operators, who perhaps felt the houses were substandard, did not welcome the proposal.

There are as yet unsubstantiated rumours of misappropriation of funds, with claims that some senior ex-officials, who used to be poorly paid domestic workers, now own construction companies that are being awarded KKHC contracts. The political appeal of KKHC and the meddling of top political figures have raised whispers about politically orchestrated cover-ups of embezzlement (see below).

This brief review indicates that, like all community based socio-economic organisations, urban housing co-operatives have their problems. These include ethical problems, some of them with legal and political implications. But these problems have not eclipsed the visible successes of some of these groups.

Some lessons on housing co-operatives as community based organisations

It can be seen from the foregoing that, as community based organisations, co-operatives have particular problems that can not be explained in terms of technical issues like efficiency, accounting or management. Theirs are problems that are closely intertwined with and embedded in the socio-economic and political environment in which they exist as organisations. Kugarika Kushinga Housing Co-operative thus owes its peculiar set of problems to this environment. The major sources of the co-operative's problems appear to be the choice of leadership, its composition, co-operators' attitude towards the leadership's performance, and the "political behaviour" of co-operatives. These are issues that need to be examined in greater detail.

As noted above, housing co-operatives like all community based organisations, elect their leaders on grounds other than performance or competence. Charisma, influence and political affiliation are some of the basic criteria for choice (see Mubvami and Kamete, 1999). In the case of KKHC, the leadership is closely linked to grassroots structures of the ruling party. This is not a deficiency originating in the co-operative movement, but is rather a response to the operating environment. In contrast to private sector companies, housing co-operatives as community organisations have agendas which are less straightforward than cost effectiveness or good returns. They have more "sophisticated" needs that do not rely on a simple customer or clientele base that can be wooed by advertising or promotional campaigns. Theirs is a complex agenda characterised by heterogeneous interests, aspirations and expectations.

Sometimes these complex agendas can be satisfied by such acts as kowtowing and singing praises. It is not surprising, therefore, that co-operatives seek alliances with institutions of power and influence. They anticipate that these alliances will help them reach their goals. So, if it is the political party that can get them access to critical resources like land, loans and technical expertise, then being conspicuously linked to the party will be an advantage. As we have seen in the case of KKHC, some misdemeanours may be overlooked as long as the perpetrator brings some tangible benefit to the organisation.

Another very important reason why housing co-operatives, and indeed most community based organisations, establish links with powerful or (potentially) influential forces is the desire to allay the fears of these forces. It is a move that is partly aimed at assuring these forces that the members are not up to "mischief". It is interesting that before KKHC was registered, the ruling party was apparently neither informed nor involved. There were suspicions that the organisers had some political agenda. At the instigation of the ruling party's officials the leader of the new co-operative was arrested. Only after assurances at meetings that the organisation had no political motives was KKHC allowed to register. A lesson was thus learnt to involve the party in the movement. The newer co-operatives took the cue and did not repeat the "mistake" of KKHC (Mubvami and Kamete, 1999).

With such an atmosphere, it could be risky to openly question, let alone fire for misconduct a party official who is a leader of a housing co-operative. The party might interpret such an act as a move, not against the errant leader, but against the party. This may explain why some members ended up whispering against the array of misdeeds chronicled above without taking any decisive action.

In view of the foregoing, it can be understood why the ruling party—ZANU-PF—always has a say in co-operatives. In Zimbabwe it is not easy to separate party and government, neither locally nor centrally. Party politics trickle over into the co-operatives. This explains why some co-operative officials can afford to violate operative legislation and statutes. The two violations mentioned in the case of KKHC (salaries and the bus) have gone unchecked possibly because of the long hand of the party.

Politicians tend to make sure that their associates obtain top positions in community organisations, including housing co-operatives. Most of the elected officials are in office due to manipulation, arm-twisting and showmanship. The members know that the party wants to use the co-operative, but they also know that they will be able to use the party to achieve their aims. It is hard to imagine a housing co-operative succeeding without a friendly shove from the party. It is plain therefore, that there is some tacit reciprocity between the party and co-operatives.

Another conclusion that can be drawn from the experience of KKHC is the tendency of most community based organisations to have misplaced optimism. This again is linked to aspirations. The co-operators in KKHC wanted houses. As their savings increased, they started to believe that they could get the best possible houses that money could buy. It should be noted that the bulk of houses in Mabvuku, where the co-operative is based, and in which all the members of the co-operators were or are lodgers, were four-roomed houses with an average floor area of 200m². The 6-roomed houses chosen by KKHC in its first phase were thus much better than what was available in the area at that time. Not surprisingly, the co-operators were unwilling to accept Housing People of Zimbabwe's advice to build one-room core houses. This overconfidence is a result of poor planning and lack of foresight. But it is also a result of an otherwise discerning leadership to go with the flow, to avoid disappointing their members.

The tendency of technical advisers only to train the top echelons in community organisations and not regular members is one of the reasons why leaders ignore legal provisions and co-operative principles and get away with it. In the case of housing co-operatives, it is mainly the management committee that is trained in key areas such as by-laws, co-operative principles, management, accounting and other areas. The general membership is normally in the dark, left to conjecture what is right and what is wrong. In cases of ignorance and uncertainty, unscrupulous leaders are able to consciously misbehave and get away with it.

GOVERNMENTAL RESPONSES TO THE URBAN HOUSING CO-OPERATIVE MOVEMENT IN ZIMBABWE

This section will start by reviewing the direct responses of government to the urban housing co-operative movement. The discussion will then move on to examine the legal and institutional framework within which housing co-operatives operate.

Central government responses to the operational problems of housing co-operatives

Housing co-operatives came up during the heyday of socialism in Zimbabwe. The ruling party was then an avowed proponent of self-reliance and collectivism. Central government welcomed housing co-operatives because they fitted within the state ideology. As will be seen, active promotion and training were provided for the first co-operatives, including KKHC. In fact central government went a step further. Having realised that the original Co-operative Societies Act of 1956 did not cover non-profit-making bodies like housing co-operatives, government progressively amended the legislation, first in 1990 and then in 1996. By 1996, the Act had been restructured to make it possible to pass Model (Housing) By-laws under the new Act.

Government also responded to the need for title and ownership, thereby making it possible for houses to remain the property of a co-operative until all members' housing needs have been satisfied. This has helped curb acrimonious conflicts and court cases brought about by people who abandoned a co-operative once they had acquired houses registered in their names. The fact that title can now remain with the co-operative rather than the individual was a government reaction meant to ensure the continued survival of a co-operative until its ultimate goal has been achieved.

Central government was quick to ensure financial viability and sound management of financial resources. By government regulation, a feasibility study is now mandatory before a co-operative is registered, and free training and auditing are regularly provided by government agencies. This was a response to the general collapse of co-operatives in the country and the frequent cases of maladministration and embezzlement of co-operative funds.

Immediately after independence the Marxist government went about promoting, establishing and financing co-operatives in every sector of the economy. As these co-operatives were more a political than an economic expression, they were hastily established without adequate preparation and management assistance. Poor management and corruption were inevitable. Neither could the co-operatives survive the eventual drying up of public funds that resulted from the economic recession and the macro-economic instability of the late 1980s and the 1990s. The new government measures on finance and administration were designed to avoid a recurrence of these developments.

Local government responses

So far local authorities have demonstrated a high level of sensitivity to the needs of housing co-operatives. Whenever land is available, the surest way of gaining access to it is to form a housing co-operative. Some smaller co-operatives have had their land requirements completely satisfied. Table 10:4 demonstrates this in the case of Harare.

The table shows that the local authority has actually exceeded the re-quirements of the co-operatives by over three per cent. It should be pointed out that this is taking place in an environment in which it is difficult to access land.

In response to the assurances by housing co-operatives that they have the capacity to provide infrastructure themselves, the Harare City Council has gone ahead to provide unserviced land to co-operatives rather than wait for the time when council will have the money to service the land (Mubvami and Kamete, 1999)

Table 10:4. *Allocation of land to smaller housing co-operatives in Harare by 1997*

Co-operative name	Membership	Plot allocated
Zvakatanga Sekuseka	240	240
Highfield	200	230
Perseverance	16	16
Kutambura	10	10
Napolo Lord Malvern	10	10
Batanayi	10	10
ZRP	75	75
Sarudzayi	18	18
PTC Trust	32	32
Progress	41	40
Kutamburira	158	158
Total	810	839

Source: Adapted from Mapedza (1996) and City of Harare (1997)

Setting up the regulatory and legislative environment

The first legislation passed for the purpose of governing the establishment, registration and operations of all co-operatives in Zimbabwe was the 1956 Co-operative Societies Act (Chapter 193). The minimum membership for any co-operative to be registered was set at ten. Other requirements included ex-plicit objectives and a name.

The Co-operative Societies Act of 1990 revised the 1956 Act. As noted above, this Act saw the registration of what is unquestionably the biggest and most renowned community based co-operative in urban Zimbabwe, Kugarika Kushinga Housing Co-operative in Harare.

In time it was realised that the 1990 Act, like its predecessor, did not address some key policy issues faced by non-profit making co-operatives like those in the housing sector. The new Co-operative Societies Act (Chapter 24:05) rectified this oversight. This 1996 Act emphasises common goals, objectives and expectations. It also has requirements on democratic control and full participation in all aspects of the collective organisation.

The latest Act also addresses a crucial anomaly. The first two Acts did not recognise community ownership. Once a house was built and allocated, title was registered in the name of the individual rather than the co-operative "... thus undermining the whole fabric of community participation ..." (Fologwe, 1997:7). The 1996 Co-operative Societies Act corrected this serious flaw. It was under this Act that the Model (Housing) By-laws were recently drawn up. The by-laws require that houses built by a co-operative be owned by it. It is only after the scheme has been wound up (that is, after all members are housed) that ownership is transferred to individuals.

In addition to the above stipulations, the by-laws require a detailed feasibility study, detailing the objectives of the housing co-operative, its membership, development plan and financial assessment. As indicated above, this stringency is a reaction to the widespread collapse and mismanagement of many co-operatives. Another reason for added emphasis on financial assessment is that local authorities want to be sure about the capacity of a given co-operative to deliver. Ultimately, it is the local authority that allocates land to the co-operatives to build houses. In doing so, the council examines the financial status of the co-operative to determine the number and value of stands to be allocated to it.

Creating the institutional framework for co-operatives

Governmental involvement in housing co-operatives can best be understood by reviewing the part played by individual government agencies at the central and local levels. Fologwe (1997) provides useful insights into government's institutional involvement in the urban housing delivery system as it affects these civic organisations.

The Ministry of National Affairs, Employment Creation and Co-operatives (MNAECC) is, in the final analysis, the institution responsible for the registration and supervision of co-operatives. The MNAECC promotes the formation of co-operatives, and the conscientisation and training of members, as well as final registration. The Registrar of Co-operatives is in this ministry. The ministry provides free services, such as training and auditing, to legally registered co-operatives (Butcher, 1990).

The Ministry of Local Government and National Housing (MLGNH) is in charge of all local authorities. This responsibility encompasses physical planning and administration. Local authorities have to operate within the ministry's guidelines. This also applies when they are dealing with co-operatives. The ministry can also issue directives, regulations and guidelines that affect the local authorities' attitudes to dealings with housing co-operatives. Having taken over the functions of the former Public Construction and National Housing ministry, MLGNH has assumed the task of setting and reviewing minimum building standards and managing the National Housing Fund (NHF), from which local authorities (LAs) borrow funds to build houses or service land. All these responsibilities have a potential either to facilitate or frustrate the efforts of housing co-operatives, in their interaction with the LAs.

The Ministry of Finance (MoF), by virtue of being the national treasurer, also makes decisions that affect co-operatives. It is this ministry that is in charge of defining the tax regimes, which have a direct effect on disposable incomes including those of co-operators. The high tax rates in Zimbabwe have been the subject of national debate and controversy for a long time. Just as important is the ministry's role as the custodian of the Building Societies Act (1965) and its 1993 amendment. This Act deals with such issues as mortgage advances, loan values and deposit and interest rates. The Banking Act is also administered by the same ministry, as are the annual Finance Acts that authorise allocations to government ministries.

The significance of the MoF to housing co-operatives lies in the fact that the latter are essentially financial groupings. The single most crucial link between a co-operative and its members are member contributions, which are seen as critical in the furtherance of the members' common socio-economic goal, namely the provision of adequate and affordable housing. It follows that any institution that is responsible for setting parameters for the national financial and macro-economic environment is of interest to co-operatives.

Local Authorities (LAs) deal directly with housing co-operatives. Urban LAs owe their existence to, and derive their power from the Urban Councils Act, a creation of central government. The LAs are responsible for the planning and management of a city or town. Physical planning, infrastructure provision, land acquisition and allocation are their domain. They also administer the housing waiting list, which is used as one of the criteria for registration of collectives and allocation of land. LA officials are responsible for vetting co-operatives in terms of viability (Fologwe, 1997). They can also suggest ceilings to membership levels and advise on the amount of contributions.

The foregoing analysis shows that government, at its various levels, has established a detailed legal and institutional regime that governs the establishment and life of housing co-operatives in Zimbabwe. Some of these parameters are a response to the real and perceived inaugural and operational problems faced by housing co-operatives, implying that officials in both central and local government have not been blind to the needs of these important institutions.

CONCLUSION:
CIVIL SOCIETY, HOUSING AND URBAN GOVERNANCE

Housing co-operatives currently play a decisive role in the delivery of urban housing in Zimbabwe. They grew to fill a void created by the failure of government and the private sector to satisfy the housing needs of the lowest echelons of the urban low-income groups.

Operational problems are experienced, especially with large co-operatives like Kugarika Kushinga. These problems have been addressed by a shift towards smaller co-operatives. Questions of conduct have also been raised. These cover a wide spectrum from violation of legal stipulations to decision-making, as well as investment. They revolve around legality, efficiency, transparency, democracy and accountability.

Government at its various levels has confirmed its commitment to making the co-operatives work. This has been proved by direct responses to the formative and operational problems of housing co-operatives in particular. Government has also created an intricate legislative, regulatory and institutional framework to superintend the running of these institutions. Local governments have, at least in recent years, been responsive towards the land requirements of co-operatives, by allowing virgin land to be allocated to these community organisations. Having said this, the bias towards co-operatives has raised questions of equity, transparency and efficiency in resource allocation.

It is party politics that enables co-operatives to function. The ruling party permeates the whole fabric of co-operatives, from conception to registration. It also greatly affects the day-to-day running of the institutions. Manipulation is manifest, as local and national politicians seek to make political capital out of the endeavours of the poor. But the reciprocity between party and co-operatives should not be overlooked.

The role of government in associations initiated and run by the poor is not unique to the housing sector. Politicians and civil servants in local and central government like to regard themselves as the champions of "their" peoples' interests. This meddling in the affairs and endeavours of the poor (who constitute the majority of the electorate) very often benefits the poor who do not mind the "interference" as long as their cause is promoted. In fact, the poor urban populations often turn to politicians and government officials for assistance in the formation and operations of their associations. They know this will help their cause, whatever selfish or altruistic motives the latter may have for assisting them.

Housing co-operatives fill a vacuum. Prior to their existence the government and other actors had shown an interest in housing less well to do urban households, but nobody had acted. What effort there had been had been limited to the upper rungs of the low-income group with the lower rungs being left to their own devices. Hence people themselves were doing what nobody else had done for them. Since these associations appeared on the housing scene, however, the state at the local and central level has been playing a critical role in helping people help themselves.

References

Ashton, E.H., 1969, "The Economics of African Housing", *The Rhodesian Journal of Economics*, 3(4):29–33.

Butcher, Colleen, 1990, "The Potential and Possible Role of Housing Co-operatives in Meeting the Shelter Needs of Low-Income Urban Households", paper prepared for the ZIRUP Annual School 1990, Harare July.

Chikowore, Enos, 1993, Address by the Minister of Ministry of Public Construction and National Housing at the Urban Councils Association of Zimbabwe Annual General Meeting held at Masvingo Civic Centre Masvingo, 19–21 May 1993.

City of Harare, 1997, "The Challenge of Infrastructure Provision for the Next 100 Years", paper prepared for the *National Housing Convention*, Victoria Falls, 24–28 November 1997.

Fologwe, Agnes, 1997, "Collective Community Participation in Housing Delivery", paper delivered at the *Housing for Africa '97 Conference*, Midrand, South Africa 4–8 August 1997.

Galante, Edward E., 1995, "The Joint Venture Approach—Zimbabwe's Experience with Public/Private Partnerships", paper presented at *The Zimbabwe National Shelter Sector Workshop*, Kadoma 26–27 September.

ILO (The International Labour Organisation, 1971, *Management and Productivity*, No. 36, 1971). Geneva: ILO.

Kamete, Amin Y., 1998a, "Continuity with Change: A Review of Zimbabwe's Urban Low-Income Housing Production System", *Development Southern Africa* (forthcoming).

—, 1998b, *Repositioning the Urban Environment Question in Zimbabwe: Environmental Sustainability and Human Sustenance—A Review of the Context and Processes*. Mimeo.

KKHC (Kugarika Kushinga Housing Co-operative), 1996, *Project proposal for Kugarika Kushinga Housing Co-operative: Crowborough North Housing Project*. Harare: KKHC.

Mafico, Christopher J.C., 1991, *Urban Low-income Housing in Zimbabwe*. Aldershot: Avebury.

Mapedza, Everisto, 1996, "An Evaluation of the Role Of Housing Co-operatives as a Solution to the Low-Income Housing Crisis: The Case of Kugarika Kushinga (Mabvuku)". Unpublished MSc. Thesis. Department of Rural and Urban Planning. Harare: University of Zimbabwe.

MPCNH (Ministry of Public Construction and National Housing), 1991, *Report on Development of Human Settlements in Zimbabwe*. Harare: Government Printers.

Mubvami, Takawira, and Amin Y. Kamete, 1999, "The Contributions of Co-operatives to Shelter Development in Zimbabwe", paper prepared for the International Co-operative Alliance and UNCHS (Habitat).

Mudonhi Judith, 1998, "A Review of the Housing Strategies Being Used in (the) Co-operative Housing Delivery System: The Case of Harare". Unpublished MSc. Thesis. Department of Rural and Urban Planning. Harare: University of Zimbabwe.

Munzwa, Killian, 1997, "Housing Co-operatives", paper presented at *The National Housing Convention*, Victoria Falls, 24–28 November 1997.

NHC (National Housing Convention), 1997, Proceedings of the National Housing Convention, Victoria Falls, 24–28 November 1997.

Nkomo, John L., 1997, Opening Address by the Minister of Local Government and National Housing to the National Housing Convention, Victoria Falls, 24–28 November 1997.

Okpala, Donatus C., 1992, "Housing Production Systems and Technologies in Developing Countries: A Review of the Experience and Possible Future Trends and Prospects", *Habitat International*, 16(3):9–32.

Payne, Arnold, 1997, Presentation to the National Housing Convention, Victoria Falls, 24–28 November 1997.

Rakodi, Carole, 1992, "Housing Markets in Third World Cities: Research and Policy into 1990s", *World Development*, 20(1):39–55.

Rakodi, Carole, and Withers, Penny, 1995, "Sites and Services: Home Ownership for the Poor? Issues for Evaluation and Zimbabwean Experience", *Habitat International*, 19(3):371–89.

Socks, Witness, 1997, Address to the Housing for Africa '97 Conference, Midrand, South Africa, August 1997.

Taimni, K.K. (ed.), 1978, *Managing the Co-operative Enterprise*. Calcutta: Minerva Associates.

Thema, Nelson N., 1997, "The Planning System and Housing Delivery" paper presented at *The National Housing Convention*, Victoria Falls, 24–28 November 1997.

UNCHS (United Nations Centre for Human Settlements [Habitat]), 1989, *Co-operative Housing: Experiences of Mutual Help*. Nairobi: UNCHS (Habitat).

Van der Linden, Jan J., 1986, *The Sites and Services Approach Renewed*. Aldershot: Gower.

Watzlawick, H., 1978, "Aspects of Co-operative Management", in Taimni, K.K. (ed.), *Managing the Co-operative Enterprise*. Calcutta: Minerva Associates.

Zimbabwe, Government of, 1995, *Global strategy to the Year 2000: Zimbabwean Report to the Fifteenth Session of the United Nations Commission on Human Settlements (Habitat)*. Harare: Government Printers.

SECTION IV

INFRASTRUCTURE AND SERVICES

In most African cities, local and central governments have failed to develop and maintain adequate institutions for urban management and infrastructure. Partly as a response to the crisis in service provision, a multitude of voluntary associations has emerged. Some associations are neighbourhood-based, others may be based on professional groupings seeking to protect their economic interests, and still others may be charity initiatives aimed at improving the lot of the poor. Whatever their origin, voluntary associations are engaged in both day-to-day matters of urban management and service provision and in building more long term alternatives to mal-functioning or abdicating public institutions.

In this section, the authors examine various associational responses to the specific situation in the city of their choice. The cross-cutting theme is the interface of public authorities and policies and the concrete actions urban residents are taking to improve their living conditions.

Gabriel Tati examines a variety of associational activities in Pointe-Noire (Congo) and Yaoundé (Cameroon). His first case is an association of land-owners in Pointe-Noire that has become the main supplier of urban land for housing purposes. He then presents the case of a neighbourhood committee which with the city authorities' approval, constructed roads and a bridge to ease access to its area. He describes how a local waste disposal association developed into a lucrative business operation serving better off neighbourhoods in Yaoundé. His final examples are traders' associations engaged in the management of public markets in both cities, and the role of parents' associations in the improvement and construction of educational facilities.

The recurrent theme throughout the chapter is the retracting state. With regime change and economic liberalisation, the state is withdrawing from service provision and subsidies. It is also giving up its institutional monopolies and easing its control on organisational life. Market forces and citizen participation open new possibilities for individuals and collectivities. Associations of various types provide new institutional frameworks within which members can set agendas and mobilise resources.

In contrast to this broad panorama of citizens' actions in two cities, Susanna Myllylä's chapter deals with one particular neighbourhood devoted to providing one specific service for the city of Cairo, namely solid waste management. She traces the story of a settlement of scavengers on the out-skirts of Cairo that in less than ten years changed from being a sorting point for garbage to a flourishing recycling industry run by the garbage workers themselves. The backdrop is a multi-million city almost choking on its own garbage, the shrinking role of public authorities in service provision and the emergence of a variety of non-governmental organisations occupying various niches in urban governance. In this particular case, a reformist NGO has served as a development catalyst for one of the most disadvantaged areas and occupational groups in the city.

The initiative to improve conditions in this particular area was taken by the city authorities as part of a programme to improve solid waste management by involving the scavengers themselves. The transition from waste collection and manual sorting to far more specialised and profitable recycling was initiated and managed by an NGO approved by the Ministry of Social Affairs, established for this particular purpose. This NGO has now developed into a multi-purpose development association run by local people. Myllylä attributes this success to the first generation leaders. They were committed, educated and charismatic leaders who worked on a voluntary basis, and supplemented their technical and administrative expertise with a holistic understanding of the problems of the area. This case is thus yet another example of the importance of choice of strategy in mobilising people for collective action.

Robert M. Mhamba and Colman Titus take us to Dar es Salaam, the capital of Tanzania, one of the fastest growing cities in sub-Saharan Africa. As in many other cases, the city government has failed to produce and maintain public utilities and services. Most residents of the city lack decent housing, access to safe water and adequate sanitation. Roads are in disrepair and are often used as dumping grounds for uncollected garbage, which pollutes air and water. This situation has led the city's residents to take a number of initiatives to providing services themselves.

The authors identify two main types of such initiatives, individual and collective ones. These can be either constructive or destructive, permanent or non-permanent, for profit or non-profit. The main part of the paper discusses various types of collective action aimed at improving conditions in given localities. Solid waste management is a case in point. Usually started by women, a number of organisations are now contracted by the City Commission to collect solid waste in their neighbourhoods and beyond for fees. They receive training and tools on condition that they provide employment. Non-profit permanent initiatives also proliferate, with a diversity of missions and objectives, ranging from building and maintaining access roads to combating illiteracy. Some are run by outsiders rather than local people and are able to attract donor funding.

Insufficient infrastructure and services have not led to demands on policy makers and government to change their modus operandi and be more efficient in their use of public resources. City-wide protests and alliances have not occurred. Rather, urban residents take initiatives to improve conditions in their particular locality. The authors conclude that service provision through community based organisations can only be a viable alternative to public utilities if the associations not only successfully mobilise resources, but also demonstrate accountability and transparency in how they manage them, and are firmly embedded in the localities they serve.

CHAPTER 11

Responses to the Urban Crisis in Cameroon and Congo: Patterns of Local Participation in Urban Management

Gabriel Tati

INTRODUCTION

The trend towards restructuring of the nation-state in Africa since the mid-1980s, characterised by radical domestic politics and economic reforms, has given rise to new directions in associational activity at the city level and in community based organisation. The collapse of government programmes in social welfare provision, resulting from drastic cuts in public spending in the wake of neo-liberal policies, which gave priority to market forces in order to promote economic growth and reshape political institutions, seems to have created conditions for the emergence of new strands in associational life. Generally, this article will argue that both political and economic restructuring, by de-emphasising state interventionism, has opened up space for associational initiatives in areas that were for a long time considered the sole preserve of the government (Rakodi, 1997:568–82). This opening-up process, it is claimed, might promote the emergence of associations that are both participatory and appreciative of governmental measures to reduce public spending. Under the reforms, community participation (associational life being one of its forms) is seen as a key element in cost-effective strategies for regeneration in urban contexts (Mayo and Craig, 1995:1–11). Promoting participation of civil society groups has thus emerged as a recurrent theme in debates about the rolling back of the state and about privatising services provision.

In African cities, people are organising themselves on a voluntary basis and to a varying degree, in response to free market (neo-liberal) strategies pursued by the state. Consequently, community organisation, wherever it is taking place, has probably more linkages with the goals of cost-sharing or cost reduction in the public sector than it had in the past. In other words, strong links may exist between activities undertaken by community based organisations and the overall state agenda to restructure social provisioning. However, the patterns of associational action in relation to the overall state agenda raise a number of problematic issues. Among the multitude of existing urban associations, some are genuinely contributing towards the achievement of efficiency in the provision of goods and services. Others may be channels of income redistribution by the reforming state, or even vehicles for rent-seeking groups taking advantage of the state's retreat. The range of possible patterns raises the question of how constructive or distortive actions of urban associations actually are in relation to the state's efforts to increase efficiency at the national level.

The present paper addresses this particular question by examining how various social groups in Cameroon and Congo have responded to the urban crisis brought about by recession, economic reforms and democratic openness. By response is meant involvement in the supply of services and goods that the public authorities had provided previously but which it could no longer sustain due to severe financial constraints. The cities of Yaoundé (the political capital of Cameroon) and Pointe-Noire (the economic capital of Congo) have been chosen as the empirical contexts under study. In each city, different forms of community participation have emerged in various sectors of social and economic life: provision of land for housing purposes, mass transportation, solid waste collection, management of public markets, and construction of educational facilities. Discussing each of these sectors in turn, the author attempts to answer the following specific questions:

1) To what extent does associational action contribute to the achievement of objectives pursued through economic and social restructuring?

2) Are the activities of associations influenced by the state apparatus?

3) How do the associations protect individuals against deprivation?

4) Do the associations represent new forms of popular resistance to state institution-building?

The paper scrutinises the actions of a few selected associations in order to ascertain whether they depart from state interests or complement them. The empirical material is drawn from observations and interviews with leaders of the civic associations, conducted by the author in Yaoundé (Cameroon) and Pointe-Noire (Congo) over the period 1990–1996. Primary data collection was supplemented by gleaning data from public records. The factors underlying the development of associations will be examined in the light of democratic pressures, decentralisation and liberalisation.

ASSOCIATIONAL ACTIVITIES: AN OVERVIEW BY SECTOR

Following the deterioration of economic conditions and the ensuing implementation of structural adjustment programmes (SAPs), the role of community based associations in providing basic social services has become increasingly important in the cities considered here. The interventions reviewed have been undertaken by such associations and represent but a few examples among many. They are not to be interpreted as generalisations of what is happening in the countries concerned.

Urban land for housing

Urban land use is a sensitive issue in Congo. From the end of the 1960s to the mid-1980s, the administration of land was under supervision by the public authorities, in keeping with the Marxist-Leninist principles that informed the country's political life at the time. Traditional or customary systems of land tenure were abolished in 1969 when the Marxist regime, led by the *Parti Con-*

golais du Travail—PCT (Congolese Labour Party), came to power. Under this regime, land, like many other national assets, was the property of the state. Hence, before the recession and implementation of the first SAP in 1986, individuals wanting to acquire land for housing were referred to the city authorities. The latter worked jointly with the district authorities and other related public agencies in the management of urban land. Progressively, with the implementation of economic reforms initiated in 1986 and the political reforms adopted in 1989 (the latter put an end to Marxist ideology), the state's influence over land management was significantly reduced. The winds of economic liberalisation did not bypass the land market, which was already characterised by high demand and distortive behaviour. In fact, in spite of state control, land for housing purposes had for several years changed hands informally between individual operators. Inefficiency in the public administration of land transactions led to the total withdrawal of the state in the mid-1980s. Officially, the withdrawal was intended to restore efficiency in the land provision system in order to increase tax revenues; it was believed that informal land transactions caused massive tax evasion. State withdrawal allowed organised private agents to operate openly. Thus, land in the urban periphery became a market commodity handled by private brokers. At the community level, several groupings of individuals have since emerged in order to seize the financial opportunities generated in real estate.

The powerful *Association des terriens de Pointe-Noire* (Association of Pointe-Noire Landowners), comprising several groupings of landowners, provides an illustration of community intervention in the urban land market.[1] Membership of the association does not involve any financial contribution. The association is led by an Executive Committee, elected for a period of two years. After completion of a term, activities undertaken by the committee are critically reviewed at a General Assembly. No auditing mechanisms are allowed to operate during the course of a term. To understand the role of the association, it is useful first to present the involvement of each grouping of landowners as an association in its own right at a lower level.

Groups of landowners may be formed either by individuals living on the city periphery, with family ties based on duration of residence in the area, or by residents living in the city, themselves or their parents originating from the same rural locality. These landowners organise themselves as sellers of land they consider their cultural property. They claim the right to sell land, with reference to traditions relating either to their ancestors or to membership in the village communities still occupying the land. Land selling in the city periphery began in the early years of the first SAP, after 1986. But only a few groups of landowners, often linked to the municipal bureaucracy, were formally allowed to sell land. Progressively, due to the substantial financial gains involved, permission to sell land was accorded to a larger number of groups as more and more landowners began to take part.

Groups of landowners are currently the main suppliers of urban land for housing purposes. The retreat of local authorities has turned these groups into

---

[1] There are similar associations in all of the big cities of Congo.

powerful urban operators. They decide which pieces of land may be sold and at what price. The public register of property is only consulted once a land title is to be recorded. It is no exaggeration to say that land selling as it has evolved so far is beyond the control of municipal authorities. From zoning to valuation of land, groupings of landowners have become powerful institutions in the land market. Each group operates in conjunction with the local leaders (*chefs de quartier*) in the land transaction procedures with buyers. The *chefs de quartier* were not elected officials but rather appointed by the PCT in accordance with the marxist-leninist principles of party organisation at the neighbourhood level. Acquisition of any official document regarding land title from the register of property or the city council is subject to possession of certified documents endorsed by both the landowner (or the group to which he/she belongs) from whom the land has been bought, and by the community leader of the area where the land is located. The government is no longer intervening in transactions about land for housing. Households wanting to buy land have to refer to the associations of landowners. Land pricing is not regulated by institutional mechanisms. Depending on the location and zoning regulations, landowners decide at will (often driven by urgent need for money) what price to charge for the plots. The same principle applies to the size of plots, regardless of demand. The size varies between 400 and 800 square meters. Generally speaking, land is sold at prices not affordable to most urban residents, given the prevailing wage rates. From 1980 to 1997, the price of an unserviced plot of land increased, in nominal terms, from 90,000 CFA francs (roughly 334 US$) to 800,000 CFA francs (roughly 2,963 US$).[2]

For many buyers, the price itself is not the main obstacle to land acquisition. It is the speculation that often occurs in the transaction process that matters most—in many cases tantamount to fraud. A plot may be sold by a landowner to several buyers, resulting in disputes between the buyers as to who is the rightful owner. Sometimes buyers have to seek recourse in the legal system to claim ownership.

In line with the landowners' interest in preserving this lucrative source of income (without any capital investment), landowners decided in 1988 to form an informal association with a view to strengthening their status. With the advent of democracy in 1990, which allowed freedom of association in Congo, the *Association des Terriens de Pointe-Noire* was authorised to operate and the rights of the landowners were reinforced. The purpose of the association is to offer a legal framework for each of the individual groups of landowners involved in land transactions. At its biennial general assembly, organisational issues are debated and membership reviewed. The association will endorse a land transaction only if the grouping involved is under its supervision.

The association of traditional landowners has adopted internal procedures in an attempt to put an end to malpractices and to protect individual

---

[2] The CFA franc is the currency of both Congo and Cameroon. It is pegged to the French currency (in 1980 one French franc equalled 50 CFA francs). The amounts have been converted into US$ at the average 1980 exchange rate, i.e. 1 US$ to 270 CFA francs. The CFA franc was devalued by 50 per cent in 1994.

buyers. For a prospective buyer the procedures require that he/she be referred to the head of the association, in order to check the terms and conditions stipulated in the contract regarding the plot he or she intends to buy. However, the procedures are hard to enforce, as many land transactions take place outside the control of the association. The increasing number of traditional landowners, attracted by the lucrative prospects for making money, makes it difficult for the leadership of the association to supervise land transactions. Neither is the modern legal system adequately equipped to adjudicate in conflicts over land. Consequently, many disputes have so far remained unresolved. Due to speculation and lack of an efficient regulatory pricing system, the cost of land transactions is rising rapidly. Besides, peripheral urban land is being occupied for housing purposes without basic infrastructure and social services. The trade in land is to a great extent driving the urban sprawl as agricultural land in the outskirts of city is progressively being converted into dwelling areas. The *laissez-faire* attitude of public authorities is fuelling this trend which, in turn, contributes to accelerating urban growth. Entire villages are literally being sold to urban dwellers for the profit of a few individuals who claim to be the traditional owners of land.

Road infrastructure

Associations involved in infrastructure seek to improve the quality of roads in order to ease the accessibility of buses and vehicles to peripheral urban dwelling areas. Towards this end local residents in the city of Pointe-Noire have organised themselves in associations called *Comité de quartier* (neighbourhood committee). Through community mobilisation they engage in construction of bridges and improvements of road quality on a continuous basis. To the south of Pointe-Noire, for instance, two densely populated neighbourhoods, *Matendé* and *Loandjili*, separated by a river, were linked by the construction of a bridge through such a community initiative. Since 1991 when the bridge was built it has been a source of revenue as vehicles, including heavy lorries, are charged a toll when crossing. The inhabitants of the two neighbourhoods raised the initial construction cost. Thereafter, they contracted an engineer for a feasibility study and subsequent implementation of the project. Their initiative was met with approval by the city council.[3]

Generally, when initiating work involving community action, the leaders of a neighbourhood committee, in consultation with the local community, identify the work to be done. The local residents may contribute to the realisation of a project either by providing labour or by a financial input. Many of these neighbourhood committees have, in practice been built on the former units which served as representations of the sole political party, the *Parti Congolais du Travail*, that ruled Congo from 1969 to 1990. With the advent of democracy, those units were transformed into neighbourhood committees for the purpose of mobilising local residents in pursuit issues of common interest.

---

[3] To express gratitude to the mayor at the time, the bridge was named after him.

Solid waste removal

Many community activities are being undertaken in this sector, albeit erratically and sporadically. They are not as well organised as other community interventions. However, there are a few examples of community organisations that may be regarded as associational responses to privatisation of social welfare, e.g. in the city of Yaoundé, where one community has organised garbage removal. Urban residents took action in order to tackle the tremendous problem of garbage accumulation, which was becoming a serious public health hazard. The association started out without an explicit name but was later referred to as *Programme Special Urbain*—PSU (Special Urban Programme). It started with a gathering of individuals in a neighbourhood of Yaoundé named *Nkoldongo*. Despite its proximity to the commercial centre of the city, ostensibly a locational advantage in terms of sanitation, the area was experiencing mounting piles of garbage. Faced with financial constraints and lack of equipment, the municipality was no longer capable of collecting the garbage. Attempts to privatise garbage collection services through contracting-out arrangements failed, because the private companies involved were not being paid according to the contract. Collection was frequently suspended because the municipality did not pay its debts. Long delays in payment by the public authorities discouraged private companies from involving themselves in garbage collection. As solid waste was accumulating on open land and in the streets, the residents of the area, under the leadership of a local businessman, began organising themselves through a neighbourhood association committed to providing waste collection services on a regular basis in order to make their housing environment more healthy. Gradually their activities became permanent and the membership of the association increased. The association gained in popularity and eventually became a well-structured organisation with an appointed management board.

As its popularity increased, the association directed its attention to other city areas affected by the problem of garbage collection. Residents living in those areas were encouraged to take part. This extension of activities changed the status of the association into a city-wide organisation. Its relationships with the city authorities also changed, in part due to a strategy of constructive co-operation with the city council adopted by its management board. This strategy proved successful when the PSU was recognised by the government of the Cameroon as a national non-government agency. This recognition also allowed the association to receive government support—e.g. use of lorries owned by the city council—as well as assistance from international donors. It is in the context of this institutionalisation of the association that the World Bank, within the framework of the Cameroon Structural Adjustment Programme, decided in 1995 to back the association's activities financially. The term "Programme" in the name of the association is a reflection of its World Bank sponsorship.

In reality, World Bank funding related to a much larger social programme: *Dimension Sociale de l'Ajustment* (Social Dimensions of Adjustment). This programme is concerned with the alleviation of transitional poverty in the context of SAP, operating as a safety net for vulnerable groups in order to ameliorate the adverse effects of SAP measures. The fact that the association had been formed by local residents of a poor area to provide common services motivated the World Bank to give support. However, financial support from the Bank had certain unexpected effects on the functioning of the association. Encouraged by World Bank support, the PSU decided to concentrate its activities in the business centre of the city, in order to enhance visibility to the funders. They also focused on more prestigious residential areas owned by the building society *Société Immobilière du Cameroun* (SIC). The intention was to show the donors that the money received was being used effectively. Garbage collection was no longer done in the high-density and poorer districts in dire need of better sanitation. Rather, the association's activities were increasingly benefiting affluent households more than less advantaged ones. In addition, members began to claim remuneration for their labour input. The grant from the World Bank was used to pay wages to the members and a large share accrued to the managing board. Consequently, individual participation waned and became highly selective and competitive because of the financial gains involved.

Due to its popularity in the city, the association gradually became a political instrument for the central government with regard to propaganda about job creation, income redistribution and community participation. It was quite difficult for the association to escape this cooption by the government, because the financial support from the World Bank was conditional on the concurrence of the government. Moreover, the management board was co-opted by the political party in power. The head of the managing board, for instance, in 1996 became an active member of the party and two years later he became the deputy mayor of Yaoundé. The recruitment of members became more and more based on regional origin, with preference given to the regions where the incumbent political party had a strong following. More importantly, relations between individual members and leaders had, to a great extent, evolved towards clientelism and regime sympathy. The association had acquired a political dimension, which changed its initial purpose. Community action, which in the initial stages was orientated towards serving the common interests of city residents, became, with the backing of the World Bank and the government, an employer organisation driven by profit considerations—both political and monetary.

Management of public markets

A public market refers to site officially designated by the municipality as a public place for selling and buying of goods, especially foodstuffs. Although there are several separate sites serving as market places in each city, they are referred to as one entity, regardless of size and location. In African cities public markets play an important role both in the economy and in social life. They are not only places where households come daily to sell fresh produce or buy manufactured goods, but also venues offering job opportunities and contributing greatly to municipal revenue through payment of taxes by the vendors. The policies regarding public markets differ between the two countries. This justifies examining the situation of Congo and Cameroon separately.

In the former, due to their vital role in urban fiscal policy, the public authorities are keenly aware that public markets ought to be incorporated in the national fiscal policy. This awareness has motivated the authorities of Pointe-Noire to apply a direct management regime in order to exercise control. Self-management by the vendors was ruled out as an option in Congo. However, direct management has not contributed to efficiency and higher productivity. Public market sites grow as the city itself grows. This growth needs to be accompanied by appropriate measures regarding the organisation of petty traders (market vendors), the distribution of stalls, the safety of assets, the healthiness of the milieu, the efficiency of tax collection and investments to improve the existing infrastructure. Unfortunately, several years under direct management did not improve the deplorable state of public markets. Despite compulsory payment of taxes—some of them unjustified—by stall owners and petty traders, the state of these public places had been deteriorating steadily. Mismanaged by the local authorities, the public markets had become unhealthy places characterised by growing insecurity, anarchy in occupancy arrangements, and endemic practices of corruption and money extortion. The vendors complained about working conditions and stopped paying taxes.

In 1987, the launching of economic reforms provided the basis for changes in the management of public markets in Congo. The need for improvement of the tax collection system compelled the local authorities to leave management in the hands of the vendors themselves. In order to restore the confidence of the petty traders, the council authorities restricted their tasks to monitoring and collection of tax. Moreover, a few taxes, regarded as unnecessary, were repealed in response to complaints by the vendors. In 1990, with the democratic opening allowing for multi-party politics and freedom of association for development action, the politicised management of the market under the PCT was abolished. Soon thereafter, the petty traders formed their own association to deal with the development of their work place. A *Comité de Marché* (market committee) was set up. Its members were chosen through an electoral process, which takes place every year. Women have always been strongly represented on those committees. Internal procedures have been adopted, such as weekly meetings to debate issues, and auditing of the activities undertaken by the committee, to ensure accountability. Since the market is generally divided into sectors selling specific goods, the committee includes a representative of each sector. The committee performs supervisory tasks to enforce decisions taken at the meetings of vendors. Among the many measures taken since the management responsibility was transferred to the traders, it is worth mentioning the supply of clean water, construction of modern latrines, rezoning of the market into areas separated by wide aisles, permitting people to walk easily in-between stalls, and reconstruction of the whole market by using cheap local material (wood). In addition, disputes over the occupancy of stalls have been contained. In the past, under the supervision of the PCT-affiliated management, such disputes occurred frequently, due to speculation and corruption in the allocation of stalls; the same stall was often allocated to more than one occupier. To put an end to this situation, the new committee of vendors conducts a survey every year to obtain information on the changing patterns of market growth. The list of stall occupiers is up-dated regularly. The charge for occupying a stall is regulated to avoid speculative behaviour, and set according to its location. The security in the market has improved significantly since lighting was installed by the committee. Overall, the self-management approach has enhanced the efficiency of the market. Productivity has increased and the public market is currently contributing to the city's fiscal income. In most respects the committee has been able to manage the market successfully, even though some problems still remain with regard to absorptive capacity. The central market, for instance, is spreading beyond its allotted site due to the increasing number of operators, both foreigners and nationals.

The situation has evolved differently in Yaoundé, where the restructuring of the tax collection system has reinforced the practice of direct management by the city authorities. This has materialised through construction of modern public markets by the local authorities, with massive funding from the World Bank and the European Union. The purpose of modern public market structures was to put an end to the proliferation of street vendors and the informal occupation of existing disorganised market places. In short, the underlying objective was to organise the petty traders by allowing them to operate in a very modern environment. Until 1987, the public markets were not as well structured as those in Congo. In addition to the construction of modern market facilities, there was also an underlying economic motive linked to municipal fiscal policy. Most petty traders had not been paying taxes because they were operating illegally on the streets. By providing them with modern infrastructure, thus instituting a mechanism of fiscal control, it was expected that the vendors would start paying fees for the occupied stalls.

However, the construction of modern market facilities led to resistance on the part of the petty traders. They disapproved of the design of the market infrastructure, arguing that it was not appropriate for the effective running of their activities. Besides, they protested against the fees charged, which were judged to be too high compared to the profits derived from their selling activities. In each informal market a protest movement gathered momentum against the decision by the municipal authorities to compel them to use the new infrastructure. The protest was dominated by groups of women called *Bayam sellers* (buyers and sellers), who formed associations in order to give more strength to their movement and to organise all vendors. From 1990 to 1994, repeated demands were made for a reduction of fees and a repeal of the compulsory use of the new facilities. In the first instance, municipal authorities rejected those demands and made several attempts, with the help of the military, to evict the vendors from their usual, informal places of activity. But resistance to military force was so strong that the demands were, in effect, partially accepted. To date, the modern market structures are only half occupied and many petty traders carry on selling their wares outside the new infrastructure. The association has remained on the alert to mobilise vendors against new attempts by the local authorities to impose excessive tax hikes.

This case provides an example of the failure of an initiative by the public authorities to incorporate a major segment of the informal sector into their efforts at economic restructuring, due to a movement of social protest. One reason for that failure seems to lie in the municipal approach, which excluded the potential beneficiaries of the investment from the design stage and set the level of stall fees without consultation.

Improvement and construction of educational facilities

Generally, the urban educational system in Cameroon and Congo has deteriorated seriously due to the recession and, consequently, to the resulting decrease in subsidies from the state. Several other causes, population growth among them, have also contributed to the deterioration. Overcrowding of existing schools is a reflection of demand exceeding supply. In response to a deteriorating educational sector, community initiatives have been taken in various ways. Two types of initiatives are examined to illustrate community involvement in efforts aimed at improving the performance of the educational sector.

The first type of community participation is designed to expand the capacity of existing schooling facilities such as classrooms, to provide teaching materials, and to create a healthier environment. Participation is facilitated through associations called *Associations des parents d'élèves* (Associations of Pupils' Parents)—in Yaoundé and Pointe-Noire as elsewhere in African cities. Such associations have been formed in virtually every school by the parents of children attending that school. Each association is an independent body with its own management board. It is also independent *vis-à-vis* the teaching staff of the school. However, this independence does not preclude collaboration between parents and teachers. Periodically, they meet to discuss issues of common concern. Through the *Association des parents d'élèves*, the parents have a permanent voice with regard to the quality of teaching their children receive. They are also involved in fundraising when additional investments are needed, through individual annual contributions by the members. Since the associations are also involved in the supervision of how funds given to the schools are used, rules of accountability have been introduced in the methods of management. The associations may also exert pressure on the local authorities in order to increase the number of teachers employed in the schools. However, demands of this nature are rarely accommodated because the government cannot meet the additional costs incurred. The associations' contributions are not adequate to cover payroll costs.

Action undertaken by the *Associations des parents d'élèves* contributes to finding appropriate solutions to common problems. Some of those problems are serious and may threaten to close some of the schools in the city. The interventions are so crucial in the management of existing public schools that it is no exaggeration to say that they have prevented several public schools from winding up altogether. The magnitude of the crisis in the public educational sector has, to a great extent, been lessened owing to parental contributions of various kinds. The associations have been institutionalised as an integral part of every school's management board. Also, the associations have jointly elected a representative body, which has an office in the Ministry of National

Education (although this does not imply that it is a governmental institution).[4] In turn, the government, through its Ministry of National Education, strongly encourages parents to become members of such associations in order to contribute directly to the education of their children. Associations' activities are regularly reported on the national radio.

The second type of community participation, and probably the most innovative, is concerned with the provision of new schools. With respect to such investments, the case of Congo is relevant because it has moved from a centralised socialist model of education to a decentralised liberal one.[5] The examination will be focused on Congo, therefore, whose educational system since independence in 1960 was an entirely governmental affair. In line with the Marxist-Leninist approach emphasising free mass education, the state was the sole provider of schooling facilities up until 1990. In contrast to Cameroon, where investments by the private sector were encouraged and promoted by incentive packages, the Congolese authorities never allowed private interests into the educational system (Makonda, 1988). With the introduction of a liberalised economy in 1986 and the collapse of the socialist regime in 1989, however, private involvement in the supply of schooling facilities was permitted. In response to the government's stabilisation measures intended to reduce budget deficits by cutting back spending, *inter alia* on education, community initiatives began to emerge in order to fill the gaps and to take advantage of the opportunities created by liberalisation of the sector. Private investors began to invest considerable amounts in the creation of new schools. Their concern was not primarily to satisfy a specific community demand for schooling facilities, but rather a response to new economic opportunities.

The magnitude of the costs for construction and running of schools necessitated involvement by many investors and groups of individuals interested in making a contribution. The investors were not a homogeneous group of residents from a specific neighbourhood. The basis of their formation was mainly financial, sometimes coupled with long experience of teaching in public schools. Progressively, this approach has resulted in the construction of many private schools. The investment funds stemmed either from individual savings or commercial bank loans.

As private schools proliferated, urban households became increasingly preoccupied with the quality of teaching. The serious deterioration of teaching conditions in the public sector contributed to a preference on the part of parents for enrolling their children in private schools, especially since tuition fees were affordable for most urban households. Investments have been made predominantly in primary and nursery (pre-school) educational structures, in the latter predominantly by businesswomen. However, initiatives towards expanding capacity in secondary education have also increased in recent years. Vocational and professional education has not been left out of the process either. Of special importance is the development of training centres in basic

---

[4] Currently, Congo is chair of an the international assembly formed by several national associations from different African countries. The assembly is recognised by UNESCO.

[5] In Cameroon, the private sector has always participated along with the public sector in the provision of education infrastructure.

computing skills, of which there are several in the two biggest cities of Cameroon. This type of investment has been facilitated by young professionals highly qualified in computing, who have not been able to find jobs in the public sector. The only option for them was to start their own businesses by forming groups of investors.

Private investment in physical schooling facilities has contributed to an increasing number of schools in the city of Pointe-Noire. Primary schools are now found everywhere, above all in poorer or peripheral urban areas. It is not uncommon to observe two or three functioning private schools in a block of 100 dwellings within the same neighbourhood. The capacity of a primary school varies between 150 and 600 pupils, even up to 1,000. Children living in the urban periphery no longer need to walk long distances to reach school. On the other hand, competition among schools is sharpening as more and more parents are becoming conscious of the performance of each school. Schools which perform poorly may not attract enough pupils. National exam results serve as performance indicators within the educational system.

On average, tuition fees in the private educational sector are affordable for many low-income parents. But they vary according to the location of the school and the type of education offered. Although some attempts have been made by the government to regulate the tuition fees in private schools, they are generally determined by the market mechanisms of supply and demand. Surprisingly, the fees are lower in Congo than in Cameroon. In primary education, for instance, the annual fee is on average 21,000 CFA in Pointe-Noire, whereas in Yaoundé it is 45,000 CFA. The fee differential may be explained with reference to the average level of household income in the respective countries. Another explanation may be found in the maturity of the private sector. In Congo, the private sector is still very young, whilst in Cameroon it is more mature, dating back at least to the 1970s.

Private investment in primary education is still expanding as more and more individuals with financial means are collectively putting their money into such ventures. Informal sources of information indicate that investment returns are high. Individuals who create a school are, in effect, shareholders, as far as their invested capital is concerned. Each member of a group of investors receives a share of the dividends, in proportion to his or her contribution to total investment. The government does not intervene in the generation of resources for private schools. Nor does it interfere in their management. The teaching staff are recruited exclusively by the funders of the school, as are the managerial staff, although the group of investors often manages the school itself. Recurrent costs are covered by tuition fees and other private revenue. The expansion of private investment in educational facilities is fuelled by growing demand for such services. The quality of education offered in private schools is said to be higher than that of public schools. The teachers are highly motivated—above all by the *regularity* of salary payments, rather than the salary level itself. Nevertheless, teachers discharge their tasks in an efficient manner. Wages are actually lower in the private sector than in the public sector. Besides, the teaching and managerial staff are not covered by career plan or social security schemes similar to those prevailing in the public sector.

On the other hand, the fact that private schools are not assisted through any kind of financial scheme put in place by the city authorities or the central government has placed the future of some of them in jeopardy. Government reports suggest that the number of schools unable to meet their costs is increasing. The schools located in poor areas are facing greater financial problems because the tuition fees they charge are too low to create a secure financial foundation. As a result, poor households in those areas may have no other option than to enrol their children in public schools. Several private schools have been forced to close due to shortage of funds. Others, in strenuous efforts to survive at any price, are pursuing strategies which may be regarded as unfair and not in line with educational ethics, in order to attract as many pupils as possible. For instance, they provide parents with misleading information about the schools performance in the national exams. They may also deliberately publicise erroneous tuition fee schedules. Once the registration done, payment of additional fees is demanded from the parents. Overall, notwithstanding some unfair practices such as these, it must be conceded that private investments made by groups of individuals have impacted positively on the educational system, in terms of both infrastructure and the quality of teaching offered. Job creation is also a beneficial spin-off from the proliferation of private educational facilities. Many university graduates, unable to find jobs in the public sector after completing their degrees, have been recruited as teachers in private schools. Recruitment is done city-wide but the teachers are required to reside in the area where the school is located.

DRAWING LESSONS FROM THE CASES EXAMINED

The foregoing examination of community initiatives—be they at the level of a district or region, a place of work, a company, or an ethnic group—has served to shed some light on what is occurring in the context of the urban crisis. The various interventions undertaken by communities in two cities—Pointe-Noire (Congo) and Yaoundé (Cameroon)—provide an illustrative picture of the urban transformation at the grassroots level. They depict how individuals are coping in a collective spirit with the withdrawal of the state from basic social services and subsidy schemes. Indeed, taking advantage of the democratic opening of the early 1990s, various forms of community based organisations are increasingly intervening in the public arena. Some have emerged during the crisis, whereas others which predate the 1990s have grown in strength with the changing economic and social context.

As evidenced by the cases studied, associational interventions are providing some basic social services that the state or the local authorities have been unable to deliver due to resource constraints. The abolition or reduction of state subsidies in the provision of social services or facilities has created the basis for community based initiatives in various spheres of urban life, producing considerable positive impacts.

Political influence has been exerted in some instances, e.g. in the cases of the *Programme Special Urbain* and the *Association des Terriens*. Notwithstanding these two cases of direct political influence or co-optation, the community based associations and their initiatives are generally not under control by the state apparatus. Their actions are driven instead by a collective will to change the urban environment without the problematic intervention of the government. This may be the main reason why such organisations generally reject any involvement of public authorities in their management. The boards of those associations are often elected democratically.

International aid agencies may also take advantage of community based organisations. It has been pointed out how the World Bank managed to convert what was, in effect, a community initiative in garbage collection into a component of its safety net package in the context Cameroon's difficult structural adjustment period. Even so, women, prominently represented in the *Programme Special Urbain* and financially backed by the World Bank, used their earned income to launch petty trading activities. By contrast, the *Association des Terriens de Pointe-Noire* case illustrates how harmful a community initiative may be to the livelihood of poor people. Villagers are losing their agricultural land and the local authorities are doing nothing to stop it. Urbanisation is encroaching on rural land, effectively converting villages adjacent to the city into city wards. The sole alternative for displaced villagers is to migrate to the city, thus contributing further to urban growth, and adding to the social problems in its wake. The city's physical growth is also influenced by the haphazard way in which landowners sell land to urban households. This is producing a pattern of urban settlement that makes the provision of basic services increasingly costly. The unchecked process of urban expansion creates a patchwork of poor settlements wherever low-income households find it possible to settle.

Whether associational actions are new forms of popular resistance to the state has been examined implicitly through the cases studied. It is acknowledged that the context of structural adjustment, accompanied by political liberalisation, is different from that characterised by authoritarianism and a one-party system. The new multi-faceted context, characterised by freedom of association, public choice considerations, state withdrawal and privatisation of social welfare seems to offer opportunities for people, of which advantage has been taken. The forms these initiatives take do not seem to fit patterns of popular resistance as reported by several authors (see for example Tripp, 1992 and MacGaffey, 1992). The assumption made here is that at the starting point of any association in a context of crisis—whether urban or nation-wide—lies a collective reaction of social frustration. In other words, a feeling of discontent with deteriorating social and economic conditions may compel individuals to take initiatives of their own to remedy the situation. The collective form of an association is chosen in order to be effective. Instead of remaining passive, people decide to act collectively in order to improve the living conditions for themselves and their children. Thus, the formation of associations is the result of a burgeoning collective reaction to deteriorating living conditions at the community level. Pooling their resources—be they human, financial or in kind—helps participants to satisfy their demand for goods and services or to secure their dwindling incomes. At a later stage, such a collective reaction build on frustration may become constructive and collaborative, and sometimes serves as an interface for complementary action undertaken by both the reforming state and communities.

CONCLUDING REMARKS

In this paper, an attempt has been made to examine emerging patterns (or models) of associational intervention at the community level, in relation to economic and political reforms. All evidence considered, it can be said that attempts to privatise social welfare within the context of political reforms may produce either positive or negative institutions in terms of participatory development.

Cameroon and Congo have initiated important economic and political reforms. Of course, there is still a long way to go; setbacks have occurred, some of them stalling the course of political reform (as in Congo in 1997). But the democratisation of state institutions launched in the early 1990s is being buttressed by community struggles at the grassroots. Policies of devolution of decision-making authority are being implemented. The interventions discussed above are but a few outcomes stemming from the combination of social and economic reforms driven by market forces, political reforms that have permitted freedom of association and cultural forces which provide a basis for community based associations. Cultural forces are derived from what Aké (1989) called "African communality". One remarkable outcome of this confrontation of the economic and social, the political and the cultural is a growing awareness among urban dwellers that, with the advent of SAP, the days of paternalistic government are over, however shaky it may have been. They are also aware that democratic opening has offered them new opportunities, even if the political system remains fragile. Through their associations, urban residents are taking concrete action in order to improve their living conditions. In the past, such action was scorned by the state apparatus, but with the new dispensation, releasing market forces as well as citizen participation, those actions are increasingly welcomed by governments. Participation through community based associations has become an institutional fact and a major factor in the advancement of economic and social development goals. At the city level, associations provide an institutional framework for collective action, by setting agendas, mobilising resources, and formulating norms and expectations—even though problems of co-ordination and regulation are largely extant. The cases examined may point to ways of strengthening or improving state-people or state-associations partnerships in strategic urban planning, provided a modus operandi can be found in the co-ordination of initiatives.

* * *

Acknowledgement

The author would like to thank Caroline Wolhuter and Alberto Gianoli for useful comments to an earlier version of this paper.

References

Makonda, A., 1988, "Une Ecole 'pour le Peuple'?", *Politique Africaine,* 31, pp. 39–44.

Aké, Claude, 1989, *Sustaining Development on the Indigenous.* Working document prepared for the World Bank. Washington, DC: The World Bank.

MacGaffey, Janet, 1992, "Initiatives à la Base: L'autre cheminement social du Zaïre et la restructuration économique", in Hyden, Goran and Michael Bratton (eds), *Gouverner l'Afrique: Vers un Partage des Roles* (French version). Boulder, CO: Lynne Rienner.

Mayo, Marjorie and Craig Gary, 1995, "Community Participation and Empowerment: The Human Face of Structural Adjustment or Tools for Democratic Transformation?", in Craig, Gary and Marjorie Mayo, (eds), *Community Empowerment. A reader in Participation and Development.* London: Zed Books.

Rakodi, Carole (ed.), 1997, "Conclusion", in Rakodi, Carole (ed.), *The Urban Challenge in Africa. Growth and Management of its Large Cities.* Tokyo: United Nations University Press.

Tripp, Aili Mari, 1992, "Organisation Locales et Participation Face à l'Etat, dans les villes de Tanzanie", in Hyden, Goran and Michael Bratton (eds), Boulder, *Gouverner l'Afrique: Vers un Partage des Roles* (French version). CO: Lynne Rienner.

CHAPTER 12

NGOs in Urban Environmental Governance:
Waste Recycling in Cairo

Susanna Myllylä

INTRODUCTION

Due to the spread of urban lifestyles, the fast growing amount of solid waste is becoming a serious environmental problem in the mega-cities of developing countries. The waste handling capacities of both the public and private sectors are lagging behind the increasing production of solid waste. People in the so-called informal sector, scavengers and other waste collectors, therefore, play a considerable part in solid waste management in urban centres. This is related to the income-generation needs of the poor: everything recyclable is collected from households. This function is usually an invisible and marginalised part of urban life, although vast amounts of different types of waste are being reused and returned to the wider production system in many cities.

For any African city to function, the informal sector is critical in solid waste management. This is evident in Greater Cairo, which has a population of 15 million people. In the past, the waste collectors, the *zabbaleen*, were sometimes banned from entering the city, due to suspected health hazards and the perceived risk of epidemics. It later transpired that non-collection of solid waste constituted an even greater health risk. Currently Cairo produces 6,500 tons of solid waste daily, half of which is collected by the city and private companies, and one-third by the *zabbaleen* (Moharram, 1994). The rest, 1,500 tonnes, is left on vacant sites in the poorest areas, which have no waste collection system at all. Part of the unrecyclable waste collected by the *zabbaleen* remains in the living habitat of the *zabbaleen*, exposing them to serious health risks. Cairo municipality has only reluctantly recognised the important role of this informal environmental service, regarding it instead as a primitive, temporary phenomenon to be wiped out later and replaced by a modern system of waste disposal (Volpi, 1997).

This article focuses on the development process among the Cairene waste recyclers resulting from the intervention of a non-governmental organisation (NGO), the Association for Protection of the Environment (APE), formed in 1984. The *zabbaleen* are a poor urban group whose informal settlement is located on an environmentally hazardous site. The majority of them are Copts (only four per cent are Muslims) and as such they represent a minority in the city as a whole. The APE was originally established from above by the city government, with professionals in charge, in order to create better living conditions in the settlement, particularly for the poorest women and girls. Another purpose was to co-ordinate the waste recyclers' work with the city-wide solid waste management system. The whole upgrading project gradually evolved into a development intervention, in which environmental issues were closely connected with income generation, women's empowerment, education and health care. Today, the APE wants to be considered a grassroots organisation, since it is run mainly by the *zabbaleen* themselves.

The material derives from the author's Ph.D. project, which analyses the urban environmental practices of NGOs and their contribution to urban governance. The data stem from both secondary material and primary sources—semi-structured interviews and informal discussions as well as observations—from the fieldwork site.

First, I will introduce the wider societal context in which the role of the *zabbaleen* and the APE may be placed and assessed. I start by looking briefly at the actors in urban governance in Cairo, and examining some characteristics of Egyptian civil society. I will concentrate on the relationship between two actors, the NGOs and the government. Thereafter, a case study of the *zabbaleen* experience is presented. Three fundamental questions are raised concerning associational life in Cairo:

1. Why have local NGOs emerged in the urban governance domain?

2. Why it is so difficult for Cairenes—especially the poor—to form grassroots associations, and what is required to mobilise people in a community or neighbourhood?

3. How can an NGO created in a top-down fashion make a holistic development intervention in a poor settlement, and how might it be transformed into a vehicle for grassroots action?

NGOs IN URBAN GOVERNANCE AND THEIR RELATIONS WITH THE STATE

In developing countries, large bureaucracies inhibit necessary urban change, while citizens find it hard to believe that governments are able to find solutions without causing them hardship or inconvenience. As a result, a rapidly growing number of private voluntary associations has emerged, including community based organisations and people's self-help activities. This change in state-society relations may be regarded as positive because non-governmental organisations can help alleviate the burden of the state, for instance, in solving environmental problems (Gomaa, 1994).

The term *governance failure* refers, on the one hand, to the inadequacy of government responses to new types of complex problems; absence of popular trust; lack of accountability; limited institutional capacities; extremely poor service delivery record, etc. On the other, it refers to the breaking down of traditional structures; an increase in the number of actors in political, economic and administrative systems; and poor co-ordination of these actors and their functions (Kooiman, 1993:2; King and Schneider, 1994:139–41; Swilling, 1997).

The scale of the current urban crisis in the developing world places humankind in an entirely new historical situation. There is no previous knowledge or tradition for coping with very large cities in these regions (Perlman,

1990). It is evident that urban knowledge has to develop from more equal partnerships between different actors at various levels of society. In the case of Cairo, the main actors in environmental governance have been listed in Figure 12:1. The share of local NGOs is becoming ever more important in the search for better urban governance (Hardoy et al., 1995:209–10). Therefore, their position and role need further examination. Theories and new approaches to local non-governmental organisations are still to be formulated, including in the field of urban studies. Underlying the entire NGO discourse is a funda-mental question: for whose benefit do NGOs operate?

Figure 12:1. *The main environmental actors in Cairo*

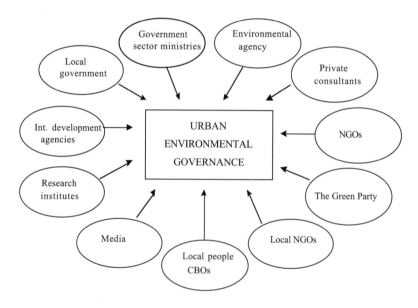

Since the 1970s, the reduced role of the state in service provision has produced a great need for gap-filling by NGOs and the private sector in Egypt (Shu-krallah, 1998). Deterioration in services has impacted adversely on the poor and other low-income groups. As a result of deteriorating socio-economic conditions, groups of Muslims and Christians have united to work together both in religious movements and in secular NGOs (Abdel Wahab, 1997).

Alongside the Egyptian government, NGOs have played an essential part in the development of an environmental policy for the country through their important role in formulating the new environmental law of 1994. Basically, the law empowers relevant NGOs to report environmental crimes. As a result, some NGOs have successfully sued local governments on such grounds (El-Ghayati, 1997). The Egyptian Environmental Affairs Agency (EEAA) has ac-knowledged the importance of NGOs by conceding that they may be instru-mental in promoting citizen participation, which is vital in tackling environ-mental problems (EnviroNet, 1994:1–2). The EEAA has also stated that it sees its relationship to NGOs as quite different from that of other government agencies, which have mainly political objectives and generally shun pressure groups or use them for their own benefit. There is yet another reason for the government's interest in NGOs: the government tries to guarantee fulfilment of its own priorities only *after* foreign donors have indicated their intention to provide financial assistance directly to NGOs. Organisations are indirectly influenced by the government and the EEAA, as reflected in the consensual and consultative role of NGOs *vis-à-vis* the government (Gomaa, 1992; 1994). However, in meetings of environmental actors, local NGOs are sometimes perceived as difficult partners: one EEAA officer stated in 1997 that these meetings are "very noisy and quarrelsome", due to "overactive" NGO representatives.

NGOs often suffer from harassment or repression by governments (Hardoy et al., 1995; Abbot 1996). The Cairene NGOs face some additional constraints. Egypt has a two-tier system of administration, whereby the central government has substantial control over local governments. Mustapha Al-Sayyid (1995:264–94) points out that only one of several criteria for a vibrant, autonomous civil society is adequately met, namely the presence of a large number of active formal associations, while freedom of expression is still very restricted.[1] In Cairo, organisations experience difficulties in keeping their autonomy and managing their own money. Inflows of funds from foreign donors must be approved by the Ministry of Social Affairs, the government body regulating the affairs of non-profit organisations. Law 32 of 1964 requires associations to register with the Ministry and to submit reports regularly. If the Ministry disapproves of the association's activities, it can assign a government employee to its board of directors, or even shut down the organisation, as has occurred in the case of some feminist associations (*Egypt Today*, 1994; Shukrallah, 1997; 1998). As a means of control, the government before 1960 absorbed many private voluntary organisations (Singerman, 1997:312, n17). Today, this law continues to create tension between the NGO sector and the government. While government provision of social services may have improved, communal participation has declined.

Violent social movements in the city may be interpreted as symptoms of urban crisis, reflecting the inability of the government to deal with urban problems (Kharoufi, 1995). When the government cannot cope with the situation, its response is repression. The political movements in Egypt (and in the Islamic world as a whole) have remained external to and alienated from organised politics, occasionally erupting into unrest (Zubaida, 1989:135). In Cairo, the food riots and other uprisings, along with the activities of some violent Islamist movements, may be seen as part of this wider crisis. The assertion that Cairo cannot be governed well is due to the paramount preoccupation with security in government circles in Egypt, which, in turn, inhibits mobilisation of people (Sullivan, 1983).

---

[1] Lloyd Sachikonye (1995:7) refers to the Western historical roots of civil society and points out that its institutions are not inherently democratic. Terje Tvedt (1998) states that there are many examples to show that strengthening some NGOs may have weakened civil society as a whole. The common belief, however, is that NGOs are important for political reform, as they exercise different sorts of pressures and controls upon government institutions (see Bratton, 1994; Harbeson et al., 1994)

OBSTACLES AND OPPORTUNITIES FOR GRASSROOTS ACTIVISM IN THE CITY

Hopkins et al. (1995) undertook a large survey on environmental awareness of Cairenes. They found that people are primarily concerned with local problems—those they can see and experience. The majority saw the inadequacy of the solid waste disposal system as the main environmental problem. Second to the waste problem was air pollution and third was water supply—its quantity and quality. Many people noted the government's favouritism towards well-to-do areas. On the other hand, people from the upper classes claimed that people of the lower social classes tend to destroy the amenities that the government has provided in the city.

The scope for environmental grassroots activism in Cairo has also been examined (Hopkins and Mehanna, 1997). It was found that while the poor tend to blame each other for environmental problems, the upper middle class tends to blame the poor. Few were ready to complain to the authorities or create pressure groups. It was concluded that, since people do not consider solutions to be within their grasp, recognition of the problems would not by itself generate grassroots activism. It was also pointed out that, although the poor were well aware of environmental problems, they felt powerless.

It is often argued that a certain passivity prevails in Egyptian society, due to political and social centralisation, compounded by a stifling bureaucracy. Thus, the power structure of society is the cause of this phenomenon. Nevertheless Diane Singerman (1997:5) refers to a system in which people have developed "a type of financial consciousness to judge and evaluate economic policy changes". By maintaining a keen awareness of what they are receiving from the government, they can protect their economic interests. Since they do not have access to formal politics "to be political, and remain out of danger, is to consume". In other words, the state has shifted the issues of formal politics from distribution and participation to the realm of consumption. The government maintains its commitment to providing certain basic goods and services to the sha'b (the common people, the grassroots) in return for political acquiescence (Singerman, 1997:245; see also Hoodfar, 1997).

The vast areas of informal settlements on the fringes of the city and the congested inner-city slums indicate that it has been very difficult for the government to meet the demand for urban housing and services in Cairo (Badran, 1994). The city has well over 100 illegal settlements (manatiq al-ashwa'yya), housing over seven million people (Bayat, 1997b). According to another estimate, more than 80 per cent of Cairo's residents are housed in unplanned and unlicensed settlements, not all inhabited only by the poor, but by the middle class as well (Salem, 1994). The illegal/informal housing, representing a large proportion of the Egyptian housing market, is financed entirely by private investment. Squatting is uncommon in Cairo, but occurs on the fringes of the built-up areas, as well as in and around tombs in a cemetery area, the City of the Dead. The overall result is low-quality development deprived of basic services and infrastructure. When these informal settlements reach a population size large enough to exert political pressure, the government is forced to provide them with infrastructure. In many instances, the authorities in Egypt have adopted a *laissez-faire* policy, ignoring illegal occupations, while at other times taking drastic action such as bulldozing poor areas (Kharoufi, 1997; Yousry and Aboul Atta, 1997). Asef Bayat (1997a, 1997b) argues that, although organised social activism is rare among Cairo's poor, this does not mean total lack of grassroots activism. He introduces the concept of *street politics* and refers to the "quiet encroachment of the ordinary" in which the squatters illegally "hook" into the city's infrastructure, thus exposing themselves to a constant risk of repression when in conflict with the authorities. Even though NGOs provide some services and donations to the needy, their ability to empower the lower class remains limited. Bayat concludes that current NGO resources cannot match the magnitude of the needs of the urban poor in Cairo.

The religious structures, the mosque or the church, with their local communal organisations, could provide a means of strengthening the weak civil society in the country. It has been suggested that these could take on a greater role as integrative welfare structures for the people at the grassroots level. An *imam* (in charge of the religious and administrative activities of a mosque) or a priest could act as a community leader. As a fundamental prerequisite, in order to enjoy the trust of the people, he would have to be well educated in both religious and administrative matters, and not closely affiliated to the government. The communities formed around mosques and other religious structures are difficult for outsiders—e.g. government officials and NGO staff—to approach without causing great suspicion on the part of local people. Hence, an *imam*, priest, or *shaykh* (a learned man who is a traditional person in a community) could act as a link or mediator between people and the government or NGOs (Sabet, 1998; Kharoufi, 1997; Singerman, 1997; Deboulet, 1996). Amr Sabet and Ari Salminen (1994) refer to these potential welfare units in the Islamic world as neighbourhood mosques. They are deformalised, decentralised, non-bureaucratic and self-sufficient communal welfare structures based on religion, and requiring minimal intervention from the state. These entities could be responsible for providing health, education, and social security in their immediate environments, through communal contributions, *zakat* income (an Islamic religious tax, which can also be used for non-Muslims; "tithe" in Christianity) and *awqaf* (religious endowments). Such services would be heavily dependent on personalised interaction among neighbours, friends and relatives living close to each other. This kind of structure, might, it is suggested, function as a redistributive mechanism in a society characterised by a very unequal income distribution.

So far, the NGOs initiated from above have been the main civic organisations in Cairo. Their founders have come from the middle and upper classes and have university degrees. The voluntary charity organisations are run by the rich (Ben Néfissa, 1995:46; Gomaa, 1995). It is common for a member of the Egyptian Green Party to establish an NGO outside the rigid and competitive political system, in order to tackle environmental issues more efficiently. This implies that attempts are being made to find new democratic channels for policy-making in environmental issues. "Having an NGO" can also be interpreted as a search for a measure of economic and political power, which, in turn, could provide opportunities for obtaining project funding from foreign donors (Myllylä, 1997). The Cairene NGOs also operate *within* the political system. A typical NGO has a member or lobbyist in the People's Assembly (Singerman, 1997:246). Many NGOs have also declared their intentions to involve the grassroots more closely in their operations (Egyptian Green Party, 1997; on the CBOs, see Kandil and Néfissa, 1995).

In Egypt, it can thus be stated that genuine people's organisations are a rare form of urban associational life. The following section gives an example of an NGO with a "reformist" development agenda. The Association for Protection of the Environment has sought to function as a development catalyst in the waste recyclers' area in Cairo, by tailoring certain environmental practices to the special socio-cultural context of this settlement. In addition, it has used the volunteer workers' personal connections to the political system.

THE *ZABBALEEN* AND THE APE

The *zabbaleen* live in seven areas outside the city proper, of which the largest is the Mokattam settlement with a population estimated at 18,000 in 1997 (Guindy, personal communication). In less than ten years, the Mokattam settlement has been transformed from a mere manual waste sorting point to a recycling industry. The *zabbaleen* have been waste collectors in Cairo for a long time, but the term recyclers is preferable because it describes better the change that has taken place in the settlement as a result of the development intervention by the APE and the other actors. Internationally, the *zabbaleen* experience has served as a model which might be emulated elsewhere in big cities of the developing world. Within Cairo, the *zabbaleen* are becoming better known through environmental awareness-raising projects among the urban population. However, in the case of such a marginalised group and its activities, the process is slow and faces many obstacles.

The *zabbaleen* settlement and early associational activities

The *zabbaleen* settlement is located to the east of Cairo, on the outskirts of the city. It is hidden in the lower part of the Mokattam limestone mountain, but above the low-income district of Manshiet Nasser. Therefore, the settlement has also been called Upper Manshiet Nasser. It is not visible from the city below, but the black smoke from its burning waste is easily recognisable amidst the huge yellowish rocks when passing the area at a distance. To visit the site one must enter through a labyrinth of houses and small roads in Manshiet Nasser below. When arriving in the closed area of the *zabbaleen*, rushing donkey carts and pick-ups filled with different types of solid waste pass by between the multi-storeyed concrete houses. Behind these houses are pigsties. All around people are sorting, moving, and reprocessing various types of household waste. The majority of the population is Coptic, while only four per cent is Muslim.

Waste villages in Egypt are an urban phenomenon dating back to the late 1940s. However, there was a professional group of waste collectors, the *zabbaleen* (singular: *zabbal*), already in the 19th century Cairo (Raymond, 1993:

243). Today's *zabbaleen* have migrated from rural areas in southern Egypt, especially from Assiut, to the capital. Being landless, illiterate peasants, unprotected by the patronage of a large landowner, they were driven by crop failure to the big city in search of a livelihood (Kamel 1994:1).

The *zabbaleen* used to set out on donkey-drawn carts to individual residences in the city, collect the waste, take it back to their settlements and sort it into separate recyclable components. The food waste was fed to pigs and other items sold to recycling centres. Thus, pig production, not recyclables, made up the bulk of their income. Keeping animals was one of the many ways in which they could hang on to their rural origins and *saidi* lifestyle (of southern Egypt). The households paid a monthly fee to a middleman, a *waahi* (originating from an oasis in the desert) who allocated concessions on collection routes to waste collectors, and also earned some profit from the sale of recyclable paper. The *zabbaleen* never received any money from the people they served (Kamel 1994:1–3). The inflow of migrants also meant prosperity to another group of middlemen, the *mu'allim* ("master", land proprietor), who settled the newcomers (Kamel 1994:101). Gradually entire *zabbaleen* families, clans and villages moved to Cairo and took over the task of paper collection from the *waahi*.

The size and number of these squatter settlements, located on the periphery of the city, have increased steadily. Numerous evictions, however, compelled many *zabbaleen* to move to other parts of Cairo, until a large number of them finally settled on the Mokattam Hills, where they built homes of tin, cardboard and fallen rocks, in anticipation of further eviction by the government. Although they felt the place to be secure, it appeared inhospitable: a deserted, rocky and sandy hill with no access to roads, water, or electricity. Fires burned constantly around the village, since all useless waste was set on fire. In the 1990s, several gigantic rocks have fallen from the cliff, killing tens of people (Kamel 1994:3–5, 104–105; *Middle East Times*, 1994:6). Kinship ties have been very strong in the settlement. Kamel (1994: 8) points out that the people formed a complex web of community and family networks, all of which share a common ethnic identity and a destiny of oppression, which served to produce a sense of solidarity.[2]

---

[2] Laila Kamel (1994) stresses that "... [i]t is vitally important to understand that our classification of the various groups of people organised in this productive activity as men, women and children is *not* how the people [the *zabbaleen*] themselves perceive their organisation. Rather, they saw themselves as *fathers* going out on the route with *sons, daughters, nieces,* and *nephews* ..." She refers to the special comprehension of the life of people whose world is formed around "an entire labyrinth of kinship ties through which they perceive themselves and their work". Coming from a *zabbaleen* family (and belonging to the first generation of waste collectors who have received formal education, i.e. one of the "new generation leaders"), Ezzat Naim Guindy (1997) confirmed this by saying that the whole Mokattam settlement actually originates from one big family, and there are strong relationships among the people (see also Rugh, 1985:206–7). In this respect, I could have used the term *community* in this article. I prefer, however, the terms *settlement*, or *neighbourhood*, because I have not studied the issue more closely, and also because the studies of Volpi and Abdel Motaal (1997) indicate that El Gam'iyya has generated tension within the settlement. John Abbot (1996:118–20) points out that "the problem which needs to be faced by urban upgrading, and similar programmes being dealt with through negotiated development, is that they cannot escape the issue of community heterogeneity" (see also Vaa, 1993). There exist many potential conflicts, for instance, between men and women, between landowners and tenants, between different organisations claiming to represent the community etc.

For a long time, the only outsiders who ventured into the Mokattam waste village were merchants of recyclables. But due to strong religious convictions, Egyptians, and some foreigners gradually became involved with this marginalised group. The area has been the object of numerous charity and development activities. In the mid-1970s, a bishop of the Coptic Orthodox Church was the first to initiate mobilisation efforts at the community level, leading to the formation of the Waste Collectors' Association, El Gam'iyya, as a community based organisation (CBO). Thus, the bishop was instrumental in legally forming a non-profit association to assist the people in times of crisis and need. The new organisation, the APE, however, criticised El Gam'iyya, because the most powerful families in the area had allegedly taken over the leadership and distributed the benefits unequally. Elena Volpi (1997) found that El Gam'iyya in the 1980s was a non-participatory organisation, with an authoritarian (or patron-client) leadership style, accountable only to a minority of zabbaleen. Hence, it has been unable to improve the situation of the poorest in the settlement. Laila Kamel (1994:12–15) argues that El Gam'iyya was, nevertheless, a milestone in transforming a private voluntary association from a charity-orientated organisation into a community based development organisation adopting self-help (el maghoud iz-zati, Deboulet, 1996:154) as its approach.

The active priest of the Catholic Church, Father Simon, is the current president of El Gam'iyya, and "the most powerful leader in the settlement", whose personal relations have helped to obtain donor funding (Volpi, 1997:25–26). The services in the settlement have extended beyond liturgy, worship and Christian education, to the establishment of schools, adult literacy classes, services for disabled children, etc. Another important person has been Soeur Emmanuelle, a Catholic nun, who has devoted her life to serving the zabbaleen. The Sisters of Charity (Mother Teresa of India) and El Gabarty Services (headed by Suzanne Mubarak, the wife of Egypt's President) have also offered health and education services to the settlement (Assaad and Garas, 1994:8–10).

Emergence of the APE

The first private voluntary organisation in the area, El Gam'iyya, became the recipient of funds for a credit programme designed to enable waste collectors to become recyclers. In the 1980s the Governorate of Cairo, i.e. the local government, sought to improve its solid waste management. The Governorate selected the Mokattam settlement for participation in a squatter settlement upgrading programme financed by the World Bank. Thus, the local government, which had not previously recognised the settlement, now favoured the upgrading programme, due to the financial support it was to receive from the World Bank (Volpi, 1997:40). In addition to improving the living conditions of the zabbaleen, it was hoped that the waste collection operations could be incorporated into the wider solid waste management system of the city (Assaad and Garas, 1994:1). The World Bank entered into a contract with a Cairene consulting firm, Environmental Quality International (EQI), specialists in solid waste management and urban upgrading programmes, in order to carry out studies on the infrastructure in the area. The EQI was to run an integrated programme to address the main question: how to upgrade the settlement in terms of environmental protection?

Before 1984, the *zabbaleen* used to sell plastic and metal waste to outsiders who recycled it. The EQI came up with the idea of establishing small workshops equipped with machines that could crush and modify different recyclable materials. It was desirable that local people be employed in such enterprises and participate in the manufacturing processes, to ensure that more of the overall economic benefits would accrue to the settlement. In addition to enhanced income generation, the other critical question was how to get rid of the waste which could not be recycled, the *zeriba* waste, i.e. manure from the organic waste fed to pigs, goats and donkeys. It was common practice to get rid of *zeriba* waste by dumping it in the streets, vacant areas, or by storing it in houses or in pits, to be sold later. These practices produced foul odours and were unhealthy and hazardous, causing skin and eye infections. To deal with the problem of the *zeriba* waste—a potential raw material for compost—the EQI studied the feasibility of establishing a composting plant to receive the organic material, ferment and separate it, and eventually sell it as powder compost for agricultural purposes in the desert areas in the country. This new project was meant both to offer solutions to environmental concerns, and to generate income for the settlement from processing residues into high quality soil nutrients.

The critical question concerning the prospects for project success was whether or not the people had the skills to run this type of venture. The EQI found that El Gam'iyya faced several problems related to the sophisticated demands of composting plant management. Therefore, the EQI decided to develop an organisation that could run the plant, in order to generate a profit, which, in turn, could fund and support all the other development activities in the settlement. A development-orientated solution was desired, rather than just a commercial enterprise; thus a producer co-operative was ruled out in favour of a private voluntary organisation. The EQI concluded that an association under the Ministry of Social Affairs would be the only viable option for the envisaged purpose. Thereafter, the EQI approached community leaders as well as outsiders, a few professionals, to form a new organisation. As a result, the Association for Protection of the Environment (APE), a nongovernmental development organisation, was established in 1984 and registered with the Ministry of Social Affairs.

The APE was expected to manage the Mokattam composting plant and initiate other development activities and services in the settlement. The main objective was "to improve the lives of the indigenous groups of waste recyclers as individuals and as a community (...) the principles of participation of the people in decision-making, and of financial and environmental sustainability were highlighted from the beginning." (Assaad and Garas, 1994:40–41). The first priority was to set up its administrative structure and to build the composting plant. In 1987 the APE Board established the first development unit: the Health and Development Committee. However, it was soon realised that applying development principles when working with poor people living under harsh conditions was no easy task. The APE had chosen to work with the most vulnerable group, the poorest young women and girls. Doaa Abdel Motaal (1997) has studied the circumstances under which the *zabbaleen* women live in Mokattam. She observed that the people in the settlement live under extremely overcrowded conditions. Each household keeps 40–50 pigs in sties in the backyards of their residential quarters. The women who sort the waste (10–12 hours daily) are even more susceptible to diseases. Most of the dwellings do not have access to running water, electricity or latrines. The purchase of water from the local church is also the responsibility of women.

Since the emergency needs of the people and adequate responses to them were regarded as important, a Crisis Management Committee was also established within the APE. According to the APE volunteers, the attempt to organise at the grassroots level proved a most difficult exercise for the *zabbaleen*, which was explained as follows (see also Wikan, 1980):

> Due to harsh conditions under which the people live and the tendency to believe in the survival of the fittest, they do not easily trust each other or outsiders. And if they trust, they trust individuals with whom they have had long contact. Workers must first prove worthy of their trust. Moreover, because of the complex family and working relations and the various charity endeavours in the settlement, people enjoy receiving but do not know the meaning of giving. If they are not sure of deserving immediate benefit from the activity, they exercise passive resistance. (Assaad and Garas, 1994:42).

The organisation faced several challenges in the beginning. First, there were very few experts in this field readily available in Egypt. Second, the rent for the plot of land, leased from the municipality, was high, which conflicted with the objective of the project, and placed an extra financial burden on the Association. Third, in plant management, the APE had to adapt job descriptions according to the level of skills and qualifications of the local people, to ensure sustainability of the project after EQI's withdrawal. Fourth, technical difficulties emerged in the operation of the plant (e.g. breakdown of equipment and lack of spare parts), which indicated that the selected technology was perhaps not appropriate. Fifth, environmental hazards from the combustion process used in the plant emerged, in the form of smoke entering living quarters. Furthermore, the established infrastructure—drinking water, sanitation and electricity—was overburdened, due to the continuous influx of new families into the area, as well as the electricity-consuming workshops. As a result, the local infrastructure functioned poorly (Assaad and Garas, 1994:36–40).

The EQI prepared a feasibility study for the composting plant and was instrumental in the formation of the APE. It also provided technical and management assistance to the organisation in the initial stage of its operation, and was represented on the Board of directors of the APE (Assaad and Garas, 1994:35). In accordance with the law, the APE, as an NGO, was governed by a General Assembly which held annual meetings and selected Board members who direct all activities of the Association. There are nine Board members, seven of whom are women. They organise all the main activities, adopt policies and are responsible for strategic planning. Both the General Assembly members and the Board members are volunteers, as required by law. Some 50 paid professional staff implement the policies and carry out practical activities. The composting plant is the basis for all activities, since its proceeds cover staff salaries and maintenance as well as overhead costs. Other activities, such as a rug-weaving centre, cover their own staff salaries, materials, machines and other direct costs.

The composting plant and rug-weaving centre

The Mokattam composting plant became the focus of the settlement and the organisation. The EQI helped in securing funding, in which Les Amis de Soeur Emmanuelle in Mokattam played a very important role. They turned to the European Union, which decided to provide support. The Ford Foundation also gave a grant. The plant was expected to upgrade the environment of the settlement as a whole by (Assaad and Garas, 1994:35–36, quoting EQI, 1984):

1. clearing streets of animal *zeribas* and other organic waste, thus encouraging improvement of the level of cleanliness and sanitation;

2. generating surplus funds that could be channelled into other activities aimed at further improving the settlement, and at providing self-support after the withdrawal of donors; and

3. increasing the effectiveness of the services provided by the *zabbaleen*.

Currently, there are two composting plants in operation, because it became necessary to double the capacity. The composting plants are located almost in the middle of the settlement.

The household waste collection work of the *zabbaleen* precedes the recycling process. A *zabbal* has to cover a route of tens of kilometres on a daily basis. He transports the collected material up the hill with two exhausted donkeys pulling his small wooden cart. Then the whole family starts sorting the material.

> Each waste collector traditionally has his own area in Cairo to collect from. In the early hours of the morning a *zabbal* goes with his son to the households and brings the waste into his house, and he starts sorting. After that the plastics, metals and papers are stored inside the house. When he has a good quantity for sale, the raw material is sold to recyclers. Then he has the leftovers from the kitchen, which he gives to animals ... and after that he collects the manure and mixes it with the leftovers from kitchen, and brings it to the Association (Guindy, 1997).

The next phase in the process is to take the *zeriba* waste to the composting site. The continuous traffic of donkey carts loaded with manure are not pulled, but rather slowed by donkeys on sliding hooves, down the steep road leading to the composting plant:

> So here [to the Association] becomes the "waste of the waste", after the animals are fed. It is then dropped into two loaders [composting machines] which sepa-

rate it ... and which have pit drums with many holes to allow the powder of the compost to fall down between the concrete walls, and the other waste comes from the other side, and we take that to be fermented again ... the waste will be kept heated under the sun for six weeks ... the loader turns it over once a week. After that we measure the temperature inside it and when we are sure that it is 70 degrees, it [the compost] is good (Guindy, 1997).

In its new form, the soil does not contain the harmful bacteria of unrefined manure, but another severe problem has arisen in the process: a high level of heavy metals in the composted soil. In order to tackle this problem of soil contamination, a pilot project was started to separate waste at source, i.e. in the households of Cairo. It took a few years for the APE to monitor and follow up the pilot project. For this purpose, a team of young men was trained to visit the households and remind them to continue sorting their waste. Two different types of experimental sites were chosen: households from both high-income and low-income areas. It appeared that the latter were more interested in the sorting process than the former. The households were given two different boxes, one for organic and the other for inorganic waste. After this experiment, the heavy metal level in the composted soil dropped considerably. The experiment reduced contamination in animals fed with the organic waste. Moreover, it had a significant effect on the life of the women because their work—separation of the waste—became less time-consuming, thus releasing time for other tasks. Currently, the APE is planning to extend the project by including new high-income areas, in which some 50,000 units (households and restaurants) will participate. Apart from its environmental objectives, the project aims at continuously enhancing the pride and reputation of the despised *zabbaleen*.

Thus, the upgrading project began with recycling of organic pig manure from *zeribas* into high-grade compost, which was sold to agricultural areas, including reclaimers of desert land. This activity generated income which was directed to a) a community based health project; b) an income-generating project for girls and women in rag and paper recycling; c) literacy classes and d) a children's club.

In 1988, a second initiative was launched by the Association, which again took charge of a settlement-wide project. The project focused on the poorest women and girls, who were taught to recycle clean rags into rugs by weaving on handlooms. Simple technology was used in teaching basic skills to girls and women who might be regarded as dispossessed. Skilled craftsmen were brought in to teach them. The Association established small private sector-type enterprises to create employment opportunities. In fundraising, it "freed itself" from Western sources and introduced the traditional system of *zakat*, allegedly forgotten in modern development work. The APE took advantage of personal networks in this fundraising campaign: owners of textile factories and shops were asked to give *zakat* in the form of rags to the project. Other types of donations (materials, machines and services) from the private sector, embassies and women's groups also contributed. The trained participants, women and girls, are now able to support their families (Kamel, 1994:23–32; Assaad and Moharram, 1994).

Recycling workshops

In the settlement, each family has specialised in a certain material, which is indicated by the type of waste piled up in front, or on the roofs, of its house: cardboard, paper, plastic, glass, tin or clothes. Women and girls sort food waste, at which they spend four to six hours daily. The simple machines in the small workshops reprocess the material collected. The plastic items are first separated by colour and stored in containers, then crushed and modified into pipes and clothes hangers, for example. Other products include shoes, textiles, pots and pans. Glass is also sorted into big containers, and sold to factories in Cairo. Plastic recycling has enabled the machine owners to increase their income significantly, but only about 100 people in the settlement own recycling machines (Volpi, 1997:21).

In the middle of the colourful plastic heaps, men cut plastic bottles into two pieces with huge scissors, for cleaning. The economic benefit deriving from recycling of plastic depends on the manufacturing process of the raw material:

> In the workshops the men sort the plastic according to type and colour. After sorting they crush it in the machine, the plastic is still dirty. Then they sell it and another person who buys it inside the community cleans it. In another process people sort and then clean it by washing in boiling water with ammonia, and after that they dry it under the sun, and then crush it in order to sell it as clean pieces, so it is ready for recycling. In the first type of process the price is cheap, and the latter is more expensive thus more profitable ... Why, then, is it not cleaned first? Maybe because there are no machines or workers for cleaning ... In the past, the El Gam'iyya used to give loans to people for machines, but not any more. Now people themselves save money and start to organise their own projects (Guindy, 1997).

The settlement receives 700 tons of solid waste daily from households, of which 250–300 tons is organic waste. The amount of unrecyclable waste is relatively small, 10–15 per cent. Since the flow of waste is so enormous, it is difficult to avoid accumulation of waste in the living environment. Unrecyclable waste is usually burned or just dumped outside the settlement. The largest dumping site is in Qattameyya, 35 kilometres from Cairo. El Gam'iyya rents trucks, for each of which a waste collector has to pay 15 Egyptian pounds, in order to get rid of his waste. Half of the people hire trucks to move unrecyclable material to Qattameyya, and another half burn the waste, or dump it in the streets. Burning environmentally noxious materials creates dangerous smoke, and the smell of manure attracts swarms of flies—all of which create exceptionally choking conditions in the settlement, especially during the hot summer months when temperatures reach 40 degrees. Even though the living conditions have improved greatly compared to the past, in some places dead animals can still be found lying in the middle of unrecyclable plastic bags, rags, discarded razors and batteries, which add to the severity of the health hazards.

The most serious problem in solid waste recycling is the type of plastic waste that cannot be reused. Due to increasing Western-style consumption in the city, the amount of unrecyclable waste is expected to grow in the future.

Anything which is not for selling ... nobody asks for black plastic bags since everyone knows you can't use them ... white bags can be recycled. Also children's diapers and family size Pepsi or Coca-Cola bottles are not recyclable. Mostly things that are burnt are these. We arranged through our team health visitors' awareness activity ... they visited the people from door to door: "if you fire the waste, your children will get sick and then you will pay about 50–60 pounds for the doctor per one child, so paying the fee for dumping is cheaper and your children are healthier" (Guindy, 1997).

One side effect of the recycling industry in the settlement has been severe air pollution from vehicles and machines, a consequence which was not taken into account initially.

The APE's relations with other associations and the government

The Association co-operates, to some extent, with the other associations in Mokattam and the neighbourhood: El Gam'iyya, El Gabarty Services, El Salam Hospital, El Mahabba Clinic and Anglo American Hospital (Kamel, 1994:126). Networking and collaboration are necessary to avoid duplication of effort. Knowledge is said to be exchanged at NGO meetings, workshops, and seminars, as organisations "train" each other (Guindy, 1997). However, at least in the case of El Gam'iyya and the APE, their relationship has not evolved without difficulty. Volpi (1997:31–32) observed that El Gam'iyya felt challenged by the APE, particularly with regard to funding. Similarly, the APE has criticised El Gam'iyya for representing only privileged families and for failing to improve the lot of the poorest and women. Furthermore, the settlement is divided into two geographical parts, each falling under the influence of one of the respective organisations.

> The antagonistic relations between the APE and El Gam'iyya prevent the self-sustainability of the activities implemented in favour of the *zabbaleen*. On the other hand, from the beneficiaries' point of view, it favours the multiplication of projects and ensures a constant influx of resources to the settlement. (Volpi, 1997:32)

The international NGO community knows the APE quite well. The Association has co-operated with several European NGOs, many of which are religious and health organisations, and with larger organisations such as Oxfam and the Ford Foundation. Moreover, the Association was selected as one of the global 500 environmental organisations by the UN Environment Programme (UNEP). Recently, the experiences of Mokattam have been replicated in Bombay and Manila (Vincentian Missionaries, 1998) because it has proven an economically sustainable and environmentally suitable solution for these cities. The co-ordinating NGO of this venture was the Mega-Cities Project, which aims at improving urban management and conditions of life in the world's largest cities (Badshah, 1995; Badshah and Lazar, 1995; *Mega-Citizen*, 1995:2).

The APE receives funds from national and international donors, e.g. the Egyptian International Co-operation Ministry and the European Union. Any funds received must be approved by the Ministry of Social Affairs; no external funds may be channelled directly. The reports from the General Assembly have to be submitted to the Ministry, which sometimes sends a representative to attend meetings.

The Association has started cultivating contacts with the Egyptian Environmental Affairs Agency (EEAA) and is approaching industry, by inviting representatives to visit the settlement. So far, interest has been only slight. Yet, it will be vital for the APE to co-operate more closely with industry. A new project proposal for spreading awareness of the *zabbaleen* among Cairenes is under consideration. It is hoped that it will be implemented with the help of the Ministry of Information and the national media, but it still requires funding. The organisation's Board members and other volunteers have several personal connections with governmental institutions and the political system, which are very important in lobbying for the goals of the APE.

AN UNFINISHED METAMORPHOSIS IN A DIFFICULT ENVIRONMENT

In many instances, NGOs have emerged as a complement to the local government's efforts to cope with various urban problems in Cairo, ushering in a new era of urban governance. Associational life in the city, however, faces a paradox. On the one hand, to engage in spontaneous grassroots activism has been very difficult for residents, due to strict government control and a lethargic bureaucracy, as well as lack of resources in the poorest communities. On the other hand, "outsiders", professionals and other educated persons from the upper classes, have founded the majority of NGOs in the environmental field. This has invoked criticisms of elitism. Nevertheless, Cairene NGOs have discovered ways of proliferating in a difficult political environment by finding sponsors in the political and administrative systems. This probably means that the *status quo* will be maintained with regard to power relations and distribution of resources.

Although the Association was initiated in a top-down fashion by outsiders, today it likes to project itself as a grassroots organisation because it is 80 per cent run by the *zabbaleen*, particularly the educated and trained "new generation leaders" (Assaad and Moharram, 1994; Guindy, 1997). The APE has not succeeded, however, in creating alternative forms of grassroots organisation. It has faced great difficulty in "promoting horizontal participation in a context traditionally foreign to this approach" (Assaad, 1993/94, quoted in Volpi, 1997:36).

The *zabbaleen* experience demonstrates how a squatter settlement upgrading project evolved into a development intervention, transforming the lives of at least a segment of the waste collectors into that of recyclers and owners of micro enterprises. Hence, despite the numerous internal difficulties El Gam'iyya and the APE are facing, their experiences in solid waste disposal as a whole is considered a successful example with potential for replication in other big cities. The case represents a peculiar phenomenon in the country. Notwithstanding the overwhelming positive international and national attention the Association has received, some Egyptian critics point out that the settlement receives a disproportionate amount of attention overshadowing the good work of other organisations and communities elsewhere in the country.

Social movement theories highlight the importance of the mobilisational strategies of organisational elites in activating people in low-income areas (Tarrow, 1991), which the case of the Mokattam settlement seems to confirm. Religion and its local structures also played an obvious part—as in other parts of Africa, where the role of missionaries has been important in organisational life (Fowler et al., 1992; Bratton, 1994; Agbola, 1994). Moreover, the technical and administrative know-how of the APE was soon complemented by social approaches, in contrast to many other cases (see e.g. Vaa, 1993).

The *zabbaleen* experience shows plainly how necessary it is to introduce appropriate solutions and to be sensitive to particular socio-environmental and cultural realities. One remaining problem is the continued exposure of the *zabbaleen* to various health risks, which raises a fundamental question: should the City sustain this activity—and if not, what can it offer these people in return? Currently, the question of land ownership need to be clarified with the municipality, in order to reduce living costs, and contribute to the sustainability of the projects. At the moment land may be purchased but it is too expensive for most of the people in the settlement. These and other matters would require better collaboration and co-ordination between the two associations. To which constituency are they primarily accountable? Bearing in mind the internal tension of most urban neighbourhoods the definition and usage of the term "community based organisation" (CBO) warrants critical re-examination.

Non-governmental organisations are newcomers in urban governance, in Cairo as elsewhere. They are often reputed to be troublemakers in the eyes of other actors. Yet, more co-operation between different actors is required in the face of complex urban challenges. In this regard NGOs have certain comparative advantages that could be exploited more widely. Although their path appears to be a rocky one, NGOs have entered urban governance to stay.

References

Books, journals and reports

Abbott, John, 1996, *Sharing the City. Community Participation in Urban Management*. London: Earthscan.

Abdel Motaal, Doaa, 1997, "Women at the Muqattam Settlement", in Volpi, Elena and Doaa Abdel Motaal (eds), *The Zabbalin Community of Muqattam*. Cairo Papers in Social Science, Vol. 19, Monograph 4. Cairo: The American University in Cairo Press.

Agbola, Tunde, 1994, "NGOs and Community Development in Urban Areas—A Nigerian Case Study", *Cities*, Vol. 11, No. 1, pp. 59–67.

Al-Sayyid, Mustapha Kamil, 1995, "A Civil Society in Egypt?", in Norton A., (ed.), *Civil Society in the Middle East*. Leiden: E.J. Brill.

Assaad, Marie and Nadra Garas, 1994, *Experiments in Community Development in a Zabbaleen Settlement*. Cairo Papers in Social Science, Vol. 16, No. 3. Cairo: The American University in Cairo Press.

Assaad, Marie and Ayman Moharram, 1994, *The Role of NGOs in Solid Waste Management*. Cairo: The Association for Protection of the Environment.

Badshah, Akhtar and Reena Lazar, 1995, "Sharing Approaches That Work: Transfer and Adaptation of Urban Innovations", *Co-operation South,* May, pp. 29–33. Technical Co-operation among Developing Countries, UN.

Bayat, Asef, 1997a, "Cairo's Poor, Dilemmas of Survival and Solidarity", *Middle East Report,* Winter, pp. 1–12,

—, 1997b, "Un-civil Society: The Politics of the 'Informal People'", *Third World Quarterly,* Vol. 18, No. 1, pp. 53–72.

Ben Néfissa, Sarah, 1995, "Associations égyptiennes: une libéralisation sous contrôle", *Monde arabe Maghreb-Machrek,* No. 150, Octobre–Décembre, pp. 40–56.

Bratton, Michael, 1994, "Civil Society and Political Transitions in Africa", in Harbeson, John W. et al. (eds), *Civil Society and the State in Africa.* Boulder: Lynne Rienner Publishers.

Deboulet, Agnés, 1996, "Devenir citadin ... Ou partir à la conquete de droits urbains élémentaires: exemples tirés de faubourgs récents du Caire", in Lussault, Michel et Pierre Signoles, (eds), 1996, *La citadinité en questions.* Fascicule de Recherches no 29 d'URBAMA, Université de Tours.

Egypt Today, 1994, "NGOs Coming into their own", 7:94 (interviews with Marlyn Tadros and Aziza Hussein, The National NGO Steering Committee).

EnviroNet, 1994, Newsletter of the Project in Development and the Environment, Vol. 3, No. 1. Asia/Near East Bureau, U.S. Agency for International Development.

Fowler, Alan, Piers Campbell and Brian Pratt, 1992, *Institutional Development & NGOs in Africa.* Oxford: INTRAC and Novib.

Gomaa, Salwa S., 1992, "Environmental Politics in Egypt", in Hopkins, Nicholas (ed.), *Environmental Challenges in Egypt and the World.* Cairo Papers in Social Science, Vol. 15, No. 4. Cairo: The American University in Cairo Press.

— ed., 1995, *Environmental Threats in Egypt: Perceptions and Actions.* Cairo Papers in Social Science, Vol. 17, No. 4. Cairo: The American University in Cairo Press.

Harbeson, John, Donald Rothchild and Naomi Chazan (eds), 1994, *Civil Society and the State in Africa.* Boulder, CO: Lynne Rienner.

Hardoy, Jorge, Diana Mitlin and David Satterthwaite, 1995, *Environmental Problems in Third World Cities.* (First ed. 1992.) London: Earthscan.

Hoodfar, Homa, 1997, *Between Marriage and the Market. Intimate Politics and Survival in Cairo.* Berkeley: University of California Press.

Hopkins, Nicholas et al., 1995, "Pollution and People in Cairo", in Gomaa, Salwa S. (ed.), *Environmental Threats in Egypt: Perceptions and Actions.* Cairo Papers in Social Science, Vol. 17, No. 4. Cairo: The American University in Cairo Press.

Hopkins, Nicholas and Sohair Mehanna, 1997, "Pollution, Popular Perceptions and Grassroots Environmental Activism", *Middle East Report,* Winter 1997, pp. 21–25.

Kandil, Amani and Sarah Ben Néfissa, 1995, *Al-Gamiyyat Al-Ahli Fi Al-Misr.* Cairo: Al Ahram Strategic Studies.

Kamel, Laila R. Iskandar, 1994, *Mokattam Garbage Village.* Cairo: Stallion Graphics.

King, Alexander and Bertrand Schneider, 1994, *The First Global Revolution.* A Report by The Council of The Club of Rome London: Simon & Schuster.

Kharoufi, Mostafa, 1994, "Reflections on a Research Field: Urban Studies in Egypt Morocco and The Sudan", in Stren, Richard (ed.), *Urban Research in the Developing World: Africa* Vol. 2. Centre for Urban and Community Studies, University of Toronto.

—, 1997, "Governance of Urban Society in North Africa: Morocco, Algeria, Tunisia and Egypt", in Swilling, Mark (ed.), *Governing Africa's Cities.* Johannesburg: Witwatersrand University Press.

Kooiman, J, 1993, "Social-Political Governance: Introduction", in Kooiman, J. (ed.), *Modern Governance—New Government-Society Interactions.* London: Sage.

Mega-Cities Project Inc., 1995, *Local Initiatives In Community Health.* New York.

Mega-Citizen, 1995, The Newsletter of the Mega-Cities Project, Vol. 2., No. 1. New York.

Middle East Times, 1994, "Zabbaleen rising to the top of the heap", 11–17 September, p. 6.

Myllylä, Susanna, 1997, "The New Dawn of Social Movements in the Southern Mediterranean Cities", in Linjakumpu, Aini and Kirsi Virtanen (eds), *Under the Olive Tree: Reconsidering Mediterranean Culture and Politics.* Tampere Peace Research Institute and the European Science Foundation.

Perlman, Janice, 1990, "A Dual Strategy for Deliberate Social Change in Cities", *Cities,* Vol. 7, No. 1, pp. 3–15.

Raymond, André, 1993, *Le Caire*. Fayard: Paris.

Rugh, Andrea, 1988, *Family in Contemporary Egypt*. (First ed. 1985.) Cairo: The American University in Cairo Press.

Sabet, Amr and Ari Salminen, 1994, "On Welfare, Administration and Communicative Action: A Local Community Islamic-Nordic Comparative View", in Ahonen, Pertti (ed.), *The Political Economy of Finnish Administration*. Tampere: Finnpublishers.

Sachikonye Lloyd, 1995, "Democracy, Civil Society and Social Movements. An Analytical Framework", in Sachikonye Lloyd (ed.), *Democracy, Civil Society and the State. Social Movements in Southern Africa*. Harare: SAPES Books.

Salem, Osama, 1994, "Urban Bias and Urban Slums", *CEDARE Chronicle*, Vol. 2, No. 2.

Shukrallah, Alaa, 1998, "NGOs and Disability Activities in Egypt", in Hossain, Farhad and Susanna Myllylä, (eds), *NGOs Under Challenge: Dynamics and Drawbacks in Development*. Ministry for Foreign Affairs of Finland, Department for International Development Co-operation, Helsinki.

Singerman, Diane, 1997, *Avenues of Participation—Family, Politics and Networks in Urban Quarters of Cairo*. Cairo: The American University in Cairo Press.

Sullivan, Earl L. (Tim), 1983, "Should Cairo be Governed?", in Lobban, Richard (ed.), *Urban Research Strategies for Egypt*. Cairo Papers in Social Science, Vol. 6, No. 2. Cairo: The American University in Cairo Press.

Swilling, Mark, ed., 1997, *Governing Africa's Cities*. Johannesburg: Witwatersrand University Press.

Tarrow, Sidney, 1991, *Struggle, Politics, and Reform: Collective Action, Social Movements, and Cycles of Protest*. Western Societies Papers. Cornell Studies in International Affairs.

Tvedt, Terje, 1998, "NGOs Role at 'the End of History': Norwegian Policy and the New Paradigm", in Hossain, Farhad and Myllylä, Susanna (eds.), *NGOs Under Challenge: Dynamics and Drawbacks in Development*. Ministry for Foreign Affairs of Finland, Department for International Development Co-operation, Helsinki.

Vaa, Mariken, 1993, "Community Participation in Urban Development Planning", *Forum for Development Studies*, 2, pp. 167–75.

Vincentian Missionaries, 1998, "The Payatas Environmental Development Programme: Micro-enterprise promotion and involvement in solid waste management in Quezon City", *Environment and Urbanisation* Vol. 10, No. 2, October 1998, pp. 55–68.

Volpi, Elena, 1997, "Community Organisation and Development", in Volpi, Elena and Abdel Motaal Doaa (eds), *The Zabbalin Community of Muqattam*. Cairo Papers in Social Science, Vol. 19, Monograph 4. Cairo: The American University in Cairo Press.

Wikan, Unni, 1980, *Life among the Poor in Cairo*. London: Tavistock Publications.

Yousry, Mahmoud and Tarek Aboul Atta, 1997, "The Challenge of Urban Growth in Cairo", in Rakodi, Carole (ed.), *The Urban Challenge in Africa, Growth and Management of Its Large Cities*. Tokyo: United Nations University Press.

Zubaida, Sami, 1989, *Islam, the People and the State. Essays on Political Ideas and Movements in the Middle East*. London: Routledge.

Personal communications

Abdel Wahab, Ayman (Researcher) Al Ahram Center for Political and Strategic Studies, March 1997, Cairo.

Assaad, Marie (Anthropologist and Volunteer), The Association for Protection of Environment, August 1994, Cairo.

Badran, Osman (Consultant and Advisor) Ministry of Reconstruction and New Communities in Egypt, September 1994, Cairo.

Badshah, Akhtar (Director of Programs), Mega-City Project, December 1995, New York.

Bayat, Asef, (Associate Professor) Dept. of Sociology, The American University in Cairo, April 1997.

The Egyptian Green Party members, April 1997, Cairo.

El-Ghayati, Sami (Chairman) Society for Preservation of Nature, April 1997, Cairo.

Gomaa, Salwa S. (Professor) Social Research Center, The American University in Cairo, February 1994 and March 1997.

Guindy, Ezzat Naim (Vice-Director of Health and Development Committee and Public Relations Officer) The Association for Protection of Environment, April 1997, Cairo.

Hopkins, Nicholas (Professor) Dept. of Anthropology, The American University in Cairo, April 1997.

Mehanna, Sohair (Senior Researcher) Social Research Center, The American University in Cairo, April 1997.

Moharram, Ayman (Veterinary Surgeon) Association for Protection of Environment, August 1994, Cairo.

Sabet, Amr (Associate Professor) Dept. of International Politics, University of Tampere, May 1998.

Shukrallah, Alaa (Chairman) The Association for Health and Environmental Development, March 1997, Heliopolis.

CHAPTER 13

Reactions to Deteriorating Provision of Public Services in Dar es Salaam

Robert M. Mhamba and Colman Titus

The nature, characteristics and repercussions of developing countries' urbanisation and the failure of state and local authorities to provide urban amenities are issues which are well documented. In response to discontent with central or local government performance, people have increasingly taken action, both individually and collectively, in order to improve their welfare. These actions may take many and varied forms, ranging from advocacy and campaigns for political, economic, social and environmental improvement to provision, production operation and maintenance of public amenities. It therefore seems appropriate to look more closely into the particular circumstances which induce people to organise themselves, and the areas of service provision their newly formed associations cater for.

This study aims at analysing peoples' response to increasing shortages of urban services and the response of central and local government to popular action. Dar es Salaam, which is the largest city in Tanzania, is taken as a case study. Given the fact that there is a proliferation of individuals and groups taking action, one may expect to find a wide set of organisations, with varied objectives and motivations. This study attempts to qualitatively analyse both individuals and associations formed within civil society. It is based on data collected through a series of interviews with informed local observers, such as City Commission officials in the Department of Community Development, government officials in the Prime Ministers Office and various professionals. Data were also obtained from voluntary associations formed in the city. In this chapter, these associations are referred to as people's organisations, POs (Turner and Hulme, 1997).

URBANISATION IN TANZANIA

The pattern of urbanisation and characteristic features of Tanzania's urban areas are quite similar to what is observed in many other low-income countries. This section aims at highlighting some particular elements of urbanisation in Tanzania. Mainland Tanzania has a total of 20 regional headquarters and a number of small urban centres, which are either district headquarters or marketing centres located close to mining or agriculturally productive areas. Apart from being administrative centres, the regional headquarters also serve as industrial, commercial and service centres. District headquarters, on the other hand, are rather small urban centres with a limited range of activities, mainly limited to commerce and small scale services.

The urban population in Tanzania has in the last three decades more than quadrupled. In 1970, only seven per cent of the country's population was living in urban areas. By 1995, the proportion had increased to 32 per cent, and is expected to be 39 per cent in 2005 (UN, 1998). This chapter explores how urban residents have responded to persistent and escalating deficiencies in urban services. The analysis begins with a general introduction to the city of Dar es Salaam, then proceeds with a presentation of how its residents have reacted to the urban problems. A typology for the classification of popular initiatives is proposed.

The City of Dar es Salaam

Dar es Salaam, which means haven of peace, is the largest and fastest growing city in Tanzania. With an estimated population of about 3 million in 1997, it is currently seven times larger than the next largest urban centre of Mwanza (Sheuya, 1997:6). The rate of growth of the city, which is between 8 and 10 per cent per year, is one of the highest in Sub-Saharan Africa. The main source of growth is in-migration of people from rural areas and from neighbouring countries. However, natural increase plays an important role too. Dar es Salaam also is the headquarters of many national organisations, industries and ministerial offices and it is where all the offices of foreign country representatives and those of various multilateral and international organisations in the country are situated.

Until June 1996, Dar es Salaam was managed by the Dar es Salaam City Council (i.e. local government) which was the highest policymaking body in the city. In June 1996, the national government decided to suspend local authorities and appointed a commission, Dar es Salaam City Commission, to manage the city. The Dar es Salaam City Council was dissolved because it failed to comply with the provisions of the Local Government Act of 1982 and conducted its affairs in a manner that was incompatible with the purpose of that act. Unfortunately, the Prime Minister's Office dissolved the Dar es Salaam City Council and appointed the City Commission without any consultation with city residents. They were thus denied the opportunity to participate in exercising power in the management of their local government's economic and social resources in a legal and formal way.

Provision of public services

Public services or utilities have to be provided, produced and maintained to ensure a sustained flow of services to the public. Ostrom et al. (1993) have distinguished between provision and production in the public realm as follows:

> Provision refers to decision made through collective-choice mechanism about: the kind of goods and services to be provided by a designated group of people; the quantity and quality of the goods and services to be provided; the degree to which private activities related to these goods and services are to be regulated; how to arrange for the production of these goods and services; how to monitor

219

the performance of those who produce these goods and services. Whereas production refers to the more technical process of transforming inputs into outputs, making a product or in many cases rendering a service. (Ostrom et al., 1993:75.)

Like in many other cities in the world, urban authorities are responsible for the provision of urban public services in Tanzania. The history of urban authorities in the country dates back to 1910, when the German administration elevated Dar es Salaam and Tanga urban centres to municipal level. At independence in addition to these two municipalities there were 11 town councils, established under the 1946 Municipalities' Act and Local Government Act of 1953 (Mateso, 1993:3). These urban authorities were responsible for providing sanitation and water supply, surveying and allocating plots and issuing building permits in their municipalities and townships respectively. In 1972, however, urban authorities were abolished and Tanzania adopted "decentralisation". The move was aimed at shifting decision-making power from state level to local level. Regional and district authorities were charged with the responsibility for all public services in both urban and rural areas. The newly established authorities however, were to concentrate on rural development, since that was the priority of the government at the time. Consequently, urban public utilities like water supply and sanitation, roads, and also urban planning and building regulations were neglected (JICA, 1997). Unplanned settlements grew rapidly, as there was no efficient and effective system to control them. As part of easing urban problems, the government adopted a system of repatriating the urban jobless, homeless and beggars by force to the rural areas. Repatriation however, proved unfruitful, as the repatriated returned to town within a few days of their repatriation.

In 1982, the government decided to reintroduce local government and the relevant institutions started to function in 1984. Apart from other functions, local governments were charged with the responsibility of providing, producing and maintaining public utilities and services in urban areas. However, urban problems persisted and are escalating. These problems include, inadequate housing, and shortage of surveyed housing plots to meet the growing housing demand (JICA, 1997). In addition, there is inadequate supply and maintenance of already available public utilities (e.g. water supply and sanitation), as well as deteriorating urban roads. In 1991 only 51 per cent of the urban population had access to tap water (Mhamba, 1996:35). As water taps in Tanzania's urban areas are almost always without water, access to adequate and safe water supply for the urban population may be far less than indicated in the official statistics. In the period 1991/92 only 14 per cent of the urban population had flush toilets; when water is short these toilets are rendered useless. About 84 per cent used pit-latrines and almost two per cent did not have any toilet (United Republic of Tanzania, 1994). However, the shortage or absence of evacuating tankers in some urban areas in the country renders pit-latrines difficult to maintain. The urban roads, macadamised during the colonial period, are now almost all dust roads with deep and sharp potholes and most of them are impassable by car. In fact some of these roads have become urban waste dumping grounds and using them is very difficult.

As a result, most urban residents in Tanzania lack decent housing, a clean and reliable water supply and functioning sanitation services. Roads are very poor and the air is polluted. Schools and health care units facilities leave much to be desired. Poor urban management and institutional bottlenecks have exacerbated these problems.

PEOPLE'S INITIATIVES TO SOLVE SERVICE PROBLEMS

People's initiatives to improve conditions in their neighbourhoods, localities or at higher levels generally have two main aspects. The first aspect relates to efforts geared towards influencing actors, such as policy makers, executives, private enterprises and NGOs to act in a way that will result in changes from unsatisfactory states of affairs. This involves actions that might induce different actors to focus their attention on alleviating existing problems. Such attempts to influence policy decisions and implementation can be done either by people individually or collectively, through open confrontation and mass protest, or advocacy, lobbying and sensitisation of the legislative and executive organs. It also involves inducing or instigating members of the public to take action against unsatisfactory states of affairs. Efforts in this respect are aimed at motivating people to act, as well as providing them with information about their rights and the proper procedures for solving their problems. Motivation touches on people's feelings, attitudes and allegiances where as information may modify thoughts, insights and beliefs (Heideman, 1992:107).

The second aspect of people's reactions to unsatisfactory states of affairs involves decisions to take matters into their own hands, i.e. to perform operations themselves, either individually or collectively, so as to solve the problems they have identified. This is a process of allocating own resources, be it time, labour or funds, so as to bring about desired changes.

The growing problems and shortages of urban utilities in Dar es Salaam have led its residents to take initiatives to provide services themselves. One can distinguish two main patterns, Individual Action Initiatives (IAI) and Collective Action Initiatives (CAI). The two patterns and their subsidiaries are represented in Figure 13:1. These two main brands of people's initiatives can be further classified according to whether they are destructive or constructive, permanent or non permanent, undertaken for profit or non-profit.

Individual action initiatives

A destructive individual action is a strategy adopted in both residential and industrial locations by individuals and industrial firms respectively. In their initiatives to provide themselves with services which the city council has failed to provide, households and industrialists adopt strategies which jeopardise the public interests. The strategy carries along with it short and long run negative effects not only for the individual, but also for the urban population and the environment as a whole. Faced with the problem of insufficient surveyed plots, residents have built their houses in unsurveyed areas without seeking any official permission. They later look for a surveyor to survey the already developed plot. This process frustrates future efforts to design urban streets,

construct urban drainage systems, install water supply systems etc. and it becomes technically impossible to straighten streets or install water supply systems without demolishing some buildings. Even if it is possible to demolish
some buildings, lack of finance to compensate the affected owners, forces the
city authorities and the national government to shy away from undertaking
such a move.

Figure 13:1. *People's initiatives in solving urban public utility or service
problems in Dar es Salaam City*

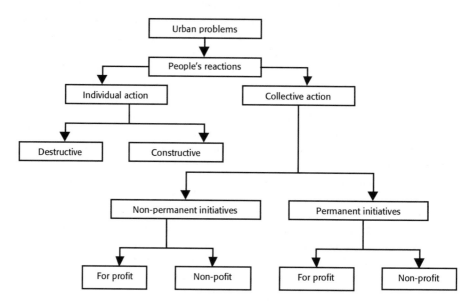

Individual destructive actions also include households' emptying of septic
tanks into the streets at night. A household using a pit latrine may dig a hole
or an opening on the side of a latrine so as to allow waste to ooze out and be
washed away by rain water. Solid waste is partly thrown on the streets or left
in open spaces at night. This is the dominant practice for the disposal of solid
waste. Apart from being a nuisance to the entire neighbourhood, it pollutes
the environment and creates more problems than it solves. In the low-density
residential areas, households may use on-site treatment of solid waste since
they have available space for it. However, that too pollutes the environment,
especially groundwater, which is the source of drinking water in many parts of
the city. In the industrial areas, untreated water from industries is allowed to
flow into the natural water courses, hazardous solid waste is thrown into open
spaces or dumping sites, which are normally located not far from the residential areas.

However, some individuals resort to constructive initiatives. These are
individuals who voluntarily decide to allocate their own resources to provide,
produce and/or maintain one or more of the public utilities or services. The
motivation may be to find a solution for their personal needs, but sometimes

benefits from their initiatives spill over to an entire neighbourhood or locality. This happens especially when benefits from a public utility or service have non-excludability characteristics, i.e. when benefits of a good or service are available to a group, whether or not members of the group contribute to their provision. Typical examples are construction and maintenance of roads.

Collective action initiatives

The second non-conventional strategy is what we call in this chapter "Collective Action Initiatives", which can be subdivided into two, depending on their time perspective. These are "Non permanent collective action" and "Permanent collective action". Both types can either be for profit or non-profit. The first category consists of individuals who organise themselves for the purpose of making money from offering a temporary solution for an iden-tified problem. The overwhelming motive behind such collective efforts is not to mitigate the problem, but rather to earn income for the day. POs of this kind exploit the existing problematic situation to generate income i.e. to seek rent from users of the utility concerned. Such initiatives are found in road construction and maintenance, especially during the rainy seasons, as well as house-to-house collection of solid waste in high-density areas.

Within the non-permanent collective action initiatives, a second category of initiative may be identified. This is when people in a neighbourhood or locality organise themselves so as to find ways of solving a shared utility problem and thus improve the state of their welfare. In this case members of this type of association expect to directly benefit from the outcomes of their initiatives. This sort of initiative may also emerge during disasters, which hit people indiscriminately. They are thus naturally forced to unite together to find emergency means to rectify the situation. Collective action initiatives in these cases have normally included efforts to pool resources, in terms of la-bour contributions and also the formation of committees to represent the af-fected neighbourhood or locality to the higher authorities to solicit assistance. Committees formed on this basis have, in some cases, eventually developed into permanent community based organisations, engaged in provision, and/or producing and maintaining one or more public services. The Hanna Nassif Development Association, which is a famous urban PO in Tanzania, is a typi-cal example.

Secondly, there are those organisations which are formed by a collective effort of the people in a community which is affected by an existing utility problem, and whose members obtain incomes from their efforts. Solid waste collection is one example, where women are particularly prominent. In Dar es Salaam, the City Commission has contracted 29 for profit people's voluntary organisations to collect solid waste. Women have formed six of them, mem-bership of which is open only to women. These include, the Kinondoni Mos-cow Women Development Association, Hanna Nassif Women Development Association, Tanzania Environmental Cleanliness Association, Skuvi 167, POCA and LIFEPRO. Among the associations of this category there is only one with only male membership, the rest having mixed membership (Table 13:1).

Table 13:1. *People's organisations dealing only with solid waste management in Dar es Salaam*

District	Solid waste collection location	Number of POs	Membership by gender
Ilala	Middle Income Area	1	Women
	Low Income Area	2	Mixed
		1	Women
Kinondoni	Middle Income Area	2	Women
		8	Mixed
		1	Men
	Low Income Area	5	Mixed
		5	Women
Temeke	Middle Income Area	3	Mixed
	Low Income Area	1	Women

Source: Dar es Salaam City Commission: Community Development Department

The main activity performed by these POs is solid waste collection (i.e. primary refuse collection), using various types of equipment to bring the solid waste to secondary collection sites. From these, Dar es Salaam City Council/Commission and private companies can easily collect and transport it to the city dumping site. These POs also remove solid waste from drainage systems, sweep streets and cut grass in their respective areas of operation. These kinds of POs are normally very active in activities related to the environment where there is a widely published donor interest in supporting local-level initiatives. Therefore members of this kind of POs use their organisation to attract donor funding. Not only that, they also use the PO as a way of getting contracts from the City administration to collect solid waste or clean the city. Since the number of this kind of POs is increasing, they are now competing for these contracts. In performing their activities, they have not restricted themselves only to their own communities, but are performing their activities all over the city where there is an identified need for their services or where they are contracted by the city administration or members of a community.

Apart from solid waste management, the City Commissions aim in contracting people's voluntary associations for solid waste management is to alleviate poverty. The City Commission, therefore, contracts these voluntary organisations to collect solid waste in middle- and low-income areas of the city, on the condition that they hire labour within the locality or neighbourhood where they are operating. The Dar es Salaam City Commission (DCC), in addition, provides training and working tools to enable the POs collect solid waste more effectively and efficiently. Training aims to provide the POs with adequate technical skills in solid waste management and also to sensitise them on issues related to sustaining a clean urban environment. The DCC expects in turn that the POs will use the knowledge gained from such training to sensitise urban residents in their respective working localities in the city.

Permanent, non-profit organisations

The last kind of people's organisation in our typology is organisations emanating from collective initiatives of some members of a community which become permanent, non-profit organisations. Normally, this type of organisation is initiated by members of the local elite, who have either some connections to the authorities or to the donor community, or both. Most have evolved from either individual destructive or individual constructive efforts into more organised collective permanent initiatives. Some have developed from temporary collective efforts or initiatives during disasters, into permanent efforts to bridge public deficiencies in provision, production and/or maintenance of public services. An example of such a voluntary people's organisation or association is the Hanna Nassif Community Development Association.

Establishment of this Development Association emanated from problems which were caused by floods in the Hanna Nassif squatter area. These destroyed houses and rendered many residents homeless. In their initiatives to solve this problem, people in the area worked as a team to reconstruct the damaged houses and also to repair tertiary roads and to construct drainage systems, which were not there before the floods. They also formed a committee which was charged with the responsibility of soliciting emergency assistance from the government, as well as from the donor community. Later the committee developed into a permanent organisation, the Hanna Nassif Development Association, which invited all interested residents in the locality to become members. The association added a further development activity when it undertook to provide residents with tap water. In addition to provision of these services, the association also took on the responsibility for operating and maintaining the facilities provided.

The financial resources required to perform these activities were met from donor contributions, membership fees and user fees, e.g. road tolls for all vehicles driving into the locality. Because of leadership conflicts, which basically were motivated by the craving of leaders to use the association's funds for personal gain, the association split (Nguluma, 1997:71–73). Some leaders withdrew and established another voluntary people's organisation within the area i.e. the Hanna NASA Development Trust. Establishment of this trust caused even more conflicts between leaders of the two associations and among members and residents in the locality as a whole. The government had to intervene to try to resolve the conflicts and, in the process, another people's organisation called "Umoja wa Maendeleo wa Wananchi wa Hanna Nassif" (UMWAHA), which can be translated as Hanna Nassif people's development association was formed. This association has undertaken development activities which were previously under the Hanna Nassif Community Development Association. UMWAHA draws its members from the two conflicting POs and from the wider Hanna Nassif locality.

As illustrated in Table 13:2, though engaged in development initiatives in one way or another, the people's organisations have demonstrated a diversity of missions, objectives and motives. The Permanent POs identified by the Dar es Salaam City Community Development Department amount to 38. Out of these, 9 deal with a number of activities geared towards development of their locality. The remaining 29 are concentrating mainly on solid waste management.

Table. 13:2 *Non-profit voluntary People's organisations (POs) in Dar es Salaam*

District	Member- ship	Name of People's Organisation	Activities that prompt- ed establishment of the organisation	Additional activities
ILALA	Male & female	Tabata Develop- ment Trust	Roads and water supply	Roads and water supply
	Male & female	Wailes Commu- nity Development Association	Overflowing drainage canals Economic activities	
	Male & female	Buguruni Development Trust	Dealing with water and health problems in their area	Maintaining tertiary roads and their bridges; building public dispen- saries; water wells; rehabilitation of tape water supply facilities; eliminating illiteracy and poverty in the locality
	Male & female	Mburahati Barafu Develop- ment Association	Connecting their locality to the main road running to city centre	Maintaining public health care units and public primary schools; digging water wells
KINONDNI	Male & female	Kijitonyama Development Co-operation	Roads and water supply	
	Male & female	Mwinyuma Community Development Association	Providing and maintain- ing infrastructure (roads, drainage system etc.) Health promotion	
	Male & female	Mbezi Msigani	Road maintenance	
	Male & female	Lubokwe	Road maintenance	
	Male & female	UMWAHA	Taking over develop- ment activities from an organisation in the neighbourhood which split into two because of leaders' fight for positions	Roads, drainage systems, water supply
	Male & female	Mpimbeki	Providing and maintain- ing infrastructure (roads, drainage system, etc.) Health promotion	

Source: Dar es Salaam City Commission and Survey Data

It would seem important at this point also to mention those non-governmental organisations which are motivated by charity, rather than by service problems experienced by members. This type of organisation is usually non-profit and permanent and formed by collective efforts of people in or from outside the community. This kind of NGOs is normally professionally staffed and seeks to aid constituents external to its own social group. Such NGOs are not directly accountable to their intended beneficiaries. They have normally engaged themselves in helping communities in Dar es Salaam to construct primary schools, provide school equipment and even offer direct assistance to individual households. Plan International is one example of such an NGO. It is working with communities in the Buguruni and Vinguguti areas, supporting primary schools and helping pupils to pay for medical costs.

Local action rather than protest

The list of invisible and indirect causes of urban problems includes unprogressive attitudes among legislative and executive actors in the central and local governments, coupled with lack of commitment and transparency. But initiatives by POs to lobby and educate policy makers and executives have not been recorded. Popular responses to the urban crisis in Dar es Salaam have not included demands on policy makers and government executives to change their modus operandi and ensure effective and efficient utilisation of public resources. Deficient urban management is an underlying cause of many of the problems the city's residents have to cope with, but has not received direct attention from urban associations. For instance, the central government's decision to abolish the Dar es Salaam City Council and replace it with the Dar es Salaam City Commission led to little protest from residents generally or voluntary associations specifically. Advocacy, lobbying and educating have tended to be focused on residents of respective localities, encouraging them to join forces to improve those conditions in their locality which have a direct impact on their livelihoods. Urban residents have pooled their resources and mobilised additional resources from outside in order to have better local infrastructure and services. Demands are not made on behalf of all residents of the city, and city-wide alliances have not occurred. The overwhelming reaction of people in the city to escalating urban problems can be said to be that of performing operations themselves, either individually or collectively. It has become the order of the day for Dar es Salaam residents to allocate their own resources, either individually or collectively, so as to bring about changes to the unsatisfactory states of affairs in their neighbourhoods or localities.

Such initiatives are popular among Dar es Salaam residents and lately they have gained support also from the city authorities and the central government. The City Commission has recognised the positive contribution of people's organisations to urban development. Through its Community Development Department, the Commission is now facilitating the establishment of Community Development Association in various localities. By pushing its responsibilities back to urban residents in this fashion, the urban authority is denying the urban residents of their right to be supplied with public goods and services by the central and local government. Given the fact that two governments collect taxes, levies and user fees from urban residents, one would expect something to be delivered in return, and also for some accountability in the way the collected revenues are spent.

INSTITUTIONS AND VOLUNTARY NON-CONVENTIONAL INITIATIVES

North (1991:97) defines institutions as:

> ... humanly devised constraints that structure political, economic and social interaction. They consist of both informal constraints (sanctions, taboos, customs, traditions, and codes of conduct), and formal rules (constitutions, laws, property rights)

Formal constraints are enforced either by the local or national government regulatory machinery, whereas the informal constraints are self-enforcing or are enforced by a community. The formal institutions or regulations in Tanzania provide for free establishment of associations. Community based organisations emanating from permanent collective action initiatives are not constrained by the enacted rules and regulations. An organisation can be set up by registration in two different ways, either by registration under Societies Registration ordinance in the Ministry of Home Affairs, or under the Trustees Incorporation Act at the Administrator General's Office.

Constraints on individual actions

Though prevalent, destructive individual actions are constrained by both formal and informal institutions. There are provisions in the laws of the Republic of Tanzania and also local government bylaws prohibiting people or companies from undertaking destructive actions. However, such laws and regulations are currently ineffective, first of all because they are very old and out of date. Most were inherited from the colonial government, with none or few amendments since then. Therefore what was a then harsh punishment is currently a joke to the offenders. A fine of 1,000 Tanzanian shillings, just enough money to buy a single meal in a cheap hotel for throwing garbage and waste in a manner which is not allowed by the law, is a very minor punishment today. Secondly, civil servants who are supposed to enforce the rules and regulations are unmotivated, due to very low remuneration. This may lead to corruption and rent seeking behaviour in some instances or complete laxity in others.

Destructive actions are also constrained by informal norms. Emptying wastewater in streets and throwing solid waste everywhere is unacceptable in any neighbourhood. That is the reason why this is done at night. The individual who does it would not like others to do it, since this would worsen an already unsatisfactory situation. However, everyone does it, expecting others will not do it; consequently, such activities go on endlessly but not openly.

On the other hand, constructive action is limited neither by formal nor by informal constraints. This is because the outcomes of such initiatives are always advantageous to the entire community or neighbourhood. Permanent community based organisations often have their origin in the initiatives of individual actors, who have pooled their resources and managed to mobilise others. Some of the permanent POs which are found in the city are, in one way or another, products of constructive individual action. Their activities do not only attract others, but also mobilise them to work jointly.

Constraints on permanent collective actions

Permanent non-profit community based organisations are not always accepted in the community. This is because their formation is based on minority objectives, in the sense that it is members of the elite who initiated their formation. Usually, it is the same people who are in the forefront of running them. Depending on the type of people residing in the neighbourhood, the elite forming these organisations range from rich people, retired senior officials and government employees from affluent neighbourhoods to relatively educated and well-off people in poor neighbourhoods. Such POs are controlled by just a few people, without any established organisational framework for ensuring accountability to their constituency.

The elite are unwilling to totally integrate community residents mainly because they obtain personal gains from the voluntary organisations. The majority in a community may enjoy the outcome of a PO's efforts, but are reluctant to support it unless they are given some say in running the organisation. Given the fact that these POs also depend to a great extent on external support, residents view the leaders as opportunistic, using the PO as a platform for personal financial gains. This contributes to the majority's reluctance to participate actively. The belief that POs are a source of enrichment leads to competition for leadership positions. Consequently a lot of time is spent on solving leadership conflicts instead of on the POs intended tasks (as Hanna Nassif described above).

The fight for leadership positions may also lead to accusations of witchcraft, jeopardising effectiveness and efficiency in the operation of the PO. Though these kinds of POs have a formal constitution, which is one of the requirements for registering, their constitutions rarely allow any input from people living in the community they are supposed to serve. The constitutions are made to suit the interests of elite members of a PO, in terms of how the leadership is elected and their terms of office. That leaders are re-elected several times is not unusual and member meetings are rarely held.

Despite the constraints discussed above, however, one should not belittle the efforts of the voluntary people's associations. They have, in many cases provided infrastructure and services where local government and national government have failed.

CONCLUSION

The aim of this chapter was to analyse how community based initiatives have developed in the city of Dar es Salaam, as a result of rapid urbanisation coupled with poor urban management and deteriorating urban public services. The analysis identified, among other things, the factors behind the initiation of community based organisations; i.e. the particular circumstances which induce people to organise themselves, and the areas of service provision for which their newly formed associations cater. The responses of central and local governments to these popular, collective actions as well as the institutional (formal and informal rules) requirements for their establishment and operation have also been described. In conclusion, some issues of sustainability of the community based efforts will be raised and some recommendations made.

The inadequate supply of public goods and services in Tanzania's urban areas has attracted an array of reactions from residents, ranging from individuals acting alone to collective reactions by people in a neighbourhood or locality within the urban area. Some individual reactions have worsened an unsatisfactory situation, while others have worked towards improving it. The positive contribution of some individual initiatives have in some cases prompted people to form associations or organisations, some of which have become permanent. However, most of the voluntary people's organisations have been initiated by one or more individuals, through mobilising and recruiting others. Most of these permanent voluntary people's organisations have broadened their activities to incorporate development activities beyond those which motivated their establishment. They tend to be male dominated, though exceptions exist in the case of POs whose members are entirely women.

To provide, produce and maintain public services in a sustained way through community based organisations will, to a great extent, depend on the sustainability of the organisations themselves. The POs can only survive if at least two conditions are fulfilled: first of all, they must be generally accepted in the community. Secondly, they must have enough capacity in terms of own resources (human, financial and material) to enable them to pursue their objectives.

Fulfilment of the first condition calls for POs to first adhere to the formal rules, i.e., to officially or formally register. This reduces the possibility of tension between the PO and local or national government. Secondly, POs must make themselves acceptable to all members of a community. This can be done through involvement of all members of the community in formulation of the PO's constitutional objectives or aims; and in the election of leaders. POs must be accountable and transparent to the community by holding regular meetings open to all residents and must openly reveal their financial statements to scrutiny. This can motivate people to have a sense of belonging to a PO. Most probably, it can also motivate members of a community to contribute their own resources to a PO, thus easing resource constraints. However, such POs cannot easily become accountable and transparent to their members without sensitising the elite which is currently leading them. Elite sensitisation could be done by NGOs and international donors, such as local representatives of Plan International; the International Labour Organisation; the World Health Organisation and UNCHS (Habitat). These organisations are already supporting some of the POs in the city of Dar es Salaam in one way or another, and should see their task as not only one of channelling funds, but also contributing towards the building of viable organisations and acceptable institutions.

References

Heidemann, Claus, 1992, *Regional Planning Methodology: The First and Only Annotated Primer on Regional Planning*. Discussion Paper, No. 16. Karlsruhe: Institut für Regionalwissenschaft der Universität Karlsruhe.

Japan International Co-operation Agency (JICA), 1997, *The Study on the Solid Waste Management for Dar es Salaam City*. Final Report, Volume 1. Kokusai Kogejo Co. Ltd.

Mateso, Peter, 1993, *Urban Planning in Tanzania, State of the Art and Proposals for Improvement*. Lizentiatenarbeit zur Erlangung des Grades des Lizentiaten der Regionalwissenschaft. Karlsruhe: Institut für Regionalwissenschaft der Universität Karlsruhe (TH).

Mhamba, Robert Mitundwa, 1996, *Bedingungen Dauerhafter Wasserver—und Abwasserentsorgung in den stadtischen Gebieten Tansanias*. Lizentiatenarbeit zur Erlangung des Grades des Lizentiaten der Regionalwissenschaft. Karlsruhe: Institut für Regionalwissenschaft der Universität Karlsruhe (TH).

Nguluma, Huba Mary, 1997, "Sustainable Human Settlement and Environment in Search of a Strategy to Improve Urban Infrastructure in Tanzania: A Case of the Hanna Nassif Upgrading Project in Dar es Salaam". MSc. Thesis. Stockholm: Royal Institute of Technology, Department of Architecture and Town Planning, Division of Built Environment Analysis.

North, Douglass C., 1991, "Institutions", *Journal of Economic Perspectives*, 5, pp. 97–112.

Ostrom, Elinor, Larry D. Schroeder and Susan G. Wynne, 1993, *Institutional Incentives and Sustainable Development—Infrastructure Policies in Perspective*. Boulder: Westview Press.

Sheuya, Shaaban, 1997, *Employment-intensive upgrading of urban unplanned settlements by communities. Practices and opportunities in Dar es Salaam, Tanzania* Dar es Salaam: International Labour Organisation (ILO) and Advisory Support, Information Services and Training for Labour-based Programs.

Turner, Mark and David Hulme, 1997, *Governance, Administration and Development, Making the State Work*. London: Macmillan Press.

UN, 1998, *World Urbanisation Prospects. The 1996 Revision*. New York: United Nations.

United Republic of Tanzania, 1994, *Environmental Statistics in Tanzania*. Dar es Salaam: Presidents Office, Planning Commission.

SECTION V

EMERGING INITIATIVES

A central theme on the preceding pages has been the economic decline and downgrading of the role of the state in Africa's towns and cities, leading to an upsurge of civil society and associations. The international community has contributed to this development through its emphasis on structural adjustment policies and an "enabling framework" (UNCHS:424), which encourages partnerships between the state and individuals, households, communities, businesses and voluntary organisations.

As we shall see in this section, however, international involvement and support to local NGOs, CBOs and other similar new bodies has not been without its problems. It has proven difficult to work out constructive relations between a weak state on the one hand, and local organisations subsuming many of the state's responsibilities on the other. The aid organisations themselves often suffer from an inadequate understanding of the competence and capacity of local organisations in their endeavours to push the "civil society agenda". As a result they have tended to become local associations in their own right (sidelining the associations they were to support), or they have become marginalised and "victims" of political processes they do not understand.

The contributions that follow reveal the importance firstly of political and economic context for enabling associations to function, and secondly of a tradition for local organisations and associations on which to base new bodies, in the form of NGOs, CBOs and CBDOs. In particular the issue of democratic rule and accountability seems to be a problem in societies with strong traditions of clear authority-structures. Community based organisations seem to function best when they have well-defined and practical objectives, and their relation with government structures is well defined.

The article by Warren Smith from South Africa describes the emergence of strong community based organisations during the time of the apartheid struggle. They had a strong leadership and a common goal, and played an important part in bringing down the apartheid regime. However, after the turn to majority rule, with the elections in 1994, CBOs have had problems defining their role. Some have been absorbed into corporatist participation systems set up by local governments, while others have tried to become autonomous development organisations. Nevertheless, Smith concludes that community based organisations do have an important role to play; asserting that it is only by co-operation between the state, CBOs and NGOs that the development challenges facing south Africa will be adequately tackled.

The contribution by Paul Robson from Luanda in Angola presents a completely different type of setting: 30 years of near continuous war, a dramatic population increase, particularly since 1992, and devastating socioeconomic conditions for the urban population have all contributed to a void of government structures as well as civil society and associations. The separation between urban and rural areas caused by the war has effectively cut ties with traditional society and modes of organisation. Urban services are primarily provided through informal (and often very expensive) networks. The few community based organisations that have emerged are generally weak and depend on foreign support. Robson draws the conclusion that a minimum of government structures and credibility must be established before community based organisations can function and contribute constructively to urban development.

Jørgen Andreasen describes a situation from Zanzibar, where the government and local organisations did have a constructive relationship under one-party rule, when authority structures and division of roles were clear. However, general economic decline and the introduction of democratic rule have weakened both institutions, at the same time as there is no tradition for popular participation. There are currently small initiatives for establishing community based organisations, but they suffer from problems of popular mobilisation and funding. Andreasen argues that funding from abroad will be essential in order to build up local associations, but is relatively pessimistic with regard to the options for developing truly democratic and well-functioning institutions.

The final contribution by Frayne, Pendleton and Pomuti presents a situation where there was a strong foreign intervention to support community based organisations, at a time when local government was also trying to establish itself after independence in Namibia in 1990. The Danish aid organisation Ibis took on such a central role that local government felt threatened, and the established Community Development Committees (CDCs) became too dependent on Ibis, both organisationally and financially. After the withdrawal of the Danish organisation in 1995, the lack of clarity about the roles of and division of responsibility between the CDCs and the government has led to confusion and frustration on both sides. The local government sees CDCs as a threat to their own position, and the CDCs have expectations for funding and other types of support from local government that is unrealistic.

In conclusion, the contributions in this section all point to the potential importance of community based organisations for urban development. At the same time, however, the weakness of the state that has contributed to their emergence represents their main problem: without a viable counterpart in the form of stronger national and local government, community based organisations cannot fulfil expectations from their communities regarding social development and representation in decision-making.

CHAPTER 14

The Changing Role of Community Based Organisations in South Africa in the 1990s, with Emphasis on Their Role in Development Projects

Warren Smit

INTRODUCTION

South Africa has a tradition of strong community based organisations (CBOs) which played a leading role in resisting apartheid government policies in the 1980s. The most important CBOs were the civic associations, which emerged in the 1980s—they were organisations which claimed to represent all residents in a particular geographic area. Changing political conditions in the early 1990s resulted in some of these CBOs beginning to play a leading role in implementing development projects in their areas, and non-governmental organisations (NGOs) began to become involved in supporting CBOs to participate in "community based development". Participation in development was not unproblematic, however, as the divergent interests within black communities, which had been submerged or suppressed during the apartheid years, emerged into the open.

After the first democratic national and provincial elections in 1994, the participation of CBOs in development projects became increasingly important. After the establishment of democratic local government in 1995–1996, the role of CBOs began to be more complicated, as there were now councillors who were the democratic representatives of communities. Existing CBOs were either absorbed into corporatist participation systems set up by local government or tried to become autonomous, sustainable development organisations, and new mutual help organisations with a focus on development also began to emerge. Simultaneously, however, there was also a drastic reduction in grant funding from international donors to CBOs and NGOs after 1994.

This paper examines the changing role of South African CBOs in relation to their participation in local development projects, with a focus on Durban, and analyses the various ways in which they have responded, and continue to respond, to the changing conditions in South Africa. First of all, the rise of the civic movement in South Africa is looked at. Second, the changing conditions of the early 1990s and the involvement of CBOs in development projects is discussed. Third, recent changing conditions and the resulting trends, such as the growth of community development corporations and mutual help organisations, are looked at. Finally, conclusions are drawn about the future of CBOs in South Africa in the new millennium.

THE RISE OF CBOs

Communities

CBOs are both products and processes of their environment—they mediate and articulate the dynamics of specific communities (BESG, 1996:6). CBOs are usually associated with less affluent areas, as a strong sense of community is generally more common in these areas. Shared experience of hard times, together with functional interdependence, generates a mutuality of feeling and purpose in less affluent areas, and this mutuality gives rise to social institutions and community spirit, although there is often as much conflict and disorder as there is cohesion and communality (for example, see Jackson, 1968: 155–60).

South Africa is unique as, over and above the sense of community prevalent in less affluent areas, apartheid policies artificially created highly spatialised communities which produced a very specific type of CBO. A strong sense of community depends upon having a strong common interest, and, in a sense, apartheid policies created strong communities by politically and economically oppressing black people and resettling them into racially and spatially segregated residential "townships" on the periphery of urban areas. The climate of common oppression and the spatial layout of apartheid towns and cities had an enormous influence on the nature of the CBOs that emerged in those areas.

The Black Consciousness Movement of the 1970s popularised the use of the term "the community" to describe residential entities such as townships (Thornton and Ramphele, 1988:35). The assumption was that a "community of purpose" always existed in these areas, especially as their residents were oppressed and economically, socially and culturally deprived. This political view of black communities as homogenous set the scene for the emergence of CBOs to represent these settlements.

Growth of the civic association movement

Black townships had a long tradition of collective action and mutual help. In the broader sense of the word, CBOs are any organisations with grassroots membership, and the first CBOs in townships were "organisations of survival", such as *stokvels* (savings clubs), burial clubs, church associations, and sports clubs (Narsoo, 1991:27). Their primary purpose was for people to help each other cope with everyday life.

In a narrower sense of the word, however, CBO is usually used to refer to organisations which claim to represent all the residents in a specific geographic area, and it was in the late 1970s and the early 1980s that what Narsoo (1991) calls "organisations of resistance" grew out of the organisations of survival. These organisations were known under a variety of names, for example, residents associations, but they were generically known as civic associations.

After the clampdown on the Black Consciousness Movement in 1977, political resistance began to be channelled into grassroots organisations that focused on living conditions and daily life (Swilling, 1993:17). The first civic associations were the Soweto Civic Association and the Port Elizabeth Black Civic Organisation which were formed in 1979–1980. In 1983 the mass political movement, the United Democratic Front (UDF), was formed, which began a campaign to form civic associations in every township in South Africa, as part of the struggle against the state (Shubane and Madiba, 1992:4).

Civic associations were theoretically democratically elected organisations claiming to represent all residents in a particular area. "The community" was seen as a cohesive, homogenous entity, and in local negotiations the civic associations always assumed that they were supported by all people in a particular township, for example, with regard to rent boycotts.

Civics were both grassroots organisations and also part of the liberation movement, specifically the African National Congress (ANC). Due to political parties such as the ANC being banned within South Africa, the civic association movement emerged as an internal counterpart to the liberation movement, parallel to the trade union movement in the workplace. Civic associations were in the forefront of mass action and resistance against the apartheid state in the mid-1980s, mainly through actions such as rent boycotts, consumer boycotts, and bus boycotts.

The civic association movement first grew in the formal townships, and civics were primarily concerned with rents and service charges, and with opposing the local authority as part of the repressive state. Squatter settlements were initially usually controlled by undemocratic "warlords" or "squatter committees", and democratic civic associations only emerged in these settlements later. Civic associations in squatter settlements were naturally mainly concerned with resisting forced removals and with development. They therefore often had a more flexible relationship with local authorities, as they were mainly concerned with issues such as land tenure, services and housing. These were the CBOs which were to later play a major role in development projects.

Typical civic association constitutions, such as that of the Zilweleni Residents Association in Durban (which could be classified as a grassroots civic association), stated the goals of the organisation as including the following:

- To "ascertain in a democratic manner, the needs, wishes and desires of the members of the Association in particular and of the community in general and to articulate, express, publicise and make known such needs, wishes and desires".

- To "resolve, arbitrate and/or mediate any disputes between members of the community".

- To "identify, develop, conduct, assist and encourage projects for the economic, educational, recreational and material well being of the members of the Association in particular and the community in general" (and "to establish sub-Committees, Trusts and Companies" , raise funds, and provide specialist services, either through its own resources or by employing consultants, for achieving these goals).

Swilling (1993:23–24) distinguished between four different types of civic associations in terms of leadership. Grassroots civic associations had accountable leadership and a well-organised grassroots base. Populist civic associations had strong, popular leadership and grassroots support, but little organisational capacity or accountability. Leadership elite civic associations had strong leadership but a weak support base. Paper civic associations were where the name of the civic existed but there was no organisation or support base, and the name of the civic association was sometimes expropriated by people for their own use.

Typical civic associations, such as the Zilweleni Residents Association, had a Committee of seven to fifteen people elected at an Annual General Meeting of the members of the Association. Any resident of the community could apply to the Committee to be a member of the Association. Annual General Meetings took place every year and Ordinary General Meetings could be called by 10 per cent of members. The quorum for General Meetings was 33 per cent of the members of the association. The reality did not always follow the constitution, however, as in practice most civic association members were "nominated" rather than democratically elected. For example, Mahura (1995:80) found that only about a third of the civic association members she interviewed in a survey in Durban had been elected.

Despite noble aims and constitutions, some civic associations did not effectively represent their communities. The view of black communities as homogenous ignored the fact that the effects of apartheid were felt differently by different people, such as the employed and unemployed, house dwellers and shack dwellers, owners and renters, and so on. In general, while there was indeed a strong communality as a result of apartheid, civic association members were often drawn from the more affluent ranks of communities and did not necessarily represent everybody (Shubane and Madiba, 1992:10–16). There are many examples of civic associations representing narrow interests rather than the interests of a community as a whole. For example, the Nonqaba civic in Mossel Bay was dominated by businessmen who were largely self-appointed and who ignored the interests of the squatters they were supposed to be representing (Pieterse and Simone, 1994:94–96). Mahura (1995:81–82) found that some civic associations had members from a wider variety of socio-economic backgrounds, including pensioners, students, and unemployed people, but that women were seldom well represented.

On the whole, though not always democratically elected or fully representative, many civic associations were recognised by their communities as leaders and were reasonably accountable to their constituencies, as they held regular report-back meetings (Mahura, 1995:83).

The rise of NGOs

The 1980s also saw the rise of the voluntary sector. At first volunteers helped CBOs by providing advice and support. Many of these voluntary organisations subsequently obtained access to foreign funding and began employing full-time staff. They were referred to as "service organisations", and later as non-governmental organisations (NGOs). In South Africa, the term "non-governmental organisation" is usually used to refer to non-profit organisations which provide some sort of professional service for community groups or another constituency (Marais, 1997:v). NGOs, like CBOs, are organisations of civil society, but are distinguished by their focus on a sector of activity, whereas CBOs are usually defined by a geographic level of organisation (Uphoff, 1993:619).

The voluntary sector was heavily funded by northern donors. As part of their policies to put pressure on the South African government, Western European and North American governments disbursed funds to the voluntary sector in South Africa for humanitarian causes.

An example of a housing NGO is the Built Environment Support Group (BESG), in Durban and Pietermaritzburg. It was formed in 1982 as a voluntary association of town planners and architects to assist community groups in their struggles around housing issues. From 1986 onwards, BESG acquired grant funding and began to employ permanent staff in order to be able to cope with the number of requests for assistance it was receiving from CBOs. NGOs such as BESG were active in resisting the policies of the state, for example, BESG fought against the attempted forced removal of the Happy Valley squatter settlement by the Pietermaritzburg City Council. The settlement had been demolished by the Council five times, but BESG was eventually able to bring enough pressure to bear on the Council for the right of the settlement to stay to be finally recognised.

THE PARTICIPATION OF CBOs IN DEVELOPMENT

Changing conditions in the early 1990s

Major changes occurred in 1990. Political parties such as the ANC were unbanned and the dismantling of apartheid began. The government underwent a shift in its policies and began negotiating with communities. For example, the government set up the Independent Development Trust (IDT) in 1990, and in 1991 the IDT announced a capital subsidy scheme to provide 100,000 subsidies of R7,500 each, which would enable households earning less than R1,000 per month to acquire a serviced site. (In 1991, 1US$=R27.74.) The scheme reflected international thinking of the time, as it was market orientated as well as focusing on self-help and community participation (Robinson et al., 1994:12–15). In contrast to an almost total lack of participation in previous development projects, it was a requirement of the scheme that community participation occur at a number of stages: application, services and standards, allocation of sites, and consolidation. There was also a focus on labour intensive construction methods.

Changing conditions such as these were also forcing civic associations to change. While in the late 1980s some civic activists had expressed the view that there was no need for local elections because civics were a democratic form of local government (Friedman and Reitzes, 1996:57), with the rapid political changes that started occurring from 1990, it became clear that the role of civic associations would have to change. The high point of the civic association movement was reached in 1992 with the formation of the South African National Civic Organisation (SANCO), but democratic government was imminent, and the civic associations began to examine the basis for their existence anew. The two possible roles were as "watchdogs" over local government or as developmental agents. This represented a significant shift, as prior to 1990, civic associations had mainly been involved in stopping development as a way of struggling against the state, for example, by burning down new school buildings. Civic associations with a developmental focus were particularly common in squatter areas, in which the organisation had usually been formed specifically to negotiate with the local authority around development issues.

Simultaneously with shifts in government policy and the interest of civic associations in getting involved in development, development practitioners had increasingly begun to recognise the need for community involvement, due to the failure of a top-down, technocratic approach which had often resulted in uninhabited "toilets in the *veld*"—sites and services projects (Bekker and Wilson, 1991). This recognition of the need for participation resulted in what has been referred to as the "take-me-to-your-leader" syndrome, as development professionals began looking for community leaders to participate in projects (Thornton and Ramphele, 1988:32).

There were a variety of different approaches to participation (Swilling, 1993:30–32). The first approach was the "rubber stamp" approach, in which a civic association simply agreed to a developer's proposal or participated in a nominal project committee in which most decisions were made by the technical staff. The second approach was to turn the civic association into a community based development organisation (CBDO), which resulted in the interests of the civic association becoming synonymous with the interests of the project. A third approach tried by some civic associations was to pressurise local government into implementing development projects that met the needs of the people. The problem with this, of course, is that the civic associations had no control over the nature and quality of the project. The fourth, and most effective way, was for the CBO to be directly involved in establishing a CBDO, such as a community based trust. The civic was thus, in theory at least, able to retain its independence from both local government and the developers and funders, while still playing a part in the process. In all, 29 per cent of IDT subsidies went to community based trusts (Robinson et al., 1994:23).

In 1994, the new democratically elected government introduced a new housing policy based on the IDT's capital subsidy scheme. Housing subsidies of up to R15,000 were made available to low-income households. Community participation in development was made an integral component of housing policy, for example, "social compacts" signifying the agreement and roles of all stakeholders had to be signed before an application for subsidies for a project could be submitted.

The government also made "development facilitation" funding available for communities to be able to participate in drawing up the proposed project details for subsidy applications. A typical development facilitation process in Malukazi, Durban, involved the twenty members of the Malukazi Development Committee in almost 30 hours of workshopping around key issues in the project proposal. Five workshops were held: on the housing subsidy scheme and levels of service, the role of the developer and the project budget, the evaluation and short-listing of developers, drafting the social compact, and completing the social compact agreement (Hodgson, 1996:84–88).

The challenges of development

One of the key challenges that civic associations had to face in getting involved in development was that communities are not homogenous, and that while the anti-apartheid struggle was based upon the theory of homogenous communities, development projects have to explicitly recognise different and conflicting interests. As Moser (1989:127) has pointed out, the reality is that "in most low-income communities there are often more conflicting interests than similarities between neighbours".

During the years of resistance, civic leaders were able to mobilise communities around key issues in reaction to repressive state action fairly easily. Proactively mobilising people for development purposes, however, proved to be considerably more difficult. For example, it soon became obvious that it was a lot harder to end a rent and service charge boycott than it was to start one. Rent and service charge boycotts had been well supported by communities, but for different reasons. Some people boycotted to withhold money from the local authorities as a form of protest, some boycotted as a way of bankrupting the state in order to bring about the collapse of apartheid, some boycotted because they were not happy with the services, and some boycotted because they could not afford to pay. As a result, civic associations which negotiated agreements with local authorities to resume rent and service charge payments often were unable to persuade their communities to resume payments (Shubane and Madiba, 1992:16–17).

Another example of the divisive nature of development was a housing project in KwaMancinza, Durban, funded by the Malaysian government, where the CBO had been demanding two room houses for all 620 households in the community. It soon became clear, however, that higher income members of the community refused to have two room houses, and would not be satisfied with anything less than a four room house with a bathroom. On the other hand, some members of the community were not able to afford even R128 per month for the two room houses and wanted smaller, cheaper houses. The more affluent residents won their demands, while the latter group were ignored by the funders.

Despite these problems, however, the participation of CBOs in development projects did have a tangible, usually positive effect. So what have been the results of such participation?

Firstly, community participation has facilitated the implementation of projects, albeit often with considerable conflict and delays, and thus greater cost. Without participation most projects would not be able to get underway, as, for example, the contractor would not be able to work in an area. Participation has also been successful in resolving disputes and preventing abuse of allocation systems, and so on.

Secondly, there has been temporary local employment and skills development—of leadership, sub-contractors, people involved in socio-economic surveys, and community liaison staff. Considerable amounts of money have thus been retained in the community, and the capacity of people to be involved in future development projects has been greatly increased. Some people involved in the projects have gone on to be permanently employed in the development field, and some sub-contractors have gone on to be successful, but many were not well trained nor well selected, and became unemployed again after the projects ended.

Thirdly, there has been a more appropriate end product, which has resulted in greater acceptance and sense of community ownership, because of community involvement in deciding on service levels, layouts and plot allocation. The community usually had minimal impact on selecting service levels or housing options due to the financial constraints imposed by the subsidy levels prescribed by government. However, it was possible to have greater impact on layouts; more appropriate layouts resulted in the case of *in situ* upgrades as community members negotiated plot boundaries and the circulation layout was usually more sensitive, with a greater emphasis on pedestrian paths. Community allocation of plots was a particularly important part of the community participation process.

The changing role of NGOs

The changing conditions of the time also resulted in NGOs changing their roles. In the 1980s NGOs had mainly supported communities in an advocacy, or advice, role. With the availability of funding for development from the IDT and other sources, with some civic associations wanting to play a role in development, and with the need of the most disadvantaged client communities for development, some NGOs began to take the step into implementation. Some NGOs saw community participation in development projects as an opportunity for building the empowerment and self-reliance of communities, so that they would be able to take care of their own needs and initiate further projects themselves. NGOs such as BESG and other affiliates of the Urban Sector Network (USN), therefore focused on supporting communities in "community based development", in which community based trusts were the developers. The support typically provided by these NGOs to CBOs included organisational development, technical advice and project management.

Case study of Zilweleni

Zilweleni, Durban, is an example of the participation of a CBO in a development project. Zilweleni ("we are struggling") was a small informal settlement of 84 families in danger of being evicted by the landowners. In 1990 the Zilweleni Residents Association (ZRA) approached BESG for assistance in negotiating around buying the land and upgrading the settlement. With BESG's assistance the ZRA obtained funding from the IDT in 1991, the land was acquired, and detailed development plans were completed by 1992.

The project was on 16 hectares of land, and consisted of providing infrastructure to 186 residential sites. The ZRA decided to implement the project itself and set up the Zilweleni Development Trust (ZDT), consisting exclusively of community members, to be the developer. The ZDT appointed BESG as the project manager and obtained bridging finance for the project.

Community members were involved in many aspects of the project, including security, site pegging, site allocations, and toilet construction. Sinqobile Contractors, a partnership of unemployed residents trained in basic building skills, was formed to undertake the construction of toilets for the project. All decisions were taken by the ZDT or at a community meeting, and the ZDT reported back to the community at monthly meetings. The ZDT estimated that they had the support of about 95 per cent of the community for the project.

This was one of the first instances where a CBDO acted as a developer in South Africa. The project was completed within budget and only four months over schedule, and the ZDT proved to be efficient and capable of handling the large sums of money associated with the project. The project proved that a community based approach can be extremely successful and that CBDOs are capable of controlling development projects. A measure of the project's success can be gauged from the fact that the community subsequently decided to change the area's name to Sinqobile ("we have won").

THE CURRENT POSITION OF CBOs

Changes 1994–1996

The period 1994–1996 saw profound changes in South Africa. Democratic national and provincial parliaments were elected in 1994, and democratic local government councils were elected in 1995–1996.

The civic movement was enormously affected. Civic associations lost many leaders to local government, and many of the representative roles performed by civic associations at the local level were taken over by political parties and elected councillors, who often viewed CBOs with suspicion. Simultaneously, there was a "declining spirit of voluntary community commitment" and the civic movement lost its sense of purpose (Mayekiso in Seekings, 1997:6). The role of civil society had been seen as revolutionary and the long-term goal had been socialism, but now civil society began to be seen either as a pliant partner of the state or as a watchdog of social democracy. In addition, apartheid had been a "social glue" that held communities together by presenting a focused target for discontent and which facilitated the building of common fronts of interests and demands. With the dismantling of apartheid, this "social glue" melted away and the diversification of interests within black communities made it increasingly difficult for any single organisation to provide collective representation for a whole community. The net result is that civic associations have been marginalised in local government and development planning, in contrast to the key role they played in the early 1990s.

The dominant trend is that most civic associations have been absorbed into, or sidelined by, local government controlled corporatist participation structures. CBOs have been co-opted into Development Forums, which act as advisory bodies to local government, and local governments have also set up "ward committees", consisting of elected residents of electoral wards chaired by local government councillors, as parallel community structures. Neither bodies can be said to be autonomous or directly involved in development, however—at best, they are involved in the formulation of local authority integrated development plans or serve as a liaison channel between councillors and residents. The degree of local government control is clearly indicated by a policy on Development Forums adopted by the two main local authorities in Durban, the North Central and South Central Councils, which, among other things, included "ensuring that Development Forums abide by the policies and procedures adopted by the Council" (Nene, 1997:13). The policy sees Development Forums as being able to influence Council decisions on development projects, for example on the selection of a contractor, by making submissions, but regards the local authority as having the final decision (Nene, 1997:11).

The corporatist model of community participation is essentially aimed at controlling the community participation process. Friedman and Reitzes (1996) see it as blurring the distinction between civil society and the state. They argue that there is a danger that the incorporation of community groups into corporatist forums will not empower civil society, but will merely bureaucratise it; civil society thus becomes an arm of the state.

Parallel to the decline of the civic movement, there was a decline in the NGO sector. With the advent of democratic government, international funding for the NGO sector started to dry up and there was also a "brain drain" of staff from NGOs to government bodies from 1994 onwards (Kraak, 1996:87–88).

In addition to these structural changes, there also began to be a change in the nature of projects. As land for development was released in the post-apartheid era, there was a shift away from *in situ* upgrading projects towards greenfield projects on land that had previously been vacant, often in well located areas. As there were usually not existing communities for such greenfield projects, this resulted in a shift to beneficiary participation rather than participation by geographically defined civic associations.

All of the above changes have had an immense impact upon CBOs. It has been well documented that there is usually a decline of social movements in post-liberation and post-revolutionary societies (Swilling, 1993:27–28). All organisations emerge in response to specific conditions; they tend to decline when those conditions change in a way that they fail to understand, and new organisations emerge. Organisations only survive if they are able to respond to the changes that are occurring

The failure of government housing policies to meet expectations, however (for example, see Bond and Tait, 1997), has meant that the need for involvement of CBOs in development is as great as it ever was. Some CBOs are evolving in response to these changing conditions, and new CBOs are emerging. There have been some civic associations that have been able to obtain funding to set up permanent community development organisations to initiate development projects, or community development corporations (CDCs), as they are sometimes called. As a response to changing conditions and alienation from traditional civic associations, new mutual help organisations, with a strong focus on development, are also emerging.

Community development corporations (CDCs)

Initially civic associations had envisaged democratic local government as providing for the basic needs of everybody, but they subsequently realised that the government would have financial constraints and competing demands placed on it, as well as the need to avoid bureaucratic, "top-down" approaches to development. Civic associations had therefore begun to investigate the possibility of community based institutions that could proactively initiate development work as a complement to government development programmes (Coovadia, 1991:347–48). Some also argued that, because of the vast differentiation between communities there was a need to move away from the top heavy, uniform structure of the civic movement towards more autonomous, locality-specific community organisations (Pieterse, 1997:12).

One popular model was that of the United States community development corporations (CDCs), which are self-sustaining organisations involved in promoting local economic development (LED) within a community. They originally started as grassroots community organisations lobbying the government for development programmes, but evolved into community based non-profit organisations engaged in housing and business development (Pieterse and Simone, 1994:52–57).

The promotion of the idea of CDCs represented a significant shift, from the idea of looking at what local government can do to what a community can do for itself (Pieterse and Simone, 1994:54). The failure of local government to meet the expectations of people as to delivery, will probably result in the increasing popularity of CDCs in the future. Funding is becoming increasingly difficult to obtain, however, and very few community organisations will be able to obtain ongoing funding to employ permanent staff. For example, Dlamini (1997) recommends that CBOs that want to become sustainable development organisations need a minimum of funding for an office, an administrator and fieldworker, and for bridging finance to help the organisation develop its own long term funding strategy.

Case study of the Southern Pinetown CBOs

The case of Southern Pinetown, Durban, is an example of CBOs attempting to transform into sustainable community development organisations. The Southern Pinetown Joint Civics Association (SPJCA) was formed by twelve development orientated civic associations in Southern Pinetown in 1993, with assistance from BESG. The SPJCA was interested in implementing a housing programme in its area based on the government consolidation subsidy. It acquired funding from the IDT for housing support centres and housing advisors, and funds from Oxfam (Canada) for the training of community members to participate in the housing delivery process.

The SPJCA set up the Sibambisene Joint Venture to undertake a pilot housing project, with BESG as the project managers. Households were able to choose how to spend their subsidies on housing, and could choose from a list of approved local builders and building materials suppliers. They were advised by the housing advisors, who also monitored the quality of construction. By the end of 1998 over 1,100 houses had been completed in the area. Ultimately, over 12,000 houses will eventually be provided in Southern Pinetown.

The CBOs' involvement in development projects has further allowed them to look at methods of sustaining the housing support centres they have built and the housing advisors they employ. It is intended that the role of the support centres and the advisors will be broadened out to provide a social service to the community that goes beyond assistance in the construction process. They have been providing training courses and have set up a training fund that can be accessed by residents in their areas who wish to start a small business or require skills training. The organisations are looking at ways of generating money through offering their expertise in the development field and by establishing concrete block manufacturing facilities, and they are planning to tender for the provision of local authority services in their areas such as mail delivery, refuse removal, and the collection of rates.

The SPJCA has since transformed into a Section 21 (not for profit) Company called the Ubhaqa Development Association. It has secured funding and has hired full-time staff members to be involved in stimulating development in its area. Its attempts to be autonomous and self-reliant have met with hostility from some local councillors, however.

Mutual help organisations

The lack of success of the government's housing policy has resulted in growth of a new type of grassroots organisation. It is essentially a reaction to popular perceptions that politicians are self-interested, that officials have stifled housing delivery with red tape, and that consultants and developers are making huge profits out of housing delivery. There has been a rejection of developer driven housing delivery and small "instant houses" of as little as 12m², and the emergence of a back-to-basics self help approach (Sokhulu, 1997).

These new organisations differ markedly from civic associations. Whereas civic associations were male dominated, political organisations with a geographically defined base, the new organisations are dominated by women, they are fiercely non-political, and membership is voluntary. Whereas civic associations had a broad focus, the new organisations focus on housing delivery.

The mutual help approach is where, in the absence of external assistance, a group of people organises itself and provides income generation opportunities, infrastructure, housing or facilities. The mutual help approach is mainly based on South Asian experience, developing out of a context of community mobilisation in poor countries with relatively weak formal sectors, so as to enable the poor to develop survival strategies for themselves, for example, the alliance of the Society for the Promotion of Area Resource Centres (SPARC), National Slum Dwellers' Federation (NSDF) and *Mahila Milan* in India.

The most important of the new mutual help umbrella organisations is the Homeless Peoples' Federation (although there are others, such as Habitat for Humanity). In 1991 a conference called "A People's Dialogue on Land and Shelter" was held in South Africa, at which about 50 squatter leaders pledged to strengthen ties between their settlements. They drew on the experiences of the SPARC/NSDF/Mahila Milan alliance in India, and went on exchange programmes to India. Out of this process the South African Homeless Peoples' Federation emerged, with a NGO called the Peoples' Dialogue as the Federation's support arm.

The Homeless People's Federation consists mainly of women (although men are not excluded) who are very poor, do not have security of tenure, and live in shack settlements, backyard shacks or hostels. The alliance sees designing and building homes as "soft skills" that people can acquire relatively easily. They see accessing and allocating land, creating systems of distribution and governance, and managing finance as "hard skills" that require the poor to organise themselves so as to be able to acquire them.

The basic building blocks of the Homeless People's Federation are Housing Savings Schemes. The process of saving money is used as a mobilising tool and a way of increasing the Federation's bargaining power. As of mid-1997, the Federation consisted of 43,000 members, with total savings of R810,000. The Federation has a loan scheme, called the uTshani Fund, which is used to lend money for housing to members. Loans are given to small groups of 10–20 members at a time

The loans are disbursed to members in the form of building materials via a Building, Information and Training (BIT) Centre. The BIT Centres are the focal point of the construction process—materials are stored there and it is the site office of the local project co-ordinator. The members themselves are responsible for undertaking the construction of the foundations and floor slabs, and builders are usually employed to build the superstructures, with some assistance from the members. The houses produced are usually quite large (up to 66m^2 in size), and are usually of adequate quality.

Kanana

The Kanana project in Gauteng is an example of community self help in action. In April 1994, 1,500 backyard shack-dwelling households in Sebokeng, Gauteng, invaded a vacant piece of land intended for industrial development next to the Golden Highway, and called it Kanana (i.e. Canaan, the promised land). Plots, roads, and sites for community facilities were laid out. The residents of Kanana were threatened with eviction to health reasons. In response, Kanana's leaders paid council workers to steal plans of the water and sewerage systems in the area and show them how to tap into the water mains so that communal standpipes could be provided. The Kanana community subsequently joined the Homeless Peoples' Federation.

Members of the Homeless People's Federation infrastructure team and the Kanana Housing Savings Scheme went on an exchange programme to the

Orangi Pilot Project in Karachi. They subsequently got a loan from the uTshani Fund and designed and constructed a water supply and sewerage network for 38 sites in Kanana. The local authority tried to prevent them from connecting up to the main sewer line, because it was already overburdened. Ten 48m² houses were also built with loans from the uTshani Fund.

Although the Homeless Peoples' Federation has won support from some national and provincial Ministers, it has often provoked strong political reactions from councillors and officials. One response from a councillor about the Kanana project was: "Those are not RDP (Reconstruction and Development Programme) houses. I will demolish them" (People's Dialogue, 1997). Peoples' Dialogue speculates that this reaction is due to newly elected councillors seeing the Homeless Peoples' Federation as a threat to their legitimacy, especially as the Federation is not aligned with any political party.

CONCLUSIONS

Conditions in South Africa have changed considerably since 1990, resulting in many opportunities for CBOs to participate in development, but also resulting in many challenges to their continued existence.

Corporatist participation systems to facilitate participation in local government affairs are not yet working well in practice, but they have the potential to become a way for civil society to influence local government development initiatives, for example, by participating in integrated development planning and budgeting. Formalised forums for structured participation are important, in order to facilitate a move from a culture of resistance to one of co-operation between local government and civil society. With more local government support, and with more autonomy and responsibility, Development Forums might be able to grow into true organs of civil society and effectively represent the needs of different interest groups in the affairs of local government, rather than merely being an extension of local bureaucracy or a training ground for aspiring politicians.

Corporatist participation in the affairs of government is however, not a substitute for civil society. Outside of the corporatist model, it is vital that there is a strong, autonomous civil society to balance and complement local government, and to contribute towards a multi-faceted approach to development, as local government can not provide for the needs of everybody on its own, nor is it always right. An effective civil society needs to consist of watchdog CBOs to keep a check on local government and developmental CBOs to fill in the gaps left by state policies and the market and to demonstrate alternative, "bottom-up" approaches to development (for example, see Uphoff, 1993:618–619). Strong civil society needs to consist of autonomous CBOs, supported by strong NGOs, operating in a voluntary pluralist mode, sometimes co-operating with and sometimes acting in opposition to the state.

Different types of CBOs need to play different roles in civil society, as the roles of "watchdog" over local government and of a developmental agent are inherently contradictory. Although traditional civic associations may continue to be represented in Development Forums, they seem to be potentially suited to play the role of watchdog CBOs. In order to be effective, non-political watchdogs of local government, however, they will need to develop their own identity separate from party politics. The support of NGOs is critical, in order to build their capacity to engage with local councillors on a more equal footing.

The two types of developmental CBOs that are emerging are CBOs that are evolving into permanent community development organisations, or CDCs, and the new mutual help organisations. Both types of developmental CBO are important, as they serve different interest groups—the former are more suited to fairly cohesive, well established residential areas with efficient CBOs, while the latter are more suited to marginalised groups not adequately represented by traditional CBOs.

These two types of developmental CBOs have the potential to become sustainable development organisations that can continue to be involved in implementing local development projects, as long as sufficient funding and cost recovery opportunities are available. NGOs have a very important role to play in supporting both types of developmental CBO, as indicated by BESG's support for the Ubhaqa Development Association and the support of Peoples' Dialogue for the Homeless Peoples' Federation. It is only by ensuring that there is a strong civil society, and by co-operation between the state, CBOs and NGOs, that the development challenges facing South Africa can be adequately tackled.

References

Bekker, Simon and Carey Wilson, 1991, "Project Development in Durban and Pietermaritzburg: A Survey of Expert Opinion", *Development Southern Africa* 8(1), pp. 85–109.

Bond, Patrick and Angela Tait, 1997, "The failure of housing policy in post-apartheid South Africa", *Urban Forum* 8(1), pp. 19–41

Built Environment Support Group, 1996, *Mechanisms for Community Participation in Urban Housing Delivery: Review of Community Based Organisations and Institutions.* Report prepared for the Community and Urban Support Services Project (CUSSP), Johannesburg.

Coovadia, Cas, 1991, "The Role of the Civic Movement", in Swilling, Mark, Richard Humphries and Khehla Shubane (eds), *Apartheid City in Transition.* Cape Town: Oxford University Press.

Dlamini, Kisa, 1997, "In the Light of the Need for the Delivery of Low Cost Housing at Scale, Is Community Participation More of a Hindrance Than Help?", paper presented at *CUSSP Housing Workshop*, Durban, 17 April, 1997.

Friedman, Steven and Maxine Reitzes, 1996, "Democratisation or Bureaucratisation? Civil Society, the Public Sphere, and the State in Post-Apartheid South Africa", *Transformation* 29, pp. 55–73.

Hodgson, Spencer, 1996, "Proactive Facilitation at Malukazi: A Case Study on the Management of Housing Facilitation". Unpublished report commissioned by the KwaZulu-Natal Provincial Housing Board, Durban.

Jackson, Brian, 1968, *Working Class Community.* London: Routledge and Kegan Paul.

Kraak, Gerald, 1996, *Development Update—An Interfund Briefing on Development and the Voluntary Sector in South Africa in 1995/1996.* Johannesburg: Interfund.

Mahura, Ntebatse, 1995, "An Evaluation of the Effectiveness of Civic Structures in Housing Development With Reference to St. Wendolins and Savannah Park". MSc. (Urban and Regional Planning) Thesis, University of Natal, Durban.

Marais, Hein, 1997, "Annual Review: The Voluntary Sector and Development in Southern Africa 1996/97", *Development Update*, 1(3), whole issue.

Moser, Caroline, 1989, "Community Participation in Urban Projects in the Third World", *Progress in Planning*, 32(2), pp. 71–133.

Narsoo, Monty, 1991, "Civil Society: A Contested Terrain", *Work in Progress*, 76, pp. 24–27.

Nene, Bheki, 1997, *Building an Understanding of Community Based Development Fora.* Durban: Urban Strategy Department, Durban Metro Council.

Peoples' Dialogue, 1997, *The Liberating Power of Self Reliance: People Centred Development in Kanana Settlement, Vaal Region, Gauteng Province.* Cape Town.

Pieterse, Edgar, 1997, "Urban Social Movements in South Africa in a 'Globalising' Era", *Urban Forum*, 8(1), pp. 1–17.

Pieterse, Edgar and AbdouMaliq Simone (eds), 1994, *Governance and Development: A Critical Analysis of Community Organisations in the Western Cape.* Cape Town: Foundation for Contemporary Research.

Robinson, Peter, Tressan Sullivan and Susan Lund, 1994, *Assessment of the Independent Development Trust's Capital Subsidy Scheme.* Cape Town: Independent Development Trust.

Seekings, Jeremy, 1997, "SANCO: Strategic Dilemmas in a Democratic South Africa", *Transformation*, 34, pp. 1–30.

Shubane, Khehla and Pumla Madiba, 1992, *The Struggle Continues? Civic Associations in the Transition.* Research Report No. 25. Johannesburg Centre for Policy Studies.

Sokhulu, J.Z., 1997, "Community Participation and Housing Development—A Community Perspective", paper presented at *CUSSP Housing Workshop*, Durban, 17 April, 1997.

Swilling, Mark, 1993, "Civic Associations in South Africa", *Urban Forum*, 4(2), pp. 15–36.

Thornton, Robert and Mamphela Ramphele, 1988, "The Quest for Community", in Boonzaier, Emile and John Sharp (eds), *South African Keywords—The Uses and Abuses of Political Concepts.* Cape Town and Johannesburg: David Philip.

Uphoff, Norman, 1993, "Grassroots Organisations and NGOs in Rural Development: Opportunities with Diminishing States and Expanding Markets", *World Development*, 21(4), pp. 607–22.

CHAPTER 15

Communities and Community Institutions in Luanda, Angola

Paul Robson

BACKGROUND TO THE STUDY

This paper is based on research carried out in December 1996 in urban areas in Angola, as part of a larger study of communities and community institutions in the country. The research examined community institutions as a potential basis for development interventions in urban areas, mainly in the capital city Luanda. The research was a response to the severe lack of information about people's living conditions, institutions and production systems in Angola.

The research project was carried out through semi-structured interviews with key informants in Government and in Non-Governmental Organisations. Case-studies in two peri-urban *bairros* (spontaneous, unserviced settlements) were carried out through semi-structured interviews and through focus-group discussions. The interviews and discussion groups focused on the growth and structure of Luanda, coping strategies, family and neighbourhood cooperation, community structures, relations with Government and views on development. Other previous studies were also re-analysed (Amado, Cruz and Hakkert, 1992; INE, 1993).

The two *bairros* which were studied in depth were Palanca and Hoji-ya-Henda. The *bairro* Palanca is inhabited by people from the north of Angola of the Bakongo group, many of whom lived in exile in Kinshasa from about 1961 to 1982. The *bairro* Hoji-ya-Henda is inhabited mainly by people from the immediate Luanda hinterland and from the Kimbundu group. Both *bairros* grew spontaneously during the 1980s and are located about 7 kilometres from the city centre ("Baixa") of Luanda.

The need for research

There has never been any significant amount of research carried out at the community level in Angola. Such research was not encouraged by the Portuguese during the colonial period, and only at the beginning of the anti-colonial struggle in 1961 was any need felt for understanding local customs, farming systems or coping mechanisms. Community based research has not been encouraged in the post-independence period either. There has been a strong belief in rapid industrialisation and modernisation, and the ability of the State to survive on off-shore production of petroleum reduced the need to understand basic socio-economic processes (Messiant, 1998). In fact, socio-economic development has become the *de facto* responsibility of donor organisations.

Knowledge about grassroots civil society is of importance for reconstruction, rehabilitation and reconciliation in Angola. The high-profile September 1995 Round Table of Donors in Brussels endorsed a Programme of Community Rehabilitation and National Reconciliation as the main vehicle for social reconstruction. This states that "Angola's overall recovery depends on the ability of the country to bring about (among other factors) the rehabilitation of economic and social infrastructure through community rehabilitation and reconstruction programmes" (Government of Angola, 1995).

Communities and community organisations in Angola are expected to play an important role in physical reconstruction, social reconstruction, peace-building, and reconciliation. This is in line with the current ideology in the international aid community, which emphasises that "civil society" has a key role in development and democratisation and that the process of developing institutions is essential, especially in Africa where there has been institutional regression (Uphoff, 1993).

Some observers have argued that the enormous changes in Angola following from war, forced population displacement, rapid urbanisation etc. have led to an individualistic society in which community organisations have disappeared. Other observers have postulated that it is only through community solidarity that most Angolans have survived the past 40 turbulent years.

URBANISATION IN ANGOLA

Urban population growth has been extremely high in Angola, even by African standards. The percentage of the population living in urban areas is now estimated at over 50 per cent (UNDP, 1997) (UNICEF/GoA, in preparation), compared to only 14 per cent in 1970 and 11 per cent in 1960 (Amado, Cruz and Hakkert, 1992). All population data in Angola are uncertain, but approximately 3 million people are now believed to live in Luanda and another 3 million live in the other major towns of Lobito, Benguela, Huambo, Lubango, Malanje and Uige. The total population in Angola is 12 million.

At the same time, the contribution of rural areas to the economy has declined dramatically. By 1996 agriculture contributed only 7 per cent of GDP, in stark contrast to the early 1970s when Angola was a large net exporter of agricultural products and the fourth largest producer of coffee for the world market (UNICEF/GoA, 1999). The petroleum sector's share of GDP reached 60 per cent in 1996, compared to insignificant levels in the 1960s.

Rapid urban population growth from 1960 to 1974 was associated with attempts by the Portuguese colonial government to accelerate economic development. Immigrants from Portugal, contract labourers brought from the central highlands to work on the railways and ports, and people from surrounding areas attracted by urban employment were the main components of urbanisation.

Since 1975, urban migration has not been caused by the attraction of urban areas or the availability of employment, but rather by push-factors in rural areas. The first twenty years of Independence have been a period of extreme turbulence, with forced population movements, destruction of infrastructure and deterioration of the agricultural sector. This turbulence continues, despite attempted peace settlements through the Bicesse and Lusaka agreements of 1991 and 1994 respectively (Tvedten, 1997).

Until recently there has been an assumption that at least some of the urban growth would be reversed with the end of conflict. But the end of conflict has proved elusive, and even when it comes it is by no means certain that people will return to rural areas. During the periods of relative peace (such as the period of "no war, no peace" between 1995 and 1997), the enhanced freedom of movement within the country led even more people to migrate to urban areas rather than return to rural areas. At the same time very few recently arrived urban dwellers are making plans for returning to rural areas, as the conflict has continued for so long and the rural economy and trade has collapsed. Despite the difficulties of urban life, the perception of rural areas is mainly negative with forced labour in the colonial era, continuous armed conflict, and inadequate social services.

A high urban birth rate also means that a large proportion of the urban population is made up of young people born in towns and cities, as children of rural people who migrated to the city. Sixty-one per cent of people in Luanda are under 20 yeas of age and 49 per cent under 15 (INE, 1993). Thirty-six per cent of the total population of Luanda was born outside the city, but only 44 per cent of the population under 30 and 13 per cent of the population under 15 were born in other areas. These young people do not consider themselves as displaced people who will eventually return to rural areas.

There is a growing realisation that reconstruction needs to take into account that present-day Angolan society is heavily urbanised. Reconstruction cannot be based on traditional perceptions of Angola as primarily a rural society: Despite this, however, there is no strategic view of urban development in Angola.

The growth of Luanda

The most spectacular growth in the urban population has taken place in Luanda, which now contains about a quarter of the total population of Angola. There has been migration to Luanda from rural as well as other urban areas, and from all provinces in the country. The siege and occupation by UNITA of cities such as Huambo, Uige, Kuito and Malanje during 1993 and 1994 were particularly important events and led to large-scale migration from these towns to the relative safety of Luanda. The population of Luanda is estimated to have grown as follows (Table 15:1).

Historically the arrival on a large scale of Portuguese settlers from 1945 onwards led to the construction of many multi-story buildings and larger, permanent houses in the "down-town" area of Luanda (presently the Municipal District of Ingombotas and parts of the Municipal District of Maianga). This led to the expulsion of the local people who already lived there to surrounding areas. The central cement city (mainly inhabited by Portuguese) became known as the "Baixa", while the surrounding, unplanned African settlements became known as *musseques* (from a local Kimbundu word describing the sandy soil of the higher areas surrounding the city). The peripheral musseques grew rapidly while older musseques, closer to the Baixa, disappeared under multi-story buildings.

Table 15:1. *Population growth, Luanda*

Year	Population	Year	Population
1930	50,000	1970	480,000
1940	61,000	1980	940,000
1950	141,000	1990	2,000,000
1960	224,000	1997	3,000,000

By 1970, the inhabited area had reached out in a semi-circle of 5 kilometres radius around the port of Luanda and the Baixa. Beyond this, industry was expanding out further along the main roads, with some small residential areas close to the main industries. However, most of the land between the main roads was uninhabited, with only vegetable gardens and *mandioca* (cassava) fields, cultivated by people who lived in Luanda but worked their fields and gardens a few days each week.

The population distribution changed markedly from 1970 to the 1990s. The flight of the Portuguese after 1975, civil conflict in the city after Independence, the arrival of Bakongo people from Kinshasa and northern Angola after 1982, and successive waves of immigrants from various parts of Angola completely changed the city. Between 1974 and 1982, the areas between the main roads became slowly occupied, and this occupation intensified after 1982. By 1986, the residential areas formed a semi-circle reaching out about 8 kilometres from the Baixa. Growth has continued since, so that the residential area now reaches more than 10 kilometres from the centre of the city. At the same time all areas of Luanda have suffered a continuous increase in population through increases in the number of people on each building plot, and in each house, and with people even occupying the edges of roads or uncompleted high-rise buildings.

Luanda communities

The population of Luanda has come from all parts of Angola at various times and has integrated in various ways. The trajectories of different population groups migrating to Luanda are complex, and not everybody migrated directly to the city from their areas of origin.

Before Independence in 1975, Ovimbundu people (speaking Umbundu) from the central plateau of Angola were forcibly recruited to work in the port and railways in Luanda and made up 20 per cent of the population of the city. Ovimbundu people were also forcibly recruited in the late colonial period to work on cotton and coffee plantations in northern Angola. As the plantations gradually collapsed from 1975 onwards, they migrated to Luanda as well. Ovimbundu people are often found living in precarious conditions on the periphery of Luanda.

Before Independence in 1975, only two per cent of the population of Luanda were Bakongo people from northern Angola. Bakongo people (speaking Kikongo) tended to migrate to Kinshasa (Belgian Congo, Republic of Zaire, Democratic Republic of Congo), especially from 1961 onwards when there was a massive flow of people following abortive uprisings against Portuguese rule in the north. Significant numbers of Bakongo returned to Angola from 1982 onwards, mainly to Luanda and not to their rural areas of origin. They tend to live in *bairros* such as Palanca and Mabor, and now make up a significant (but unknown) percentage of the city population. Many Bakongo returned to Angola with educational qualifications that they had obtained in exile, and with an outlook on life that they had learned in Kinshasa.

The other significant population group in Luanda is the Ambundu (speaking Kimbundu) from the hinterland of Luanda, who in 1970 represented 68 per cent of the city population. They are still probably the largest group in Luanda. Certain areas contain high concentrations of Ambundu people from particular areas (such as Malanje or Catete) while other areas contain more mixed populations.

The way that migrants integrate themselves in the city is still not fully understood. Most migrants initially seem to go to a *bairro* where they have family members, or people from their immediate area of origin. They stay with them for some time before they find land where they can build their own houses, sometimes in more peripheral area of the city where there are also people from their area of origin. But it is not always the case that *bairros* are populated by people from the same region: Viana II on the outskirts of the city has residents from fourteen of the eighteen Provinces of Angola, and many other *bairros* also have mixed populations.

Survival in the city

Migrants from rural areas come to a city with few services and few employment opportunities. The current population of Luanda is about 3 million, with services designed for a city of only 500,000. Residents are particularly concerned about the poor water and electricity supply, poor schools and medical services, deteriorating roads and inadequate security.

Findings from our 1996 survey indicate that the lowest levels of government administration function very poorly, and respondents argue that the Government Administration is hardly visible. Communal Administrators report neither receiving a budget to maintain and operate the offices nor a salary. The Municipal Districts, which are comprised of two or three *Comunas*, are perceived as marginal with limited budgets and depending on the Provincial Government of the City of Luanda for supply of services.

Only thirty-five per cent of incidents of sickness are treated by public health services, with 42 per cent being treated by private services and 24 per cent by self-medication. The poorest section of the population usually cannot afford medical consultations, and buy medicines in the market without seeking medical advice.

Furthermore, most parts of the city outside the Baixa area do not have piped water, and people purchase their water from private water-sellers who are supplied by private water tankers. The price of water is high, being highest (about 15 US$ per cubic metre) on the southern periphery of the city which is furthest from the main water pipes and the River Bengo (the main source of water). While aid organisations have defined certain groups of the population as particularly vulnerable (street children, war-disabled, some groups of displaced people) the opinion of most people is that there are large sections of the population who do not have an adequate income and are vulnerable to a whole range of shocks, such as poverty, illness, and crime.

The income of a typical family comes from a number of different sources and from different family members. More men than women are employed, but as many as 58 per cent of women are economically active. A young woman will often look after many children from her extended family to make it possible for other women from the family to generate income. It is only innovative social organisation like this that makes it possible for a family to survive in present day Luanda.

An analysis of one extended family (Van der Winden, 1996), revealed a monthly income of 780 US$ for 10 adults and 13 children. Three women with informal economic activities contributed 55 per cent of the income, and small scale agricultural activities contributed 18 per cent. Twenty-seven per cent came from formal sector employment, though this may be atypical, as this family had one member paid by an international aid organisation. Those employed by the State receive much lower and irregular salaries.

Thus the majority of families in Luanda depend on the informal sector market and petty trading for their survival. This means long hours of work by women, which in turn depends on co-operation between members of a family and between neighbours for child-care and housework. Figures of the National Statistical Institute indicate that 50 per cent of the households in Luanda have at least one member involved in small scale trading (in markets or on the street) (INE, 1996). The ease with which it is possible to begin informal trading and the small amount of capital required makes it an attractive prospect, but profit margins are very low. INE data indicate that the more people in a family who are employed, the poorer is the family. For most families the informal labour market is characterised by a large number of low-paying jobs which each contribute a small amount to the family income.

The informal labour market is a relatively recent phenomenon, but continues to expand. Competition to enter it is high, which lower profits. Women who sell fish usually sell between one and three boxes per day, and the profit is about 3 US$ per box. This is barely enough to feed a family.

There is no official poverty line for Angola, nor defined criteria to determine one (Lopes, 1993). The National Statistical Institute (INE) has defined its own criteria and indicates that 60 per cent of the Angolan population are below this poverty-line and 10 per cent are in extreme poverty, with more than 70 per cent of family expenditure being used for food (INE, 1996).

There are few data available to show differences in income levels and poverty between the different areas of the city. Data are unreliable and are generally aggregated to the level of Municipal Districts, which are made up of different types of *bairros*. Health data indicate lower morbidity and mortality in the Districts of Maianga and Ingombotas than in Districts which contain more spontaneous peri-urban *musseques*. But all health indicators show very poor health, and declining health conditions over the last 20 years.

ORGANISATIONS AND ASSOCIATIONS
Traditional organisations

"Traditional" institutions of solidarity, to which all members of an area belong by birth and which regulate all aspects of life, still exist in many places in Angola. The pastoral population in Southern Angola could not have survived without institutions regulating vital aspects of the life of the community, such as migration patterns, use of water, and numbers of cattle. The national animal of Angola, Palanca Negra Gigante, has survived in the Malanje Province thanks to protection by traditional leaders. Also development projects in some rural areas have been based on "natural" forms of solidarity which unite a whole village.

In all rural areas of Angola, as well as in some urban areas, there are still traditional leaders or *sobas* (Neto, 1998). However, conflict and instability have affected the role of *sobas*. In some areas the Soba is someone in whom a community has confidence. In others the Soba is appointed from outside and mainly acts as an intermediary in the transmission of information between the village and lower levels of the State Administration (Andrade et al., 1998; Pacheco and Ryle, 1998).

In Luanda no remnants of "traditional" organisational structures have been identified, and the word Soba is not used. There are no leaders who are able to speak for all the people living in one area, even when people have recently arrived from the same area of origin. Migrants become urbanised rapidly, and rural values and institutions seem to disappear quickly.

Neither has it been possible to identify organisations which link people with their areas of origin. Home area associations, which are an important feature of African cities such as Khartoum and Addis Ababa, are not found in Luanda. Most people seem to lose contact with their rural areas of origin, partly because the difficulties of travel are so great. This is a concern for people, as they are not able to help their family members in rural areas. Some people report that they travel outside Luanda, but to areas with easier access such as Kwanza Sul (where it is possible to buy agricultural produce) or the Lundas (the diamond-mining areas) and not to their own areas of origin.

Although no "traditional" organisational structures have been identified, Bakongo-people living in Luanda place particular emphasis on their traditional culture and the role of solidarity. They express a greater belief in the concept of community, show more recognition of being part of a specific group and tend to work together. They conceptualise this as *sangolo sako*, which signifies the link to an African tradition of individual or collective self-help. The Bakongo believe that taking initiatives will attract support from others. They contrast this tendency with other Angolans, who they feel have been heavily influenced by European colonial and post-independence paternalism which makes them wait for help instead of taking initiatives themselves.

Official organisations

Residents' Committees were organised by the Government in all urban areas in 1983, as a means of communication between urban populations and the State. Members of the Residents' Committees were elected and the Committees functioned for some time. However, these committees are currently not functioning. People knew of their existence, but they were unable to say what they did or when they had last met. The explanation that residents give for their disappearance is that there are no clear Government counterparts with which such committees could maintain dialogue, and hence that they could rarely resolve problems and became redundant.

A similar reason was given for the lack of other kinds of autonomous residents' committees. There is little reason to create such organisations if there are no effective local government bodies with which to speak. Another reason given is that there is very little experience with such organisations, in either pre-Independence or post-Independence Angola.

Organisations inspired by NGOs

Despite the lack of tradition and political climate for local organisations, international NGOs have had positive experiences with supporting the few committees that exist for concrete tasks such as water-points committees and Parents' Committees in schools. This indicates that there is potential for organising communities, when this helps to resolve a problem being given high priority by the community itself.

Water committees are responsible for maintaining a water-point, and for collecting money from users for its maintenance and upkeep. Committees of this type are elected by the users, keep the latter informed about the management of the water-point and liaise with the Luanda Water Company. Parents' committees work with the Director of a school, collect funds for school maintenance and monitor the work of the school staff. Parents' Committees have been encouraged by the Ministry of Education.

Both Water Committees and Parents' Committees have succeeded in organising residents of peri-urban *bairros*, and in creating a dialogue with state service providers. In both cases, the input of NGOs has been important for structuring the Committees and creating linkages with the relevant state agencies. NGOs have helped create systems of financial management; carried out leadership training to create accountable and transparent organisations; helped to create an environment of trust between the users and the State service supplier; and dealt with technical aspects of water supply and primary education, which allow residents to participate in a functioning service.

Residents have been less willing to organise when they do not feel that there is a concrete problem to which to relate. It has, in other words, often been necessary to construct a water point before a Water Committee can be organised. Committees bring together people in the same *bairro* who already know each other, who already see each other regularly, and who have common goals which can be dealt with fairly quickly.

Ad-hoc *bairro* organisations

In the two *bairros* studied, Palanca and Hoji-ya-Henda, community organisations were identified which had been established to resolve specific problems and had had a short life span. Families who do not have electricity develop relations with those who have, in order to iron clothes or watch television, and some other service is arranged in return. Families who have poor access to water develop relations with people who have better access to wash their clothes, and some other service is arranged in return etc.

Groups of families join together to repair holes in a street or to remove rubbish. Sporting, cultural and recreation groups have been established and are important for young people. Groups of young people join together to organise an excursion or a sporting event. These recreational groups are small and get little financial assistance. Nevertheless they help create a community feeling.

Residents of the *bairro* of Palanca reported ad-hoc community organisations of this type more frequently than residents of the *bairro* of Hoji-ya-Henda. Palanca is as noted a *bairro* where almost all the residents come from the north of Angola and share a common set of values which emphasise self-help and mutual assistance. Hoji-ya-Henda is a *bairro* with people from more diverse origins, though most are from the Luanda hinterland and from the Ambundu group. They themselves say that they have lost much of their traditional African solidarity, often do not share common values, and have less experience in community organisation than people from the north of Angola. Residents of Hoji-ya-Henda *bairro* also say that even mutual assistance between neighbours or members of an extended family is difficult under the existing economic circumstances.

Ad-hoc organisations in the informal economy

As was noted previously, most people survive through their participation in the informal economy in petty trading on the street and in markets. Their ability to participate in the informal economy depends on developing networks. Women represent the majority of the traders, leaving their children with extended family members or friends and neighbours. Vital knowledge about available goods and where they can be bought and sold also comes through networks. These networks are fluid and to some extent "hidden", as people prefer that outsiders, who may be potential competitors, know little about them.

Some of these networks are "horizontal", in that they are formed between equals who have similar interests. But some are "vertical", with a strong aspect of exploitation and divergence of interest. Longer-term residents, with accumulated assets and superior knowledge, act as gatekeepers to networks of information and services. Those who have sufficient assets or contacts to be involved in wholesale trading are at an advantage in trading networks, as the profit margin in the wholesaling of fish (from the port to the market) is five times higher than at the retail stage (in the market and to the door).

The informal market is not without its rules: it is, in some respects, organised. The huge market of Roque Santeiro in Luanda (where several hundred thousand people pass through every day) appears anarchic, but has rules which control the hours of operation, what is sold where, where marketing stalls are located and how an individual gains access to a place to sell. No one is able, or willing, to say how such rules are set or how they are enforced. They create order in a context where the State has not been able to create order: most participants welcome the informal organisation, even though it seems to benefit longer-term and influential residents more than newcomers. The strong correlation between sectors of trade and certain ethno-linguistic groups indicates that access to trade sectors depends on contacts made through extended family links and other people from the same area of origin.

Many people who are involved in petty trading are also involved in an informal savings and credit system known as *kixikila*. A group of between 10 and 15 people who know each other well, and have regular face-to-face contact, put money into the *kixikila* regularly: the whole amount is put at the disposition of one of the members in a system of rotation. This gives each member access to a large sum of money once or twice a year, which permits purchase of large quantities of goods or investment. *Kixikila* is similar to *Xitique* found in urban areas in southern Mozambique, and to rotating savings societies found in almost every country in Asia and Africa. Similar credit institutions existed in Europe in the past and in some cases, financed small scale industrial development (Putnam, 1993). *Kixikila* was reported to have disappeared between 1994 and 1996 (a period of very rapid currency devaluation) but is now reported to have re-appeared and grown in importance, to the extent of financing the import of cars and lorries. The institution of *kixikila* is an indicator of a high degree of mutual trust between workmates, friends or neighbours in an environment which is usually depicted as being devoid of such trust.

Local NGOs

Local NGOs have been established by people from the two *bairros* under study since the revision of the Constitution in 1990 made this legal. They vary in size, competence and capacity, but most of them are small with limited funding. The NGOs fill gaps in service provision left by the State and the private sector. However, many residents remark that they have little information about the local NGOs and are not actively involved in their work.

Local NGOs have only recently begun to work with long-term social mobilisation, to help resolve conflicts and to raise the level of trust in a community. Residents express a desire that NGOs begin to help them create a dialogue with Government. However, the NGOs themselves are reluctant to take on this role, as they have little experience with being intermediaries and do not want to become involved in what should be direct communication between communities and the Government.

The local NGOs argue that they are almost completely dependent on foreign donors, and thus have to define their strategy on the basis of the strategy of the latter. This limits them to short-term actions, and to providing services in the same way as private service-providers (i.e. without involvement by the users).

Local NGOs also report that it is difficult for them to obtain help to build their own capacity, and to cover their running costs. They normally receive a series of small grants, which implies considerable administrative work. They have grown during a period in which foreign donors have been looking for partners to implement emergency programmes, and now face a challenge in adjusting to the donors' new agenda of rehabilitation and development.

Churches

Churches are important institutions in peri-urban Luanda. The large denominations (Roman Catholic, Salvation Army, Baptists, Methodists) are represented, as well as a proliferation of very small Churches. The latter are the most visible and best-organised organisations in peri-urban areas.

Peri-urban residents explain that the rapid growth in the number of churches in their areas has taken place because the churches act as a refuge in times of turbulent and difficult conditions. They act as a substitute for "traditional" structures which have disappeared. But although they are well rooted in peri-urban *bairros*, they do not represent the complete *bairro* or even a sub-area. In some cases they exclude part of the population, or even create divisions in the community. Some residents feel that the large number of very small churches is a particular cause for concern. Where they provide services, such as health-posts, they rarely collaborate among themselves and are unwilling to follow the standards set by the relevant Ministries.

SOME CONCLUSIONS ON URBAN ASSOCIATIONS AND RECONSTRUCTION

We have argued that migrating to an urban area in Angola implies an abrupt break with "traditional" rural forms of solidarity. The function of rural forms of solidarity has been taken over by informal forms of organisation, as well as churches. Both types of institutions fill the gap created by the inadequate services provided by the State and the private sector. It will require time and energy to build the necessary trust and linkages, and to define the rules of co-operation necessary to function constructively.

People from the northern Angola, who historically have experience from the urban context of Kinshasa, bring a set of shared values which allows them to recreate forms of solidarity more easily. People from other areas do not yet have the same experience of creating their own associations or NGOs, even though they argue that such institutions have the potential to resolve practical problems in their *bairro*. Activities which involve collecting or saving money, are said to present particular difficulties, because money tends to disappear.

However, the institution of *kixikila* indicates that, under certain circumstances, trust and appropriate mechanisms of monitoring can be developed. Where there has been some success in organising collection of funds (e.g. for managing water points or improving schools), it has involved long-term social mobilisation, usually by an NGO, to help resolve conflicts, raise the level of trust, develop a transparent leadership and create appropriate rules.

Duffield (1994) uses Angola as an example of a complex political emergency where not only economic and physical infrastructure have been damaged, but also the country's institutions and organisations: cultural, educational and health structures; market and business networks; human resources and skills; and social, civil and political organisations have all disintegrated and left an institutional void, undermining the foundations upon which conventional social relations are based and upon which recovery should be built. The associational forms which currently exist in peri-urban Luanda do little to fill this institutional void. The state has retreated, but the market and collective action have only partially occupied the space.

Residents state that life in urban areas is costly, and that there are important services which simply do not exist. The residents of both *bairros* studied reported difficulties in their relations with Government, but they still argue that development of civil society requires a more active role by the State rather than its retreat.

There is a potential to link local initiatives with the relevant government structures. However, this necessitates a re-definition of the role of the State, to actively link with local initiatives and work at the micro-level. The fact that community initiatives do not produce a response from Government creates a feeling of cynicism and frustration. This is particularly true among people from the north of Angola living in Palanca, who feel that the State is against them due to their ethnic background. People from the north of Angola feel that their greater propensity to take initiatives or organise themselves creates misunderstandings with other Angolans, who are influenced by paternalism or dependency in their relations with institutions such as the state and the Church.

In the peri-urban areas of Luanda, there are initiatives which at present are directed mainly towards family and individual survival. There is, as we have argued, a potential for community-level responses when there is adequate response by other parties. Residents of peri-urban *bairros* are only interested in organising themselves around activities which they feel can resolve their problems on a more permanent basis. Because of promises made in the past that did not bear fruit, communities tend to be wary of promises, plans and fine words.

It is currently mainly NGOs that are concerned about the institutional void in the poor areas of Luanda. The State has not shown much sign of being aware of this problem, and continues to be more concerned with technical than institutional development. The "international community" appears mainly to see the solution in terms of the creation of multi-party democracy or, in the case of the World Bank, privatisation of State services. We have argued that the concept of community based rehabilitation advocated by NGOs is still valid, and that the creation of sustainable institutions is potentially an important contribution to peace-building, rehabilitation, reconstruction and development in Angola.

References

Amado, F., F. Cruz and R. Hakkert, 1992, "A urbanizacão e desurbanizacão", *Cadernos de Populacão e Desenvolvimento*. Year 1, Vol. 1, No. 1. Luanda: Ministério do Plano and FNUAP.

Andrade, Filomena, Paulo de Carvalho and Gabriela Cohen, 1998, "Deslocados: estudos de casos—Malanje e Benguela", in *Comunidades e Instituicões Comunitárias em Angola na Perspectiva do Pós-Guerra*. Luanda: ADRA—Angola, Development Workshop—Angola, Alternatives (Canada) and Save the Children Fund (UK).

Duffield, Mark, 1994, *Complex Political Emergencies with Reference to Angola and Bosnia; An Exploratory Report for UNICEF*. School of Public Policy, University of Birmingham, UK.

Government of Angola, 1995, *First Roundtable Conference of Donors: Programme of Community rehabilitation and national reconciliation*. Luanda.

INE, 1993, *Inqérito socio-demográfico e emprego na cidade de Luanda (Junho–Julho 1993); resultados definitivos, populacão, emprego e desemprego*. Luanda: Instituto Nacional de Estatística.

—, 1996, *Perfil da pobreza em Angola*. Luanda: Instituto Nacional de Estatística.

Lopes, Teresinha, 1993, *Sistemas de acompanhamento da pobreza*. Luanda: Secretariado de Estado do Planeamento and UNICEF.

Messiant, Christine, 1998, "Conhecimentos, poderes, intervencões, comunidades—da guerra ... paz", in *Comunidades e Instituicões Comunitá rias em Angola na Perspectiva do Pós-Guerra*. Luanda: ADRA—Angola, Development Workshop—Angola, Alternatives (Canada) and Save the Children Fund (UK).

Neto, Maria de Conceicão, 1998, "Contribuicão a um enquadramento histórico da situacão actual", in *Comunidades e Instituicões Comunitárias em Angola na Perspectiva do Pós-Guerra*. Luanda: ADRA—Angola, Development Workshop—Angola, Alternatives (Canada) and Save the Children Fund (UK).

Pacheco, Fernando and John Ryle, 1998, "Comunidades rurais de Huambo", in *Comunidades e Instituicões Comunitárias em Angola na Perspectiva do Pós-Guerra*. Luanda: ADRA—Angola, Development Workshop—Angola, Alternatives (Canada) and Save the Children Fund (UK).

Putnam, Robert D., 1993, *Making Democracy Work: Civil Traditions in Modern Italy*. Princeton NJ: Princeton University Press.

Tvedten, Inge, 1997, *Angola. Struggle for Peace and Reconstruction*. Boulder, CO: Westview Press.

UNDP, 1997, *Relatório do Desenvolvimento Humano, Angola 1997*. Luanda: UNDP.

UNICEF/GoA, 1999, "A Brighter Future for Angola's Children. A Situation Analysis of Children". Mimeo. Luanda: UNICEF and Government of Angola.

Uphoff, Norman, 1993, "Grassroots organisations and NGOs in Rural Development: Opportunities with Diminishing States and Expanding Markets", in *World Development*, Vol. 21, No. 4, pp 607–22.

Van der Winden, Bob (ed.), 1996, *A Family of the Musseque (Survival and Development in Post-War Angola)*. Oxford: One World Action and Worldview.

CHAPTER 16

The Legacy of Mobilisation from Above: Participation in a Zanzibar Neighbourhood

Jørgen Andreasen

Since Independence in 1961, the Government of Tanzania has been very concerned with common people's access to power—in theory, in official statements and in legislation. The political will to foster community based development was demonstrated in 1967 when the then ruling Party, TANU, and the Government very vigorously produced the Arusha Declaration and subsequently adopted a policy of socialism and self-reliance. The present conception of local government is enshrined in the constitution of the United Republic of Tanzania. Sub-section (1) of section 146 of the constitution provides that:

> Local Government Authorities exist for the purposes of consolidating and giving more power to the people. The Local Government Authorities shall be entitled and competent to participate, and to involve the people in the planning and implementation of development programmes within their respective areas of authority and generally throughout the country.

When practised, however, participation was rarely conceived by those holding power as a democratic right or by the communities concerned as a voluntary activity. Community participation was often reduced to top-down information campaigns and mobilisation of individual labour inputs.

In the 1970s and 1980s, the initiative for local development was concentrated with the single party, TANU (Tanganyika National Union) in the Mainland and ASP (Afro Shirazi Party) in Zanzibar and from 1977, CCM in both places (Chama Cha Mapinduzi—the party of the revolution), as it still is in Zanzibar. All over Tanzania, people joined forces with the Government in collective efforts to build schools, dig drains, etc., mobilised and guided by the Party. In many places this type of intervention has been a positive experience. In others the Government did not fulfil its role and the process at times left deep rifts between people and the Government, due to the undemocratic approaches adopted.

With the transition to a multi-party system, and with declining trust in the old system, this type of participation is today rare. As mentioned above, the "CCM branch" has little ability to mobilise people. At the local level, the official status of "ten-cell leaders" (*balozi*) disappeared and was not replaced by anyone else below the level of the *sheha*, the lowest level officer in the local administrative hierarchy, responsible for ca. 500 plots.[1] The development of

---

[1] The *sheha* should, today, be assisted by ten assistant *shehas*.

new local organisations is restrained by the fact that the old and sometimes distrusted leadership is in many places still in power, often supported by government structures at higher levels. In Zanzibar the CCM party retains very strong power. Some people, therefore, look at interventions and initiatives from the side of the Government with suspicion.

In practice, however, there is a growing interest by the government in people's participation, not primarily as a result of converted politicians and government administrators, but spurred by the increasing inability of the Government to deliver the services and the projects that they earlier could. Therefore, Central and Local Government has an objective interest in passing on the tasks that they have limited resources to implement to the lower levels of the state and to the users themselves.

Tanzania goes along with the general international trend towards support to decentralisation, to NGOs and community based organisations. The growing number of CBOs and NGOs over the last ten years suggests that a new and potential development force is being formed, even if such organisations still need the formal or tacit acceptance of the ruling party and the government. In 1993, a little over 200 NGOs were registered in Tanzania (mainland only). By the end of 1994, there were 813 NGOs, and estimates early in 1997 suggested there were more than two thousand (UNCHS, 1997). Unofficial estimates suggest that there were over one hundred NGOs and CBOs in Zanzibar by 1998.

It remains, both in the Tanzania mainland and in Zanzibar, to be seen how a government with a political base in the old, ruling party will in its endeavours to enable community development be able to disengage from the party structures, and from local leaders who are regarded by some basically as mechanisms of exploitation, and from whom people expect little service. Findings from Moshi (Nnkya, 1996) and villages outside Moshi (Lerise, 1996) demonstrated that, in the practice of planning, little regard is paid to popular participation, although this is politically advocated and legally instituted in the Constitution and the Town and Country Planning Act. Studies by UCLAS, on the other hand, suggest that, with political liberalisation in the 1990s, community initiatives are increasingly important in local development and maintenance of the communal space and the environment, mainly in urban areas and particularly in Dar es Salaam. These initiatives build, to some extent, on structures inherited from the one-party period.

The study

This study of people's participation in local development and maintenance of the communal space and the environment in Zanzibar Town was conducted in 1996–97, when the legacy of the one-party system still dominated development, but when community based organisations (CBOs) and non-governmental organisations (NGOs) had started mushrooming.

What would warrant people to invest time and resources in collective actions related to the public space? Like in Europe, in Tanzania services and infrastructure are supposed to be planned, delivered and managed by the government. Local participation, however, has been an important ingredient in national policies since independence, and with varying enthusiasm people have contributed to local development to a greater extent than in Europe.

The findings presented here stem from a study which is part of a research programme on the performance of planning in Tanzania conducted by Urban and Rural Planning Department of UCLAS in Dar es Salaam in co-operation with the School of Architecture in Copenhagen.[2]

The intention was to study successful examples of community initiatives in local development of environment and infrastructure, to examine the 'social capital' existing in a neighbourhood, to ascertain who participates in what, and to understand how the government and other external actors approach the challenge of development. The concept of "social capital" is borrowed from Putman (1993) and refers to the capacity for communal action, facilitated by associational ties.

Kwahani, a neighbourhood in the Ng'ambo area surrounding the old Zanzibar Town, was identified by local partners as the urban area with the most active local organisations. Public sector planners, as well as new NGOs, emphasised that Kwahani is an interesting area. The main reason for this appeared to be the very active chairman of the local Baja group, with a good talent for catching attention and sometimes funds for local activities. We also collected data in Mkunazini and Vuga in the Stone Town.

Interviews were conducted through an interpreter or by Kiswahili speaking interviewers, and a few in English. The statements of the persons interviewed are obviously subjective and their interpretation of events may very well be influenced by their allegiance in present party politics. It proved difficult and was deemed not advisable to establish contact with key persons affiliated with the opposition, whose views are, therefore, not available. Qualitative interviews were conducted with 17 household heads in Kwahani and 12 with local leaders, as well as with central government officers and politicians. A list of events of collective activities was prepared and checked in a structured survey with 79 residents in Kwahani. In addition, 18 interviews were conducted in the Stone Town, but only in one case is this part of our data set referred to here.

The study focuses on the neighbourhoods and resident households rather than on specific organisations and associations, or projects and programmes. The research project aims in the coming years, to conduct a longitudinal study of events in selected neighbourhoods, recording the local development as it evolves through both the communities' own efforts and also as a result of interventions by government agencies or other outside actors.

---

[2] The study was conducted in Zanzibar in the period November 1996 to June 1997 and supported under the Danida funded ENRECA research programme. The author was throughout the process of data collection and analysis assisted by Ghalib Omar, Marcos Burra and Peter Mandwa.

NOTES ON THE HISTORY OF ZANZIBAR

In 1964, following a revolution that ousted the sultan and curbed the power of non-African groups, Zanzibar merged with Tanganyika to form the United Republic of Tanzania under a constitution that gave Zanzibar its own house of representatives. The ministries of defence, foreign affairs and home affairs are under the United Republic of Tanzania. The remaining ministries are independent in Zanzibar and in the Mainland. Socialist policies and a constitution designed in the Mainland were transferred to Zanzibar. Since the late 1980s, liberalisation and multi-partyism have been officially introduced in Zanzibar, like in the Mainland, but in practice the CCM maintains a very strong hold on power.

Although Zanzibar became a part of Tanzania and shares many characteristics with the mainland, it constitutes a fairly different context. It is a region with a specific and quite distinct social, ethnic, economic and political history. Centuries of integration into the trading networks of the Indian Ocean; prosperous production of cloves, using slaves, a slave trade and exports of ivory from the mainland; the establishment of a large non-African community from India, Persia and the Arab peninsula; and the predominance of Islam all contributed to the different profile of Zanzibar. The sultans remained as rulers until the revolution in 1964, although since the beginning of this century, under strong British domination, they were in reality dispossessed of power and wealth.

The revolution, headed by the late Sheikh Karume, ended the traditional power of the sultan's regime and wealthy non-African land owners and traders. It was enthusiastically supported by the majority of Africans, and many promises by the new government were fulfilled. The government did in fact deliver: Nationalisation of property; land to the landless; employment in new state farms and industries; public works creating a feeling of national dignity such as the airport, highways, hospitals, international style hotels, and multi-storey houses for urban dwellers and agricultural labourers. Housing had, in Zanzibar a particularly central role as a vehicle for political mobilisation and "nation building".

Communities based on ethnic and religious affiliations lost much of their strength after the revolution. The administrative divisions and the lines now drawn on maps for party "branches", *shehias*, and ten-cells with elected *balozis* were closely connected with an understanding of a community as a geographically defined unit. This was a logical approach in a new society, where the ruling party emphasised nation building and de-emphasised ethnic, tribal and other divisions.

Until recently, under the one-party system, people did at least formally have access to decision-making through a representative system, with a ten-cell leader at the lowest level, and a "branch chairman" covering a neighbourhood. A *sheha* (two in Kwahani, each covering around 50 *balozis*), a councillor (*diwani*) and sometimes a member of parliament complete the list of elected representatives related to a neighbourhood.

Participation

The new leaders, headed by the late Sheikh Karume, were inspired to mobilise people for development by socialism as it had developed in eastern Europe and China. *Maendeleo* (development) and later *ujamaa* (connoting "togetherness" or "socialism") were catchwords. Efforts were channelled into public works, including public institutions, *ujamaa* villages and blocks of flats. Substantial assistance was provided to Zanzibar by the DDR, counter-acting early assistance to the mainland from West Germany.

People offered voluntary inputs, and many did not get or expect a dwelling or other assets as an individual reward. It is obvious, however, that participation was *called* from above and that the entire process was non-democratic. A local leader loyal to the ruling party put it like this:

> The year 1964 marked the end of Indian, Arabic and Comorian communities. Now people were acting together. When a call was made for people to join in construction of government houses, everybody, whether Indian ... [or] African, joined in. This spirit of self help started and was at its peak during the rule of the late Sheikh Abeid Amaan Karume but immediately after the take over by his successor [former president] Aboud Jumbe, it weakened and collapsed. If Karume would be alive, self-help would be still there today.

Many associations were initiated by the Party in the form of classic socialist institutions, such as, in Kwahani, the co-operative shop Sisi kwa Sisi (later named Ushirika wa Tumacho), the Ndara Ndara cultural group, the building of Party offices, the Ujenzi wa Taifa washing places and the Hatuna Baya co-operative.

In spite of critical views on the late Sheikh Karume, his era remains in the minds of many people as the "good old days" when dignity was restored, when there was a communal spirit and participation by people. The following are quotes from interviews with people and local leaders in the neighbour-hoods selected for detailed study. They reflect positive views on the early pe-riod of the revolutionary government, but also disappointment with how things have developed. According to a Kwahani *sheha*:

> Mzee Karume was a gifted individual, he was able to mobilise people for devel-opment activities, all the roads, Maendeleo housing, health and education pro-jects ... people volunteered in large numbers to build all you see today here in this country. There is a big difference today, people have lost the participation and the voluntary self-help spirit; the present generation and the leaders have not been able to continue on that spirit. ... The old people would say: "We have done our part. ... Let the young people do those activities now". How-ever, the youth has no motivation to do that, they will tell you that the time for self-help activities have passed—we need employment to keep ourselves tack-ling the hardships of life.

A Kwahani *balozi* provided a picture of an ageing and tired nation:

> Our nation was still very young when participation in nation building was ac-tive. As a young nation the people had youthful energy and they were eager for advancement. Because of this youthful energy whatever Karume asked the peo-

ple to do they did it. It is in that way that projects like construction of the Michenzani and Kilimani flats, construction of old people's home and establishment of ujamaa villages were undertaken. As days pass, the nation is becoming mature, now we have many officers, directors, ministers and secretaries. As time went by the youthful eagerness continued to fade away It is like a man becoming five years old then ten, twenty and later on forty. Through out this growing process the ability of that person will continue to decline.

It is evident that times have changed, and that the young generation is not interested in political and ideological food, but in concrete activities to secure jobs and incomes. It is also characteristic, that while housing and agriculture predominated as issues in the 1960s (the house and the hoe were characteristic electoral symbols of politicians), today the environment is in the foreground as an issue motivating voluntary collective action.

An old widow also lamented on the fact that, nowadays, during the last decade:

> ... leaders do not emphasise the self-help spirit in development activities ... we are not called to attend meetings related to carrying out improvements of the environment in our area. Long time ago, our branch leaders would call a meeting; people attended and were eager to participate in activities related to nation building. We participated in building houses in Michenzani, Kilimani, Kikwajuni ... we went to all those areas. These days it is difficult to get people to do the same things. Times have changed. ... The new generation is not much enthusiastic about carrying out development, the Karume style; likewise present leaders fail to mobilise people on these issues.

Although the period leads to the expression of a good deal of nostalgia, there are opposing views: "... Even during the Karume period people were not willing to participate in nation building, their participation was a result of pressure which Karume exerted. After his death many people were happy because they would no longer be made to participate in nation building projects".[3] A *sheha* in the neighbouring Jang'ombe area explains: "... because it was the beginning of the Nation building work, sometimes [Karume] had to use force to get things done. However, now people are better informed. They understand many things, so normal mobilisation could suffice."

The dynamics of economic development and the high level of mobilisation were short-lived. Sheikh Karume was assassinated in 1972. The clove industry collapsed and, during the next two decades, the capacity to deliver and manage development and to sustain existing projects gradually declined, like in the remaining part of Tanzania. Development requiring capital soon faced difficulties.

Maintenance of the many nationalised properties has never been organised, which has contributed to an appalling collapse of precious multi-storey buildings in the Stone Town. People in Kwahani recall many communal projects in the early years after the revolution and in recent years, but in the

---

[3] Statement by a female head of household in the Stone Town, presumably voting with the opposition

1970s and 1980s, no local projects and or participation in collective action come to mind.

THE CASE OF KWAHANI

Kwahani is a neighbourhood, one kilometre to the south of the Stone Town, consisting of two *shehias*. Kwahani was opened for development in the 1940s to accommodate an increasing population in the Ng'ambo area. Plots of 12 x 18 metres laid out in a regular pattern were formally allocated to people in 1958. Since then, the majority of the plots have been developed, with very few exceptions, according to regulations. By 1997 Kwahani accommodated approximately 6,000 persons in about 1,000 houses. The majority of persons in the area vote for the ruling party (84%).

The building unit is a classical swahili house with 4–6 rooms, a small backyard with a back-building containing kitchen and toilet, and a room often used for residential purposes. This unit has proved to be robust, flexible for a variety of uses, easy to manage, and where it is the space for several families (fully rented or shared with the owner), internal co-operation and mutual relations are generally reported to be good.

In Kwahani unemployment of the youth, accompanied by drug traffic and other criminality, is considered a major issue, and constituted the motivation for The Baja Social Group to start their community based organisation. The most conspicuous physical and environmental problem is annual flooding that over the years has silted up large areas, requiring people to successively move floors, doors, windows and roofs upwards, since the 1970s more than one metre. The area also suffers from serious problems of garbage collection, inadequate water supply, blocked or absent drainage.

Neither people themselves, nor local leaders, the Municipality or occasional visiting donors had by 1997 made any serious progress in solving these problems, although periodic cleaning of drains takes place. A local group, the Baja Social Group, has taken initiatives to combat unemployment by employing young people in environmental improvements and in carpentry.

In contrast to the larger space, collective action is common in a social space including up to 6–7 houses in whatever direction (mainly along the same street) where people know each other, share events linked with daily life and deaths, help each other when the need the arises, and in a few reported cases join hands to solve problems like water or sewage leakage.

The involvement of people in collective activities and decision making

A local leader in Kwahani loyal to the ruling party was asked how people in fact do influence decisions today. He replied by describing the idealised model which in reality ceased to operate many years ago:

> The people of this area always sit with the party leaders, and they give their ideas ... and they say what is their problems. And the government and the party leaders will help them. [They may go] to the diwani. If he cannot solve the problem he will lead them to where to go, or he himself calls upon someone, who may come here, and they look at the problem together.

There was, during the many interviews with households in Kwahani, no evidence of this type of process. According to the Kwahani *diwani*, the more important channel for people to be heard is the direct approach: "So many people approach me. Most of them are bringing issues of illegal or haphazard construction, and the lack of waste collection, especially those who are close to the dumping points. Some are coming with the general environment question of the area." However, he also admits that his ability to move matters in the Council is limited because there are many demands from councillors, and only limited funds are available.

Only one household respondent described attempts to raise a question and have it moved up in the system, a young man in Kwahani with a past in the local CCM youth committee: "This [youth] committee sometimes calls us to tell the youth what we should do in our area ... Then we, the youth reply 'yes it is a good idea', we are going to do it, but then nothing is done [from their side]. ... Many projects which we planned to do, especially dealing with the youth, never continued."

Little concern is devoted to the communal social services and physical infrastructure which are considered to be "public works", the responsibility of the municipality. This also applies to the seasonal flooding that has been a problem for the inhabitants for 25 years. The issue has repeatedly been brought to the Municipality and the Government. Funds were set aside, but no action was ever taken. However, by the end of 1998, Japanese aid through JICA, was funding the construction of a major drain. However, this collapsed in January 1999 due to poor engineering.

No forum exists for a local discussion. Meetings are rarely held. People cannot arrange meetings without formal, written permission by the District Commissioner. Participation in communal space therefore becomes a directive from above. During our study, we came across only one example of local mobilisation as a reaction against public sector intervention. In the early 1970s, influentials had built their houses in an area located at a higher level than Kwahani. They, the big people, decided to drain their area by directing the flow of water to Kwahani, where soon flooding problems appeared. People organised and blocked the new drain with cement, sending the water back. This minor insurgence, however, did not succeed and had never been followed by any other active resistance. In the study of Kwahani, for more than 20 years, up to 1991, then, there is no record and no recollection of communal activities or mobilisation—neither from below nor from above!

MOBILISING PEOPLE FROM ABOVE

As explained earlier, people in Kwahani have had little real potential and/or possibility to organise collective activities and influence decisions from below. At the same time, local leaders face problems in mobilising people from above. A *sheha* explained that, in the period before multi-partyism, if he called people to participate in the self-help activities, it was a matter of minutes before they all came. Another *sheha*, from neighbouring Jang'ombe explained:

I have been visiting opposition branches as well to ask them to come and join in the work—although they didn't turn up. ... They are very difficult to deal with. I have sent letters and reminders to the opposition secretary. He read them. I waited for his people to come, they didn't come. I went to him again. He told me that his people had refused to attend the work. ... Out of ten attendants only one would come from the opposition.

He is aware of his officially party-neutral position: "I have to respect them all, the *sheha* is required to perform his duties as non-partisan and not leaning to one side."

When the multi-party system was introduced, the *balozi* lost his/her position as a person chosen by the local community as a whole (or the ten plots involved). Today, the lowest level administrative person is the *sheha*, who is in theory non-partisan. Many expectations point to the *sheha* as the person to take the lead, although few people interviewed in this study recall meetings ever being called by him or her. Some people (with a preference for the opposition?) see the *sheha* as part of the old system. According to some in Kwahani, services of the *sheha* are only obtainable upon payment.

The *diwani* paints a different and more optimistic picture: People "are willing and they are ready. In fact they are already mobilised. If you just group them and ask them they will be willing." Also the Municipal Town Director believes that people can be easily mobilised from above, but he has little confidence in the local leaders and gives credence to the central administration as the locomotive in local development:

> ... the sheha may go and educate [people] that there will be this and that development going on, and then he goes away. He is not seen anymore, and of course nothing will happen. ... If *we* concentrate, actually, on these places ... we go to the place ..., call the people and tell the them that we need to do this and this and this and we want your contribution to this, physically or whatever ..., but we want the contribution, and they are willing. ... It needs proper organisation, that we go there on the site, the Director of the Municipal Council himself, the District Commissioner, the Regional Commissioner, the constituency members say a member of the House of Representatives, and one parliamentary elected member. So we go together and call the people, and this thing I think should be [done].

The non-participation in top-down mobilisation should not be exaggerated. The structured survey of Kwahani residents' participation suggests that 6–8 per cent of households participate in drain cleaning and water projects, which amounts to a substantial contribution (60–80 households over some years). But it is purely delivery of unpaid labour for collective activities planned, decided, called and directed from above.

The potential for collective activities at the micro level

At the street level, where formal organisation and mobilisation is not an issue, there are many examples of spontaneous and mostly "invisible" structures of co-operation. In Kwahani there are examples of spontaneous and *ad hoc* communal actions, for instance when once a septic tank burst, when there are funerals or where families need help to move their belongings when a house is flooded.

Reference is made by many to the concept of *ujirani* , i.e. "neighbourliness", the relationship that exists between neighbours—*majirani*—living in an area within which people recognise one another as neighbours. There are formal administrative divisions by ward, but they have little meaning to people in Kwahani as references to places of common interest and belonging. The definition of *majirani* and how big an area *ujirani* covers varies. Some respondents were very precise counting the nearest six or seven houses on both sides of the street as close *majirani*, others vaguer.

A *balozi* in Kwahani provided a very positive impression of strong feelings of *ujirani*. He attributed this to Koranic verses: "a neighbour is like a brother or sister. When you are in trouble, they will come for your help even before your natural relatives arrive to give help. In Kwahani many people know one another, you can go up to the seventh house in any direction, people will still know you. Neighbours help one another in a number of ways, if you are sick or if you don't have something, you can go to your neighbour and explain to him your problem, and he will help you. Neighbours like to sit together on barazas and conduct their talks. At Kwahani families sharing a house live together like relatives."

This view of good relations is generally confirmed by the interviews, although older people explain that it is now disintegrating. During the colonial period people used to help one another. They would go to a colleague and help him to build his house or work on his farm without any payment, only food.

Ujarani also varies between people and areas. In the Stone Town, it is not untypical or surprising to find reservations with respect to interaction with neighbours, because the previous community patterns were broken up by the revolution and people have been brought together by coincidence in the tenements. A Stone Town married woman explained: "Every one is on his own. Unless there is a serious issue like somebody has lost a relative or some one is injured and needs to be sent to hospital, there is not much interaction among neighbours. If you go to other people many people will say, 'She is a trouble seeker; she is after problems, isn't it?'" Even in Kwahani such views are entertained, here cynically expressed by a man living for thirty years in the same house: "in Kwahani, neighbours' interaction is more limited to '*salaam aleikum*'. People don't know one another, there is no one to help another, you can sleep with hunger, the other person will just laugh at you, this is the culture of this place."

The historian, professor Abdul Sheriff explains: "The way we live in town; we do not live in communities. If we were, it is many years ago. The concept of community is a little bit broader here in town than it is in the rural areas." While community based programmes operate in the villages, "in town it is not that easy to have that system in operation because of the nature of the habitation of people in town". Many recent cases of local CBOs created by residents for service development in Dar es Salaam, however, suggest that it is not urban society *per se* that lacks the "social capital" to undertake self-help projects.

Community based organisations: The Baja Social Group

One important reason for focusing on Kwahani was the existence of the Baja Social Group, a local CBO formed in 1991 by 14 young men to combat the growing rate of unemployment, accompanied by drug traffic and robberies, by creating self employment activities locally and positive role models for young people. The group also decided to address the environmental degradation of the area related to sanitation and solid waste disposal. The group wanted to train the community to practice good hygiene in their environment. The activities included waste collection and separation for recycling; vegetable gardens; welding services and a carpentry workshop, linked with training; a blending machine for coconut pulp and a machine for the extraction of oil from coconut pulp. Also Baja (i.e. the present young leader Mr. Makame) has taken initiatives to solve the flooding problem, to get drains cleaned and to improve the water supply.

The efforts are backed by a nominal contribution from a donor (UNDP), but results are very limited and the initiatives attract few local residents. Problems relate for example to the availability of even limited funds to maintain wheelbarrows, and to continuity of activities and the organisation.

Our study showed that, nevertheless, 20 per cent of the households interviewed in Kwahani had, at some time, subscribed to the Baja garbage collection operation, and 10 per cent had joined the youth training programme. For an almost non-supported, locally initiated activity it is, indeed, a good start.

Another CBO, the Kwahani Development Committee, was started in 1996, initiated by CCM politicians, and the local member of the House of Representatives, but it has been less successful. It received some assistance from local donors to develop a kindergarten and a health clinic. Funds were inadequate to complete the projects, they were stopped by the Ministry of Education for lack of toilets. A letter soliciting support that was submitted in 1996 to the Government remained unanswered by September 1998, and the committee had not followed up on the matter. It is worth noting that during the 8 months of field work in Kwahani, no one ever mentioned this relatively official committee, which was "discovered" by coincidence by the researchers in 1998. By 1999 the Committee had been given access to the process of development of a major drain with aid from Japanese JICA.

Who participates in what?

Through interviews with households and leaders, we recorded a list of collective undertakings since independence (Appendix 1) It is evident that collective action was extensive around the 1964 revolution, that very little occurred in the 1970s and 1980s, and that a new wave of activities appeared in the 1990s. Admittedly, we cannot completely exclude the possibility that faulty memory is responsible for the few events reported by people in the 1970s and 1980s.

There is, however, excellent recollection of the events during the revolution one to two decades earlier.

Subsequently, in a structured interview with ca. 10 per cent of households we asked about the knowledge of and participation in the various events. The proportion of possible activities or events in which the respondent could have participated was computed for the eight most significant events (those with developmental aspects, but excluding for example meetings called to inform residents about polio vaccination). The local activity scoring the highest on participation (over 70 per cent of those interviewed) is street cleaning, promoted periodically through radio and television campaigns. In spite of its top-down nature and the lack of dialogue, this form of communication of an important message appears, indeed, to be a more effective tool than local leaders knocking on doors.

Table 16:1. *Per cent of activities in which respondents participated*

		Participated in activity	Heard of activity	Never heard of activity
1996–97	Cleaning environment radio/television campaigns	73	25	2
1997	Cleaning of drains	8	53	39
1996	Cleaning of drains	7	54	39
1993	Vegetable garden (Baja)	2	48	50
1992	Improving water supply system	6	17	77
1992	Youth training in welding and carpentry (Baja)	10	17	73
1991	Garbage collection (Baja)	21	27	52
1991	Baja group founded	0	71	29

Participation is higher for long term residents than newcomers (16 compared to 3 per cent of possible participants), for owners than for tenants (16 compared to 5 per cent); and for women compared to men (13 to 9 per cent). Age and ethnic origin does not affect participation significantly.

What is perhaps more important than active participation is the high proportion of people that had never heard about the cited event. In other words, there are not only problems, of government delivery and support, the blocking of local initiatives (unless approved by the party) and limited knowledge of how to organise communal activities and democratic processes, there is also a big problem of basic communication. A German project linked with environment and street cleaning appears, as earlier mentioned, to have been very successful in creating awareness of environmental issues through radio and television. The approach, however, is directed to the individual and does not encourage local organisation and democratic leadership.

NGOs

The NGOs and community based organisations constitute a growing development force in Zanzibar, in spite of the present difficulties. In the post-revolution period the Party almost completely monopolised local organisation. Hence, associations with a democratic structure are rare. Where an association exists, it is often generated by an influential person, usually with acceptance by or linkage to the Party, and it involves participants to a varying degree. People with relations to NGOs suggest that there is a strong fear of the ruling party and the government. In this political climate, it is unlikely that new organisations could exist without explicit or tacit acceptance by the government.

Interviews with NGO representatives suggest that most of them are aware of the importance of keeping clear of party politics. For example, people with a known relation to the ruling party explain that they face difficulties in acting as NGO builders, particularly in neighbourhoods which are dominated by the opposition. One example is KAMUJAMU, an NGO committee established and registered in 1993 and operating in Mkunazini in the Stone Town, with ambitious environmental objectives. It is run by a well-educated, retired government officer. One million tsh (1US$=600 tsh) has been collected for various purposes and deposited in a bank. Projects aim at a) environmental improvement; b) small scale community economic activities; c) hygiene activities; d) collection of waste paper and marketing it on the mainland; e) collection of scrap metal to be sent for recycling to the mainland; f) educating and creating awareness in the community. Nothing has been implemented and participation is very limited, which, according to the founder, may be due to people suspecting CCM linkages.

Most of the NGOs, however, share the views also expressed by the government that people have to contribute to development. One NGO leader explained that participation is necessary because the government cannot be expected (any more) to deliver everything. "[People] feel that the government is responsible for everything, whether you are talking of hospitals, education or housing. Which is of course now a very wrong concept, not very realistic. ... So we need to change that attitude to make them feel that their development has to be contributed by themselves."

The number of CBOs and NGOs is growing fast. A list compiled in 1997 included 22 associations, believed to be the majority of non-governmental and community based organisations in Zanzibar at that time, and included professional organisations and trade unions (Appendix II). By early 1999, the Chief Minister's Office estimated that the number had reached 87. This included two umbrella organisations, Umoja wa Walemavu Zanzibar (Zanzibar Association of the Disabled) and Association of Non-Governmental Organisations of Zanzibar (Angoza). A meeting held at Angoza in November 1996 was attended by a great variety of organisations. Only a few had a territorial definition: In the environmental field some groups of young people had started garbage collection as a paid service in some settlements. In villages on the east coast of Unguja, the Department for Environment supports women in their efforts to develop water supply. The community and NGO groups are, however, very fragile and break down easily. Angoza has only limited capacity to support them. Another support organisation for NGOs is the NGO Resource Centre established with support from the Aga Khan Trust. It has assisted communities in rural areas with research, setting up of local organisations, etc., but it has, from the year 2000 concentrated its assistance to NGOs.

Finally, the Association of Disabled has, for many years, supported the creation of small NGOs in a variety of fields. Its leader explained about the difficulties facing new NGOs:

> ... it could be a group which has been experiencing oppression, not getting the basic human rights, and they feel that they have to raise their voice. ... This is how we got the formation of women's organisations, [the] disabled organisation ... they do not get a fair share.

The formation of new NGOs suffers from problems encountered also in other developing countries concerning leadership and hidden objectives. The leader continued:

> People who are a little bit educated feel that they can start as catalysts and organise ... so that they can be able to mobilise people. Even the existing NGOs ... still find that the capacity of the leadership itself is very low. ... Do they have a mission? Or have they just formed an NGO because they are fund driven? There is a lot of money in aid. There is a lot of money in environment. Clever people say, "aha, we have to start an NGO to be able to tap these funds". ... Of course in this respect I could also blame the donor agencies, they give some sort of incentives. These NGOs that exist ... very few have been built with a touch of the grassroots.

SUMMARY

The study was conducted in 1996–97, a period in which public infrastructure and environmental services had almost collapsed; the long established ruling party and the opposition had to find their feet in a multi-party, democratic system. The development capacity of the government was at a very low level, and the potential of the communities had not yet been mobilised. Non-governmental organisations were weathering through the trials and errors of local democracy and self-help development. Very few organisations in the urban area could be characterised as community based. There were, indeed, organisations formed by small groups of people in some neighbourhoods, but they were neither representative nor effectively linked with the residents. For example, 29 per cent of the residents in Kwahani had never heard about one of the most successful local organisations in their area, Baja Social Group.

The main findings are :

- we are witnessing a transition period, in which the legacy of the old one party system is limiting the people in deciding on their local affairs and the fuller development of an NGO and CBO sector;

- the government has lost its ability to deliver most services and infrastructure and most residents acknowledge the need for people to contribute to development;

- the government and local leaders have very little ability to mobilise people and there is wide distrust of the ruling party;

– some government officers are increasingly concerned with participatory approaches;

– local communities, NGOs and government staff are, even if they agree to join forces, constrained by a severe lack of experience and skills in handling more democratic decision making processes in planning and implementation of projects;

– some NGOs have emerged mainly to take advantage of donor funding.

The study suggests that, in spite of different motives and approaches, the government, the municipality, local politicians and leaders, as well as NGOs, all share the view that services and infrastructure cannot any longer be provided without people's contributions.

With the continuing legacy of the one party era, participation is synonymous with mobilisation from the top. The local leaders' and the government's conception of participation is the act of passing on to people important information or running a campaign, or mobilising unpaid labour for local public works projects that cannot be implemented due to limited government resources. In other words, the system operates as a top-down system, as it did under the sultans, under the British and under Karume.

The propositions in this chapter are that involvement of people in their local affairs is very limited and that there is a deficit in 'democratic capital' and approaches. There are hardly any local associations. The urban neighbourhoods are becoming increasingly heterogeneous and communities have an ethnic and religious base rather than a spatial/territorial basis.

Responses to the centrally designed attempts to mobilise people for local development have declined ever since the early 1970s. What was possible in the post-revolution period is not possible today. It is agreed by all people interviewed, including officials and politicians, that the government and the party retain strong power, but that they have little ability to mobilise people to contribute to development. In practice, the political—administrative structure of the one-party system is still in place. As a *balozi* in Kwahani explains, "I must emphasise that in Zanzibar, we are so much used to the party/branch system—even if you go to the rural areas—that it has been accepted by many as a mobilisation point."

The political life and thereby the context for participation and associational life has been changing rapidly in the 1990s, due to economic liberalisation (and until recently access to foreign markets and capital) and the beginnings of changes in power relations. The period is one of transition. Many observations made before mid-1997 may not reflect the situation in 2000. Visits made in September 1998 and February 1999 suggest that many officials in the government are moving into new approaches, e.g. in the Directorate for Lands and in the Directorate for Community Development. Also, new community initiatives are recorded for every visit and CBOs, NGOs and their resource centres are continuously making progress, albeit with great difficulty, partly because the ruling party and the government hesitate to reconsider their routines of centralised decision making and control over local development.

Examples of new organisations are Semuso, working for local water supply, drains, roads and electricity, and a CBO in Mtoni Mwanyanya, working for basic infrastructure.

The way ahead

Independent community initiatives are rare and not likely to become an important development factor in the near future. Few people in the neighbourhoods have the experience, knowledge, skills or courage to form new organisations and to organise collective action comprising more than a dozen or so households. Even if they could, none would be able to operate without substantial support from the government or from donors.

The limited trust in the government and the limited funds available make the growing NGO sector the most dynamic actor for support to local development, but it in turn needs funding from outside Zanzibar. It is important, however, also to back up the staff and departments of the government and the municipality that try hard to apply new and more democratic approaches to development. They are, moreover, the persons who understand and can co-operate with NGOs and CBOs.

The growing NGO sector will be unable to sustain growth without funding from outside Zanzibar. However, from within the new NGOs themselves, there are strong warnings against the institutionalisation of and drive for donor funding, that could threaten the goals of development in the interest of common people. With regard to alliances or partnerships with the government, many express the view that if local development CBOs and NGOs are used as a vehicle to attract political backing to certain political parties, and as a platform for party struggles, it is unlikely that democratic structures and local involvement will develop. If an NGO receives assistance from the current government, it will inevitably be seen as related to the ruling party. Hence, even with the best intentions, the present government should not be an important actor in the development of local associations.

Community based organisations, NGOs, government and municipal staff all lack experience and knowledge of ways to build up and support local initiatives. There is no doubt that methodological training and more resources could assist many young people in the government and in the non-governmental associations change attitudes to work with and not for the grassroots. Donors could, with limited funds, provide important incentives. First and foremost, there is a need for time and patience to develop democratic practices in local development and in the planning approaches applied by the government. External support to NGOs and CBOs—and some relevant government projects—should be handled with great care and with insight into who are drivers and who are passengers, who will benefit and what are the prospects of democratic development.

Finally, in any discussion of external assistance, it is important to stress that long term and low key projects are needed, projects that do not suffocate local initiatives. It is appropriate to give the last word to the *sheha* in Jang'ombe who, like most others, has lost trust in the government providing the needed improvements, but who nevertheless is hesitant also when assistance from donors is suggested. If the government wanted to take on itself a role as facilitator or enabler, rather than one providing prescriptions and dictates, there is indeed, a local platform for taking the first careful steps.

> I think that people mobilising themselves without government [intervention] could be a better idea. However, when there are deficiencies in necessary resources like in the case of our drainage, then the government acts like the father to fill the gap ...

References

Lerise, Fred Simon, 1996, *Planning at the End of the River—Land and Water Use Management in Chekereni Village, Moshi District—Tanzania.* Copenhagen: Institute of Town and Landscape Planning, Royal Danish Academy of Fine Arts.

Nnkya, Tumsifu J., 1996, *Planning in Practice and Democracy in Tanzania.* Copenhagen: Institute of Town and Landscape Planning, Royal Danish Academy of Fine Arts.

Putnam, Robert D., 1993, *Making Democracy Work. Civic Traditions in Modern Italy.* Princeton, NJ: Princeton University Press.

UNCHS, 1997, *Appraisal for the Habitat Supported Community Development Programme—Tanzania.* Nairobi: UNCHS.

APPENDIX I

EVENTS OF COLLECTIVE ACTION IN KWAHANI SINCE INDEPENDENCE

1997 cleaning of drains
1996 improvements Kwahani rd
1996 improvements Kwahani rd
1996 polio meetings
1995 2nd meeting allocations small scale enterprises
1995 orientation meetings elections
1994 drainage rehabilitation meeting
1994 street lights installed
1994 1st meeting allocations for small scale enterprises
1993 actions for environment cleanliness tv/radio
1992 water supply improved
1992 meeting improvement water supply—Baja
1992 youth training in welding and carpentry—Baja
1992 garbage collection started—Baja
1991 Baja group formed
1976 attempts to block drain after two inlets constructed in 1974
1970 Hatuna Baya Co-op formed
1964 Ujenzi wa taifa—washing places constructed
1964 water and roads works
1964 Khani house converted
1964 party offices constructed
1964 Sisi kwa Sisi converted to Tumacho Co-op
1964 and before: participation in urban improvements

APPENDIX II

CBOS AND NGO'S ESTABLISHED IN ZANZIBAR TOWN IN 1997
(Compiled by Suleiman M. Nasser, Codecoz, January 1997)

1. Zanzibar Association for Farmers and Fishermen Development (ZAFFIDE).
   Activities: training, financial assistance to farmers /fishermen.
2. Catalyst Organisation for Women Progress in Zanzibar (CORPS).
3. Zanzibar Entrepreneurship Development Organisation (ZEDO).
4. Disabled Association of Zanzibar
   Activities: Loan, train in projects, sensitise disabled to establish income generating activities.
5. Zanzibar Women Development Organisation
   Activities: mobilising young females school leavers to establish income generating groups and assisting them in seeking donors and support.
6. Zanzibar Association of Blind (ZANAB)
   Activities: treatment, develop activities, train of blind people
7. Zanzibar Orphan Trust
   Activities: Assist Orphans to get uniform, text books and food
8. Zanzibar Tour Operators
   Activities: An association of business people engaged in tour operation
9. Umoja wa Maskari Wastaafu (Veterans)
   Activities: Printing machine, security guard, carpentry workshops, petty business.
10. Zanzibar Nursing Association
11. ZAFA+
    Moral backing to HIV patients.
12. Zanzibar Youth for Self Reliance
    Activities: Promotion of unemployed youths to be Self-reliant
13. Diabetic Association of Zanzibar
    Activities: Awareness and to give moral backing to patients
14. Zanzibar Dairy Farmers Association (ZADFA)
    Activities: Deals with dairy production
15. Zanzibar Wood Workers Association
    Activities: Association of people engage in carpentry
16. Beitrus Building Brigade (BBB)
    Activities: Production of building materials
17. Zanzibar Women Entrepreneur Trust Fund
    Activities: Provide credit scheme for business women
18. Kamati ya Maendeleo na Ustawi wa Jimbo la Mkunazini (KAMUJAMU) 1993
    Activities: Environmentally related projects in the Stone Town.
19. BAJA Social Group in Kwahani. 1990.
    Activities: Environmental improvements and employment of the young.
20. Community Participation and Health Education (CPHE)
    Activities: Rehabilitation and improvement of Zanzibar Municipality's sewerage, drainage and solid waste disposal system.
21. Zanzibar Women Corporation (ZAWCO) 1990
    Activities: Community development projects (water) in rural areas
22. Community Development and Environmental Conservation in Zanzibar (CODECOZ) 1994
    Activities Research, education, project planning and management, evaluation and monitoring for local communities. Sustainable development.

CHAPTER 17

Urban Development and Community Participation in Oshakati, Northern Namibia

Bruce Frayne, Wade Pendleton and Akiser Pomuti

INTRODUCTION

The rapid and sustained urbanisation phenomenon witnessed across much of the Africa continent over the past fifty years has precipitated an urban management crisis, with formal services and infrastructure simply unable to meet the burgeoning demand amongst the poorer sectors of society (World Bank, 1994; McDonald, 1997, 1998; Potter and Lloyd-Evans, 1998). In response to this growing shortage of physical and social infrastructure in many African cities, citizens are increasingly finding ways in which to manage their own needs. The significant rise in common-interest associations is closely related to this prevailing urbanisation within a context of increasing democratisation and decentralisation of urban governance, and marks the ingenuity and perseverance of common people to improve their circumstances, in spite of the overwhelming odds against their tenacious efforts at urban survival (Haviland, 1993:291; Mabogunje, 1990). The importance of these associations for urban dwellers, whether by individual choice or community need, is related to the opportunities they provide for social support, leadership opportunities, fund raising, management of financial resources, organisational skills, and other functions related to community development. Such associations may be seen as replacing the more traditional groupings in African society, which are based on kinship, marriage, age, and gender (Gmelch, 1996).

In the Namibian context, there were relatively few common-interest associations prior to independence, and the country thus differs from much of sub-Saharan Africa, and in particular from countries in East and West Africa, where such associations proliferate (Little, 1964; MacCarney et al., 1995). Namibia's small and sparsely distributed population, together with a relatively recent onset of rapid urban growth and urbanisation, has certainly mitigated against the development of significant urban associations. Another important reason for the limited number of associations is that during the *apartheid* era people were reluctant to belong to any clubs or civic groups other than those related to church and sports activities. People were afraid of being accused of political activity that was anti-South African, as such an accusation brought with it interrogations and possible imprisonment (Bauer, 1998). Another key limiting factor was that during the Namibian War of Liberation, which lasted from the 1960s until 1989, northern Namibia was an active war zone and people were subjected to military harassment, curfews, and relocation (CIIR/BCC, 1981).

Situated deep within this former war zone, Oshakati has been described as an atypical African town, in that it lacks a historical and a traditional basis for its existence (Tvedten and Hangula, 1993:6). It was a small colonial administrative centre until the mid-1970s, when it became a military base. It was a major military centre for South African military operations against the military wing (PLAN) of the South West African People's Organisation (SWAPO). Oshakati is also atypical because of the many non-productive service businesses that dominate its economy, such as bottle stores, *cuca* shops (informal drinking establishments), garages, general dealer stores, and supermarkets (Pendleton et al., 1992). There is very little manufacturing industry in Oshakati. Although the town Oshakati provided employment for some and was a migration destination for many, it was not a good environment for community development or for the development of common-interest associations. As a result, people received little experience in participation or leadership with organisations of this type.

In addition to these exogenous factors precipitated by the peculiarities of the colonial state in Namibia, traditional institutions in Owambo society are largely authoritarian and hierarchical, with little scope for the formation and role of *ad hoc* socio-political associations within village life (Williams, 1991). The system of headmen and their deputies (sub-headman) under a chief fosters a paternal relationship between patrons and the general population falling under the control of that patronage. In particular, decisions on resource allocation are made by the headmen according to prevailing social norms of traditional society, rather than by a more transparent and democratic negotiation between associations of common-interest and the traditional authorities. For example, the traditional system of land allocation has been maintained in the informal settlements of Oshakati, where "location headmen" act on behalf of the traditional authority by allocating land to new arrivals in the urban areas, rather than deferring such decisions to the municipal authority (Frayne and Pomuti, 1997; Adams and Vale, 1990). The strong hierarchical structure of traditional Owambo society is further evident in the paternal relationship between the development-oriented civic associations in Oshakati and the municipality. In general, these associations expect the municipality to take care of their needs for land and infrastructure in the same benevolent, albeit authoritative fashion, as do the headmen in both urban and village settings (Frayne and Pomuti, 1998).

Given the oppressive history of Namibian society, and the hierarchical and largely authoritarian structure of Owambo society, spontaneous self-generated common-interest associations remain largely undeveloped in Oshakati, with externally initiated and supported civic associations dominating. This study provides an analysis of development-oriented associations in selected informal communities in the municipal area of Oshakati, and draws out lessons for the function and role of community based associations in the urban development process within a context of rapid urbanisation, limited urban resources and newly established and democratised urban governance. The paper is based on quantitative and qualitative data collected through a long-term involvement in the Osahakti and its shantytowns by the authors (see e.g.

Frayne et al., 1993; Tvedten and Pomuti, 1994; Frayne and Pomuti, 1997 and 1998; Pendleton and Frayne, 1998).

ASSOCIATIONS IN OSHAKATI

Oshakati is currently the fastest growing urban centre in Namibia, and estimates suggest that the population of the town will double in size within approximately nine years (Frayne and Pomuti, 1997:14). In 1993, the population was estimated to be 35,000; by 1997, this estimate had risen to 50,000.[1] At current growth rates, by 2006, the population is likely to be in the region of 100,000. As a further marker of growth, in 1990 there were five informal settlements within the Oshakati town boundaries; by 1997 four more informal settlements had emerged. This rapid urbanisation is also occurring in the adjacent and contiguous municipality of Ongwediva, and about 30 km to the south in the town of Ondangwa. The growing importance of this urban nexus is well recognised by government. Within the next decade, the combined population of the three proximate urban centres of Oshakati, Ongwediva and Ondangwa might well exceed 200,000, which is the current size of the capital city of Windhoek. This represents phenomenal growth, and the concomitant challenges to the newly established municipalities to provide at least some level of service infrastructure within a poorly developed economic system and narrow formal tax base are likely to sharpen as a result (Frayne, 1998).

This study has its roots in the history of the Ibis (WUS-Denmark) Oshakati Human Settlement Improvement Project (OHSIP), which commenced in 1993. The main aim of OHSIP was to upgrade basic service infrastructure in selected informal settlements within Oshakati, including roads, electricity and sanitation and to improve the urban layout where appropriate (Hangula, 1993; Tvedten and Hangula, 1994). At that time, Oshakati comprised a formal, serviced urban area, surrounded by five informal settlements. In addition to technical and infrastructural support, OHSIP sought to build the capacity of community level associations to better enable them to actively participate in their own development, within four of the five informal settlements. These community organisations became known as Community Development Committees, or CDCs. CDCs were democratically elected bodies with ten members, constituting themselves by selecting four office-bearers and managers of different sub-committees.

A landmark meeting was held between all the four CDCs established during OHSIP on 25 March 1995, which resulted in the establishment and implementation of four Community Based Development Organisations, known as CBDOs. The CDCs remained in place as the executive committees of these development organisations. In addition to the mutual acceptance of the CBDO Constitution, which outlines in detail the legalese required to es-

---

[1] The point that population numbers do fluctuate on a seasonal basis as a result of links to the rural areas and crop production is made in the 1994 Baseline Study (Tvedten and Pomuti: 11). This is important to bear in mind when working with these population figures that they are only estimates, and may well vary on a seasonal basis. However, they do provide a good indicator of the magnitude of growth.

tablish and run such organisations, it was agreed that the CBDOs would become the development organisations at community level which could help to concretise development objectives, mobilise resources and negotiate projects at local, regional, national and international levels. The CBDOs also made provision for including traditional leaders and their important functions within the CBDO development objectives. Headmen were generally included in the CDC membership, thus linking communities to these development institutions through their respected leaders.

The CDCs and CBDOs were to be funded through the establishment of a community based brick-making business known as the OEAU. This acronym derives from the first letters of the four communities involved: Oneshila, Evululuko, Amukambya (now called Oshoopala), and Uupindi. The profits from the brick-making were to be used to finance the CDCs in order to ensure their continued operation. In addition, the OEAU was also to draw on local labour thus contributing to employment in participating communities.

More than three years later, the CDCs are in various states of breakdown; the CBDOs are weak and ineffectual; and the OEAU brick-making project has all but come to a standstill, although Uupindi and Evululuko are still making some bricks at the Uupindi site. The result is that CDC members have become disillusioned (with the exception of one or two committed members), the CDCs are not receiving an income from the OEAU, and they have become fragmented and ineffectual in meeting their development objectives.

The remaining five settlements of Sky, Ompumbu, Kanjengedi, Oshimbangu and Eemwandi, which were not part of the OHSIP project, do not have formally constituted development associations. Kanjengedi is the only part-exception, in that the community has, on its own initiative, established a CDC which is active and dynamic, although it could benefit from further direction and focus. Notwithstanding Kanjengedi, the communities rely primarily on their traditional leaders (urban headmen and village headmen) to deal not only with disputes and discipline, but also with the allocation of land.

As a parallel and important association, the National Housing Action Group (NHAG) has established housing unions in each of the informal communities, which are active both in the housing domain and with regard to general development concerns and needs. These unions act to an extent as CDCs in those communities where CDCs have not been established (non-OHSIP areas). Sky, for example, has an active NHAG Committee that deals with issues beyond housing. The Sky NHAG Committee manages and controls the payment of water tariffs to the Oshakati Town Council on behalf of the community. In communities with CDCs, there appears to be a trend where CDC members are active in the housing unions because NHAG has greater resources than do the CDCs, given that the OEAU brick-making operation has ceased to function effectively (Frayne and Pomuti, 1997).

Three important things happened when the OHSIP project ended in 1995. The first was that the technical assistance in the form of expertise and project funds ceased. The second was that Oshakati was proclaimed as a municipal local authority, and saw the establishment and increasing participation of the Oshakati Town Council in the management of the town. The third was that, although OHSIP was terminated, Ibis continued to support the institutional and capacity-building efforts initiated during OHSIP in the informal settlement areas through their CBDO Support Function (CSF). Although its CSF in Oshakati was providing support to the CDCs, it was not directed by any formal programme or clearly formulated strategy. This reduced the potential impact of Ibis activities on the continued growth and function of the community based development organisations. In contrast, through its Oshakati Town Council Support Programme, Ibis was (and still is) providing a direct and effective support service to the fledgling municipality.

It was therefore decided that Ibis should develop and implement a Community Support Programme to run in tandem with the Oshakati Town Council Support Programme. Moreover, Ibis recognised that the objective of setting up self-sufficient and self-sustaining community based organisations during the OHSIP phase had largely failed, and that the CDCs in fact required additional support during the post-OHSIP era. A longer-term approach to achieving the goal of self-sustainability was considered to be a more appropriate strategy.

Four communities were chosen for the research, on the basis of their unique characteristics and potential to reveal information which would assist Ibis in identifying and developing appropriate institutional vehicles for implementing the Community Support Programme. The following communities were selected:

1. *Uupindi*: an OHSIP community with a CDC that is weak and poorly functioning.
2. *Evululuko*: an OHSIP community with a CDC that is relatively strong and active.
3. *Sky*: an "illegal" informal settlement with no CDC, but spontaneous community organisations, including a Housing Union.
4. *Ompumbu*: a peripheral community located within the municipal boundary, but in agricultural fields, with an active Housing Union, but no CDC.

The discussion that follows highlights a range of social, cultural and practical issues that dominate associational life in the four informal settlements that were selected for this study. In particular, the functioning of the institutions set up by OHSIP, and other associations that exist are examined. This institutional review forms the basis for an analysis of the utility of externally initiated community based development organisations.

INSTITUTIONAL REVIEW

Former OHSIP communities

The communities of Uupindi and Evululuko are both OHSIP beneficiaries, and although they represent opposite ends of the spectrum in terms of post-OHSIP efficacy of their respective CBDOs and elected CDCs,[2] they have much in common. The withdrawal of direct support from the external project agency (Ibis) after the completion of OHSIP has impacted both CDCs negatively, reducing their ability to function as coherent and focused grassroots development organisations.

Uupindi is an informal settlement that falls within the Oshakati municipal boundary. It lies to the north west of the formal town of Oshakati, and is in close proximity to the centre of the town. With a population of 7200, and an estimated annual rate of growth over the past five years of 14 per cent (Frayne and Pomuti, 1997), Uupindi is an important residential area. As a beneficiary of OHSIP, Uupindi has roads that are sufficiently well developed to ensure vehicular and pedestrian access during the rainy season, as well as VIP latrines, potable water supplies and power. Further, its prominence as a former OHSIP settlement has ensured that the Oshakati Town Council has recognised Uupindi as a legitimate settlement in Oshakati, despite its informal status. This situation implies a degree of tenure security for residents, although there are conflicts between the municipal authorities and the local residents, particularly regarding methods of land allocation and settlement.[3]

Uupindi has suffered financially in the post-OHSIP era, both from a lack of income and from poor financial management. Perhaps the key factor in the demise of the CDC is the failure of the OEAU to continue to provide the level of support that was possible in earlier years. Also very important within a context of limited accounting skills is the fact that the OHSIP accountant, who had ready access to the books of any CDC at any time, was not replaced once the OHSIP project came to an end. Certainly the Uupindi CDC members quoted this as a major factor in creating opportunities for fraud, as the "watch dog" had been removed. Members were equally clear that they would welcome some form of outside assistance again to help fill the post-OHSIP gap.

It appears that the financial problems facing this CDC, including those of alleged fraud and corruption, are partly the result of the withdrawal of OHSIP expertise with no replacement, and partly the result of a lack of local level financial expertise. These two factors have combined to provide a very loose, often verbal, accounting system, with no legal recourse thus far in cases of open fraud. Feelings of powerlessness and impotence together with a lack of expert backup, have left the CDC demoralised, impoverished and unable to cope properly. The expertise to undertake much needed financial planning and forward planning are absent.

Having said this, the Uupindi CDC has continued to function financially, albeit in a less than optimal manner. This is testimony to both the sheer determination of certain key people to ensure that it continues to function, and the honesty of those same people. This is clearly an indication of the kind of

---

[2] The distinction between the CBDOs and their respective CDCs is not strictly followed in this report, as the CDCs are the focus of the study, and the term 'CDC' is the preferred term within the study area. However the reader's attention is drawn to the technical distinction highlighted here.

[3] Traditional land allocation methods through the Location Headman, versus permission to occupy provided by the local authority.

potential that exists within the Uupindi CDC to see through the struggle of rebuilding the financial integrity of the organisation. It is noteworthy that the Uupindi CDC has been able to continue to operate on a very limited budget derived from the brick-making operation and the community crèche. The CDC's operational budget totals some N$700 per month. This represents self-generated income, and is therefore the basis of a self-sustaining financial system.

Like Uupindi, Evululuko is an informal settlement that falls within the Oshakati municipal boundary, and is also an OHSIP beneficiary. Evululuko is growing fast, and has a current population of approximately 3500, and an estimated annual rate of growth over the past five years of 15 per cent (Frayne and Pomuti, 1997). Similarities between Uupindi and Evululuko include issues of access to land, the perceived lack of action by the municipal authorities, reliance on the location headman for land allocation, a lack of secure tenure, and so forth. Nonetheless, Evululuko remains the strongest and most effective CDC of the four OHSIP communities, even though success in this respect is a matter of degree. Evululuko also has difficulties, and the key factor which undermines the continued operation of the Evululuko CDC is the lack of internal cohesion, precipitated by financial difficulties.[4]

Due to internal disputes and a degree of fragmentation within the CDC, the current office bearers and members consider themselves to be temporary executive officers within the organisation. They perceive themselves as keeping operations going until the next election, as required in terms of the current CDC Constitution. Again, like Uupindi, while the CDC wants to hold elections and believes it is important to do so. However, members are concerned that they do not have the resources (personnel, expertise and finances) to properly organise and hold a successful election.

The CDC is a member of the OEAU Brick-Making Company and has derived an income from the brick-making activities. However, financial difficulties have meant a cessation of funds flowing into the CDC, and it claims to have received no income from this source for more than a year. The CDC has its own brick-making enterprise, which appears to be an attempt to replace the income lost to the OEAU. Although a small scale operation, the brick-making ensured a steady income for the Evululuko CDC for a year. This contributed directly to the ability of the CDC to continue to function more effectively than the Uupindi CDC. In addition, the CDC runs a crèche from its premises, which provides additional and important income for the CDC. The crèche is not as lucrative as the Uupindi crèche, and thus provides a small income.

The key difference between the two CDCs is that Evululuko appears not to be suffering from internal corruption, which helps to maintain a degree of morale within the CDC itself. Nonetheless, the mismanagement and apparent corruption within the OEAU has been cited as a major source of concern, and indeed financial hardship, for the Evululuko CDC.

---

[4] It should be emphasised in this regard that the CDC considers its own financial affairs to be in order, but that the lack of income from the OEAU is where the real financial management problems occur.

Like the case of Uupindi, the Evululuko CDC is clear that it lacks expertise to properly manage the finances of the CDC, and the organisation is worse off as a result of the withdrawal of the OSHIP accountant who provided much needed support. The accounting system requires upgrading, and the treasurer, at least requires some training. Both Evululuko and Uupindi have their own businesses, and therefore urgently require the implementation of more transparent and documented systems of materials acquisition, production inputs and costs, output (stock) records, debtors and creditor records, and the like.

Given this background to the two communities, it is instructive at this point to consider in some detail the key issues that the CDCs themselves identify as being central to their inability to function effectively in the post-OHSIP era. These issues are presented according to the broad areas of common concern between the Uupindi and Evululuko CDCs, and quotes from the interviews held are included where illustrative of the issue under discussion.

Institutional responsibilities

Members of both CDCs stated clearly that they view themselves as the minions of the Oshakati Town Council, and that they need to be both guided and given the support and resources they require by it. However, the CDCs believe that the Oshakati Town Council is not fulfilling its responsibilities as their "development agency". Also, the CDCs feel that the Oshakati Town Council has accorded them a low status in Oshakati, and that this perception, and the consequent lack of support undermines the operation of the CDC. Members stated that:

- Although they are our leaders, the door of the Oshakati Town Council is always closed to us.
- Our development problems are actually the responsibility of the Oshakati Town Council.
- Even though the Oshakati Town Council is alive and can see, it gives no support to the CDC.
- The lack of Oshakati Town Council action, and ignoring us, is a block to our development-why do they do this?

Although not unique to either Uupindi or Evululuko, this strong perception of a hierarchical relationship between the Oshakati Town Council and each CDC is evidence of a lack of understanding on the part of the CDCs of the role of a local authority in an urban area, as well as a poor comprehension of the financial and budgetary systems employed by municipalities in general.

Literacy versus education

From the above point, it is clear that the CDCs do not understand how a local authority works, and how development finance and infrastructure come about. The CDCs identified this as a problem and a constraint on their continued functioning, and raised the need for an educational endeavour to improve their understanding of their role in their own development, and in particular, the role of the Oshakati Town Council with respect to the Local Authorities Act of 1992 (Republic of Namibia, 1992) and municipal systems of urban governance. Members report that:

- We are alive because we can see, but we need to know what is in the mind of the Oshakati Town Council.

- Development is like a rock. We need come together with the Oshakati Town Council to agree on key issues so that together we can lift the rock of development. It is too heavy for only one person.

The CDC members are also clear that for them education does not mean literacy, but rather information and support. Education is therefore used as a term in its narrowest sense (information needs). Support is needed to give members the tools they need to be able to engage with change agents and the Oshakati Town Council, and to have recourse to their members, and the justice system (legal support).

Lack of management control and support

The CDCs were clear in their identification of the lack of support for their efforts from the Oshakati Town Council as a key problem. They are uncertain about how to proceed on many fronts, including financial management, project development and implementation, and identifying and accessing potential sources of support (both technical and financial).

The control issue relates to the financial aspects of the CDCs. While the Uupindi CDC recognised that corruption is a major obstacle to its success, the Evululuko CDC members believe they do not suffer from corruption. However, the members of both CDCs are aware that they need assistance to tighten up their financial management. The CDCs feel that they do not have a sufficiently well developed system of management and control, and that support in developing such a system will be of significant benefit to the organisation. In support of this need, members say that:

- We do not have proper accounting systems, and although we try, our books are in a mess. We need to sort this out.

- We are under pressure from our community to explain ourselves and their money, but what can we say when we have no support?

Constitution

Members of both the Uupindi and Evululuko CDCs expressed concern over the complexity of their Constitutions, claiming that they are difficult to read, understand and implement. The form and content of the documents require a high degree of literacy and a degree of legal fluency to interpret. With regard to implementation, the CDC members do not feel that they have the power to enforce the requirements and conditions of their Constitutions. For example, the absence of the Uupindi CDC Treasurer from meetings has placed her in conflict with the requirement of the Constitution, which demands that she be replaced. Yet the CDC is unable to remove her from office, as she will not accept the legitimacy of their actions, despite the Constitution. The CDC has no direct means of enforcing such a regulation where the offending party refuses to accept the sanction of the CDC. The call from both CDCs is for a far simpler charter of rights and responsibilities. In the words of the CDC members:

- We all know what happens to our money, but does the CDC have the power to take action? Therefore we need help.
- You must be a lawyer to read this Constitution.

Internal conflicts

The Uupindi CDC believes that many of its difficulties stem from internal problems. These include financial mismanagement, lack of accountability, disillusionment, lack of commitment (except for a select few), lack of external support and guidance post-OHSIP, poor leadership, and the lack of overall and understandable objectives for the CDC. The Evululuko CDC members similarly feel that the key internal conflicts are the result of a lack of support and guidance after the withdrawal of OHSIP. With little external support for what they believe to still be very young organisations, the CDCs were bound to flounder, as has happened. In addition, the financial demise of the OEAU and the consequent lack of income for the CDCs are seen to have precipitated the disinterest and despondency that has come to characterise them. As one member reported:

- OHSIP left a big gap when they went home, and we have now got problems in the CDC because we cannot agree on many issues.

In addition, the Evululuko CDC members claim that there has been some conflict between the four office bearers and the managers of the sub-committees, with accusations of inactivity and mismanagement flowing both ways. The CDC analyses this conflict and subsequent break up as really having its roots in the lack of role clarity for the CDC and its sub-committees, lack of support, financial pressure and frustration with the Oshakati Town Council, which has not provided any of the resources which the CDCs need.

Non-OHSIP communities

Sky

The non-OHSIP communities of Sky and Ompumbu are significantly different from each other, both historically and in terms of associational life. Sky is an informal settlement of approximately 2,000 people, located in the central area of Oshakati. The location of the settlement is in conflict with the preliminary Town Planning Scheme of the Oshakati Municipality, being situated on land designated for commercial use. As a result, the Municipality has been reluctant to recognise Sky as a legitimate settlement. Sky is therefore viewed as a "temporary" and informal urban settlement, unlike the former OHSIP communities, which although informal, can expect to be upgraded to formal status in due course. However, residents of Sky are convinced that they will remain on the site, and that if not, a suitable alternative will be found. This attitude makes for a community intent on improving its situation, irrespective of municipal views.

Notwithstanding their determination, this situation of non-recognition and impermanence places Sky in a difficult position, as the community urgently requires certain basic infrastructure to ensure safe water, sanitation and environmental health (poor drainage and a lack of toilet facilities create a significant health threat to residents). Yet investment by the community is risky given the poor tenure security, and likewise, the local authority is not in a position to invest in infrastructure as long as the settlement remains in conflict with the Town Planning Scheme.

While Sky has no community based development committee in place, they do have an active Water Committee and a NHAG Housing Union (key individuals are members of both organisations). The purpose of the Water Committee is to ensure that the community pays for the water drawn from the municipal pipeline. Each household makes mandatory contributions on a regular basis to the Water Committee, which in turn pays the municipal water tariff. This tradition of endogenously driven community co-operation makes Sky an unusual settlement within Oshakati. The key difference between Sky and other informal settlements in the area is that the community has, on its own initiative, organised itself into a functioning committee, which is able to collect subscriptions and meet obligations. It is noteworthy that, in contrast to the OHSIP-initiated CDCs of Uupindi and Evululuko, which are struggling to maintain internal coherence and legitimacy within their broader communities, the Water Committee in Sky is viewed as both legitimate and important to residents of the settlement. The high payment rate by the residents of Sky for their water service is evidence of the general level of support for this self-initiated association. Again in contrast with the CDCs, members of the Water Committee are eager and confident of their ability to engage in the development process. In their words:

 - We are already trying to develop our community.
 - We have spoken to Oshakati Town Council Health Inspector, and she has visited us to experience our problems and needs.
 - We are not a CDC, no, but we can become such a thing.

The organisational capacity is therefore present to both establish and manage a CDC. In addition, despite generally low incomes and high unemployment levels, our findings suggests that, in addition to the water tariffs, households would be willing to contribute towards other forms of development, as long as they had confidence that the money was going to be used for the intended purpose. However, it is important to emphasise that Sky residents are not sure of exactly what a CDC is, or what its role is *vis-à-vis* development. Thus conceptual understanding is poor, although the desire to learn more and consider establishing a CDC is high. In fact members of the two committees in Sky are creative about how to proceed, and discussed the idea of inviting other CDC members to address them in this matter.

Ompumbu

Ompumbu is, in some ways, a unique informal settlement in the urban area of Oshakati. It is situated on the boundary of the town, amongst remaining agricultural fields. Itself non-agricultural, it has direct links to the neighbouring rural village. Thus while it has a location (urban) headman, as with the other informal settlements in Oshakati, the links to the village headman are direct and important in the lives of the Ompumbu residents. Its peripheral location places it in the unfortunate position of being neither rural nor truly urban, and because of distance, residents have limited access to urban facilities and infrastructure offered in Oshakati. Ompumbu is small, with a population of some 250. Net growth has been limited in recent years, although as an annualised percentage, it is high at approximately 13 per cent. The income levels in Ompumbu are low, and there is a large percentage of older people.

The settlement is not particularly dynamic with regard to institutional initiatives, which may be due in part to the geographically peripheral nature of the settlement, and in part to the apparent lack of formal education and organisational ability among the older adults who can take on associational responsibilities. With the notable exception of the Penduleni Housing Union (PHU), which is a NHAG activity, there are no community based institutions in Ompumbu. Notwithstanding this situation, the community, represented by the PHU and other *ad hoc* invitees, at meetings with the research team, were clear that they wanted and believed that they would benefit from establishing a CDC. Although their knowledge of the details of OHSIP and the resultant CDCs was limited, they had an intuitive sense about the kinds of development activities a CDC ought to be involved in. As members of the community said:

- There is no land which does not have a King, and therefore we need to be led into the future.
- As a committee is always the voice of the people, it can take action and address needs.

While there was clear consensus that a CDC is a desirable goal, there was less clarity on the technical aspects of the process of establishing such an organisation, as well as the structure of such a community based entity. The primary issue was that most people had little experience of formally constituted committees, and what they really consist of. The PHU members were more informed and experienced in this regard, thus providing a positive means by which joint membership might help drive and strengthen any initiative to establish a CDC in Ompumbu. The opinion was expressed that the existing CDC communities could provide a resource for Ompumbu, as they consider the issue of setting up a CDC.

Income levels in Ompumbu are low, with few internal resources. However, people are adamant that they are prepared to volunteer their time and effort to setting up a CDC. The example of the PHU was given, where success has been achieved without salaries being paid. This situation provides an opportunity for the establishment of a CDC (or equivalent) in Ompumbu, without significant injections of cash. In addition, the potential financial viability of the existing CDCs, based on crèche income and limited brick-making activities, suggests that Ompumbu could follow such an example with the right inputs and support, leading towards a sustainable community based development organisation.

ANALYSIS OF THE FINDINGS

The analysis presents a synthesis of the key practical and conceptual issues that emerge from the research findings presented in the preceding section. This analysis will provide a basis on which to consider future structures and roles of civic associations in relation to social and service development needs in informal urban settlements like those in Oshakati.

Legal status of CDCs

Currently CDCs have no legal status *per se*. This has been identified as a major constraint by CDC members. Indeed, with no legal status, CDCs will increasingly experience difficulties in meeting their development objectives. Internal issues are difficult to address outside of the law. Similarly, the procurement of funds for projects is made more difficult when the responsible body is not a legal entity. In support of this view, many countries, not least South Africa, have ensured that community based organisations become legal entities before they are able to receive government funding. This helps to ensure that funds are not given to an individual on a discretionary basis, and the organisation can in turn be more accountable to its members and constituency. In addition, the establishment of a legal entity helps to define membership, rights and obligations, which can help to ensure better functioning of office bearers and members, while protecting individuals and groups legally within the organisation.

This is not the case at present. For example, if a project is funded for a particular CDC, and funds are disbursed to the treasurer for deposit into the CDC account, there is no legal mechanism to ensure that this in fact happens. Furthermore, there is no legal mechanism to bring a perpetrator to justice in the event of misappropriation of funds. Leaving such matters to the goodwill of individuals is seldom a suitable method, and the experiences of the CDCs stand testimony to this assertion.

Options available to community based organisations include the formation of trusts, charities, or non-profit companies. The legal documents are not complex for the establishment of such legal entities, and define the rights and obligations of all members and beneficiaries. This is clearly important in situations where CDCs manage services and money on behalf of communities. While legal entities are not a sure method of stopping corruption, they certainly do close loopholes, increase the confidence of potential supporters and funders, and make recourse to legal action more possible than under the current situation.

Simplifying the constitution of CDCs

In addition to the formation of legal entities it is important to simplify the CDC constitutions, as well as creating much simpler versions for any new community based organisations which may be developed. CDCs have elaborate and complex constitutions that are difficult to interpret and implement, yet CDCs have no legal standing as such. Empowerment appears unlikely under such a scenario.

What is therefore required is a more accessible constitution, perhaps in the format of a charter of rights and responsibilities, which can then serve as a guide document to the CDCs. With the concomitant establishment of legal entities, gross transgressions of these broad rights and responsibilities can be legally actioned if required. Complex constitutions do not in themselves ensure responsible organisational functioning, and given that the general sentiment is that they are largely unworkable (poorly understood and not readily implemented), a revision seems appropriate.

Support and training

The study shows that both CDC and non-CDC communities require varying levels of support and training in practical matters, particularly book keeping and management. Illiteracy *per se* does not appear to be a central obstacle to the functioning of the CDCs, nor to the establishment of other community based organisations in non-OHSIP settlements. What is lacking though is support for a mix of functions and activities in all cases.

In the case of OHSIP communities, the withdrawal of OHSIP has frequently been cited as a major cause of internal difficulties experienced by the CDCs. OHSIP left a support vacuum, and CDCs have had unfulfilled expectations of the Oshakati Municipality taking over the support function for which OHSIP was responsible. This is not the role of the local authority, and communities have begun to realise this. Although Ibis did put in place its Community Support Function, perceived as a means of filling the post-OHSIP vacuum, it has simply proved to be too big a task for a staff of two to undertake effectively. Although staff recognise the various levels of support required, they do not have the resources to systematically address the needs. Thus any kind of community support programme will have to address directly the need of CDCs for institutional support, and if relevant, beyond to other informal settlements in Oshakati. However, without reorienting the CDCs away from the current expectations they have of local authority, to a more autonomous and externally focused strategy, efforts at providing technical support are unlikely to be successful. Therefore "education" and "training" are two sides of the same coin, and a community support strategy will need to both recognise and incorporate these two dimensions.

Financial support

The study reveals that despite, the apparent disarray regarding the finances of the two CDCs examined, these organisations were in fact able to operate in a financially sustainable way. That is, they have been able to continue to operate through self-generated income. While the current level of income is certainly less than optimal, the system is working. Given that the CDCs can and do run on about N$700–800 per month, generated from own sources, the Community Support Programme should not inject money into the CDCs. (In 1999, 1US$=N$6.15.) Indeed, based on previous experience, this may well serve to undermine the self-sustaining nature of the system, and create socio-cultural openings for mismanagement. The Community Support Programme should focus on supporting and enhancing the current management and accounting systems, and where appropriate provide support around existing and new self-initiated projects at community level. That is, what exists and is working should be focused on as part of the broad empowerment and self-sustaining objectives of a Community Support Programme.

The CDCs, the Oshakati Town Council and urban development

The principal issue highlighted by this study is the so-called "parent-child" relationship which exists between the CDCs and the Oshakati Town Council, as well as between non-CDC communities and the Oshakati Town Council. It appears to stem in part from the history of OHSIP and the idea that the municipality was a replacement for OHSIP. It also has its roots in a cultural heritage of hierarchical and authoritarian structures, indigenous to the region. The result is a top-down system of authority, where the CDCs and other communities view themselves as "subordinate" to the municipality. The notion of the CDCs being interest groups which are quite separate in all ways from the municipality appears to be a new concept. However, this fact of independence has not escaped the municipal authorities, who clearly understand that community based organisations are not organs of state by any manner or means, but rather autonomous interest groups. This stance is clearly supported both by the function of the municipality and the statutes laid down in the Local Authorities Act (i.e. the stance of the local authority in this matter is a legitimate one).

Another dimension leading to the current hierarchical perceptions is embedded in the lack of understanding of how a municipality works, how it is funded and how it funds capital projects, and in turn, how a community does or does not benefit from the system. In addition, the fact that the functions and roles of local authorities are described legally in the Local Authorities Act is not generally known. The attitude of the local authority is generally interpreted, within the dominant socio-cultural context of the area, as a hostile "parent" mistreating a "child", rather than being understood within the context of the Act and the broader functions and responsibilities of local authorities generally.

This relationship between community based organisations and the local authority needs to change as an important component of any Community Support Programme that might be implemented. Furthermore, it is in the longer-term interests of these communities to properly understand their place in the scheme of things and to take on the persona of "independent interest group" rather than "child and victim". That is, the Community Support Programme needs to address both sides of the coin: to unravel what at first glance appears to be a weak and ineffectual CDC, but is in fact a systemic problem, rather than a lack of potential at local level. A Community Support Programme ought to introduce education regarding the legal and financial functioning of the municipality to bring communities to the point of understanding their situation and potential development role. This should assist in the task of empowering communities to become proper interest groups within the urban setting, and helping them to clearly define their roles in their own development. Such education will assist in breaking the current attitude of dependency fostered by the cultural norms of the society, thus enabling CDCs to make informed and realistic decisions and actions regarding their situations.

Relationship between the CDCs

A common complaint in the sample settlements, as well as the other CDCs in Oshakati, was the lack of interaction between the different communities. People felt that they were isolated from each other, unable to share common problems, ideas or solutions. Clearly this perception is founded on the current situation in Oshakati. With poor political representation at municipal level, and no alternative structure for bringing different interest groups together, the informal settlements are indeed isolated from one another and the broader activities of the more formal sectors of the society.

This situation appears to have had a negative impact on the development of effective and integrated community based organisations in Oshakati's informal settlements. Not only is there a clear lack of understanding between OHSIP and non-OHSIP communities of the role of CDCs and the beneficial development which OHSIP brought to a select few communities, but there appears also to be a degree of envy (and even mistrust) between the CDCs themselves, and between CDC and non-CDC communities. Yet it is evident that people want to have more open communications between settlements, and that people perceive the potential benefits of working more closely with their neighbours.

The non-CDC communities see the potential of gaining information and having access to precedents regarding the establishment of a similar structure to the existing CDCs in their own communities. The CDC communities believe that they stand to gain by pooling ideas, and in some cases resources, as a means of improving their function and output. In particular, the fact that the CDCs are generally facing issues of financial misappropriation yet are unsure of how to proceed with rectifying the situation, provides a good example of how more open communication might benefit all parties concerned in finding a solution to the problem. At a more general level, discussions regarding the role of CDCs, potential projects and funding sources, could all serve to better the current situation of CDCs. People interviewed even went as far as to identify potential benefits in organising elections as one process, pooling expertise and resources, rather than proceeding on an individual and unsatisfactory basis.

As a result of these findings, a model for co-operation between all settlements can be developed. The idea of the model is that, rather than having a number of separate CBDOs, each with its own CDC, consideration should be given to establishing one larger CBDO which represents the various participating communities within Oshakati. Operating at local level, one could retain (or develop in non-CDC communities) the CDCs, responsible for local development actions. This model would help to maximise the co-operative benefits available such as legal expertise, project development, liaison with the local authority, fund-seeking, NGO communication, and so on, while simultane-ously ensuring that the different communities retain their autonomy and are not hindered by possible inefficiencies within other communities. The CDCs would continue to operate as they do, but would have a mechanism for liaison and co-operation with other community based organisations.

In summary, the main findings indicate that not only is there scope for immediate and specific input in the form of a Community Support Programme at community level for both CDC and non-CDC communities, but that all communities indicated their willingness to participate in an Ibis initiated Community Support Programme. The study indicates that there are longer term needs of both CDC and non-CDC communities which a Community Support Programme could address, and which are crucial to empowering, democratising, and sustaining the development process at community level in Oshakati. There is also a range of short-term needs that are hindering com-munities from becoming self-sustaining and active interest groups, concerned with improving their living conditions.

IMPLICATIONS FOR A COMMUNITY SUPPORT PROGRAMME

With the right inputs, the CDCs can become self-sustaining community based interest groups that will be able to mobilise resources and realise development objectives. However, this situation will only be achieved if the time frame of the process is sufficiently long term. It would be unrealistic to imagine that two or three years of input into the Community Support Programme will yield self-financing and self-sustaining CDCs. Ibis as a development organisation ought more realistically to take the position that what they are doing is initi-ating a long term community development strategy, laying the foundation for communities to better meet their development needs and participate in the development process. In addition, and central to any externally driven project or initiative, is the need to ensure that the process is in accordance with local knowledge, ideas and needs (Vivian, 1991:1–25). In practical terms, this means that local people must be involved in the decision-making processes about what the CDCs will do and how they will be organised. Letting people speak for themselves may appear as a self-evident objective and activity within the design of such projects. However, its is seldom that local people really have a tangible and concrete input to the project development and process. All too often, and usually with the best of intentions, external organisations en-gage in so-called participatory projects at the local institutional level, where the objectives of democracy, organisational structure and management are in effect foisted on participants in a socially coercive manner. Power relations are for the most part unequal, with the external agent being dominant. The pro-ject objectives are set *a priori* by the change agent, and not often as a result of direct and mutually supportive negotiations between parties. As Chambers (1985:95–96) comments, it is crucial that local or indigenous beliefs and prac-tices be taken into account for development projects to be successful. The initiative to establish CDCs remains a donor-driven rather than a community-driven activity, perhaps flagging up an important underlying cause of post-OHSIP failure.

If the view is taken that Ibis, or any change agent, is only a catalyst in the process of community level democratisation and empowerment, and the parallel process of assisting communities to meet their own basic needs (poverty alleviation), then Ibis should be able to meet its objectives successfully. On the other hand, if Ibis considers the establishment of fully operational CDCs that are in direct dialogue with the Oshakati Town Council as the goal by the time they end their involvement in Oshakati, then measured by these criteria, Ibis may well fail in its task. However, based on current understanding of the different dynamics in Oshakati, it is believed that a realistic approach is to develop a Community Support Programme which extends well beyond Ibis' planned involvement in the area and that Ibis should view its role as initiator and catalyst in the development process at community level. The implication of this approach is that the Community Support Programme, or any similar community based development initiative, ought to be defined by the longer term development needs of the communities themselves, rather than by the *a priori* goals and objectives of the change agent. This position does not negate the need for specific projects, as catalysts in their own right. While the analysis suggests that a Community Support Programme should address the longer term, process-oriented needs of the informal settlements in Oshakati as the primary objective, there is also scope for the Community Support Programme to address some of the shorter-term needs, on a project basis. Such projects could act as important learning and capacity building experiences for communities, as well as potential "bridges" between the Oshakati Town Council and community based development organisations in the town. The possible projects identified in the course of the study are as follows:

1. Garbage Collection and Recycling Project initiated by the Ibis Urban Group within the Oshakati Town Council.

2. Water Protection and Payment Project which the Oshakati Town Council is eager to implement. The Oshakati Town Council is willing to use communities to identify illegal water points, and to develop ways in which existing taps can be protected and paid for. The Oshakati Town Council is also willing to finance such a project, which would mean additional income for participating communities.

3. Reception Area for Migrants: the need for a reception area and land allocation system for squatters and migrants is very important to the future development of Oshakati. This fact has been recognised by the technical staff of the Oshakati Town Council, and would be welcomed by communities within Oshakati.

4. Rubbish Dump Clean-up and Control: the municipal dump is a serious threat to the health of Oshakati residents. Not only are livestock feeding off the dump, but so are children and adults. Basic fencing and a system of controlling access and protecting the fencing is needed urgently. Com-

munities (in particular Ompumbu) have expressed their willingness to assist the Oshakati Town Council in finding a solution to this problem.

5. Nutrition Outreach Project: Already identified as critical by the Oshakati Town Council Health Inspector, such a project could have a direct and positive impact on levels of child health, which is a critical factor for future development. Such a project is by nature inter-sectoral, and so could have not only an integrating effect at a number of levels, but could also help communities, Ibis and other NGOs, and the Oshakati Town Council to identify in a real and hands-on manner some of the development needs facing communities in Oshakati. For example, hygiene, potable water, income needs, educational needs, and so forth could be better understood through a nutrition outreach programme.

6. Land Tenure Project: Security of tenure is a major obstacle to development from both community and Oshakati Town Council perspectives. Engaging the Oshakati Town Council and the communities in a project could, by using an actual settlement, address a wide range of related issues. Moreover, such a project could provide a powerful means by which to open communication channels and introduce and build integrated and participatory planning methods in Oshakati.

7. Charter of Rights, Roles and Responsibilities: An important project which could facilitate communications and planning and development activities amongst interest groups and the Oshakati Town Council would be to draw up simple and clear charters of the rights, roles and responsibilities of the various institutions and/or organisations involved in the development process. This project would have to involve a high degree of participatory activity between the major stake holders and role players in Oshakati.

8. OEAU Co-operative: The current initiative to transform the OEAU from a business to a community based co-operative should be pursued. This would be an important step in improving the financial autonomy of the CDCs and CBDOs. In addition, ways of extending the OEAU, or replicating a similar project within the non-OHSIP communities could be considered.

9. NHAG Housing Unions as Development Agencies: it is often preferable to use existing structures as a foundation for achieving other goals. In this case it is suggested that ways of extending the functions of the NHAG housing unions to include larger development concerns at community level could provide an important project and component of a Community Support Programme. This is especially relevant in non-OHSIP communities.

10. Eco-House Project: This is a project which has a range of potential benefits for both communities and the Oshakati Town Council. The eco-house project provides a means by which communities and the Oshakati Town Council can co-operate on experimenting with alternative and cost-effective development options. Testing out a range of options in this

way will help to achieve agreement on the levels of technology which might be used in future projects within Oshakati.

11. Oshakati Population Census: There are no hard data regarding population for Oshakati, and this creates problems on a number of fronts for the Oshakati Town Council and other planning and development agencies. The Council has suggested that a population census is needed forthwith, and that they may be prepared to support such a project. A census would provide an ideal opportunity to involve all communities.

Given the short term involvement of Ibis in the Community Support Programme that it is developing and will implement, and the long term process of developing sustainable institutional structures at community level, which it has been suggested might be the mainstay of the Community Support Programme, part of the Ibis strategy should be to explore alternative sources of support for the CDCs to continue the process established through this Ibis initiative. Continuity therefore remains a key factor in helping to ensure positive outcomes of development efforts, and potential exists within the Oshakati context to draw on the resources and expertise of a number of non-governmental organisations.

CONCLUSIONS

Oshakati is growing rapidly and is expected to become the second largest urban area in Namibia. The major part of this growth comes from the poorest sectors of society, marked by an urban population with few skills or resources, but with a high level of demand for urban social services and physical infrastructure. What is clear is that the Oshakati Municipality will continue to be unable to meet this expected rise in demand for services under the current situation of high urbanisation and decentralisation, which implies greater fiscal responsibility at the local level. Community based organisations will have to develop and rise to the challenge of contributing to their own needs. The extent to which these findings and conclusions regarding civic-oriented, community based organisations in Oshakati can be generalised to other urban environments in sub-Saharan Africa depends primarily on context. In other words, situations that display similar characteristics to Oshakati may be able to draw effectively on some of the practical and conceptual issues raised in this study. Having said that, rapid urbanisation, population growth, environmental stress, economic limitations, and poorly resourced local authorities are characteristics that many emergent and long-standing urban places in sub-Saharan Africa have in common with Oshakati. While scale and context may vary, many of the challenges facing urban managers and communities in African towns and cities are common features of the political and urban landscapes, and the socio-economic dynamic.

In dealing with these challenges of limited resources and rapid urban growth, this study suggests that self-driven and self-sustaining action by community organisations is one avenue open to communities to empower themselves. Ultimately, it is through association and solidarity at the local community level that a working partnership with the local authority might be forged. Indeed, this is perhaps one of the few options open to both the under-resourced municipalities and the expanding, poorer urban communities of African urban places like Oshakati.

References

Adams, F., W. Werner and P. Vale, 1990, *The Land Issue in Namibia: An Inquiry*. NISER Research Report No. 1. Windhoek: University of Namibia.

Bauer, G., 1998, *Labor and Democracy in Namibia, 1971–1996*. Athens: Ohio University Press.

Chambers, E., 1985, *Applied Anthropology*. Engelwood Cliffes, NJ: Prentice-Hall.

CIIR/BCC, 1981, *Namibia in the 1980s*. London: The Catholic Institute for International Relations and The British Council of Churches.

Frayne, B., 1998, *Considerations of Planning Theory and Practice in Namibia*. SSD Research Report No.18. Windhoek: University of Namibia.

Frayne, B. and A. Pomuti, 1998, *Institutional Review of Four Selected Communities in Oshakati, Northern Namibia*. Commissioned SSD Report for Ibis Namibia (WUS-Denmark). Windhoek: University of Namibia.

—, 1997, *Oshakati Status Quo Report*. Commissioned SSD Report for Ibis Namibia (WUS-Denmark). Windhoek: University of Namibia.

Frayne, B., A. du Plessis, D. Simon, R. Hopson, M. Schabler and C. Tapscott, 1993, *Regional Development Strategy for Oshana, Omusati, Ohangwena and Oshikoto*. SSD Research Report No. 13. Windhoek: University of Namibia.

Gmelch, G., 1996, "Introduction: Migration and the Adaptation to City Life", in Gmelch, G. and W. Zenner (eds), *Urban Life*. Prospect Heights, Illinois: Waveland.

Hangula, L., 1993, *The Oshakati Human Settlement Improvement Project: The Town of Oshakati—A Historical Background*. SSD Discussion Paper No. 2. Windhoek: University of Namibia.

Haviland, W.A., 1993, *Cultural Anthropology*. Forth Worth: Harcourt Brace College Publishers.

Little, K., 1964, "The Role of Voluntary Associations in West African Urbanisation", in van den Berghe, Pierre (ed.), *Africa: Social Problems of Change and Conflict*. San Francisco: Chandler.

Mabogunje, A.L., 1990, "Urban Planning and the Post-Colonial State in Africa: A Research Overvie", *African Studies Review*, Vol. 33, No. 2, September 1990:121–203.

McCarney, Patricia, Mohamed Halfani and Alfredo Rodriguez, 1995, "Towards an Understanding of Governance: The Emergence of an Idea and Its Implications for Urban research in Developing Countries", in Stren, R. and J.K. Bell (eds), *Perspectives on the City, Urban Research in the Developing World*, Vol. 4. Toronto: University of Toronto Press.

McDonald, D., 1998, "Three Steps Forward, Two Steps Back: Ideology and Urban Ecology in the New South Africa", *Review of African Political Economy*, 75:73–88.

—, 1997, "City Limits: New Public-Private Partnerships for Improving Cities May Not Meet UN Habitat II Conference Expectations", *Alternatives*, 23(2):26–32.

Pendleton, W. and B. Frayne, 1998, *Report of the Findings of the Namibian Migration Project*. Windhoek: SSD Research Report No. 35. Windhoek: University of Namibia.

Pendleton, W., D. LeBeau and C. Tapscott, 1992, *Socio-Economic Study of the Ondangwa/Oshakati Nexus Area*. NISER Research Report. Windhoek: University of Namibia.

Potter, R. and S. Lloyd-Evans, 1998, *The City in the Developing World*. Harlow: Longman.

Republic of Namibia, 1992, *Promulgation of the Local Authorities Act (Act 23 of 1992)*. Government Gazette 470. Windhoek: Government Printers.

Tötemeyer, G., 1992, *The Reconstruction of the Namibian National, Regional and Local State*. NISER Research Report No. 7. Windhoek: University of Namibia.

Tvedten, I. and A. Pomuti, 1994, *The Oshakati Human Settlement Improvement Project: A Socio-Economic Baseline Study*. SSD Discussion Paper No. 9. Windhoek: University of Namibia

Tvedten, I. and L. Hangula, 1993, *The Oshakati Human Settlement Improvement Project: A Preliminary Socio-Economic Assessment*. SSD Discussion Paper No. 1. Windhoek: University of Namibia.

Vivian, J., 1991, *Greening at the Grass Roots: People's Participation in Sustainable Development.* Discussion Paper No. 22. Geneva: United Nations Research Institute for Social Development.

Williams, F., 1991. *Precolonial Communities of Southwestern Africa.* Windhoek: National Archives of Namibia.

World Bank, 1994, *World Development Report: Infrastructure for Development.* New York: Oxford University Press.

Abbreviations

ACCEN	Ayawaso Committee for a Clean Environment
AGO	Anti-Government Organisation
AMA	Accra Metropolitan Area
ANC	African National Congress
APE	Association for Protection of the Environment
ASP	Afro Shirazi Party
BESG	Built Environment Support Group
BIT	Building, Information and Training
CAI	Collective Action Initiative
CBDO	Community Based Development Organisation
CBO	Community Based Organisation
CCAP	Church of the Central African Presbyterian
CCM	Chama Cha Mapinduzi, Revolutionary Party of Tanzania
CDC	Community Based Committees
CFA	Communauté Financière Africaine
CFH	Civic Forum for Housing
CO	Charity Organisation,
COUD	Centre des Oeuvres Universitaires de Dakar, Dakar University Service Centre
CPP	Convention People's Party
CSO	Civil Society Organisation
DACF	District Assembly Common Fund
DCC	Dar es Salaam City Commission
DDC	District Development Committee
DDR	Deutsche Demokratische Republik
DEM	Dahira des Etudiants Mourides, Association of Mouride Students
EEAA	Egyptian Environmental Affairs Agency
EQI	Environmental Quality International
GAMA	Greater Accra Metropolitan Area
GANGO	Gap-Filling Non-Governmental Organisation
GO	Grassroots Organisation
GONGO	Government Non-Governmental Organisation
HPZ	Housing People of Zimbabwe
IAI	Individual Action Initiatives
IDT	Independent Development Trust
ILO	International Labour Organisation
INE	Instituto Nacional de Estatística, National Statistical Institute
IO	Independent Organisation
IPC	Investment Promotion Centre
JICA	Japan International Co-operation Agency
KKHC	Kugarika Kushinga Housing Co-operative
MLC	Mowenderi Land-Buying Company
MONGO	My Own Non-Governmental Organisation
MoF	Ministry of Finance

NGI	Non-Governmental Individual
NGO	Non-Governmental Organisation
NHAG	National Housing Action Group
NHCT	National Housing Construction Trust
NHF	National Housing Fund
NSDF	National Slum Dwellers' Federation
OBSP	Occupation Building Servicing Planning
OEAU	Oneshila, Evululuko, Amukambya, Uupindi (community based brick-making business in four communities in Oshakati,Namibia)
OHSIP	Oshakati Human Settlement Improvement Project
PCT	Parti Congolais du Travail, Congolese Labour Party
PHU	Penduleni Housing Union
PLAN	People's Liberation Army of Namibia
PNDC	Provisional National Defence Council
PO	People's Organisation, Private Organisation
PSBO	Planning Servicing Building Occupation
PSU	Programme Special Urbain
PVDO	Private Voluntary Development Organisation
PVO	Private Voluntary Organisation
QUANGO	Quasi-Non-Governmental Organisation
RAES	Regroupement des Anciens Etudiants et Sympathisants
RDP	Reconstructing and Development Programme
SANCO	South African National Civic Organisation
SAP	Structural Adjustment Policy
SIC	Société Immobilière du Cameroun
SPARC	Society for the Promotion of Area Resource Centres
SPJCA	Southern Pinetown Joint Civics Association
SWAPO	South West African People's Organisation
TANU	Tanganyika National Union
TCPD	Town and Country Planning Department
UCLAS	University College of Land and Agricultural Sciences
UDF	United Democratic Front
UGLBC	Uasin Gishu Land-Buying Company
UMWA	Umoja wa Maendeleo wa Wananchi wa Hanna Nassif (Hanna Nassif People's Development Association)
UN	United Nations
UNEP	United Nations Environment Programme
UNCHS	United Nations Centre for Human Settlements
UNICEF	United Nations (International) Children's (Emergency) Fund
USN	Urban Sector Network
VO	Voluntary Organisation
WUS	World University Service
ZANU-PF	Zimbabwe African National Union-Patriotic Front
ZDT	Zilweleni Development Trust
ZRA	Zilweleni Residents Association

Glossary

adiyya	devotional gift
awqaf	religious endowment
baay laat	a long tunic with wide sleeves and embroidered neckline
bairro	unauthorised settlements
balozi	ten-cell leader
daira	association of (urbanised) disciples
dara	collective work group in service of a *shaykh*
diawrigne	leader, chief
diayanté	a sacred pact or contract
diwani	councillor
harambee	development through co-operative self-help
imam	priest
jebbelu	oath of allegiance to a *marabout*, in particular Mouride
kalela	recreational dance
khalifa general	administrator/religious leader, head of Mouride brotherhood
kixikila	informal savings and credit system
kukula	growth
kulipiritsa nkhuku	monetary penalty (lit.: "pay a chicken")
kusamala	care for
ku tawuni	in town
lilila	communal work parties
luholiswane	informal savings and credit system
maendeleo	development
magal	Mouride religious celebration
majirani	neighbour
malume	mother's brother
manatiq al-ashwa'yya	unauthorised settlement
marabout	religious notable
Mouriddiya	the Mouride brotherhood
mu'allim	master, land proprietor
mudzi	home village
mzimu	ire of the dead
ngoma	dance among the Ngoni people
nyau/gule wamkulu	dance and secret society among the Chewa
obadwa	locally born resident
obwera	arrived resident
Qâdiriyya	Sufi brotherhood
saidi	lifestyle of people from southern Egypt
salaam aleikum	greeting; peace upon you
sangolo sako	individual or collective self-help
serigne	Sufi religious leader
sha'b	the common people, the grassroots
sobas	traditional leaders (Angola)
shaykh	Sufi leader, marabout

sheha	lowest level officer in the local administration
stokvels	saving clubs
tijani	member of *Tijanniya*
Tijanniya	Sufi order or brotherhood
thangata	work party, forced labour
thiof	with style and resources (only about males)
turuq (*tariqa*, pl.)	Islamic Sufi-based brotherhood
ujamaa	togetherness/socialism
ujirani	neighbourliness
waahi	a person originating from an oasis
xitique	informal savings and credit system
zabbaleen	waste collector
zakat	Islamic religious tax
zeriba	waste which cannot be recycled
ziyara	devotional visit

Biographical Notes

Jørgen Andreasen (b. 1942) received his Ph.D. degree in architecture from the Royal Danish Academy of Fine Arts in Copenhagen in 1988. He is currently an Associate Professor at the Department of Human Settlements, School of Architecture of Royal Danish Academy of Fine Arts in Copenhagen. His research interests are urban development, urban planning, community and housing.

Harri Englund (b. 1966) obtained his Ph.D. in social anthropology from the University of Manchester in 1995. He is currently a research fellow at the Nordic Africa Institute in Uppsala, Sweden, and his research focuses on ethnography, migration, politics, pentecostalism and Malawi.

Katherine V. Gough (b. 1963) is an Associate Professor at the Department of Geography, University of Copenhagen. She obtained her Ph.D. degree in geography from the University of London in 1992. Her research interests include development geography, Third World urbanisation, urban governance and civil society, land and housing markets, household housing and employment strategies, sub-Saharan Africa and Latin America.

Cheikh Gueye (b. 1966) is currently employed at ENDA Tiers Monde, Dakar. He holds a Doctorate of University Louis Pasteur (Strasbourg) from 1999. His research addresses cities, governance, religious cities and urban invention.

Amin Y. Kamete II (b. 1967). He obtained his M.Sc. in rural and urban planning from the University of Zimbabwe in 1994. He is a lecturer at the Department of Rural and Urban Planning, University of Zimbabwe. His research interests include housing, urban management, urban governance, urban economies, local economic development, and sustainable human settlements.

Sarah Karirah Gitau (b. 1961) obtained her Ph.D. degree in urban planning from the University of Central England in 1996. She is currently a lecturer at the Faculty of Architecture at the University of Nairobi. Her research covers urban poverty, sustainable livelihoods and community participation.

Ilda Lourenço-Lindell (b. 1965) is a doctoral student in the Department of Human Geography, University of Stockholm where she obtained her M.Sc. in 1993. Her research interests are African cities, urban poverty, informality and social networks.

Robert M. Mhamba (b. 1959) is currently an assistant lecturer at the Institute of Development Studies, University of Dar es Salaam. He obtained his Licentiate degree in Regional Sciences from the Technical University of Karlsruhe, Germany, in 1996. His research interests include inter-sectoral linkages, local level provision of social amenities, institutions and socio-economic development and information communication technology.

Miranda Miles (b. 1966) is currently a lecturer at the Department of Geography and Environmental Studies, University of the Witwatersrand, Johannesburg, where she also obtained her Ph.D. degree in 1997. Her research focuses on development issues, gender and housing, land-use and transportation integration, gender and migration.

Susanna Myllylä (b. 1964) holds a Ph.D. degree in administrative sciences from the Department of Regional Studies, University of Tampere, Finland. Currently she is a senior researcher at the Department of Regional Studies and Environmental Policy, Tampere University and her research interests are urban governance in the Third World, large cities, new social movements, NGOs, environment, Cairo and Delhi.

Yomi Oruwari is trained as an architect, and practised some years in Lagos and Port Harcourt before she joined the Department of Architecture at the Rivers State University of Science and Technology where she is a senior lecturer in planning. She holds a Ph.D. (1993) from the University of Port Harcourt, Nigeria. Her research interests are housing, migration, urban studies, gender and development.

Wade Pendleton (b. 1941) obtained his Ph.D. in social anthropology from the University of California (Berkeley) in 1970. He is a Professor on leave of absence from San Diego State University, Anthropology Department, San Diego, California, and currently employed as a Research Associate at the Southern African Migration Project (SAMP). His research interests include migration, urbanisation, applied research and Southern Africa.

Paul Robson (b. 1952) is a researcher at the Development Workshop, Luanda, Angola. He received his B.A. in geography from the University of Cambridge in 1974. His research focuses on social change in Angola, civil society at the grassroots, participation and collective action.

AbdouMaliq Simone (b. 1952) is a visiting research scholar at the Institute of African Studies, Columbia University; New York. He obtained his Ph.D. from the Wright Institute in 1979. His research interests include African political imaginaries, urban practices, new geographies of belonging and becoming, migration and African real economies.

Warren Smit (b. 1967) is a senior researcher at the Development Action Group, Cape Town, South Africa. He obtained his Master's degree in city and regional planning from the University of Cape Town in 1993. His major research topics are housing policy, housing delivery, local government, community based organisations, urban development and urban planning.

Gabriel Tati (b. 1959) obtained his Ph.D. in urban studies from the University of Bristol in 2000. He is currently a lecturer at the University of Swaziland. Research interests include the public-private partnership in the provision of urban services, urban sprawling and local institutions in land property development, the relationship between African immigrant entrepreneurship, ethnic networks and appropriation of public space in the urban context.

Colman Titus (b. 1966) is currently a Ph.D. graduate student at the Department of Sociology, University of Minnesota, USA. He obtained a B.A. in economics in 1994 and an M.A. in demography in 1996 from the University of Dar es Salaam, Tanzania. His research interests are urban development, urban sprawl, informal sector, urban community, urban governance and inner city problems.

Arne Tostensen (b. 1948) is senior research fellow at the Chr. Michelsen Institute in Bergen, Norway. He obtained his Mag. Art. degree in sociology from the University of

Oslo in 1976. His research subjects include urbanisation, labour migration, poverty, regional integration, democratisation, human rights and aid.

Inge Tvedten (b. 1954) is currently senior researcher at the Chr. Michelsen Institute in Bergen, Norway. He holds a Mag. Art. degree in Social Anthropology from the University of Bergen. His research interests are urban development and urban poverty, natural resource management and small-scale fisheries, development co-operation institutional development and political and economic conditions in Angola.

Mariken Vaa (b. 1937) obtained her Mag. Art. degree in sociology from the University of Oslo in 1967. She is currently the programme co-ordinator of the *Cities, Governance and Civil Society in Africa* research programme at the Nordic Africa Institute in Uppsala, Sweden. Her research interests include urban governance and service provision, women and development and poverty.

Paul W.K. Yankson (b. 1949) is Professor at the Department of Geography, University of Ghana, Legon, Ghana. His research interests include urban and regional development, urban management and the urban informal economy.

Index

A

Abidjan (*see also* Ivory Coast), 123
Accra (*see also* Ghana), 124, 127, 128, 132–137, 139–141
  Accra Metropolitan Authority (AMA), 136, 137
  Ayawaso Committee for a Clean Environment (ACCEN), 138
  basic services, 132
  civil society, 140
  community based organisations (CBOs), 127, 132, 139
  community development, 138
  customary land tenure, 135
  demand for land, 134
  Department of Feeder Roads, 136
  East Legon, 135
  East Legon Extension Residents' Association, 137
  environmental sanitation, 138
  Gabwe, 134
  Ghana Electricity Company, 136
  Ghana Water and Sewage Company, 137
  indigenous settlements, 134
  lack of services, 139
  land, 133, 137, 138, 140
  land disputes, 135
  land market, 133
  lobbying, 141
  Muslims, 140
  Nima, 137
  non-governmental organisations (NGOs), 127, 132, 139
  overcrowding, 138
  peri-urban area, 133
  population density, 139
  population growth, 132
  poverty, 139
  provision of services, 133
  rents, 138
  residents' associations, 132, 136, 137
  self-help groups, 138
  service provision, 133, 137, 138, 140, 141
  traditional authorities, 140
  urban environment, 132
  urban management, 127, 140
Addis Ababa, 9, 256
African cities, 5, 8–11, 21, 24, 27, 30, 34, 35, 46, 48–50, 61, 74, 127, 128, 139, 180, 182, 188, 191, 256, 282
  associational life, 11
  employment, 10
  environmental problems, 10
  formal economy, 10
  infant mortality, 10
  informal economy, 10
  physical infrastructure, 10
  poverty, 10
  service provision, 10
African NGO Habitat Caucus, 48
Aga Khan Trust, 275
agency, 47, 50, 146, 187, 287, 289
Alexandria, 9
Amadou Bamba, 108–110, 112, 113–119, 122
anarchism, 12
Angola (*see also* Luanda), 22, 58, 233, 250–258, 260, 261
  community based organisations, 233
  community solidarity, 251
  economy, 251
  international NGOs, 257
  National Statistical Institute (INE), 255
  peace settlements, 252
  residents' committees, 257
  resistance movements, 22
  urban growth, 251
  urban population, 252
apartheid, 28, 61, 93, 232, 234–238, 240, 242, 282
Arab peninsula, 266
associational dynamics, 61
  Dakar, 61
  Johannesburg, 61
associational life, 11, 13, 14, 20, 23, 24, 27, 30, 52, 90, 95, 96, 102, 104, 130, 131, 182, 199, 213, 277, 286, 291
  poverty gender, 23
  typology, 14
  usage, 11
  women's groups, 23
associations, 11, 14–24, 30, 32, 43, 51–52, 59, 66–68, 78, 96, 104, 109, 110, 130–132, 137, 141, 147–152, 159, 164, 178, 183, 185, 186, 191, 195, 196, 199, 201, 212, 214, 218, 223, 225, 230, 232, 233, 235–239, 242, 244, 245, 256, 260, 267, 275, 278, 282–286
  accountability, 23